CLARENDON LAW SERIES

Edited by
TONY HONORÉ AND JOSEPH RAZ

CLARENDON LAW SERIES

Edited by
TONY HONORÉ AND JOSEPH RAZ

CLARENDON LAW SERIES

NORM AND NATURE

The Movements of Legal Thought

Roger A. Shiner

CLARENDON PRESS · OXFORD

1992

Oxford University Press, Walton Street, Oxford OX2 6DP
Oxford New York Toronto
Delhi Bombay Calcutta Madras Karachi
Petaling Jaya Singapore Hong Kong Tokyo
Nairobi Dar es Salaam Cape Town
Melbourne Auckland
and associated companies in
Berlin Ibadan

Oxford is a trade mark of Oxford University Press

Published in the United States
by Oxford University Press, New York

British Library Cataloguing in Publication Data

Library of Congress Cataloging in Publication Data
Shiner, Roger A.
Norm and nature : the movements of legal thought / Roger A.
Shiner.
(Clarendon law series)
Includes bibliographical references (p.) and index.
1. Legal positivism.   2. Natural law.   3. Law—Philosophy.
I. Title.   II. Series.
K331.S55   1992
340'.11—dc20   92–6062
ISBN 0-19-825719-8

Typeset by Pentacor PLC, High Wycombe, Bucks.

Printed and bound in
Great Britain by Biddles Ltd,
Guildford and King's Lynn

To
Alfred and Myrat Shiner

CONTENTS

Part III Anti-Positivism

ACKNOWLEDGEMENTS

This book has been a long time in production. Some thoughts in it go back to the first paper I ever wrote in philosophy of law, in 1977. Such an elephantine gestation implies the accumulation of many debts; I ask indulgence for an acknowledgement section of some length, and none the less for the omission of any who deserve to be there.

That first paper was presented to the Pacific North West Philosophy Colloquium at Central Washington University, Ellensberg, in November 1977. Richard Wasserstrom was in the audience. Not only did he ask politely a number of searching questions, from finding the answers to which much was learnt. He also spent an hour afterwards assuring a shaking neophyte that there really were interesting things being said and worthwhile ideas being expressed. Such kindness and courtesy was and still is much appreciated. I hope this book does not cause him regret.

General thanks are due to many generations of students in my classes in philosophy of law at the University of Alberta. I have been fortunate to have had in those classes over the years many fine minds, many persons willing to discuss questions the instructor found interesting even if little would be learnt directly applicable to course examinations, and a remarkable overlap of the two categories. Special thanks are due to those students with whom I have had the challenge of working on theses in philosophy of law— Jerry Bickenbach, Bob Reiter, and Tim Dare; I owe much to them. I would also like to thank Jeff McLaughlin for help with proof-reading this book.

Over the years, different versions of the ideas expressed here have been presented to departments, conferences, and colloquia too numerous to mention. The group that has heard the most of these early versions, and from the most to the least confused of said versions, is that of my colleagues in the Canadian chapter of the International Society for Philosophy of Law and Social Philosophy. They have been unfailingly supportive, while unfailingly critical, sceptical even. It has been a privilege to be part of such an intellectually strong and personally congenial group. I mention in particular Brenda Baker, Dick Bronaugh, Wes Cragg, Marsha

Hanen, Michael Hartney, Barry Hoffmaster, Wayne Sumner, and Wil Waluchow; their interests overlapped so much more with mine that they wrote and said more about my work than did others.

Wil Waluchow deserves a special mention because I was fortunate to have him as a colleague for two years in Alberta. I have never discussed philosophy of law so intensively either before or since. Our conversations, though now made fewer by distance, have taught me so much, as have his written comments on my work. I am grateful too to Wil for letting me see in advance of publication so much of his own writing. I hope the disagreement with his views in this book will be seen as the mark of respect for a good friend that it is.

The first complete draft was written during 1984–5 in Oxford. One great pleasure of that year was meeting Denise Réaume and Les Green. There are unquestionably parts of this book which would not have the shape or content that they have without the criticism and advice of Les and Denise, both during that year and the time since. Their friendship has meant much both intellectually and personally.

I had the chance to present the ideas in the book as a series of seminars in the Department of Philosophy at the University of Waterloo in the spring of 1986. I am very grateful to Michael McDonald and Jan Zwicky (though both have now moved on) for arranging my appointment as Visiting Professor for the session. The chance to think continuously and to have the leisure to rewrite continuously in conjunction with energetic criticism was enormously valuable. The five weeks in Waterloo were among the most productive in the development of this book.

I was able to present amounts of the material in 1986–7 while Visiting Research Fellow in the Department of Jurisprudence, University of Glasgow. Tom Campbell and his colleagues were a willing and stimulating audience. Neil MacCormick was a genial and critical host on the number of occasions during that year when I ventured across country to Edinburgh. Later still, in 1989, Dick Bronaugh and Barry Hoffmaster invited me for a week to the University of Western Ontario. They and their students provided a valuable testing-ground for several parts of the book.

The year in Oxford would not have been possible without a Release Time Stipend from the Social Sciences and Humanities Council of Canada. I am very grateful to the Council for such tangible support. I would also like to thank the Master and Fellows of Balliol College, and the Faculty of Jurisprudence at Oxford, for their hospitality during that year. The near-final draft of the book was written in 1989–90 when I was appointed to a McCalla Research Professorship in the Faculty of Arts, University of Alberta. I am grateful to the University and the Faculty for this support.

Some of the material in this book has been previously published in a somewhat different form; I am grateful for permission to use the material here. The material has appeared in the following articles: 'Exclusionary Reasons and the Explanation of Behaviour', *Ratio Juris* 5 (1992), 1–22; 'The Acceptance of a Legal System', *Canadian Journal of Law and Jurisprudence*, 3 (1990), 81–106; 'Law and Authority', *Canadian Journal of Law and Jurisprudence*, 2 (1989), 3–18; 'Adjudication, Coherence, and Moral Value', in Anne F. Bayefsky (ed.), *Legal Theory Meets Legal Practice* (Edmonton, AB: Academic Printing and Publishing, 1988), 87–107 (by permission of Academic Printing and Publishing); 'Justice in the Garden of Eden', *Philosophy*, 63 (1988), 301–16 (by permission of the Royal Institute of Philosophy); 'Hermeneutics and the Internal Point of View to Law', in Carla Faralli and Enrico Pattaro (eds.), *Reason in Law*, ii (Milan: Giuffre, 1988), 211–23 (by permission of Dott. A. Giuffrè Editore S.p.A); 'Aristotle's Theory of Equity', in S. Panagiotou (ed.), *Justice, Law, and Method in Plato and Aristotle* (Edmonton, AB: Academic Printing and Publishing, 1987), 173–91 (by permission of Academic Printing and Publishing); 'Rules vs Rights: A Paradigmatically Philosophical Dispute', in D. N. MacCormick, S. Panou, and L. L. Vallauri (eds.), *Conditions of Validity and Cognition in Modern Legal Thought* (Stuttgart: Franz Steiner, 1985), 61–7 (by permission of Franz Steiner Verlag).

It remains to thank three individuals, to each of whom in different ways I owe more than words can express. For almost a decade Joseph Raz has been encouraging me in this project, even at a time when the visible evidence for its likely success was slight. On the occasions when we have met, particularly during the year in Oxford, his courteous, patient, but unerringly apt questions and ruminations have pointed me to many productive lines of thought and away from many sterile ones. The amount I have learnt from his published writings will be evident from the text and the index. I consider myself extraordinarily lucky to have had the support and the criticism of one of the finest minds in philosophy of law.

Two of the finest minds, in fact. My debt to Antony Duff is huge. He too has been encouraging the project for almost a decade. He has read during this time far more of the bits and pieces that surfaced than anyone else, no matter how exploratory or bitty. He read the first draft, and the whole of the near-final draft; in the latter case especially he has saved me from many unclarities and the odd foolishness. He has been the very paradigm of a sympathetic but thorough and probing critic. Some of the comments I received from him were scarcely shorter than that on which they commented. As a friend, there were many times in the early years of the work when he had a confidence in both the worth and the eventual completion of the project that its author did not have. He and Sandra Marshall helped me through dark nights of the soul with warmth and love. Every philosopher should be lucky enough to have such philosophical friends.

My final and greatest debt is to Janet Sisson. She gave freely of her expertise when the project veered into adjacent areas of philosophy where she knows much more than I. She has been always willing to join me in trying to think through ideas of all degrees of inchoateness. She has used her skill as a photographer in thinking of and producing the cover image. Those are just the identifiable contributions to this work. Since we met, she has been there throughout my life as its ground and its strength. Though there are many ways in which and many persons of which it is true that without them this book could not have been written, hers is the deepest and she the one of which it is true most of all.

The book is dedicated to my parents, with sadness that my mother did not live to see its completion.

R. A. S.

INTRODUCTION

1. MOVEMENT IN LEGAL THOUGHT

One recent study of law and legal theory begins with the bold assertion that 'the nature of law debate, as currently conducted, is largely meaningless' (Soper, *A Theory of Law*, preface, vii). Soper has in mind traditional arguments in analytical jurisprudence about the nature of law. He urges as remedy that theorists take seriously, not the analytical project of presenting a piece of 'descriptive metaphysics' (a theoretical account of the nature of law), but the normative project of producing a moral justification of law—a piece of 'revisionary metaphysics' which should not shrink from the criticism of existing legal forms and institutions in the name of right and justice.[1] One motivating idea in my study is that the first of Soper's claims has force. There are indeed limitations to what can be achieved by present strategies for theorizing about law when understood as their devotees understand them. A second motivating idea in my study is that Soper's two alternatives are false alternatives: the legal theorist is not forced to choose either sterile analysis or enthusiastic censoriousness. To think that the legal theorist is faced with only these alternatives is a mistake at the level of meta-legal theory, a meta-philosophical mistake. The purpose of the present study is not to produce a novel and original contribution to conventional analytical jurisprudence in accord with the latter's own self-understanding. On the other hand, I do not eschew the task which traditional analytical jurisprudence sets itself of sharpening and deepening our understanding of legality, law, and their relationship to each other and to human society. I aim at this latter goal indirectly, by aiming directly to present in a different light the nature and achievements of traditional legal theory. If we are able to gain a better view of what is happening in traditional analytical jurisprudence, then we shall just by the completion of that task be

---

[1] I appropriate the terms 'descriptive metaphysics' and 'revisionary metaphysics' from Peter Strawson; cf. *Individuals* (Garden City, NY, 1963), 9 ff.

better able to understand that which analytical jurisprudence purports to analyse—the human social institution of law.

I take the task of modern legal theory, the enterprise to which this study is a contribution, to be to advance our understanding of *modern law*—that is, of the institution of law as it is in contemporary society. The contemporary institution of law is of course a historical phenomenon, or rather a social, cultural, and *a fortiori* historical phenomenon. Legal systems are not like fossils, though they may contain them. A fossil is unchanged since it was formed, and by discovery alone is part of contemporary life. But, however much its historical roots may have contributed to its present form, and therefore however much the theorist at her peril ignores those roots in the attempt to discern this form, a contemporary legal system is not unchanged by history. Rather, it is the present product of those forces which have created it. In so far as contemporary elements of the contemporary institution are of central concern, therefore, their influence on legal theory is to be found in contemporary legal theory. I also limit myself largely to material relative to common law systems of the anglophone world, since these are the systems with which I and most anglophone legal theorists are best acquainted.

The ambiguity in the term 'movement' in my title is intentional. 'Movement' may refer to a group of persons united by common beliefs and pursuing a common goal—as when we speak of 'The Trade Union Movement' or 'The Oxford Movement'. In this sense, there are (very broadly) three main 'movements' in legal thought—legal positivism, anti-positivism or natural law theory, and legal realism or legal instrumentalism or Critical Legal Studies. These movements provide the primary source material for the present discussion. 'Movement' may also refer to an event in the world—paradigmatically, a variation of position or place, whether literal or metaphorical. This second sense is fundamentally important to the argument of this study, for in the application to legal theory of this concept of 'movement' lies the originality of the work. The book interprets legal theory as a set of dynamic conceptual relations: it aims to be, not a map nor even a relief model, but a *working* relief model of legal theory. Legal theory is not a static array of statement, argument, and rebuttal. It is an endless conversation, a complex interaction of intuition, suggestion, claim, and response. Philosophical theories have been likened to maps, or even relief models, of the world.[2] It might be an advance over the scientistic ambitions of traditional philosophy to leave behind the desire for the one true theoretical map, and to realize that a plurality of maps might be needed if we are to relieve philosophical puzzlement. But such a view still represents the task of philosophy as static description, and as such is still in thrall to the methods of descriptive science.

Movements presuppose forces to bring them about. Traditionally, the prime motive force in philosophical discussion has been a belief in the existence of mistakes. One philosopher represents another as in error, and seeks to correct the error. The prime motive force in this study is the belief in accuracy, the belief that legal theories contain intuitive insights into the nature of law.[3] The text of this study is (pre-)occupied with legal theory, and thus it may seem that the study is only about legal theory, that it presents only a theory of legal theory and not a theory of law. That would be an erroneous impression. The sub-text of the study is that, given the assumption of intuitive insight on the part of legal theorists, to trace the movements of legal theory is to chart what it is that evokes those movements—namely, the nature of law itself. Law will be understood best by seeing it as something whose nature is recoverable by legal theory only in the examination of the dynamic interaction of one account of law with another.

Even these thoughts are not yet precise enough to express the methodology of this study. One might suppose that anti-positivism—traditional natural law theory, for example—would be represented as responding to the *mistakes* of legal positivism, and vice versa. Such a supposition is only partially true. Indeed, unless anti-positivism thought that positivism were mistaken, it would not seek to prove to positivism the error of its ways. That is a sad truth in point of psychological fact about the human predicament;

[2] By John Wisdom, *Philosophy and Psycho-analysis* (Oxford, 1969), 19, and Renford Bambrough, 'Principia Metaphysica', *Philosophy*, 39 (1964), 97–8. For my views on these wider questions of philosophical method, cf. 'From Epistemology to Romance via Wisdom', in Ilham Dilman (ed.), *Philosophy and Life* (Boston, Mass., 1984), esp. 300–11.

[3] 'If philosophy is the criticism a culture produces of itself, and proceeds essentially by criticizing past efforts at this criticism, then Wittgenstein's originality lies in having developed modes of criticism that are not moralistic, that is, that do not leave the critic imagining himself free of the faults he sees around him' (Stanley Cavell, *The Claim of Reason* (Oxford, 1979), 175). This study tries also to be not 'moralistic'.

philosophers have found it very hard not to philosophize 'moralistically'. However, there is a difference between the criticism that a legal theory has omitted altogether to mention a significant feature of law or is *toto caelo* mistaken in its approach to law, and the criticism that a theory has begun on the right path but has not gone far enough down it or is travelling on the right path but has gone too far. That is, a theory may seek to build its own position on the supposed mistakes of its opponents, or it may seek to build its position on the supposed *insights* of its opponents. One important theme in much of what follows is the way that positivism and anti-positivism build on points each thinks the other has right but not right enough, or has right but too right.

It might be supposed that if I am prepared so to represent positivism and anti-positivism, then all the talk about 'movement' and 'dynamically related theories' is unnecessary. For, presumably, if there can be 'too right' and 'not right enough', then there can be 'exactly right'. Am I not myself still using here the representationalist language I was disparaging? Why cannot there be a static theoretical map of law which, unlike positivism and anti-positivism, does get things exactly right? Certainly, one prominent feature of analytical jurisprudence of the last decade has been the emergence of what I shall call Compatibilism—the line of argument that attempts to show that anything worth while in the opposition to positivism, and in particular in Ronald Dworkin's opposition to positivism, can be incorporated into a legal theory which remains none the less positivistic in its outlook. I include also as part of Compatibilism that congeneric line of argument which confesses bafflement as to what the exact disagreement is between positivism and its opponents, or between Dworkin and H. L. A. Hart. Compatibilism constitutes a plausible and valuable challenge to the view presented in this study. I will discuss Compatibilism in Part IV, Chapter 12, below, and much will turn on whether I am able to show it to be mistaken.

I have spoken almost entirely so far of legal positivism and anti-positivism. In the words of Tony Honoré's highly apt image (*Making Law Bind*, 32–3), they are the perennial finalists in the World Cup of jurisprudence, and they are also the protagonists here. Their dominance can be explained. An assumption of this work not defended in it otherwise than by being put to work is that there is something in the world that philosophy of law is the philosophy of—namely, *law*. Pre-philosophically, or pre-analytically, there are in the world laws, legal rules, legal doctrines, legal institutions, and legal systems. Philosophy aims to give a perspicuous representation of these entities in response to puzzlement about their nature. Philosophy of law is in that respect no different from philosophy of science, or philosophy of art, or philosophy of mind. Science and art exist as human enterprises before any attempts by philosophers to understand their nature. Slightly more controversially, perhaps, but as truly, minds exist before philosophy of mind in the sense that one person tells another that he is in pain or what she is thinking prior to any attempt by philosophers whether reductionists or dualists to understand what it is for there to be minds, pains, and thoughts. Given that these facts are so, then philosophical theories which take the form of denying the existence of the pre-philosophical entities must always yield pride of place to those which assume the existence of such entities and seek to analyse, understand, or interpret them, even if reductionistically. Thus, in the present case, both legal positivism and antipositivism assume directly the existence of law, legal rules, institutions, and systems, even though each has very different ideas about their perspicuous representation. Legal realism and its associates at face value deny, if not the existence, at least the significance for legal theory of legal rules, doctrines, institutions, and systems. Therefore, whatever the value of legal realism as a moral or political or social theory, it is bound to be of lesser importance in the philosophy of law.

2. THE PRIMACY OF POSITIVISM

So far in these introductory remarks I have spoken of positivism and anti-positivism equally. However, they are not equal. Legal theory must always begin with legal positivism. The reason is not far to seek. I spoke above of the pre-philosophical existence of law, legal rules, institutions, and systems. In the same spirit I offer as a pre-philosophical characterization of law the claim that a legal system is a particular kind of institutionalized normative system— for so it is.

The concept of 'law' is one with which we are all perfectly familiar. Law is a pervasive feature of modern society. From a relatively early stage in our growth in and into the world, we become aware (not albeit under this description) of a set of norms the source of which lies beyond our family, friends, school, church, club, or other local persons and institutions; which are noted and treated with varying degrees of respect by those who in their turn are influential over us; whose application is mediated by men and women in navy-blue uniforms, gowns and wigs, and so forth, and whose exploits are fodder for numerous favourite novels, movies, and TV programmes; which represent and reflect in some broad sense what is good, what is just, what is meet to be done; which control and confine the impermissible, the unjust, and the bad; which define forms and procedures for various activities. We might also become aware that possession of such norms is not a peculiarity of our country, but is a feature of most other countries too, though we might learn that the details vary, and even that such norms are elsewhere to a large degree, and even in our own country sadly not infrequently, manipulated in the goal of evil and self-interest rather than the common good. We learn of our own exposure to these norms, that they guide and impose limits on our conduct, whether in themselves or in virtue of the consequences of a failure to observe them. The fact of the existence of a law is a reason for action; laws are normative. We might learn at some suitable stage of our growth of the relation between the existence and content of these norms and the wishes, decisions, and ideas of individual citizens and groups of citizens. Laws do not come piecemeal, but are organized into groups and structures—into systems. Unlike the norms of etiquette, or fashion, or even morality, legal rules come into existence, vary, and pass away by formal means—by the operations of legal institutions. In such a way do we acquire on a pre-analytic level the concept of 'law', whatever it is for something to be a 'concept', and whatever it is to 'acquire' a concept. We swallow the concept down, to use Wittgenstein's phrase,[4] along with everything else that helps us to grow and nurtures us.

Now, in reciting the above facts, I do not take myself to be

---

[4] 'A child . . . doesn't learn *at all* that that mountain has existed for a long time: that is, the question whether it is so doesn't arise at all. It swallows this consequence down, so to speak, together with *what* it learns' (*On Certainty* (New York, 1972), s. 143; Wittgenstein's emphasis). Cf. also my 'Wittgenstein and the Foundations of Knowledge', *Proceedings of the Aristotelian Society*, 77 (1977–8)'.

saying anything of any philosophical interest or controversy. I am not offering these facts in a spirit of naïve realism, saying simultaneously to begin and conclude philosophical debate that law is what it is and not another thing. My point is simply this. When, for example, G. E. Moore said in his famous British Academy lecture in 1939 'Here is one hand' and held up a hand,[5] this much occurred. Moore rightly indicated that which those philosophers concerned to understand our knowledge of the external world are concerned to understand—the normal case at the level of commonsensical human understanding of perceptual knowledge. *That* (and here I point to Moore's performance) is the thing which (this part of) epistemology is aimed at understanding. The recitation in the previous paragraph of plain facts about our life in the contemporary social world is offered in the same spirit. *Those* (and here I point to the entities of which the above recitation details our pre-analytic grasp) are the entities that legal theory is aimed at understanding and analytical jurisprudence aimed at analysing. A boring, but an incontestable point—I submit.

Since, however, the point is incontestable, we may begin reflection there. And when we do, we notice that we are referring to a certain set of human practices. Again, I intend that term in as pre-analytic and philosophically aseptic a way as is possible. We are referring to a set of *practices*, not of carpentry tools or works of art or marsupials or emotions, even though it might be philosophically illuminating to consider whether such practices are (like) tools, (like) works of art, (like) kangaroos, (like) romantic love. It is intrinsic to the term 'law' to refer to, to be semantically connected with, the given range of human practices that the above recitation of pre-analytic facts picks out. The recitation, however, is couched in very general and very woolly terms—it is intended to, and does, merely gesture in the direction of a multiplicity of detail in the actual entities in question.

None the less, it is possible to distil out of all that multiplicity of diffuse and diverse detail, while still remaining at the level of pre-analytic triviality, a lowest common denominator which is crucial to the possibility of picking out at all the cluster of entities—the facts that legal norms have a source which is external to the

[5] Cf. Moore, *Philosophical Papers* (London, 1959), 146-7.

individual and is social; that the practices in relation to the creation, interpretation, and enforcement of these norms are institutionalized; that the norms are related in complicated ways to other social norms, ways which cannot amount to identity; and so forth. Note how different my language has now become. This last sentence clearly uses the language of technical legal theory, the language of analytical jurisprudence itself. The above recitation of pre-analytic facts does not use such language. None the less, my intention is that the technical language be understood here at this point in my argument as no more, though no less, than a translation into such language of the recitation of plain, non-technical, incontestable, and boring facts about the concept of 'law'. We would not be able to differentiate the entities the legal theorist is concerned to understand from other social institutions and practices unless they possessed certain observable features (nor would the term 'law' have empirical reference unless this were so). The features picked out by the recitation informally and formally by its technical (or better, 'quasi-technical') translation are the required observable features.

Consider now some of the characteristic claims made by legal positivism—law is a set of commands set by superior to inferior; in the combination of two types of social rule primary and secondary lies the key to the science of jurisprudence; law is the most important institutionalized normative system; law is a set of conventional rules for the solution of co-ordination problems; and so forth. Legal positivism, I claim, is no more and no less than the attempt to redescribe in a less trivial way (and therefore less incontestable way—but we'll let that pass for now) at the technical level the entities picked out in the pre-analytic recitation and its quasi-technical counterpart. But positivism's attempt is not just an attempt at redescription. It is also an attempt to offer a theory, a descriptive theory, which gives those entities in themselves the status of the essence of law; which attempts to analyse the concept of law without remainder in terms of those entities; which offers a definition, or at least a fundamental characterization, of law in terms of those entities. Positivism does not claim in a spirit of stating a boringly obvious pre-analytic truism, as I have claimed in the spirit of stating a boringly obvious pre-analytic truism, that the concept of 'law' is the concept which picks out that range of social practices. Positivism claims as a result of its reflective and analytical activities that it really is the essence of law to be just that set of human practices. Positivism offers its conclusions not as boring truisms but as profound insights.

This fact has two consequences for the project in this study of trying to understand better the nature of law by trying better to understand the nature of legal theory. First, since our concept of 'law' in the truistic sense just is the concept which picks out that range of human practices positivism makes central to its analysis, positivism in one sense cannot be wrong. Any attempt to analyse law must not only include, but also begin with, the entities picked out in the pre-analytic recitation, and therefore the entities emphasized by positivism. If the theorist strayed so far from positivism that she presented a theory the vocabulary of which referred to none of the entities to which the vocabulary of positivism refers, her theory would not be, and could not be, a theory of law. It might be a theory of ethics, or practical reasoning, or etiquette, or agreements among gentlemen, or family customs; but it would not be a theory of law. Both anti-positivism and legal realism in their different ways remove these dull pre-analytic facts about law from centre stage. They are thus in an important sense *paradoxical* theories of law. The instinct to believe a theory of law which reiterates plain truths about the concept of law rather than a theory which offers paradoxes is very powerful, and rightly so. Positivism therefore has the legal theorist on a piece of elastic; the further one goes away from positivism, the stronger is the pull to return to it.

3. THE LIMITATIONS OF POSITIVISM

Positivism, however, pays a price for its centrality. Because positivism in its core reiteration simply reproduces accurately what we already know at the level of pre-analytic grasp before we begin jurisprudential reflection, positivism cannot in itself help those who are puzzled at the philosophical level about the nature of law. Positivism, as does any philosophical theory, simply reminds us of the familiar. It does so, however, in a particular way—it reminds us of what is familiar about the familiar. This is, to be fair, not to say that positivism is useless; to those theories which attempt to reduce law to something else—predictions of what persons in wigs will say, for example—it is a proper antidote. Moreover, a positivism which describes very carefully and organizes a very large number of the features of legal rules, institutions, and systems can be of great value to those whose puzzlement with law derives from a superficial understanding of law. But these points about positivism do show that positivism cannot succeed as a theory of law in the way that traditional analytical jurisprudence supposes that it can—namely, by being simultaneously both the most descriptively accurate and the most philosophically illuminating theory of law. We must desert positivism in order to grasp both those aspects of the nature of law which non-positivistic theories are better placed to illuminate and those aspects of law which positivistic theories are better placed to illuminate. To borrow a turn of phrase from Francis Sparshott,[6] the concept of law which positivism offers is the concept of what is in common to a set of practices; as such, positivism has no inner resources of its own, nothing on which to draw in order to provide that illumination from a source external to the practices of law which a deeper understanding of law requires. Positivism has and must have a privileged position among theories of law, for the reasons given. But it pays for that privilege in that many of its duties are to fulfil purely ceremonial engagements.

I have used modalities in talking about the place of positivism—theorizing about law *must* begin with positivism, *must* return to positivism, and so forth. What is the justification for these modalities? Why cannot legal theory begin with classical Natural Law as a paradigm form of anti-positivism? One sufficient answer is the historical one. Classically, the Greeks began legal theory at the point at which the distinction was articulated between *nomos* and *phusis*. I pass over a question which would in another context need discussion—the question of whether *nomos* means 'law', 'convention', or something of both, or what. What is clear is the contrast between it and *phusis*, 'nature'. Natural law theory asks us to see positive law/enacted law/black-letter law/human law as related in deep and important ways to *phusis*, to human nature. Natural law theory regards *phusis* as superior to *nomos*, whether by way of making normative recommendations as to how positive

---

[6] *The Theory of the Arts* (Princeton, NJ, 1982), 458. The methodology of Sparshott's book has had much influence on the present study.

law should be justified or theoretical recommendations as to how to conceive of law itself. But this priority cannot be a conceptual or analytic priority, for the following reason. The term 'law' itself in the expression 'natural law' is, or at least if the natural law theorist wants to dispute with the positivist it must be, a term whose reference is the same social institutions and practices that positivistic theory picks out as the essence of law. Natural law theory asks us to see *those practices*—sc. the practices of *nomos*— as more deeply related to *phusis* than positivism represents them as being. Natural law theory could not make that claim unless we already had the concept of law as a certain social entity, a certain set of social practices. Thus, the reason why we 'cannot begin with natural law' is this. In formulating the very claim that legal theory should begin with natural law, one has already used the term 'law' in its primary sense—the sense we all 'swallow down' as we grow up; the sense that dictionary definitions aim to specify, the sense that the recitation on pages 5–6 of boring pre-analytic facts amplifies. And that sense, for what it is worth for it to do so, belongs to positivism. Positivism begins with that sense.

Positivism also ends with that sense, and I have indicated that this is a weakness in positivism. It is of course a weakness that anti-positivist theories are peculiarly well placed to exploit. Lon Fuller's central image of the eight ways to fail to make law (*The Morality of Law*, 33–41) argues for the claim that the central character of law itself cannot be adequately characterized in vocabulary that is devoid of moral content. Patrick Devlin argues[7] that it is of the nature of at any rate the criminal law to be an enforcement of the morality of the society whose law it is. Dworkin claims that instinct in positive law itself are certain duties and entitlements the nature of which cannot be adequately represented with the conceptual resources provided to the legal theorist by legal positivism.[8] John Finnis argues for a fundamental connection of law with practical reasonableness in a wider sense and with basic human value.[9] Derek Beyleveld and Roger

---

[7] *The Enforcement of Morals* (London, 1965), *passim*. Note that this is a claim with which in fact Ronald Dworkin does not disagree—his dispute with Devlin is simply over what is to count as a moral position. Cf. *Taking Rights Seriously* (2nd edn., Cambridge, Mass., 1978), ch. 10.

[8] *Taking Rights Seriously*, esp. chs. 2–4.

[9] *Natural Law and Natural Rights* (Oxford, 1980), esp. chs. 3–6.

Brownsword regard legal validity as dependent on consistency with some essential moral requirement.[10] These archetypical lines of argument embody the thought that the nature of *law*—that is to say, the entity the factual recitation of pages 5–6 picks out—cannot be adequately represented by a theory that does not represent law as connected with fundamental value by a deeper conceptual connection than positivism can acknowledge.

In order fully to appreciate the nature of law, all these writers suggest, the theorist must venture beyond the limits of law as specified by positivism into areas of social life which positivism would regard as outside law. Anti-positivism, therefore, must be taken seriously because it too is in a deep sense correct. It has a piece that only it can contribute to the puzzle that is legal theory. To see the essential connection of law with wider society one must look outside law. If that is true, then it seems we must acknowledge the following fact about anti-positivism. Just as it was necessary to acknowledge that positivism had the legal theorist on the end of a piece of elastic, so that she would always feel the pull of positivism when she ventures away from positivism, so also anti-positivism has the legal theorist on another piece of elastic, so that as she responds to the pull of positivism by returning towards it she will feel the pull of anti-positivism, and the nearer to positivism, the stronger the pull.

4. THE ARGUMENT OF THE STUDY

I said at the beginning of this introduction that this study aimed to pursue a project in analytical jurisprudence while presuming a different model for analytical jurisprudence itself than that assumed by traditional/conventional versions of analytical jurisprudence. We are now in a position to see what I am claiming. If the above schematic account of the relations between positivistic and anti-positivist legal theories is correct, then it will obscure the nature of the contribution, and the content of the contribution, each kind of theory makes to a deeper understanding of law to represent at the meta-theoretical level the different theories as static descriptive maps. That, however, is the way that traditional

---

[10] *Law As a Moral Judgment* (London, 1986), esp. chs. 1, 4–5.

analytical jurisprudence thinks of legal theories—as careful mappings, with various degrees of accuracy, of the legal landscape.

The model presupposed by this study is, on the contrary, *dynamic*—that is, one sees past the different theories to the entities they illuminate, not by seeing the different theories as partial pictures juxtaposed, but as partial theories *interacting* with each other, and by that interaction providing the deeper understanding sought in legal theorizing.

The general shape of this interaction, and thus of the main argument of this study, is as follows. I consider the opposition of positivism and anti-positivism theory as taking place on seven fronts, all of which have been the focus of attention in recent legal theory. The seven are: law as a reason for action; the authority of law; the point of view of legal thought; the acceptance of law; judicial discretion and legal principle; legal interpretation and the semantics for propositions of law; law and the common good. I begin in Part I with the characterization of what I shall call 'simple' positivism—a theory of law in positivistic style which enunciates the separation of law and morality in a blunt and uncompromising, and hence unsubtle, fashion. I shall set out the view taken by simple positivism on each of the seven issues just mentioned. I shall turn in Part II to 'sophisticated' positivism. Sophisticated positivism perceives defects in simple positivism, but defects which, it believes, can none the less be remedied without giving up the fundamental commitments of positivism on each of the seven issues. For example,[11] simple positivism represents the authority of law as authority in name only—law has force only in that it is a set of commands backed up by an efficacious threat to visit with evil in the case of non-compliance. Sophisticated positivism tries first to say that laws are social rules and not commands backed by threats, but this thesis does not yield any account of the authority of law. Sophisticated positivism then represents law as indeed being fundamentally connected with authority, but by necessarily claiming, not necessarily having, authority. In other words, sophisticated positivism, as presented in Part II, is positivism in the best versions that positivism itself believes it has found for itself.

In Parts I and II I shall in effect have traced seven different lines

---

[11] The story will be spelt out at greater length anon—see Chs. 1.2 and 2.2 below.

of argument in positivistic legal thought, seven different paths which positivism has followed in order to find ground free from discomfort. Part III presents the responses of anti-positivism on these same seven issues.

Anti-positivism will be shown to argue that each of the seven paths if followed to its destination leads to anti-positivist positions, and thus that the roots of anti-positivism are in the insights of positivism itself.[12] The paths began, we must remember, with simple positivism. Therefore, embedded in law according to the commonsensical account of law with which positivism begins are features of law which bring about the movement of legal theory away from simple positivism through sophisticated positivism to anti-positivism. For example, anti-positivism argues that once the need is appreciated to connect law with authority in order adequately to explain the nature of law, the need cannot be met by anything less than a connection of law with the having of authority, a connection, not a separation, of law and morality.[13] Part III will be the longest part, for the reason that the arguments of positivism are well known; the arguments for anti-positivism, by contrast, need greater explication and defence.

Part IV, Chapter 11, considers positivism's response to the arguments of anti-positivism. The general form of this response is that anti-positivism has gone so far down the path away from the truths that are the intuitive heart of positivism that anti-positivism is no longer a theory of law at all. If the argument to this point of the study is sound, the inevitable dynamic of legal thought will have been exposed. I will have shown both that legal theory must desert legal positivism and that it must return to positivism; both that legal theory must end up in anti-positivism and that it cannot remain there. In Chapter 12 I argue, as promised, for the impossibility of Compatibilism—the general position that positivism and anti-positivism can be made compatible with each other in some

---

[12] In an essay published after this manuscript was first accepted, Jeffrey Goldsworthy presents an anti-positivistic theory of law resting 'on premises accepted by positivists themselves' ('The Self-destruction of Legal Positivism', *Oxford Journal of Legal Studies*, 10 (1990), 486). He argues that anti-positivism is the correct theory of law, and the focus for his argument to self-destruction is on Raz's theory of legal validity in *The Authority of Law* (Oxford, 1979), ch. 8. I do not consider legal validity here. Moreover, as will be clear, my final conclusion is not that an anti-positivist theory of law is correct. Goldsworthy's view is therefore at best a complement to my own.

[13] Cf. Ch. 4 below for the full argument.

stable third or middle-ground theory of law. Finally, in Chapter 13, I attempt to relate the picture of legal theory here developed to wider issues in both metaphysical and political theory, in order to show how the local conflicts in legal theory which I have considered have deeper roots in wider global conflicts. These wider considerations will complete and strengthen the argument for the inevitability of the movements of legal thought between the poles of Norm and Nature. The conclusion summarizes the picture of law itself that emerges from the picture of legal theory. The summary may seem on its own and out of context commonplace and trivial; but it must be seen as given full meaning by all the pages and the arguments that have preceded it.

Part I
Simple Positivism

1

SIMPLE POSITIVISM

1. INTRODUCTION

I have said that legal theory must begin with positivism. Let us therefore so begin, and in particular with what I am calling 'simple positivism'. 'Simple' here is not intended to connote 'simple-minded' or 'intellectually deficient'. Indeed, the work which perhaps comes closest to being simple positivism, John Austin's jurisprudence, is intellectually thorough and sensitive work. 'Simple' connotes 'pure', 'unadulterated', 'straightforward'; it does connote a lack of complexity, but not so as to imply this lack to be a defect. Matisse is not a worse painter than Monet or Géricault just because his canvases are in some proper sense 'simpler'. Introductory jurisprudence standardly identifies something known as 'The Command Theory of Law', which is to be found in Austin's writings. I have no interest here in the narrow question of whether it is correct to speak of laws as commands of the sovereign, for two reasons—Austin himself had a great deal more to say about law than the claim that laws are commands of the sovereign, and, second, so much more that we can see it is neither in any interesting sense straightforwardly true nor in any interesting sense straightforwardly false to say that laws are commands of the sovereign. For example, on the one hand, it is not at all obvious, as Hart has remarked (*The Concept of Law*, 27–33), how laws which facilitate the variation of interpersonal legal relations or laws which define the extent of a court's jurisdiction are commands. On the other hand, to speak of laws as commands is one attempt to expose the feature of law others have attempted to expose by speaking of laws as 'exclusionary' or 'peremptory' reasons[1]—the feature that laws present themselves to us as

---

[1] Chiefly Raz; cf. *Practical Reason and Norms* (London, 1975), 35–48, 141–8, and elsewhere. See also Hart, *Essay on Bentham* (Oxford, 1982), ch. 10, 'Commands and authoritative legal reasons'.

reasons for action of a special kind. My interest here is more ambitious. I aim to uncover the deeper thoughts about the nature of law which underlie the surface claims of a theory like the Command Theory, and to open the gate to the seven paths of legal theory that I have mentioned. The Command Theory is important, not because of anything intrinsic to the claim that laws are commands of the sovereign, but rather because it is a palmary example of a whole way of thinking about the institution of law. Simple positivism is that way of thinking.

It is important to realize that I am not describing any single historical figure. My characterization of simple positivism is 'literary' in its approach in the following sense. The author of a novel or play, for instance, makes initial and protected choices as to the who, what, where, when, and why of the work. It is up to the author whether the central character is a medieval king or a contemporary psychiatrist, whether the action takes place in Toronto or Tuktoyaktuk. The constraints to which the author is subjected appear only after those initial choices have been made.[2] Crudely, no novelist can be criticized just for making the central character a contemporary psychiatrist or setting the work in Toronto; such choices are entirely within the conventions of the novel. But, if the protagonist is a contemporary psychiatrist or set in Toronto, then it is extremely unlikely that room may be found also for a medieval king without straining credulity and coherence or scenes in Tuktoyaktuk without describing travel. So also, any choice I now make as to what will constitute simple positivism is to a point protected from criticism, for I might have chosen to write a different book within the genre of treatise on legal theory. But I do thereby bind myself to showing how beginning *here* and going on like *this* results in a book which has something important to say about legal theory. In that way I am committed to the task of being coherent with and remaining faithful to a discipline with a history and a content. The reader must decide at the end of the study whether the commitment has been discharged.

---

[2] I ignore here issues raised by Stanley Fish's claim (*Doing What Comes Naturally* (Durham, NC, 1989), 95–6), contesting views about legal and literary interpretation he attributes to Ronald Dworkin, that the very choice to write a work in a certain genre—a novel, for instance—already imposes constraints in the form of the conventions of the genre. I am concerned only with choices within a genre.

Let us, then, begin the exposition of simple positivism, and thus begin the story this study tells.

2. LAW AS A REASON FOR ACTION

Law falls within the scope of the practical. The fact that something is required or prohibited by law is a reason for action. That remark is intended as aseptically as possible from the point of view of theory. Perhaps the minimal way to conceive of laws as reasons for action is by the following image—a train bearing down is a reason for action for one crossing the railway track. Here, a whole range of goals is assumed to which the remaining on or fleeing from the railway track is related as brute means to desired end. In itself, the fact of a train proceeding at speed down the track is just that—a fact. It comes to have relevance for action only because the fact comes within the purview of some person's goal-directed behaviour. One might think of legal realism or rule-scepticism as thinking of laws as providing reasons for action in just this fashion. It is just a dull fact that certain persons—persons some call 'sovereigns', for example—have performed certain actions—some call those actions 'enacting laws'. It is another dull fact that certain other actions— some call those actions 'breaking the law'—will likely have certain consequences, for example incarceration. The obtaining of such facts may come within the purview of certain goals—worthy ones like improving the lot of marginalized peoples or unworthy ones like obtaining funds for the support of terrorism. The existence of laws as facts is made into a reason for action only by the existence of such goals and by the facts coming within the purview of the goals.

Simple positivism does not hold to such a minimal view of the way that laws provide reasons for action, but only just does it not so hold. To the rule-sceptic, there is no relevant difference at all between the ascribed normativity of the train *qua* model and the ascribed normativity of the existence of law *qua* thing modelled. Rule-scepticism so construed gives no theoretical role to the fact that the existence of a law is an institutional fact. Simple positivism does think that it is important to recognize laws are institutional facts—commands of the sovereign, for example—and that the normativity of law is in some way connected with this kind of factuality. Unless the command emanates from one to whom others are in a habit of obedience and who is himself (herself/themselves) not in a habit of obedience to any human superior, the command will not be that special kind of command which constitutes a law.[3] It is easy to overlook how subtle is Austin's taxonomy here. Commands are distinguished from other forms of imperative: those commands of the sovereign which are laws are distinguished both from those commands of others which are not laws and those commands of the sovereign which are not laws: positive law is distinguished from other kinds of law.[4] There is no initial way to explain these subtleties other than as the rejection of the rule-sceptic's crude model for the way that law provides a reason for action.

None the less, simple positivism does not move very far beyond rule-scepticism. For simple positivism, what it is for a norm to be a law cannot be stated without making some reference to institutionalization. None the less, what it is for the norm to be a reason for action can be stated without reference to institutionalization. The norm's force as a reason is derived from the fact that the command is backed by a threat or sanction—the norm-subject will be visited with evil if he or she does not comply with the command. 'Being liable to evil from you if I comply not with a wish which you signify, I am *bound* or *obliged* by your command, or I lie under a *duty* to obey it.'[5] Austin sees that theory cannot adequately represent the way that law is a reason for action unless the way that law is a reason for action is represented as the imposition of an institutional requirement. However, he offers as enough to satisfy that constraint the fact that the norm-subject will be visited with evil by the sovereign in the event of non-compliance. On such a view the connection between the evil and its source is causal and contingent, not conceptual.

Imagine oneself now in the position of a norm-subject contemplating a course of action. The fact of the sovereign having commanded thus and so enters into the practical reasoning merely in a very simple form—there is a law prohibiting me from doing X; I will be visited with evil if I do X; therefore, I have good reason

---

[3] John Austin, *The Province of Jurisprudence Determined* (London, 1954), Lecture VI, 192–5.

[4] Ibid., Lecture I, 18–23.

[5] Ibid., 14; Austin's emphasis.

not to do *X*. But this is an unrealistically simple example. Suppose that there are other benefit-producing practical reasons for disobeying the law, whether worthy or unworthy. How is the conflict between the putative visiting with evil and the putative benefits to be represented? Simple positivism cannot say more than that the evil goes one side of the scale and the good on the other, and that one will outweigh the other. 'Obligation' and 'duty' in Austin's account are place-holders for very weighty reasons for action to be thrown into the balance of reasons for action. The analysis of laws as institutional facts plays no significant part in the analysis of laws as reasons for action. Never mind that laws are institutional facts, they are still simply reasons for action to be weighed in the general balance of reasons for action. To that degree, simple positivism shares common ground with legal realism or rule-scepticism on the way that laws are reasons for action. Both for simple positivism and for legal realism, decision-making in relation to law is particularistic. Even though the commands of the sovereign may be, as Austin insists, phrased in general terms, the generality is not entrenched; it may be overridden at any time in some particular case by weightier reasons for the risk of being visited with evil.[6]

3. LAW AND AUTHORITY

Austin is famous for claiming that 'the existence of law is one thing, its merit or demerit another'.[7] This central thesis of the separation of law and morality, in the eyes of many theorists both positivist and anti-positivist, defines positivism. Different things might be and are meant by different people when speaking of the separation of law and morality. In many circumstances it is important to distinguish these different things, although the distinctions are not my concern here.[8] The separation thesis, as it might be called, is an essential part of simple positivism. So, I am

---

[6] The terminology of 'particularistic' and 'entrenched' is borrowed from Frederick Schauer, *Playing By the Rules* (Oxford, 1991); cf. ch. 5 and esp. 77–8.

[7] Ibid., Lecture V, 184.

[8] Hart, for example, in ch. 9 of *The Concept of Law* (Oxford, 1961) distinguishes 6 different ways in which law and morality might be 'connected', each of which he thinks compatible with positivism. See also Ch. 12.2 below on the issue of whether it is compatible with positivism that courts sometimes engage in moral argument.

interested in what stances one who holds that 'the existence of law is one thing, its merit or demerit another' is thereby committed to taking on a wider range of issues. I treat the separation thesis in the immediately following paragraphs, not as a general thesis about the nature of law, but as a thesis about the authority of law. In accordance with the separation thesis, simple positivism leads to a particular conception of the authority of law, or the legitimacy of a legal system.

The nature of authority has been much debated by legal and political philosophy, and the terminology is not stable. I shall begin by stipulating how I understand some of the key terms. I consider authority here as a property of laws and of legal systems. Authority must be distinguished primarily from power, efficacy, and validity. Authority is not the same as power. A person or institution may have the power to affect the way that people behave, but lack authority because he, she, or it is purely coercive. Authority is not the same thing as efficacy; efficacy simply means that there is conformity to the rules of the system, whether willing conformity or not. But it is possible for there to be conformity to the laws of a successful repressive system, and such a system would not have authority. Authority is not the same as validity. To be valid is to be pedigreed by the rule of recognition of the legal system. A legal rule may have that property, and yet lack authority because it is not a rule which there is any obligation to obey. If the law has authority, then the demands that the law makes of us it has a right to make of us; its requirements are such that we ought to conform to them. Theorists sometimes distinguish between 'legitimate authority' and 'de facto authority'. It follows from the above that in my terminology 'authority' means 'legitimate authority' as that term has been typically understood—authority which issues directives we have an obligation to obey. 'Legitimate authority' is pleonastic; 'de facto authority' is an ill-formed expression.[9]

Given such a construal of authority, the judgement that a particular law or system of laws possesses authority for simple positivism will be a judgement of, for example and in most likelihood, morality. The practitioner of censorious jurisprudence, whether lay or professional, will have implicitly or explicitly a conception of what the content of law ought to be. This conception

---

[9] See also Ch. 4.8 below.

may be directly moral—'It is morally unjust to give police the power summarily to suspend driving licences'—or indirectly moral—'There are sound economic reasons for limiting liability in negligence for purely economic loss, and morality permits the issue to be decided on economic grounds'. The law will be judged authoritative—morally deserving of obedience and respect—just in case it conforms to that content. *But*—whether or not a given law or legal system in fact does have authority in such a fashion, it is still *the law*—'the existence of law . . .'. Those standards which supply law with authority are not the standards which supply law with its status as law. The latter are internal to law; the former are external to law.

4. THE EXTERNAL POINT OF VIEW TO LAW

Simple positivism claims that it is not only possible but necessary for the legal theorist to take the external point of view to all law and the whole of legal system. It is important to note that 'external' here is a term of art. It is not a plainly factual property of plain fact situations. It is in origin a spatial metaphor, and its origin must be kept in mind when considering its use in legal theory. The presuppositions of the metaphor are that law is thought of in spatial-metaphorical terms, as consisting in a bounded domain. There is an 'inside' and an 'outside' to that domain, as there is an 'inside' and an 'outside' to the beer garden at the jazz festival, marked as such by some 'fence'. In the case of law, the 'fence' is the criterion which determines the extension of the term 'law' by defining the validity or 'pedigree'[10] of laws. To understand law, one has to understand that domain and what happens within it. In order to reach such understanding, however, one does not have to enter the domain. In order to see what is happening in the beer garden, it is sufficient to peer over the fence.

The metaphor is now beginning to strain. The claim that the legal theorist may wholly understand law from the external point of view is not a claim about empirical possibilities—not a claim (controversial, and probably false) that the theorist is able to understand what happens in a court of law or a legislature without

---

[10] The image is Dworkin's; cf. *Taking Rights Seriously*, 17.

ever sitting in the spectators' gallery or going on a guided tour. Rather, the thought is this. There are certain characteristic attitudes and commitments on the part of those for whom the law is an enterprise in which they have faith and to which they are dedicated, those for whom law is imbued with a moral character. The legal theorist can in principle offer as full and as accurate a theory about law as anyone could wish for without sharing any of those attitudes and commitments. To theorize about law without a pro-attitude and without commitment is what it is to study and analyse the law 'from the external point of view'. The law is an object which the theorist may treat as if it were inanimate, an object to which the investigator is 'external'.

Part of what motivates the externality thesis, as we may call it, is the following fact. In the normal, clear case we indeed can tell for some given particular law,[11] independently of whether we think the law in question to be a good or a bad law and of whether we are or are not norm-subjects of the legal system to which the law in question belongs, whether it is pedigreed and what its consequences are for possible courses of action. We can also seemingly give a clear sense to the notion of 'external'. Since I am not a citizen of Spain, I remain in some quite reasonable sense 'external' to the Spanish legal system unless I go to Spain for a holiday, travel on a Spanish aircraft or ship, seek to contract with a Spanish business, propose marriage to or assault a Spanish citizen, and so forth. The Spanish legal system seems to be a bounded domain which I do not have to enter unless I choose to do so, just like the beer garden at the jazz festival. Moreover, the Spanish legal system is just so far quite typical of legal systems. Seve Ballasteros or Angel Romero bear exactly the same relationship to the Canadian legal system. It is therefore easy to suppose that it is in the nature of legal systems to be such bounded domains, and therefore that the legal theorist who aspires to universality and not merely to a given legal dogmatics may in principle and legitimately occupy a position external to all such domains.

Another motivation for the externality thesis, and one which is in part underwritten by the first, is a certain ideal of theoretical

---

[11] There is a distinction between we the public, to whom laws expressed in largely ordinary language are clear, and we the legal profession, to whom, in addition, laws expressed in well-understood technical vocabulary are clear. This distinction does not affect my point here.

enquiry—the ideal of scientific detachment and independence. Life is full of stories of how theorists and investigators have failed to prove what they claimed to have proved, or have failed to discover what they claimed to have discovered, because they were misled or even blinded by emotion and prejudice.[12] Legal science, as much as any other science, needs to be kept pure from such adulterations. One way to assist legal science in this endeavour is to keep pure the object of legal science itself, the law. One way to do that is to define law in terms which prescind from the possible intentionality of legal events. We have a very clear model for externality in our relationship to inanimate and spatially bounded physical objects. If the domain of law is similarly construed, then the same model for externality can be applied.

A third motivation for the externality thesis comes from certain politico-moral ideas which are deeply rooted in democratic ideology. The existence of the law's demands represents an incursion into the domain (those spatial metaphors again) of personal freedom and autonomy. In order to preserve the boundaries of this latter domain as wide as possible, the law must be conceived so as to make it always possible to regard the decision to obey or disobey the law as one which the individual freely makes. Any claim that the law is innately binding upon the individual is an attempt to imprison the individual within the law's domain. It would be like stipulating it to be mandatory for all attending the jazz festival to enter the beer tent and buy beer, instead of leaving it as a free individual choice. The theoretical representation of law as a bounded domain which an individual is free to enter or not at will seems an important politico-moral constraint on analytical jurisprudence. To analyse law so that the external point of view may be taken to all law satisfies that constraint.

5. THE ACCEPTANCE OF LAW

Simple positivism claims that it is a contingent truth about some given society how far the law in that society is accepted as

[12] Stephen Jay Gould's *The Mismeasure of Man* (New York, 1981) tells a fascinating cautionary tale, as does John Michell's *Eccentric Lives and Peculiar Notions* (London, 1989).

legitimate. Note that the claim here is not that it is a contingent truth how far the law in any given society *is* legitimate. In one way, whether this latter fact obtains merely contingently is not one issue in the overall debate between positivism and natural law theory; it is the pivotal issue in the overall debate. In another way, in some more specific form, this issue of contingency is addressed when we consider whether law is merely contingently authoritative,[13] or when we consider whether law is merely contingently for the common good.[14] The claim that it is a contingent truth about some given society how far the law in that society is accepted as legitimate is a claim about the attitudes of people in a society towards the law of that society. It is a claim that there is no such connection of any interest to analytical jurisprudence. Such connections may be of interest to the sociologist, the psychologist, the criminologist, ..., but not to the analytical theorist who studies the concept of law.

The phrase 'accept as legitimate' is in the idiolect of the present study almost a pleonasm. That is to say, to accept the law is to accept it as legitimate; to accept the law is to accept it as creating obligations ('genuine obligations' is also pleonastic). We need both nominal and verbal forms. The nominal form 'acceptance of the law's demands', for example, sounds correct and 'acceptance of the legitimacy of the law's demands' awkward. 'He accepts the law' sounds incomplete, and 'He accepts that the law's demands are legitimate' the filled-out story.

Support for this thesis about the contingency of acceptance comes from two places. First, the separation thesis says that a law's status as law has nothing to do with its content. The separation thesis so understood is a negative thesis, but it has an obvious positive correlate—that the status of a law as law is a matter of its source or pedigree. The pedigree of a law is dependent on human intention in the general sense that a given act of law-making, of pedigreeing, is an intentional act (another pleonasm), whether by an individual or a group of lawmakers. But there is no other connection to human intention, according to simple positivism. The status of any given law as law is not dependent on its efficacy; a law that is no longer efficacious is still a law if it has been duly

---

[13] Cf. Chs. 2.2 and 4.
[14] Cf. Chs. 2.7 and 9.

enacted and not duly repealed. It might belong to the sociology of law to determine why a particular law is not efficacious, or whether a particular proposed law will be efficacious. But such projects do not fall within the province of jurisprudence, since they do not have to do with the determination of what it is for a law to be law. The claim may be made that efficacy is a necessary condition for the existence of a legal *system*. It falls within the province of jurisprudence to make that claim. Simple positivism makes such a claim. The claim is, though, largely uncontroversial. Legal theorists almost all agree that efficacy is a necessary condition for the existence of a legal system.[15] Since the interest of this study is in what divides legal theorists, little attention will be paid to efficacy here.

The second source of support lies in the notion of laws as commands backed by sanctions, and the idea that the proper source of law, the sovereign, is defined in part by the presence of a habit of obedience towards that sovereign. A 'habit' is a certain pattern of behaviour; we can speak of a habit of a group when the habits so understood of the members of the group converge. 'Behaviour' here is construed as the 'colourless movements' of behaviouristic psychology—the movements of human bodies considered as inert matter, as opposed to bodily movements considered as the movements of persons.[16] Thus, that aspect of the life of the norm-subjects of the laws which contributes to the laws being laws is an aspect which can be defined without reference to human intentionality. Likewise, there is no need to interpret the conformity to law which makes a system efficacious as any more than 'colourless movements'. That a law or set of laws is accepted, on the other hand, is a fact about the intentional stance of the norm-subjects. If the law's status as law can be defined without reference to that fact, then the relation of law's status as law to that fact is one of contingency.[17]

---

[15] Raz does not regard efficacy as a necessary condition. His 'strong social thesis' claims that the existence and content of every law is determined by a social source, as opposed to the 'weak social thesis' which demands as conditions institutionality and efficacy: see *The Authority of Law*, 46–7.

[16] The expression 'colourless movements' was coined by the psychologist C. L. Hull. Cf. *The Principles of Behavior* (New York, 1943), 25.

[17] Note that this 'behaviouristic' position is a sufficient condition of regarding the existence of law and the acceptance of law as contingently connected. It is not a necessary condition. It may be claimed that even if we regard the general stance

6. PRINCIPLE AND DISCRETION

To understand the position of simple positivism on the interrelated issues of legal principle and judicial discretion, we must begin with a position yet more 'simple'. Recent jurisprudence has given us two narratives of legal palaeontology to which we may appeal. First, Hart uses as a foil for the interpretation of contemporary municipal legal systems a postulated 'society without a legislature, courts or officials of any kind . . . a social structure of primary rules of obligation . . . alone' (*The Concept of Law*, 89). Second, Lon Fuller's egregious but jurisprudentially instructive monarch Rex I begins his would-be law-making activities by repealing all law, to clean the slate. He then 'announce[s] to his subjects that henceforth he [will] act as a judge in any disputes that might arise among them' (*The Morality of Law*, 34). The societies of the two narratives are differently primitive. Hart's society has rules but no institutions for dispute-settlement; Fuller's Rex I is an institution for dispute-settlement but he has no rules. Within legal philosophy, we cannot decide which is more primitive; an aggregation with neither rules nor institutions for dispute-settlement constitutes a state of nature, and thus falls wholly beyond the boundaries of legal philosophy.

Both Hart and Fuller rely on and exploit the pre-jurisprudential intuition that some minimal conditions have to be met before we have a plausible candidate even for the beginnings of law. Law presupposes at a minimum a degree of institutionalization and a degree of 'ruled-ness'. What Raz has called 'systems of absolute discretion' (*Practical Reason and Norms*, 137–41) may have quite complex institutions for dispute-settlement, much more than Fuller's solitary monarch, but, lacking rules, they do not have law. The ideal of the rule of law embodies at least the formal thought that the law must be capable of guiding the behaviour of its subjects.[18] Likewise, Hart's primitive society may have a rich network of primary rules, but lacking anything in the form of an

---

towards law as intentional, that stance may only be contingently one of acceptance. I believe that this issue is far from a simple one. I address it elsewhere in this study (see Chs. 2.4 and 6 below). For the moment, I abide by the attribution to simple positivism of a particularly crude and parsimonious position.

[18] Cf. Raz, *The Authority of Law*, 214. Schauer (*Playing By the Rules* (Oxford, 1991), 169) claims that only jurisdictional rules are required to create the minimally

institution for dispute-settlement, it lacks law, for a legal system is an institutionalized normative system.[19]

Simple positivism is the position that articulates this pre-jurisprudential intuition and no more than this intuition. There are institutionalized rules for dispute-settlement, and institutionalized rules for defining those institutions: law comprises just exactly those rules. According to simple positivism, law as such is no less and no more than, for example, the commands of the sovereign— 'black-letter law', 'settled law', law that is 'on the books', are other kindred terms. Contrary to what is claimed by legal realism, statutes and common law precedential rules are not sources of law, but the law itself. Contrary to what might be claimed by anti-positivism, nothing else but statutes and common law precedential rules comprise the law.

Simple positivism need not deny the existence of judge-made law, nor, in order to admit judge-made law, need it transmogrify judge-made law into really a command of the legislature for so long as the legislature does not override judge-made rules. The fundamental notion of a 'sovereign' is elastic enough to divide the rights of sovereignty between legislature and courts. After all, from the point of view of norm-subjects who will be visited with evil if they do not comply, the subtleties of the distinction between legislation and common law ruling seem of remote interest.

Despite the best intentions (or even, one may suppose, despite the worst), statutes and common law rules will be clear—provide clear guidance for the subjects, subtend clear decisions for the judges and courts—only up to a point: the better the draftsperson, the longer it takes to reach the point. When that point is reached, and the content of the law is no longer clear, then, and only then, for simple positivism, the dispute-settler has discretion on how to dispose of the dispute. Simple positivism holds to the 'two step' theory of adjudication—apply black-letter law to the extent that and just to the extent that black-letter law is clearly applicable to

necessary 'ruled-ness'. Thus he seems to accept *contra* Raz that a 'system of absolute discretion' is a legal system. Raz clearly thinks his 'capacity to guide' criterion is formal, not substantive; otherwise his positivism would be endangered. But Fuller's story of Rex suggests a difficulty. Is the requirement that there be enough discernible consistency on the part of the decision-maker(s) from one decision to the next for the subjects to be able to guide their behaviour a formal or a substantive constraint on the presence of law? I leave the issue for contemplation.

[19] Cf. Raz, *Practical Reason and Norms*, 123 ff.

the instant case: if there is a residue of recalcitrant issues that cannot be so decided, then go 'outside the law' to decide them by the use of judicial discretion. Discretion in adjudication does not exist as the hole within a doughnut,[20] but rather as the infinite space surrounding a bounded whole. The judge is held to be under an institutional duty to remain 'within the law', to apply black-letter law, for as far as and only for as far as black-letter law is dispositive of the instant case. When judicial duty runs out, judicial discretion takes over.

There is an important distinction between 'exercising discretion' and 'having discretion'.[21] The latter concept is the analytically more important concept. To say that a judge in some case 'has discretion' is to make a remark about the structural relationship between pre-existing authoritative standards and the decision that has to be taken in the instant case. Those standards do not determine the decision in the way that they would determine a decision for a case that unambiguously fell under them. The standards do not determine the decision at all once the matter has gone 'beyond' their scope. Whether or not a judge has discretion in some case is therefore a structural property of a particular piece of adjudication. However, we all know what it is for a judge to act as though he or she 'has discretion', whether in fact he or she does have discretion or not. Lord Denning has been everyone's favourite example—here is one who frequently took an expansive view of the extent to which a decision in an instant case was determined by existing black-letter law. A judge exercises discretion when, whether entitled to or not, he or she behaves as a judge who has discretion is entitled to behave—he or she treats black-letter law as not dispositive of the case.

Dworkin has usefully distinguished three different kinds of 'discretion' relevant to the nature of adjudication—two different kinds of so-called 'weak discretion', and 'strong discretion' (*Taking Rights Seriously*, 31–2). First, a decision may be 'discretionary' if there is no review of it—but that does not imply that there are no institutionally relevant standards controlling the decision; so the discretion is 'weak'.[22] Second, a decision may

---

[20] *Pace* Dworkin, *Taking Rights Seriously*, 31.

[21] The distinction is articulated clearly by Wilfrid Waluchow in his essay 'Strong Discretion', *Philosophical Quarterly*, 33 (1983), 333–5.

[22] Compare the position of Hart's scorer when a scoring rule is already in place

require the use of judgement by the decision-maker, where there are indeed standards relevant to the decision but it is unreasonable or impossible to express them in a sufficiently fine-grained way to determine the decision: here too the discretion is 'weak'. But, third, there may be cases where the decision is simply not controlled by standards set by the authority in whose name the decision is made: here the decision-maker's discretion is 'strong'. Simple positivism says that the judge in a hard case—that is, a case where the judge must go 'outside black-letter law' to adjudicate the case—does have strong discretion.

Simple positivism is not committed to the putative evil of 'mechanical jurisprudence', although 'mechanical jurisprudence' and simple positivism share some common ground. Both agree on an overriding judicial duty to apply black-letter law just in case the law is clear and clearly applicable to the instant fact situation. 'Mechanical jurisprudence' only makes sense as an ideal for adjudication if it makes the mistake of thinking that the law is always clear. That this is a correct characterization of 'mechanical jurisprudence' may be shown. Let us stipulate a distinction between 'easy cases' and 'hard cases'.[23] 'Easy cases' are cases in which an existing part of black-letter law—a statute or a common law rule—is unambiguously and uncontroversially, given the fact situation before the court, *ceteris paribus*, dispositive of the case. 'Hard cases' are cases for which black-letter law is not thus dispositive. One who says that a particular decision reached formalistically by 'mechanical jurisprudence' is a bad decision, an unjust decision, a violation of legality, will have in mind one of two things. They will mean either (*a*) the decision is indeed a correct application of a clear law, but the law itself is bad/unjust; or (*b*) the judge thinks that the law is clear, but really the law is not clear, and with a bit of imagination the judge could have seen what she so stubbornly failed to see, that a more just decision equally consistent with the fact situation and black-letter law could have

to be applied by the scorer, as opposed to that in the game of 'scorer's discretion' where the scorer determines the scoring rule at his or her discretion (*The Concept of Law*, 138–44).

[23] In the sense that the following is not meant to represent any particular theorist's antecedent understanding of these terms, but the way they will be used in this study. As Schauer has correctly underlined, such an understanding of 'easy cases' and 'hard cases' is required to bring out the full force of Dworkin's attack on legal positivism: cf. 'Rules and the Rule of Law', *Harvard Journal of Law and*

been reached. As Frederick Schauer has cogently argued,[24] formalism as a vice is best understood as the failure to follow a rule-avoiding norm made available by the legal system when the purposes of the legal system would be best served by following said norm. It is unfair to law-abiding judges to say that a type (*a*) case is a case of the vice known as formalism or as 'mechanical jurisprudence'—provided that the case genuinely is as the specification of type (*a*) cases specifies it has to be.[25] In reality, the vast majority of accusations of formalism or 'mechanical jurisprudence' involve type (*b*) cases. But if that is true, then the characterization of 'mechanical jurisprudence' in the previous paragraph is correct.

Simple positivism in avoiding 'mechanical jurisprudence' cannot reduce all type (*b*) cases to type (*a*) cases, for that is empirically implausible. Instead, simple positivism says that, in order to decide 'hard cases', the judge may go 'outside the law'. The judge may also not go outside the law—she may give a particular narrow reading of some key term in the statute, for example, or of the ratio of some precedent case so that it may be distinguished from the instant case. But then the judge runs the risk of criticism on grounds of 'mechanical jurisprudence' or 'formalism'. The thought is that only a decision in an easy case in accord with existing black-letter law is a decision 'inside the law'. All other decisions require the judge to go 'outside the law'. But once the judge is 'outside the law', then of course tautologically there can be no intra-legal standards, and therefore, for the simple positivist just as much of a tautology, no legal standards to guide the judge.

Simple positivism is not committed, however, to adjudication 'outside the law' being beyond all criticism—it is not committed to adjudication in hard cases falling under the principle that *de gustibus non est disputandum*. Adjudication is a human intellectual

---

Public Policy, 14 (1991), 668 ff. For *Henningsen* v. *Bloomfield Motors, Inc.* (32 NJ 358 (1960)) is an *easy* case. In New Jersey contract law in 1960, there was no prior institutional backing for the doctrines that consumers' waivers of warranties were void when they were unconscionable. Dworkin's strong claim is that even so the principle of unconscionability is binding on the court because it is a requirement of justice, a claim no positivist can accept. On the extent to which Dworkin unchangingly held such a strong view, see Ch. 8, sections 3–4 and Ch. 12, section 3 below.

[24] 'Formalism', *Yale Law Journal*, 97 (1988), 511–20.
[25] Cf. ibid. 520; see also F. Schauer, *Playing By the Rules* (Oxford, 1991), chs. 5–8, on the strength of the case for requiring formalistic local decision-making by, e.g., lower courts in a jurisdictional hierarchy.

activity, and as such it may be criticized by general standards of rationality appropriate to any such human activity. It is also the case that a decision in a hard case may be criticized on moral grounds, or on economic grounds, or perhaps even on aesthetic grounds. But simple positivism can permit no pretence that grounds such as these are *legal* grounds for criticism of a legal decision. Since such criticisms apply standards that are not pedigreed, not 'set by the authority concerned',[26] no legal official can be legally criticized for failing to meet them.

7. INTERPRETATION AND SEMANTICS

The nature of legal interpretation is a much-debated topic. Legal interpretation must be interpretation of something, of some legal text. The term 'text' has become in some recent philosophy multifarious and slippery. In literary theory there has been much attention paid to the notion of the interpretation of a text. There is clearly some intuitive attractiveness to the idea that legal interpretation can usefully be compared with literary interpretation. Both are enterprises that deal extensively with written texts; in both interpretations, rather than mere description or evaluation, is a favoured strategy; both have a similar conflict between independence of and vulnerability to wider social and political issues.[27]

One version of the story that 'Law is like Literature' takes law to be like literature, or legal interpretation to be like literary interpretation, on the deconstructionist version of literary interpretation. Literary formalism, as typified by the 'New Criticism' of several decades ago, claims that a set of black-letter inscriptions constitute a text, and that literary interpretation and criticism is a matter of discovering the antecedently determined meaning of that text. The message of literary theory and philosophy of literature of more recent times—hermeneutics, structuralism, post-structuralism, deconstructionism (never mind the genuine differences between these theoretical programmes)—is that such a formalist account of the literary text is naïve and mistaken. Either there are no texts, in

---

[26] Cf. Dworkin, *Taking Rights Seriously*, 32.
[27] Although I think there are also significant disanalogies between legal texts and literary texts. Cf. 'The Hermeneutics of Adjudication', in Evan Simpson (ed.), *Antifoundationalism and Practical Reasoning* (Edmonton, AB, 1987).

the class or anywhere else, or the text is the black-letter document in interdependence with its broader social context. To deny intentionalism and the relevance of readers' responses is the (postmodern) version of the Intentional Fallacy.

Such a repudiation of critical formalism in literary theory on technical grounds seems to transfer easily in legal theory to legal formalism. Legal formalism requires the presence of clear legal texts. The particular denial of 'the metaphysics of presence' in legal theory is the denial of any such thing as 'legal doctrine'—a stable set of rules and ideas to be found in black-letter law. Instead, the sceptics, such as many devotees of Critical Legal Studies, argue that a given legal text contains nothing whatever which constrains its interpreter. A judge who feels bound to interpret a statute a particular way because, in her view, that is what the wording of the statute means is simply applying her own political ideology to the unfortunate defendant in question. So proceeds the marginalization of marginalized peoples. Likewise, for legal realists and other rule-sceptics, the claim that legal interpretation is interpretation of a text does not exclude the possibility that the putative material facts of the case have to be interpreted too. Everything that goes on in a court of law, it may be said, has the status of a narrative.[28] All is interpretation: adjudication is interpretation, and so political, all the way down.

Simple positivism rejects this extreme position.[29] For simple positivism, 'interpretation' contrasts with 'observation' or 'description' or 'necessary implication'—the plain meaning of a piece of language or the nature of plain facts can be 'read off' its/their face(s); no interpretation is needed. There are two steps in the adjudicative process—first, the determination of what the text actually says, or what the material facts actually are; second, a phase which it may (or may not) be appropriate to call 'interpretation'. For simple positivism, interpretation can begin only where straightforward observation or description, or unproblematic inference, ends.

---

[28] For a sophisticated defence of this view, see Bert van Roermund, 'On "Narrative Coherence" in Legal Contexts', in Carla Faralli and Enrico Pattaro (eds.), *Reason in Law*, iii (Milan, 1988); id., 'Narrative Coherence and the Guises of Legalism', in Patrick Nerhot (ed.), *Law, Interpretation and Reality* (Norwell, Mass., 1990).

[29] To that extent the debate with some modern theories is not bypassed. But it is not engaged in this book.

But where is that? Here it seems possible for there to be different simple positivisms. For example, both a theory that put great store in the intentions of the framers of a constitutional document and a theory that confined the interpreter to the language 'within the four corners' of the document itself may be versions of simple positivism. The theoretical spirit in which these things are said is crucial. The difference between different views emerges when one asks, 'In what does interpretation consist, given that interpretation begins where description and necessary implication end?' Again, it is possible to imagine different versions of simple positivism. One might hold that it cannot consist in anything except an expression of opinion, or of emotion, by the adjudicator—as Hume once put it, 'after every circumstance, every relation is known, the understanding has no further room to operate, nor any object on which it could employ itself. The approbation or blame which then ensues, cannot be the work of the judgment, but of the heart'.[30] But such a view is not so much a theory of interpretation as a denial of interpretation, given that interpretation is supposed to be a rational activity.

Another version of simple positivism might hold that interpretation is an idiosyncratic use of the reason, and that adjudication at the 'second step' is interpretation, but that the determination of the nature of interpretation is no more within the province of jurisprudence than is the establishment of correlations between consumed breakfasts and proffered rulings. The requirements to abide by the framers' intentions or to 'remain within the four corners' would be seen as requirements of political morality, not impositions upon the judge by the character of legal interpretation itself. For simple positivism there is no such special character. Whatever requirements bind the judge at a stage of adjudication beyond the determination of meaning and facts, they are extra-legal requirements.

Unlike legal realism or rule-scepticism, simple positivism believes, furthermore, that propositions of law are as such capable of having truth-values. For the legal realist, a proposition of law can be true or false only if it is translated into a prediction about what the courts will do, or into a proposition about what people believe to be obligatory, or politically appropriate, or something

---

[30] *Enquiry into the Principles of Morals* (Oxford, 1975 [1777]), Appendix I, 290.

of the kind. But for the simple positivist it will on the material facts be just true, if it is true, that the defendant has no grounds for succeeding in his request for a mistrial, or that Tom's contract is valid—no reconstruction into some other form of proposition is necessary.

Simple positivism, in other words, is, in the sense in which the term is used in philosophy of language, 'realist' about the semantics for propositions of law. By 'realist' in this sense, I mean one who believes that if a proposition of law is true, that is because there is some fact in the world which makes it true, and if it is false, that is because any fact in the world which would make it true is absent. It is not difficult to see that this 'realism' follows naturally from simple positivism's being both simple and positivism. For any form of positivism, a proposition which asserts what the law is on some matter stands in a certain relationship to certain facts. For such a proposition can be acceptably asserted if and only if a certain kind of fact obtains—namely, the sovereign has commanded that the law is thus and so, or the Queen in Parliament has enacted the same, or whatever. Now, that the sovereign has so commanded is, if it is, a fact in the world. For simple positivism, this fact in the world makes true the pure legal proposition that the law is thus and so, and its absence would make that proposition false. Similarly, for an applied legal proposition, a verdict like 'Tom's contract is valid' or 'the defendant is guilty', there will be facts in the world about Tom's and others' actions, or about the defendant's and others' actions, which, together with facts about the sovereign's commands, make the applied proposition of law true, or, if they are absent, false.[31]

8. LAW AND THE COMMON GOOD

People typically have ideals about law—law that is perceived to function or in fact does function solely to advance the interests of the ruling class, or of the wicked dictator, or the sleazier political ends of the party in power, is thought to be a perversion of those ideals. Legal theory is in disagreement as to how to represent these

[31] I am adapting here Raz's distinction between 'pure' and 'applied' legal statements; cf. *The Concept of a Legal System* (Oxford, 1980), 218 ff.; *The Authority of Law*, 62.

dull facts at the theoretical level. Simple positivism, believing as it does that the existence of law is one thing, its merit or demerit another, argues that the failure of the law to conform to ideals of legality, or the success of the law in promoting the goals of capitalism or the ruling class, or in marginalizing sections of the population, does not in any way impugn the status as law of what is, if it is, otherwise properly pedigreed law. In this sense, simple positivism is compatible with radical critiques of law which emphasize positive law's gendered, or racist, or capitalist character.

But suppose that we try not to be pessimistic. Suppose we reject the bleaker descriptions of the world's scene as it appears from its margins. We argue that as a matter of fact the bulk of black-letter law in our country and in the countries of which we have experience indeed is for the general welfare of the citizens of those countries. In those countries the black-letter law seems indeed to be an 'ordinance of reason for the common good', and to have been promulgated by persons with a genuine and warm care for the community.[32] Simple positivism says that such an account of how it is in some country or set of countries is true, if it is true, contingently. It does not follow from the concept of law itself that the account is true: it is false that, were the account not true, there would not be law in those countries. The law in those countries, as in any others, has the content that it has because the lawmakers enacted it that way. Further explanations—in terms of domination and hierarchy, for example—of why the lawmakers enacted law that way belong to the sociology of law, not to legal philosophy. If the lawmakers had enacted different laws, then life might be more, or less, nasty and brutish, but the law would still be the law. Law may have any content you like, and still be law.

9. CONCLUSION

These remarks conclude my account of simple positivism. It may be conveniently summarized in the following seven theses:

  1. Law provides a reason for action which is a reason 'on the balance of reasons'.

[32] Cf. St Thomas Aquinas, *On Law, Morality and Politics* (Indianapolis, 1988), Q. 90, A. 4.

2. The authority of law derives from standards entirely external to law.
3. It is possible to take the external point of view altogether to law.
4. It is a contingent truth about some given society how far law in that society is accepted as legitimate.
5. Law consists of statutes and common-law precedential rules, and adjudication in hard cases is strongly discretionary.
6. Legal interpretation is 'mechanical', and the semantics for propositions of law is 'realist'.
7. It is contingent whether the law in any particular society is 'for the common good' of that society.

I emphasize again that simple positivism is an author's construction, not a palaeontologist's or a historian's discovery. I have been trying to paint the kind of picture that would be painted by a positivist who paints in large blocks of primary colours. The aim is not to show positivism in an unfavourable light by presenting what might seem to some the most implausible version of the theory. I am not at this point concerned to assert either that simple positivism is a plausible theory of law or that it is an implausible theory of law. It is of course true that many theorists will find simple positivism as characterized here to be an implausible theory of law, and a good many of them will be theorists who are none the less fully committed positivists. Conventional jurisprudence sees more subtle, more sophisticated, more elaborate positivistic theories of law as primarily reactions to anti-positivism, to natural law theory. I believe, however, that we cannot understand such theories unless we see them as they will be presented here—as primarily reactions to simpler and cruder versions of positivism. Sophisticated positivism—the subject of Part II—says what it says, not so much because it believes anti-positivism to be false, although it does believe that, as because it believes simple positivism to be false. Sophisticated positivism believes simple positivism to be inadequate as a defence of positivism. We will learn most from sophisticated positivism by understanding its motivation in those terms. Or so I hope to show.

Part II

Sophisticated Positivism

2

SOPHISTICATED POSITIVISM

Legal positivism in the last thirty-odd years has not defended simple positivism. Recent positivist writings have been philosophically more technical and sensitive. To put it succinctly, simple positivism has been replaced by sophisticated positivism. In this Part I lay out sophisticated positivism, as the development of lines of thought which began in simple positivism. We begin as before with law as a reason for action.

Simple positivism's conception of the way that laws provide reasons for action did not fare well in a comparison with rule-scepticism (Chapter 1.2 above). Given that one had reason to obey the law only if one would be visited with evil if one did not comply, it was of little additional significance that the evil emanated from an institutional source, the sovereign. Simple positivism looked at the law purely instrumentally, and so regarded the fact that something was required or prohibited by law as but one reason to be weighed in the balance of reasons. Simple positivism as much as legal realism based legal reasoning on a 'bad man's' view of the law.

The first attempt by sophisticated positivism to avoid such a mistake lies in Hart's distinction between laws as obligation-imposing rules requiring the internal point of view and threats as obliging obedience through coercion (*The Concept of Law*, 80–1). The point is not to deny the bad man his view of the law for his part; if he internalized the law's demands and accepted them as legitimate, then in all likelihood he would not be 'bad'—cases of iniquitous legal systems apart. The point is to have legal theory not take the bad man's view of the law as paradigmatic for the law's status in practical reasoning. Rather, law cannot be understood without attention being paid to the point of view of those who deem law to present a genuine reason for action of a non-coercive kind, even if there are as well those who perceive law only as a coercive reason for action.

Whatever might be the advantages otherwise of insisting on the need to make reference to the internal point of view, such a reference does not succeed, however, in escaping the model of law as a reason for action to be weighed in the balance of reasons. To look at law instrumentally is sufficient, but not necessary, for mistakenly regarding law as a reason for action in terms of the model of a reason to be weighed in the balance of reasons. Hart's theory makes this mistake as well.

There is a certain feature of law which neither Austin nor Hart acknowledges, and the failure to do so is at the root of the difficulty examined here. We may approach an account of the feature as follows. Suppose a driver, who reasons, 'If I drive at 80 k.p.h. rather than 50 k.p.h., I will not arrive late for my appointment. On the other hand, I will use more gasoline, and gasoline is not cheap.' The cost of arriving late is weighed in the balance against the cost of gasoline, and a practical decision taken. The road down which the driver is travelling, however, has a legal speed limit of 50 k.p.h. The driver now reasons, 'If I drive . . . On the other hand, . . . [as before]. Moreover, if I travel at over 50 k.p.h., I am likely to be fined, and this possible cost is to be added to the cost of gasoline as a reason for driving at 50 k.p.h.' Perhaps the driver now drives at 50 k.p.h., perhaps not. The point is that, for this driver so reasoning, the fact of the speed limit is an extra factor added in to the balance of reasons. It will tip the balance in favour of observing the speed limit or not, according to the weight attached to it, to arriving at the appointment on time, to the cost of gasoline, etc. As a reason for action, the speed limit is functioning in the reasoning exactly as any other reason for action.

The above is a sketch of an Austinian account of law as an element in practical reasoning. Suppose we change the example, and postulate a magistrate, as an official of the system, faced with enforcing the speed-limit regulation against a defendant who has sought his or her day in court. The magistrate, as an official of a genuine legal system, has *ex hypothesi* the internal point of view towards the speed-limit regulation.[1] For positivism, the existence

---

[1] See Hart's account of the minimal necessary and sufficient conditions for the existence of a legal system at *The Concept of Law*, 113.

of law is a social fact. The magistrate with the internal point of view has that point of view towards this social fact. The magistrate accepts, not only that the demand to keep to 50 k.p.h. is a proper demand, but also that legal demands generally are proper demands. Note, however, that for the magistrate the propriety of the existence of the speed-limit regulation is a reason for the action, 'Find this defendant guilty if he or she is proved beyond reasonable doubt to have driven at speeds in excess of limits prescribed by law'. That action is not the action the possible reasons for which we are now exploring. This latter action is that of driving within the speed limits. It may arguably follow (and, according to Hart's theory, will so follow) from the fact that the speed-limit regulation is a valid regulation, that officials have *qua* officials the internal point of view towards enforcement of the regulation. But it does not follow that any given official *qua* private citizen has the internal point of view towards staying within the speed limit on some actual occasion. The speed-limit regulation may be one of those 'primary rules which apply to officials in their merely personal capacity which they need only obey' (*The Concept of Law*, 113). In Hart's minimal legal system, therefore, laws are still, for those whose conduct is directly affected by them, reasons for action on the Austinian model.

Even if we suppose a 'healthy' and not a minimal legal system—a system, that is, in which the internal point of view towards the primary rules is widespread among private citizens and officials in their merely personal capacity—we still have the 'balance of reasons' model for laws as reasons for action. As far as the structure of the driver's reasoning is concerned, the law's demands are simply added to the balance of reasons. The demands are entered under the description 'proper demands', not the description 'evils with which I will be visited if I do not comply'. None the less, they will be assigned weight and, through that weight, will tip the balance of reasons however they tip it. The driver may regard the fact of there being a speed limit as overwhelmingly weighty for reasons of safety without having any particular point of view towards the law. But, given that the existence of law is a social fact, then the internal commitment to the propriety of the law's demands is just the form that the assignment of weight takes in this driver, as opposed to the Austinian 'bad' driver who keeps the limit only out of the fear of evil. Because Hart still looks at the role of law in practical reasoning in terms of an alteration in the balance of reasons, then the difference between the driver with the internal point of view and the driver with the 'bad man's' point of view is a difference *external* to law as a reason for action. If that is so, then Hart has not succeeded in showing his own view to be an improvement over the Austinian model of how laws are reasons for action.

Raz's account of laws in relation to practical reasoning gives a stronger basis for the rejection of laws as commands backed by threats. In his view, the existence of a law in some way functions to replace a process of weighing reasons in the balance. There is a point in practical reasoning at which the questioning, 'Why do you do that?' is just stopped by the answers, 'The law requires it', 'The law forbids such-and-such'. We have the sense that to go on to question the justification for the law's demanding or forbidding is to enter a new and different phase in the questioning, rather than to continue the questioning in an unbroken line.[2]

When a court orders a separated spouse to pay $500 a month in maintenance to the other partner, then the person ordered has a reason to pay the maintenance, for the fact that an action is ordered by the court is a reason for performing the action. That reason goes into the balance of reasons. But, one might suppose, viewed simply in the balance of reasons it is not necessarily a decisive reason, for one could give the money instead to the Canadian Abortion Rights Action League, or one could put it away for a holiday in Tahiti, and in the balance of reasons these might or might not outweigh the fact that the court ordered one to pay the maintenance. But the order's status as a legal order is so far underdescribed. By virtue of the order being an order of the law, not only does one have a reason for paying the maintenance; one also has a reason for disregarding the reasons against paying it— the fact that more good would be done by supporting CARAL, or more happiness brought into existence by holidaying in Tahiti. It is an essential feature of legal norms, as it is of promises, military commands, decisions, blanket rules to proceed in certain ways without deliberation, . . . [the list is not, nor is it intended to be,

---

[2] Note that I focus here only on the general issue of the kind of reason for action that the law in Raz's view is. I do not say anything about the specific version of that kind of reason that the law in Raz's view is. Such matters belong to Raz's views on law and authority, which are discussed in Ch. 2.2 below.

complete] that they function in relation to some reason to perform act A, not only as straightforward reasons for a particular action A, but also to exclude reasons against doing A.

By such reasoning Raz introduces the category of 'exclusionary' reasons for action. Reasons for action which bear directly on what to do, and go into the balance of reasons, are first-order reasons. Reasons which are reasons for acting in relation to given first-order reasons are second-order reasons. These may be positive (reasons for acting on certain reasons) or negative (reasons to refrain from acting on certain reasons). Second-order reasons which function to exclude action on the basis of the first-order reasons which fall within their scope are exclusionary reasons. The reasons for action represented by the social facts of permissions or legal requirements are at least first-order reasons for action—that I promised to do A, or that the law requires me to do A, are each reasons for doing A. But these social facts are also second-order, exclusionary reasons, excluding from the practical reasoning reasons against doing A. Only so, claims Raz, can we explain the tension that arises when a person sees that performing A is warranted by the balance of reasons but performing A is forbidden by law. Conflicts between first-order ordinary reasons and second-order exclusionary reasons are resolved, not by the relative strength of the two competing reasons, but, as Raz puts it (*Practical Reason and Norms*, 40), by a general principle of practical reasoning which determines that exclusionary reasons always prevail.[3]

By distinguishing first-order from exclusionary reasons, and by identifying a legal system as a system of exclusionary reasons, Raz opens up the possibility of genuinely distinguishing law as a reason for action from a coercive command as a reason for action, since a coercive command, as Hart rightly saw, can only be a first-order reason for action.

---

[3] Raz's view is actually less dramatic than this bald statement implies. There may be conflicts of weight between second-order reasons themselves. Moreover, exclusionary reasons have the dimension of scope; they exclude only first-order reasons within their scope. Thus by either route a given exclusionary reason may be defeated, and some action ostensibly debarred is thereby reinstated as the thing to do. The true principle is not, 'Always act in accordance with exclusionary reasons', but 'One ought, all things considered, always to act for an undefeated reason'.

2. LAW AND AUTHORITY

Law operates in the domain of the practical. The fact that something is required by or prohibited by law is a reason for action on the part of the norm-subject. A law or legal system has authority only if the existence of the law or the fact that some rule is part of the system is a reason for action. However, even simple positivism satisfies this condition—that I will be visited with evil if I do not comply with the sovereign's directive gives me a reason for action. I weigh the evil in the balance against the benefit which will accrue to me—the gold bullion, or the advancement of marginalized peoples. The authority of law, for simple positivism, amounts to the fact that the balance comes down on the side of avoiding the expected evil of obedience, not gaining the expected benefit of disobedience.

There are two different strands of argument in the rejection by sophisticated positivism of the simple account.[4] First, the simple account is mistaken in defining law without any reference to the internal point of view towards law.[5] Law will not be law unless it is accepted by its norm-subjects in some way or other as making justified demands on them. Second, the simple view misrepresents the way in which the fact that there is a law on some matter constitutes, if it does, a reason for action. Laws would not be simply very weighty first-order reasons. Rather, laws would be reasons for not straightforwardly acting on the balance of first-order reasons; they would be 'exclusionary' reasons for action.[6]

It is important to distinguish these two lines of argument, because they are there but not clearly distinguished in perhaps the most sophisticated positivistic account of the authority of law, that of Joseph Raz. In *The Concept of Law* Hart is sparing in his references to the notion of the authority of law; none the less, he has an implicit account of the notion. On page 196 of that book he writes: 'Without their voluntary co-operation, thus creating *authority*, . . .' (his emphasis). He thus implies that whatever

---

[4] See Ch. 2.1 above.

[5] Cf. Hart, *The Concept of Law*, 55 ff.

[6] This latter argument is prominent in Raz's writings about authority—see *The Authority of Law*, chs. 1–2, *The Morality of Freedom*, chs. 2–3. On the notion of 'exclusionary reason', see Ch. 2.1 above. In this study I refer primarily to the account of authority in *The Morality of Freedom*, rather than that in *Practical Reason and Norms* and *The Authority of Law*, which is less fully developed.

internal point of view is implied by 'voluntary co-operation' is a necessary condition for the authority of law. Notoriously, however, problems begin with Hart's account when one asks who 'they' are. Chapter 6 of *The Concept of Law* makes it clear that the minimum necessary 'they' for a normative system to be a legal system are the officials of the system. A system which, as far as its non-officials are concerned, is wholly coercive although one in which the officials are voluntarily co-operative, however unhealthy, is still a legal system. Simple positivism's mistake retrospectively seems not so much to be leaving out the internal point of view of the citizens as leaving out the internal point of view of the sovereign.[7]

Hart returns to the topic of authority in the last chapter of *Essay on Bentham*. He introduces the concept of 'peremptory reason' (253), which seems to be a less technically elucidated version of Raz's 'exclusionary reason'. Hart then uses the concept to define practical authority: 'to have such [sc. practical] authority is to have one's expression of intention as to the actions of others accepted as peremptory content-independent reasons for action' (258). He then remarks that 'the general recognition in a society of the commander's words as peremptory reasons for action is equivalent to the existence of a social rule' (ibid.). This suggests that practical authority exists only in a 'healthy' legal system, where the internal point of view towards the laws is widespread. If that is Hart's view, it only underlines the force of the claims by others that the minimal legal system of *The Concept of Law*, 6.2, is indeed a coercive system, not one with authority. The later view also erodes any distinction between 'believed to be authoritative' and 'actually authoritative' by collapsing the latter into the former. It would allow a dictator to be a practical authority provided his or her propaganda machines were sufficiently powerful.

Raz's theory is a good deal richer. He lays down as part of his account of the authority of law what he calls the 'Dependence Thesis'—that 'all authoritative directives should be based, in the main, on reasons which already independently apply to the subjects of the directives and are relevant to their action in the 'circumstances covered by the directives' (*The Morality of Freedom*,

---

[7] Criticism much along these lines is urged by Michael Payne, 'Hart's Concept of a Legal System', *William and Mary Law Review*, 18 (1976), John Hodson, 'Hart on the Internal Aspect of Rules', *Archiv für Rechts- und Sozialphilosophie*, 62 (1976), and Goldsworthy, 'Self-destruction'.

47). This thesis is combined with two other claims, that the 'service' conception of authority is the correct conception, and that authority should be conceived on the model of the activities of an arbitrator.[8] According to the service conception of authority, the role and primary function of authorities is to serve the governed by mediating between people and the right reasons which apply to them. The arbitrator is a good model for authority because he or she cannot simply decide the dispute in terms of his or her own ideas about what is best, but must decide the dispute in trust for the disputants in terms of the reasons which apply to them in their situation. This does not necessarily mean furthering their self-interests, but only helping them to act on reasons that bind them (*The Morality of Law*, 56); a person may be bound to act on a reason which does not further his or her self-interest.

Raz thus puts a constraint on authority that authority serve the governed. How far has he thereby distanced himself from the thought that a system which is seen by the governed as coercive may none the less be authoritative? This is not an easy question to answer. For the officials of a minimal Hartian legal system *sub specie aeternatis* may be highly enlightened and the citizens from the same perspective saturated with false consciousness. In order to serve the governed it may be necessary continuously to coerce them in their own interest. How is this appalling Temple of Sarastro[9] to be avoided within the service conception of authority? Raz's answer can only be alluded to here, for it is a lengthy argument that political autonomy is a fundamental value, and no scheme can be authoritative unless it promotes autonomy.[10]

The internal point of view of the citizen towards the law, and not merely that of the official, thus becomes an integral part of Raz's sophisticated positivistic theory of the authority of law. But now there is a difficulty. To remain a version of positivism, the theory cannot say that law is law only if it actually does serve the interests of the governed, although that may serve as a constraint on whether some normative system already identified as a legal system is authoritative, or some directive already identified as a legal directive is authoritative. On the other hand, the theory must

---

[8] Cf. *The Morality of Freedom*, 41–2, 56–9.

[9] With acknowledgements to Isaiah Berlin, *Four Essays on Liberty* (London, 1969), 145–54, not to mention Mozart.

[10] Cf. *The Morality of Freedom*, chs. 11–15.

avoid the complete separation of law and authority characteristic of unsubtle positivism. Raz's solution is to distinguish between what it is to claim authority and what it is to have authority. In Raz's view, it is in the nature of law to claim authority, but it is not in the nature of law to have authority. It is intrinsic to law that it claims its demands on us are justified, where 'justification' is constrained by the service conception of authority. Law will have authority just in case its claims to have authority are justified. The system of tribunals that is the law, in order to be law, must claim to serve the governed in the sense noted. It is not necessary for law to be law that the claim is sound.

I said earlier that the above represented one of two strands of argument in Raz's attempt to move positivism away from the problems of the simple account. Let us now turn to the second strand, which is represented by the doctrine of exclusionary reasons. An exclusionary reason is a second-order reason for action which has the effect of excluding, not outweighing, the first-order reasons which fall within its scope. Raz appeals again to the arbitrator model—once a dispute is handed over to an arbitrator, then those first-order reasons with which the disputants were wrestling become excluded from further consideration. The recommendation handed down by the arbitrator becomes an exclusionary reason for the course of action the arbitrator recommends. The notion of exclusionary reason is a formal, content-independent notion. Its working is as well illustrated by the case of an idiotic military order,[11] as by the more congenial case of a conscientious arbitrator. The conscientiousness of the arbitrator belongs to a different part of the sophisticated account of authority from the analysis of authority as a species of exclusionary reason.

None the less, to be a reason for action means that one who acts in accordance with that reason acts well by some standard of worth in action. So a positivist cannot claim that the fact that there is a law requiring X just in itself is a reason for action. A positivist can only argue that it is in the nature of law to *claim* to be an *exclusionary* reason for action, rather than to claim to be some other kind of reason for action. The positivist's point is still important. To use Raz's example (*The Morality of Freedom*, 25),

[11] An order to paint coal white is the traditional case.

the law may be justified in coercing persons suffering from infectious diseases by forcibly confining them, but it does not follow that in doing so it was exercising authority over them. It was not presenting itself to them as an exclusionary reason for action.

It is still necessary to be careful about how the position being developed here is a positivistic position. Recall the dependence thesis, that all authoritative directives should be based, in the main, on reasons which already independently apply to the subjects of the directives and are relevant to their action in the circumstances covered by the directives. Raz sees this thesis as supporting what he calls the pre-emption thesis, that 'the fact that an authority requires performance of an action is a reason for its performance which is not to be added to all other relevant reasons when assessing what to do, but should exclude and take the place of some of them' (*The Morality of Freedom*, 46). He points out that phrased thus the pre-emption thesis is only about legitimate authorities (ibid.), because it uses the notion of exclusionary reason in substantial mode, 'is [sc. genuinely] a reason'. But if that is so, then the claim that a particular event or fact is a pre-emptive reason for action would be a claim that could be made only by resort to evaluative argument. Now, Raz's version of positivism he calls the 'Sources Thesis', which specifies that the existence and content of laws can be identified by reference to social facts alone, without resort to any evaluative argument.[12] So it cannot be consistent with a positivism based on the Sources Thesis to say that laws are intrinsically exclusionary reasons for action, or are intrinsically authoritative directives.

Raz's response to this difficulty seems to consist of two different lines of argument, but the relations between them are not clear. In the first place (*The Morality of Freedom*, 35–7), he argues that authoritative utterances are 'content-independent' reasons; there is 'no direct connection' between the reason and the action for which it is a reason. What it is for a reason and an action to be 'directly connected' is not explained; it is merely said that an authority could equally well command one action or its contradictory. However, there seems to be a link with a feature of the

---

[12] This formulation is taken from 'Authority, Law and Morality', *Monist*, 68 (1985), 296; see also *The Authority of Law*, 47 *et seq*. The 'Sources Thesis' is also called the 'Strong Social Thesis'. I discuss the difference between the 'Strong Social Thesis' and the 'Weak Social Thesis' in Ch. 12.2 below.

service conception of authority and the arbitrator model. An arbitrator's decision must be identifiable as such independently of the reasons on which the arbitrator relies in giving the decision. So it seems that a decision can be a decision of an authority only if it is identifiable as the authority's decision independently of the reasons on which the authority relies in giving its decision. A criticism of Dworkin[13] shows what this means—if it is a constraint on a decision in a hard case being genuinely a judicial decision that it is the correct decision from the point of view of political morality, then the necessary condition for that decision being the decision of an authority fails.[14] The fact that authoritative utterances are content-independent reasons allows them also to satisfy the 'separate identification' condition, as it might be called, for exclusionary or pre-emptive reasons.

The second line of argument relies on the fact that laws as such merely claim to be authoritative, and *a fortiori* exclusionary or pre-emptive reasons. The intuition behind this line of argument is easy to see. Claiming is an activity; there are criteria for claiming; these criteria are non-evaluative; that someone is claiming something can be established without resort to any evaluative argument. In fact, that someone is claiming something is, in some sense of the term, a social fact. When the lawmaker enacts a law, the lawmaker is claiming to utter an authoritative directive. So the making of a law is a social fact. The Sources Thesis says that a law has a source or is source based if its contents and existence can be identified by reference to social facts alone, without resort to any evaluative argument. If laws are claims, then the Sources Thesis is satisfied.

In short, Raz's version of sophisticated positivism says that laws are claims to be authoritative utterances. There are three parts to this claim: (i) they are social facts which can be identified as obtaining without resort to evaluative argument; (ii) they have a content, but that content can be identified without resort to evaluative argument; (iii) they claim to be dependent and pre-emptive reasons for action. The third is the crucial part, for (iii) is

[13] 'Authority, Law and Morality', 310. I am neither asserting nor denying that this is a valid criticism of Dworkin; I am merely quoting the criticism in order to clarify Raz's view.
[14] Thus, paradoxically, a theory like Dworkin's cannot, in Raz's view, represent judges as authorities because on Dworkin's theory judges fail this requirement for separate identification.

held to represent a more appropriate conception of how laws relate to the reasons people actually have for action than either an account which represents laws as commands backed by threats to visit with evil, or as obligation-imposing rules accepted as such by legal officials alone.

3. LEGAL THEORY AND THE INTERNAL POINT OF VIEW

Simple positivism was characterized in Chapter 1.4 above in terms of the external point of view to law. Simple positivism treats the law from the external point of view by regarding the legal system and its operations as an inanimate machine. Hart in *The Concept of Law* (87) describes such a position—the observer is content merely to record regularities of observable behaviour. If 'behaviour' is taken 'colourlessly',[15] then we might as well be talking about the behaviour of a machine. The external observer sees human social life in general and law-abiding social life in particular as simply patterns of regularities, patterns of convergent events, and no more. Simple positivism so understood exemplifies positivism in the philosophy of (social) science applied to the study of law. Donald Black, for example, in the name of methodologically proper sociology of law, calls for the 'scientific analysis of legal life *as a system of behaviour*':[16]

Law consists in observable acts, not in rules as the concept of rule or norm is employed in the literature of jurisprudence and in everyday legal language . . . law is not what lawyers regard as binding or obligatory precepts, but rather, for example, the observable dispositions of judges, policemen, prosecutors, or administrative officials. ('Boundaries', 46)

Black states that his 'sociological conception of law is very different from but not incompatible with . . . the rule-oriented jurisprudence of Hart' in *The Concept of Law*.[17] Hart himself is far less sure about the matter. Not only is there the well-known and tantalizingly allusive comment in the Preface that *The Concept of*

---

[15] For this image, see page 29 above.

[16] 'The Boundaries of Legal Sociology', in id. and Maureen Mileski (eds.), *The Social Organization of Law* (New York, 1973), 42: his emphasis; for a full account of Black's view, see his *The Behavior of Law*.

[17] Ibid., n. 11.

Law 'may be regarded as an essay in descriptive sociology'. There is also a strenuous repudiation of 'the external point of view' as the perspective from which the legal theorist may properly understand the nature of law. We will begin examination of sophisticated positivism's account of the point of view of legal theory by discussing Hart.

In the development of Hart's theory, there are two distinct elements that respond to the case of the external observer as so characterized. First, Hart is quite clear that to represent the complex social institution that is a legal system as simply a system of observable regularities in colourless movements is profoundly to misunderstand such an institution. The misunderstanding is profound, because no attention is paid to a highly distinctive feature of legal systems, the *internal* point of view which exists towards them on the part of some at least of their norm-subjects. On the other hand, and second, it is also clear from the reference to 'descriptive sociology' that Hart none the less takes seriously ·the thought that the job of legal theory is to describe accurately the nature of a particular social institution, and, in a manner faithful to legal positivism, to do so in a way which requires the making of no value judgements about the nature and content of the institution and its norms. He therefore postulates a different point of view, that of an observer who 'may, without accepting the rules himself, assert that the group accepts the rules, and thus may from outside refer to the way in which *they* are concerned with them from the internal point of view'.[18] Such an observer both observes from a position of non-commitment and pays due regard to the internal point of view.

How far has Hart advanced beyond simple positivism? Here, first, is an important though highly condensed point made by Raz. In explicating Hart's views, Raz deliberately eschews the expression 'internal point of view' because, he says, Hart seems to use the phrase for 'three different, though interrelated, purposes' (*The Concept of a Legal System*, 148):

(1) It designates certain facts which are part of the existence-condition of rules.
(2) It designates certain truth-conditions of certain statements or certain implications of making them.

---

[18] *The Concept of Law*, 87; Hart's emphasis.

(3) It designates a certain attitude to norms which can be called 'acceptance of norms'.

Raz is quite right that the expression 'internal point of view' is used in this non-univocal way. If I understand this allusive quote aright, the 'facts' referred to in (1) are states of affairs such that when they obtain part of what it is for social rules to be in force obtains. There is a semantic rule that 'There is a rule R in social group G' is true if and only if the members of G have a certain attitude towards deviations from the rule, etc., and . . . . This attitude is the 'critical reflective attitude' of *The Concept of Law*, page 56, and elsewhere. Thus (3) and (1) are connected in that the facts referred to in (1) amount to the existence of the attitude referred to in (3). (1) and (2) are connected in that this semantic rule identifies the facts referred to in (1) as the truth-conditions referred to in (2).

Hart's claim about the internal point of view is thus a claim about semantics—a claim about what has to be the case in the world if a certain kind of statement is to be true. Hart's empiricist opponent—John Austin, or Oliver Wendell Holmes, for example, or Donald Black conceived as a competitor to Hart—maps semantically statements asserting the existence of legal rules on to convergent patterns of behavioural events. Hart says that this is wrong, for one must map semantically statements asserting the existence of rules on to convergent patterns of behavioural events plus the existence of the critical reflective attitude/internal point of view. John Austin, Holmes, and Black have got the semantics wrong; he, Hart, has got them right.[19] Construed in this fashion, Hart's position in *The Concept of Law* is 'descriptive sociology' in that it is a piece of theory-construction in the sociology of law. It tells the social scientist both that the term 'rule' must appear in the vocabulary of her theory, and it specifies the semantics for the term.

If, however, such is the correct construal of the emphasis on the internal point of view, then it is not clear that Hart in fact has moved away from the 'extreme' external point of view of the pure observer

---

[19] Peter Hacker and Neil MacCormick interpret Hart's emphasis on the internal point of view similarly. 'Hart is denying the possibility of explaining rules solely by reference to external realities of behaviour . . . [There is a] further necessary element [of] attitude among members of a group whose behaviour does reveal such patterning' (D. N. MacCormick, *H. L. A. Hart* (Stanford, Calif., 1981), 30). 'Legal phenomena . . . can only be understood if reference is made to the attitudes of human beings towards their behaviour' (Peter Hacker, 'Hart's Philosophy of Law', in P. M. S. Hacker and J. Raz (eds.), *Law, Morality and Society* (Oxford, 1977), 9).

observing mere regularities. Here are two reasons for saying that. The first reason is that a sophisticated externalistic methodology for sociology of law is still possible, if the needed improvement to simple positivism is simply reference to a critical reflective attitude. The position of Harré and Secord with respect to the nature of social theorizing provides a suitable model. They offer in *The Explanation of Social Behaviour* what they call, not unself-consciously, an 'anthropomorphic model of man'.[20] Such a model takes full account, it is claimed, of those features of the world which distinguish persons from machines. Harré and Secord distinguish their approach from empiricism; they allow for a much richer explanatory role for theories, and deploy the Kuhnian notion of 'paradigm'. They insist on the importance of making room within any social theory for 'personal reports as a crucial element', and say they are attempting 'to bring into behavioural science the phenomenal experience of individuals'. It is essential, they say, to take self-reports seriously in arriving at adequate explanations of behaviour. 'Explaining behavioural phenomena involves identifying the "generative mechanisms" that give rise to the behaviour.' These mechanisms are self-directive, and the main process involved in them is 'self-direction according to the meaning ascribed to the situation'.

Nothing in Hart's characterization of the internal point of view precludes it and any resultant theory of law being construed in terms of a pure external model like that of Harré and Secord. The question of whether an adequate theory for the nature of law must include 'rule' in its vocabulary and reference to the internal point of view in the semantics for 'rule' is quite independent of the question in the philosophy of mind as to whether mental states such as attitudes are to be construed without remainder as behavioural dispositions. Thus Rolf Sartorius has rightly questioned 'whether the reflective critical attitudes in terms of which the internal aspect is seemingly defined amount to anything more than the complex behaviour in which they are said to be displayed'.[21] James Harris likewise includes 'expressed criticisms, demands and acknowledgements' as part of the 'external aspect' of legal behaviour (*Law and Legal Science*, 56–7). He proposes to

[20] All quotes in this paragraph are taken from *The Explanation of Social Behaviour* (Oxford, 1972), 7–9.
[21] 'Positivism and the Foundation of Legal Authority', in Ruth Gavison (ed.), *Issues in Contemporary Legal Philosophy* (Oxford, 1984), 47: his emphasis. Hart

interpret the 'real' (as it were; this is my term) 'internal aspect' as internal soliloquies. Unsurprisingly, Harris is sceptical as to whether sociology of law, and legal theory *qua* descriptive sociology, could have much interest in such soliloquies. Harris may be right that, if soliloquizing is all that possession of the internal point of view can amount to, it is not of much interest to legal theory. Note, though, that, even if the internal point of view is but internal soliloquizing, and even if as such legal theory must make reference to it, these supposed truths are *still* compatible with the external point of view on the part of legal theory. It ought not to be beyond the power of imaginative behaviouristic psychology to come up with a dispositional account of soliloquizing.

As the second reason for claiming that Hart has not moved beyond the external point of view for legal theory, consider the reaction of a sociologist of law to Hart's view. J. P. Gibbs distinguishes sharply between the task of theory-construction and the task of theory-verification.[22] When Hart makes his claims about mandatory reference to the internal point of view, Gibbs sees him to be engaged in the task of theory-construction, despite Hart offering the claims as conceptual analysis. So the crucial questions for Gibbs are: Do the empirical data about behaviour in conformity with law support the theoretical claim that behaviour in conformity with law is accompanied by a critical reflective attitude? If not, what other theory does adequately explain the empirical data? The degree of internalization of laws, Gibbs says (ibid. 437–8), is an empirical matter. He goes on to give a theory of internalization which makes reference to the three factors of evaluative consistency with law, cognitive awareness of law, and acquiescence in the law's demands. He claims this theory to be an empirically/descriptively more adequate theory than what Hart says about the internal point of view. In much the same spirit, Martin Krygier ('Social Theory', 174–5) points out that anthropological studies identify societies of which it is plausible to say they have social norms, and yet there is no empirical evidence of attitudes

---

himself refers to the criticism of deviation and so forth as being from the external point of view 'further regularities' (*The Concept of Law*, 87), and as 'an observable fact of social life' (ibid. 134).

[22] 'Definitions of Law and Empirical Questions', *Law and Society Review*, 2 (1968), 430.

which could be candidates for the internal point of view.[23] My claim is not that Gibbs and Krygier show Hart's theory of law to be inadequate: I am not participating in that debate. There are genuine questions here about how to construe the enterprise of analytical jurisprudence and its relation to sociology of law. My claim is that, *if* descriptive theory-construction is the name of the game, then nothing in Hart's methodological strategies forbids such criticism. Hart insists, if law as a social institution is to be adequately understood, on the need to add to facts about the existence of convergent patterns of behaviour facts about the existence of critical reflective attitudes. If all Hart has contributed to legal theory is this insistence on the need for the extra reference, then he is still occupying the external observer point of view and has to answer the charges of those also occupying such a point of view that his explanatory theory is mistaken.

The difficulties for Hart's account just rehearsed manifestly depend upon the interpretation of it as a putative contribution to theory-construction *qua* specifying the vocabulary and semantics for a theory. The expression 'reference', which Hart himself uses on page 87 of *The Concept of Law*, gives rise to this interpretation. However, a later passage in *The Concept of Law* suggests a quite different way of taking the failure of what I am calling simple positivism with respect to the theorist's point of view. On page 88 Hart writes:

What the external point of view, which limits itself to the observable regularities of behaviour, *cannot reproduce* is the way in which the rules function as rules in the life of those who normally are the majority of society. (my emphasis)

To be adequate, legal theory must not merely 'make reference to' the internal point of view; it must *reproduce* the internal point of view. These are quite separate points; the second is much stronger than the first.[24] What, however, is it to 'reproduce' the way the

---

[23] 'The Concept of Law and Social Theory', *Oxford Journal of Legal Studies*, 2 (1982), 174–5.
[24] Michael Martin (*The Legal Philosophy of H. L. A. Hart* (Philadelphia, 1987), 17–18) makes two mistakes in treating this issue. First, he mistakenly regards the second demand as a mere reformulation of the first. Second, he mistakenly takes the second demand to be the claim that 'a legal theorist who desires to understand a legal system must view the legal system from the internal point of view'. Ch. 5

rules function? In some way it must be that the legal theorist's account perspicuously represents how it is with those who have the critical reflective attitude towards the rules and who regard them as in some sense proper standards for conduct. That means more than including a reference to an attitude; it requires something like displaying the interior content of such an attitude, saying what it is like to live in the world of those who have the attitude. The crucial issue is—does that task require the theorist accomplishing it to have the attitude in question or does it not? If the theorist is to remain in some worthwhile way 'external' to those who have the attitude, the task cannot require that the theorist herself have the attitude.

On pages 86–8 of *The Concept of Law*, Hart seems to distinguish between an 'extreme external point of view' which fails to make reference to the internal point of view, and a 'moderate external point of view'—the point of view of the observer who understands well that rule-following is taking place, who understands the internal point of view of those who accept the rules, but who is still 'external' to the system of rules in that she does not share this internal point of view. These allusive and elusive sentences comprise all Hart himself has to say on the topic of the point of view of legal theory. He is silent on how to explicate that point of view in the concepts of philosophy of social science. It has fallen to later interpreters to supply the missing articulation. In the philosophy of social science, there exists in opposition to empiricist/positivist theories of social science the hermeneutic or *Verstehen* approach to social theorizing. Hacker ('Hart's Philosophy', 8–18) and MacCormick (*H. L. A. Hart*, 29–44) have each linked the passages in *The Concept of Law* to this alternate perspective. 'One of the salient themes of hermeneutics is that description of distinctively human phenomena must involve understanding the situation described as it is apprehended by the agent whose behaviour is to be explained and understood' (Hacker, 'Hart's Philosophy', 9). Both Hacker and MacCormick have hailed Hart's emphasis on the need to reproduce the internal point of view as the introduction of the hermeneutic conception of social theorizing

below will discuss whether a case can be made out for the truth of the claim in quotes. Whether the claim can be made out or not, it is certainly not one that Hart makes, and for the plain reason that it is incompatible with legal positivism. It is not possible to take the internal point of view to a set of legal rules and make no value judgements about them.

to the British tradition of analytical jurisprudence, and thus as a significant departure from that tradition's previous association with Millian empiricism. On this account, Hart's importance lies in the signposts he erected, rather than the goals he reached.

Hacker's discussion is primarily expository: although he refers twice to Hart's 'hermeneutical methodology', he says little to help us see in what this consists but sticks very close to the vocabulary and concepts of Hart's original discussion. MacCormick, on the other hand, self-consciously goes beyond *The Concept of Law* to attempt to finish a cogent line of argument he sees as started but not fulfilled in that book. We shall therefore find in MacCormick's theory a more plausible form of sophisticated positivism. MacCormick refers to the point of view he constructs as 'the hermeneutic point of view'. Since I wish still to postpone (to Chapter 5) determination of whether in fact sophisticated positivism has absorbed the lessons of hermeneutic social theory, I shall not use this terminology, but speak instead of 'the moderate point of view'.

MacCormick has two different lines of argument for the moderate point of view as the proper point of view for positivistic legal theory. He does not clearly distinguish them, but they are there. The first and weakest line of argument may be called the 'Cartesian' line. It bases the distinction between the extreme external point of view and the moderate point of view on the distinction between publicly observable behaviour and the mental state behind the behaviour. The extreme external point of view is concerned only with publicly observable behaviour, whereas the moderate point of view deploys 'an awareness of the content of our conscious thoughts and processes of thinking' which goes beyond behaviour (*Legal Reasoning and Legal Theory*, 284). MacCormick quotes (ibid. 275) a splendid passage from *Gulliver's Travels* in which the Lilliputians describe a certain object in what MacCormick asserts to be an 'accurate external description of the thing in terms of its visual appearance and auditory manifestations'. We regular folks of course realize it is a description of a watch. The tale 'dramatizes the difference between seeing activities only as they manifest themselves externally to the senses, and seeing them with understanding, understanding in terms of the categories used by the agents themselves' (ibid. 279). Just as the realization that this is a watch 'goes beyond' awareness of its external, sensory properties, so also awareness that a particular pattern of behaviour is, for example, fraudulent misrepresentation goes beyond awareness of its external, sensory properties. But any such diagnosis is still 'external'—in principle it can be made by any observer who knows to what set of sensory properties the group who use it apply the term 'fraudulent misrepresentation', even though the observer does not consider herself bound by the correlative norm of avoiding fraudulent misrepresentation. MacCormick himself refers to this as a 'mentalistic view' of the internal point of view (ibid. 284).

The difficulty with the Cartesian line will be evident from the preceding discussion. A behaviouristically inclined social theorist is going to reduce these extra 'mentalistic' elements to other patterns of observable behaviour. Our response to a watch and the Lilliputians' response to a watch are on this view just two different convergent patterns of behavioural events. So, in so far as the Cartesian line relies for its plausibility on the claim that social theorizing about law 'goes beyond' publicly observable behaviour, that claim is not secured, and the Cartesian line fails. Since the Cartesian line is found only in the earlier version of MacCormick's argument, in *Legal Reasoning and Legal Theory*, it may be speculated that MacCormick himself wisely no longer wishes to support it.

MacCormick's second line of argument for defending the claim that there is a moderate point of view both hermeneutic and external relies on distinguishing between two aspects of the full internal point of view itself. The full internal point of view, he claims, has

both a cognitive element and a volitional element. The cognitive element covers not only discernment of convergent patterns of behaviour, but also a capacity to appraise actual doings or contemplated doings against that abstract and general pattern, and to register instances conforming to, not conforming to, or irrelevant to the pattern . . . The element of volition or will comprehends some wish or preference that the act, or abstention from acting, be done when the envisaged circumstances obtain. (*H. L. A. Hart*, 33).

MacCormick acknowledges that the 'volitional' here plausibly includes also the 'emotional', provided the latter is not understood narrowly in terms of occurrent feelings (*H. L. A. Hart*, 34; cf. *The*

Concept of Law, 56). In terms of the cognition/volition distinction, the moderate point of view

requires (a) full sharing in the cognitive element of the internal point of view—the understanding of the patterns of behaviour as such, and (b) full appreciation of, but no necessary sharing in, the volitional element, the will or preference for the conformity to the pattern as a standard. (*H. L. A. Hart*, 38)

Such a one [sc. one with the moderate point of view] shares in the cognitive element of [the internal point of view], and gives full cognitive recognition to and appreciation of the latter's volitional element. Thus he can understand rules and standards for what they are, but does not endorse them for his own part in stating or describing them or discussing their correct application. (*H. L. A. Hart*, 43)

MacCormick illustrates what he means by mentioning certain cases. He can fully understand cognitively the rules and articles of faith of the Scottish Presbyterian Church as those who live by such rules understand them, without having their volitional commitment to the rules (*H. L. A. Hart*, 38). A non-believer who has a friend he supposes to be one of the faithful can say with perfect propriety, 'You ought to go to Mass today' (*H. L. A. Hart*, 39). He (MacCormick) can truly say 'Soviet citizens may not hold or deal in foreign currencies' while having little liking for the political and legal principles of the USSR (as it then was, as they say) (*H. L. A. Hart*, 40).

Raz uses essentially the same kind of case to present a different but related articulation of a 'moderate point of view', one that is to be available for legal theory. Raz introduces the notion of what he calls 'detached legal statements'.[25] A detached legal statement is an example of the general class of 'statements from a point of view'.[26] The characteristics of statements from a point of view are that they presuppose a system of norms which is accepted as valid by some group; they are true or false in terms of the existence and content of such norms; they can be asserted by a person who has a practical interest in what is required by such norms even though that person does not him- or herself accept the norms as valid (cf.

---

[25] Cf. *The Concept of a Legal System*, 234–6; 'Legal Validity', in *The Authority of Law*, 153–9.
[26] Cf. *Practical Reason and Norms*, 170–7; 'Promises and Obligations', in P. M. S. Hacker and J. Raz (eds.), *Law, Morality and Society* (Oxford, 1977), 225.

Practical Reason and Norms, 177). They are 'to be found whenever a person advises or informs another on his normative situation in contexts which make it clear that the advice or information is given from a point of view or on the basis of certain assumptions which are not necessarily shared by the speaker' (*The Authority of Law*, 156). Thus detached legal statements are statements from the legal point of view (or from the point of view of legal science). They are statements of the positive law of some jurisdiction which does not carry the full normative force of legal statements made by one who accepts the legal norms in question. These latter statements Raz refers to as 'committed' or 'ordinary' legal statements. In general, Raz says, 'this third kind of statement [sc. the detached legal statement; 'third' as opposed to the 'external statement' and the 'internal statement'] is characteristic of the lawyer and law teacher [insofar as] they are not primarily concerned in applying the law to themselves or others but in warning others of what they ought to do according to law' (*The Authority of Law*, 155). Raz then gives the familiar-looking case of a Catholic expert in Rabbinical law advising his friend who is an orthodox but relatively ill-informed Jew. He also gives the example of one who is not a vegetarian saying to a friend who is, 'You ought not to eat this dish. It contains meat' (*Practical Reason and Norms*, 175–6).[27]

Over and above the intuitive appeal of the concept of 'detached legal statement', the theoretical grounding for it is in the philosophy of language, unlike that of MacCormick's 'moderate point of view' which is, as we have seen, grounded in the philosophy of mind. The thought is this. Both Jim, who is a vegetarian, and Kim, who is not a vegetarian, may say to Tim, who is a vegetarian, 'You ought not to eat this dish'. Both Jim and Kim mean the same thing by what they say—that Tim ought not to eat the dish. Jim, however, also believes that he, Jim, ought not to eat the dish, because he, Jim, believes that eating meat is wrong. Kim,

---

[27] Raz has clearly struck here the right chord, since the concept of detached legal statements has been taken up with approbation by other theorists—Hart (*Essays on Bentham*, 153–61), MacCormick ('Normativity', 108–13), David Lyons, ('Comment: The Normativity of Law', in Ruth Gavison (ed.), *Issues in Contemporary Legal Philosophy* (Oxford, 1987), 121–4), and, among positivism's opponents, Finnis (*Natural Law and Natural Rights*, 234–7). It is also very plausibly a close relative of Kelsen's conception of the science of law and its deliverances—see e.g. *Pure Theory of Law* (Berkeley and Los Angeles, 1967), chs. 3 and 8.

on the other hand, does not believe that she, Kim, ought not to eat the dish; in fact, she, Kim, cannot wait to get at it. We characterize the difference between Jim and Kim by saying that Jim says 'You ought not to eat this dish' with the force of commitment while Kim says it with the force of detachment. Jim makes a committed or ordinary (quasi-)legal statement; Kim makes a detached (quasi-)legal statement.

It may be that philosophy of mind and philosophy of language can help each other out here—so that we analyse the state of mind expressed by one who in saying certain words makes a detached legal statement as being that of having a cognitive grasp of the system of norms in issue but no volitional commitment to them. But there seems no necessary connection between these two lines of thought in sophisticated positivism. The notion of 'the moderate point of view' constitutes an attempt by sophisticated positivism to take seriously theory of law as a branch of social theory, and to take seriously also important criticisms of empiricist social theory. The notion of 'detached legal statements' takes seriously theses in the philosophy of language. Together, they constitute a sophisticated attempt to move away from construing the point of view of legal theory as a purely external perspective on the law as a social institution, while none the less remaining firmly positivistic by denying that legal theory need be committed to the acceptability of the statements of law it utters.

4. THE ACCEPTANCE OF LAW

Simple positivism eschewed any connection between the status of the law as law and the fact of its being accepted by its norm-subjects as making legitimate demands upon them. Simple positivism achieved this disconnection by characterizing the norm-subjects' conformity to law in terms which prescinded from the intentional aspect of human action. No actual legal philosopher has defended simple positivism in this stark form.[28] However, we must begin there in order to understand how sophisticated positivism is to be understood as an improvement over simple positivism.

Let us recall first familiar arguments from *The Concept of Law*.

[28] *A fortiori* and in particular, not John Austin; see below.

Austin defined laws as commands of the sovereign, and the sovereign as a person or group of persons to whom the bulk of a given society are in a habit of obedience. Hart claims (54 ff.) that: (i) we should interpret 'habit' in Austin's theory as a convergent pattern of behaviour; (ii) that such habits constitute an example of the external aspect of human life; (iii) that habitual behaviour is significantly different from rule-governed behaviour—social rules differ from habits in adding to the existence of convergent patterns of behaviour criticism of deviation, acceptance that deviation is a good reason for criticism, and the internalization of the pattern of behaviour as a general standard binding on the group including the individual so internalizing;[29] (iv) that Austin's major error is to omit the 'internal aspect' of rules. The law is an example of a rule-governed practice, as opposed to a mere aggregate of convergent patterns of behaviour. Therefore, Austin's theory fails as a theory of law. The point of my philosophical fiction of simple positivism and its devotion to 'colourless movements' should now be clear. Hart takes Austin to be a simple positivist in the manner described in Chapter 1.5 above. We shall come later (Chapter 6 below) to the question of how far Hart's characterization of Austin is adequate, and of what follows if it is not.

Hart also charges Austin with further inadequacies, which are corollaries of the failure to distinguish rules from habits and of the interpretation of laws as the commands of a sovereign. The notion of 'habit of obedience' clearly has to do with the efficacy of law. Austin explains both efficacy and obedience in terms of the fact that the sovereign's commands are backed by threats to visit with evil non-compliance. Austin asserts further that the coercion afforded by commands backed up with threats is that in which legal obligation and duty consist. Hart rejects these further doctrines also. He distinguishes 'being obliged' and 'being under an obligation' (cf. *The Concept of Law*, 80–1), and claims that Austin shows only why a subject may be 'obliged' to obey the law, not how he or she may be 'under an obligation'. The underlying assumption is that properly speaking laws create obligations; they do not merely oblige. If therefore a theory cannot show how laws

---

[29] Hart speaks of the latter as 'implicit' in the 2 previous elements; I leave unaddressed the question of whether the 'internal aspect' of rules is only the third element, or whether it is all 3 elements, or whether it matters which.

create obligations, but only how they oblige, it must be inadequate as a theory of law.

So far so good. But now things begin to get more complicated for sophisticated positivism. The first complication is easily absorbed. It cannot be a requirement of law as a system of obligation-imposing rules that every single subject of the rules has the internal point of view to the rules. There is no contradiction in asserting that some recalcitrant who has the external point of view to law none the less has an obligation to obey the law. It seems perfectly proper to substitute for the excessively stringent requirement of unanimity a lesser requirement that some suitable percentage less than 100 per cent of the group who are the subjects of the rules having the internal point of view to the rules is sufficient (whether by itself or in conjunction with other requirements) to show that the rules generally impose obligations on all members of the group. Moreover, for those who do have the internal point of view, it seems unreasonable to require that they have it towards each and every rule of the system, but only to the majority of rules, say, or to fundamental rules in the hierarchy of rules, rules which give the system its distinctive flavour or character. A range of cases must be acknowledged.

But now there are further complexities. A legal system is in fact not only an institutionalized normative system, but a very complicated one. Two major coarse-grained distinctions may be made in its mode of operation. The first is between the role of citizen and the role of official. The system requires for its operation and maintenance a body of persons occupying various official roles within the system, whose responsibilities have to do with the creation, variation, application, and enforcement of the rules of the system. The second distinction, a congener of the first, is between two systematically different kinds of rules of the system, those which directly impose duties upon the subjects or which provide facilities for the subjects to create and vary legal relations, and those which control the operations and maintenance of the system by the officials.[30] It seems paradoxical to say that the

[30] I realize I am opting here for one construal of the status of facilitating rules. Since they are neither 'rules about rules' nor duty-imposing rules, they do not fit happily into the 'primary rule'/'secondary rule' distinction, at least as that was made by Hart in ch. 5 sect. 3 of *The Concept of Law*. On the ambiguities in the primary rule/secondary rule distinction, see R. Sartorius, 'Hart's Concept of Law', in Robert S. Summers (ed.), *More Essays in Legal Philosophy* (Oxford, 1971), 136–8.

secondary rules of the system, being not obligation-imposing rules, are not rules of the system, when in some sense without them there would not be a legal system. A scarcely weaker claim may be made about facilitating rules, in that the existence of formal and institutionalized procedures for the creation of voluntary obligations (for example) is a trademark of law. So how might one take these two fundamental distinctions on board without letting go of the idea that a legal system is a system of obligation-imposing rules?

An antecedent commitment to positivism makes the following solution to this problem irresistibly tempting. Positive law gets to exist as positive law by having undergone some appropriate procedure of enactment or recognition—and those terms are to be understood widely enough to satisfy the most enthusiastic devotee of judge-made, common law. But along with the acknowledgement of this fact must go the acknowledgement that a second mode of existence for laws is created, one which is additional to the mode of existence as the product of a social practice embodying the internal point of view. This is the mode of existence through validity, in the sense of creation in accord with procedural rules of recognition (cf. *The Concept of Law*, 97–102). Acknowledgement of this second mode of existence not only seems to accord with the special role of officials and secondary rules, but also with the positivistic requirement of a content-independent test for law—for that a rule is created in accordance with due procedure is so (or not, as the case may be) independently of the content of the rule.

But now the issue of the status of legal rules as obligation-imposing rules has to be reconsidered. For, if it is sufficient for a rule to exist that it is valid, and if it is sufficient for a rule to impose an obligation that it is valid, then it is clearly the case that a rule may impose an obligation through being valid even when no one has the internal point of view towards that rule. And now we have an apparent substantial tension between the thought that rules impose obligations only if a suitable number of the group whose rules they are have the internal point of view towards the rules and the thought that a rule may impose obligations through existing as valid even when no one has the internal point of view towards the rule.

Again, sheer facts about how the legal system operates impel the theorist towards the following argument. The central role(s) in the operation of the system is/are the officials' role(s). The central part of their role is the use of the secondary rules. Indeed, unless there are officials and they do meaningfully create, change, apply, and enforce the secondary rules to the extent appropriate, there would be nothing to indicate the existence of a legal system rather than a purely customary normative system such as a morality (cf. *The Concept of Law*, 89–96). Thus it seems obvious that:

There are therefore two minimum conditions necessary and sufficient for the existence of a legal system. On the one hand those rules of behaviour which are valid according to the system's ultimate criteria of validity must be generally obeyed, and, on the other hand, its rules of recognition specifying the criteria of legal validity and its rules of change and adjudication must be effectively accepted as common public standards of official behaviour by its officials. (*The Concept of Law*, 113)

Hart goes on to add that the officials in their capacity as private citizens are in the same position as any other private citizens with regard to the primary rules; that is, they need only obey such rules, as opposed to having the internal point of view towards them. In short, a legal system exists as such when no one has the internal point of view towards the primary rules, and the officials alone have the internal point of view towards the secondary rules. A censorial concern for the quality of life in a society might lead to hope that the internal point of view will be more widespread, for then the society will be more 'healthy' (cf. *The Concept of Law*, 113). But from the perspective of analytical jurisprudence, the minimal case is undeniably a legal system (*The Concept of Law*, 114).[31]

One more piece of fine-tuning is needed for sophisticated positivism to sound clearly. What kind of attitude constitutes the internal point of view which is required of the officials? It would again be excessive to require that the officials' acceptance had to be a full-blooded commitment to the moral worth of the secondary rules. This is not merely because not all secondary rules will raise moral issues—some procedures may be more matters of economic

---

[31] Jules Coleman's theory that 'law is ultimately conventional: that the authority of law is ultimately a matter of its acceptance by officials' ('Negative Positivism', 148) amounts to the same view as Hart's in the present context.

convenience or traditional etiquette than of natural justice.[32] It is so in part because 'acceptance' may be properly taken to cover a range of attitudes other than, and from the moral point of view weaker than, a commitment to moral worth. The underlying reasoning seems at least in part again purely factual—it is just *true* that officials have a variety of attitudes towards the secondary rules and yet none the less regard them as 'common public standards of official behaviour'. But putative factual evidence is not germane to the theoretical issue at stake. A non-positivistic theory which argues that a legal system will not be worthy of the term unless its rules are such as to merit moral commitment will also likely argue as well that the officials will only discharge their duties in a proper spirit when they themselves make a similar moral commitment. Beyleveld and Brownsword, for example (cf. *Law As a Moral Judgment*, ch. 8), not only require that in general laws must pass a moral test to be valid, but also that officials must as a minimum make a good-faith attempt to enact laws which pass a moral test; unless the attempt is successful, the officials do not deserve the name. Thus it is an expression of legitimate opposition to positivism to say that officials who have less than a full moral commitment to the 'common public standard' are officials in name only. Positivism therefore has a significant theoretical interest in arguing that a range of attitudes other than full moral commitment none the less count as possession of the internal point of view to the secondary rules. We find in fact that this claim is made. On page 198 of *The Concept of Law* Hart argues that voluntary acceptance of the system still counts as the internal point of view when it is based on 'calculation of long-term self-interest; disinterested interest in others; an unreflecting inherited or traditional attitude; or the mere wish to do as others do'. Honoré seems to argue for an even weaker requirement—that membership in a group requires understanding of the nature and activities of the group 'minus professed rejection' rather than 'plus acceptance' (*Making Law Bind*, 36). Sophisticated positivism sees that the theory of law as a set of social rules requires in some form the presence of the internal point of view as well as convergent patterns of behaviour. However, in the spirit of the separation of

[32] For a subtle discussion of the relation between issues of economics and issues of justice, see R. Dworkin, 'Principle, Policy, Procedure', *A Matter of Principle* (Cambridge, Mass., 1985), ch. 3.

the existence of law and the merit of law, sophisticated positivism makes the specification of the content of the internal point of view as 'thin' and formal as possible.

In sum, sophisticated positivism's account of the acceptance of law is thus. It is a mistake to think that law is law when it is an entire system of coercive commands. Some persons at least must accept the law as a binding standard for behaviour. But it is sufficient for law that this acceptance be confined to the stance of the officials of the system towards the secondary rules of the system, and that the content of this acceptance be interpreted as thinly and minimally as possible. A range of pro-attitudes falling well short of a full commitment to the moral worth of the law will satisfy the requirement of acceptance.

5. PRINCIPLE AND DISCRETION

5.1. Introduction

Simple positivism presented a simple view of adjudication. The judge has available two adjudicatory strategies—either apply black-letter rules deductively and mechanically; or go 'outside' the black-letter rules and adjudicate on a discretionary basis. The first strategy is designed for 'core' or 'easy' cases, and the second for 'penumbral' or 'hard' cases. One reason for intuitive dissatisfaction with this simple account appears to be empirical. Inspection of case-law reports reveals a phenomenological level at which simple positivism fails to preserve the phenomena. Cases are often decided, or so the text of the reports seems to suggest, by a procedure which is neither a matter of 'mechanical' derivation from black-letter rule nor a matter of 'going outside the law'. Instead, the court seems to appeal to a different kind of legal standard, one expressed in such terms as 'No one shall profit from his own wrong', 'One who does not choose to read a contract before signing it cannot later relieve himself of its burdens', and the like. It is characteristic of these standards that they are expressed quite generally and even vaguely; they seem to be legally grounded in that they reflect ideas embodied in black-letter law; yet they have never passed a positivistic test of 'pedigree'. Thus their very existence seems to indicate a weakness in the simple positivist's account of adjudication. Simple positivism has no room for standards which are genuinely legal and yet not black-letter rules. Let us call these general legal standards which seem to have no home in simple positivism 'legal principles'.

Dworkin's famous original attack on positivism's 'model of rules'[33] took the form of saying that legal principles were 'requirements of justice or fairness or some other dimension of morality', and that positivism's inability to incorporate principles into its theory was symptomatic of positivism's deep failure to understand the relation between law and morality, and equally deep failure to take rights seriously. The initial premiss for this far-reaching argument is no more than the modest claim rehearsed above—that the simple positivism described in Chapter 1.5 cannot account for the use in adjudication of general legal standards. In acknowledging that Dworkin is right in asserting the modest claim, I do not mean to be endorsing all of his far more extensive claims. Indeed, the present section will explore the possibilities for a sophisticated positivistic account of 'legal principles'—that is, for an account which recognizes the limitations of simple positivism, but thinks that the phenomena can be preserved without giving up positivism. The term 'legal principle' in this section is therefore simply a term which identifies certain phenomena: it is in itself part of the vocabulary neither of a Dworkinian theory of adjudication nor of a positivistic rebuttal.

One further caveat must be entered. In his 1967 paper, Dworkin presented the issue between himself and positivism in a misleading way. *Hart's theory*, he implied, is a theory about what the law consists of: it consists essentially of rules—primary rules, secondary rules, and the ultimate rule of recognition. All rules except the ultimate rule of recognition exist by satisfying conditions for their existence laid down by the ultimate rule of recognition. Hard cases will arise, the disposition of which is not wholly determined by the existing body of rules as formulated. Since there are no other relevant authoritative legal materials, adjudication in hard cases is a matter of judicial creativity, a law-producing or discretionary activity. *Dworkin's theory*, he implied, is also a theory about what the law consists of. In his theory, the law consists partly of rules, as Hart suggests, but it also consists of another kind of legal standard, legal principles. Legal principles do not exist by courtesy

---

[33] 'Is law a system of rules?' (1967), reprinted as ch. 2 of *Taking Rights Seriously*.

of the ultimate rule of recogition; they are standards to be observed because they are requirements of justice or fairness or some other dimension of morality. Courts are as bound to follow legal principles as they are to follow precedents or statutes. Because principles comprehend all possibilities, there is no such thing as judicial discretion except by explicit delegation.

Expressed in this way, the dispute seems easy to resolve. Hart makes two connected claims about the law—it contains only rules and therefore also room for discretion. Dworkin denies these two claims—the law also contains principles and therefore no room for discretion. This seems like one theorist saying there is only one strand in the helical structure of DNA, and another theorist saying, 'No, there are two strands'. *This* dispute we know how to solve. We test the theories against what DNA actually contains. So why should we not do the same thing with the dispute over what the law contains? Law libraries groan under the weight of volumes of law reports. Do those books contain principles or not? Just look around.

Dworkin proceeds in just this way. He makes the disagreement over the existence of legal principles seem straightforwardly empirical. He introduces principles by citing two cases—*Riggs* v. *Palmer*,[34] in which a major role is played by the 'principle' that no one shall profit from his own wrong, and *Henningsen* v. *Bloomfield Motors, Inc.*,[35] which features several 'principles', including, for example, the principle that the courts will not permit themselves to be used as instruments of inequity and injustice. Having presented these two cases as illustrative of the entities he is referring to, Dworkin continues: 'Once we identify legal principles as separate sorts of standard, different from legal rules, we are suddenly aware of them all around us. Law teachers teach them, lawbooks cite them, legal historians celebrate them' (*Taking Rights Seriously*, 28). By implication, the positivist is too foolish to notice such plain facts.

There are two different models for a factual dispute. The first model is a dispute between one who says there is cheese in the refrigerator and one who denies it, and there is cheese in the refrigerator and the denier fails to see what is before his eyes. He would have agreed that there was cheese in the refrigerator if he had seen what the other saw. Dworkin implies that the positivist's

---

[34] 22 NE 188 (1889).   [35] 32 NJ 358 (1960).

denial of principles is to be construed on such a model. But this is a mistake. The positivist who has been denying the existence of principles and has them thrust in her face by Dworkin's two cases is, if anything, like the second model for a factual disagreement. The second model is a dispute where the parties see exactly the same thing and describe it differently. On this model, the positivist, in accepting Dworkin's claim that there are legal principles, would be like an obtuse Australian who, after living years in England, suddenly realizes that all around are white swans, and not just very large white ducks. Even though the Australian's discovery is not like Captain Cook's discovery of black swans, for it comes by reflection on what is observed, it is still a discovery of the factual truth, and a correction of a previous factual error.

Even this second model, however, does not accurately represent the dispute between Dworkin and positivism over the existence of legal principles. Unlike our hypothetical Australian, the positivist is very well aware of the existence of legal standards phrased in a form like 'No one shall profit from his own wrong', or 'You must take reasonable care to avoid acts or omissions which you can reasonably see would be likely to injure your neighbour',[36] and the plausibility of calling such standards 'principles'. Even Austin had no doubts about the existence of 'principles, notions and distinctions common to various systems', and he thought it an important part of 'general jurisprudence or philosophy of law' to examine such principles. He even went so far as to postulate that of such principles 'some may be deemed necessary' to 'any system of law as evolved in a refined community'.[37] The appropriate parallel here is not the ornithological parallel, but with Dr Johnson purporting to refute Bishop Berkeley by kicking a stone. Johnson interprets Berkeley's denial of matter as a denial that there are such things as stones, and so he kicks one to prove Berkeley's error. But Berkeley is not claiming that there are no stones as that claim might be made by a gardener who has finished riddling the potato patch. He has not merely failed to see the stones that Dr Johnson sees. He has a different philosophical account of what it is to be a stone. Likewise the difference between Dworkin and the

---

[36] *Donoghue* v. *Stevenson* [1932] AC 562, per Lord Atkin, at 580.
[37] *Lectures on Jurisprudence* (4th edn., London, 1873), ii. 1107–8.

positivist does not turn on one person making a factual claim the other person denies. It turns on the theoretical account to be given of the notion of a legal 'principle', of what it would be to give a perspicuous representation of legal principles from the point of view of legal theory.

We must therefore distinguish carefully two different senses of 'principle'—one sense in which 'principle' is a pre-philosophical term such as might be used by any legal theorist to identify a legal standard phrased in general terms and which therefore carries no commitment to any legal theory; and one sense in which 'principle' is a term of art used as part of the vocabulary of a given particular legal theory. Dworkin makes the term 'principle' into a term of art in a particular legal theory: the positivist who in response to Dworkin also gives an account of what it is for a standard to be a 'principle' is also making the term into a term of art in a particular legal theory. It follows that there is no sense of 'principle' which both is not a term of art and secures the truth of positivism, nor one which both is not a term of art and secures the truth of Dworkin's theory. Austin's use of 'principle' is arguably altogether non-technical and pre-philosophical, and therefore not a contribution to Dworkin's debate with positivism. But it grounds no rebuttal of Dworkin either.

To show that 'principle' can be a legitimate term of art within positivism, one must do more than remark that positivists have used the term. One must present arguments. Let us therefore turn to the arguments that have been presented.

Simple positivism does not represent a legal system as a system of absolute discretion. The adjudicator is constrained in two ways, by the rules of settled law, and by general standards of rationality. The adjudicator may also be exposed to criticism on a variety of non-legal grounds. The first line of resistance to simple positivism is that all this is not enough: it must be possible to criticize the adjudicator on legal grounds. Formalism, we said in Chapter 1.6, is a vice when it leads the judge to follow a rule of settled law when the legal system itself makes available a 'rule-avoiding' norm. It is clearly very attractive to suppose that 'legal principles' are precisely the kind of rule-avoiding norms which it is proper to expect judges to respect.[38] The second line of resistance draws on

[38] Note that the above sentences are quite neutral as to what it is for a legal standard to be a 'legal principle'.

the fact, also noted in Chapter 1.6, that consistency with settled law when settled law does cover the case in question is also a requirement in adjudication. One might think that talk about 'rule-avoiding norms' means that the virtue of consistency has to be sacrificed in the name of justice. But if 'principles' are conceived of as general standards existing 'above' black-letter rules, covering the interstices between such rules and therefore constraining interstitial adjudication, then consistency need not be sacrificed to justice. Consistency must simply be construed more broadly, and seemingly more fundamentally, as consistency with principle.

Dworkin exploits each of these lines of thought in both the rhetoric and the argument of his original attack on positivism, not to mention the moral halo worn by the notion of 'principle' in post-Kantian thought.[39] The challenge to sophisticated positivism will be to follow these lines of thought to a point which respects their weight while remaining within the bounds of a positivistic theory of law. I shall present the two connected strands in sophisticated positivism—first, the possibilities for a positivistic account of 'legal principles', and, second, the possibilities for 'rule-avoiding' constraints on adjudicators which are none the less properly legal from a positivist point of view.

5.2. Principle

Let me first note that, while views held by Hart often appear in the characteristics of sophisticated rather than simple positivism, on this particular issue Hart's theory is a version of simple positivism. This will have been evident from the deployment in the text so far of key terms in Hart's vocabulary, 'core', 'penumbra', 'discretion', 'rule', and the like. The initial attempt to offer a sophisticated positivistic account of legal principles is presented as a necessary modification of Hart's theory, while otherwise remaining close to a fundamental positivism. Raz concedes that Dworkin's criticism forces such a modification.[40] He faults Dworkin for not realizing that the issue of legal rules versus legal principles cannot be considered in isolation from the issue of the individuation of laws (825–32). Dworkin is tacitly assuming a criterion of individuation

---

[39] Who would want to have their case heard by an 'unprincipled' judge? Not I.
[40] 'Legal Principles and the Limits of Law', *Yale Law Journal*, 81 (1972), 852–3. All references in this and the next two paragraphs are to this paper.

for laws which picks out only rules genuinely to count as laws. But there is no reason, Raz urges, independent of the issue between Dworkin and positivism, to accept this criterion. Rather, if another criterion is as or more adequate, and from it a different account of legal rules and principles follows, Dworkin's criticism of positivism are beside the point.

Raz offers a classificatory scheme within which legal rules and legal principles are subdivisions of 'general legal norms', as opposed to 'particular legal norms' (824 n. 4). He has two different and complementary strategies for a sophisticated positivistic account of legal principles. First, he points to the work of legal textbook writers and legal opinion writers who concentrate on the content of positive law and describe its content while being indifferent to the exact way in which the lawmaker generated that content. He writes:

We often have need to refer summarily to a body of legal rules without specifying their content in detail . . . These references usually take the form of a statement of a principle, but they are not statements of the contents of laws of a special type, namely legal principles. They are merely a brief allusion to a number of rules . . . Some apparent statements of principles are merely abbreviated references to a number of laws, not statements of the content of one complete legal principle. (828–9)

According to this line of thought, legal principles have a positivistic 'pedigree' simply because they are shorthand for a set of pedigreed rules of black-letter law. Their extension is exactly the extension of the rules which they collect.[41]

Raz's second strategy for accounting for principles, and the one which in his view involves a modification of Hart's theory, is based on the identification of legal standards which are quite deliberately vague and general. Such general standards, like formal rules, have a source or pedigree. But, whereas a legal rule is pedigreed by one legally authoritative act of a court or legislature, a principle derives its pedigree from a series of such acts: its source is a developed custom among adjudicatory bodies of considering themselves bound to follow the principle in question (848). 'Principles evolved by the courts become binding by becoming a

---

[41] Sartorius, 'Social Policy', 156, talks in defence of positivism of principles being 'embedded' in first-order legal materials.

judicial custom. They are part of the law because they are accepted by the courts' (853). The modification to Hart's theory lies in the fact that these judicial customs which 'recognize' certain norms as legal principles must be of the same status as, and cannot be a part of, the 'ultimate rule of recognition' which for Hart grounds legal validity. The ultimate rule of recognition is explicitly customary, for Hart (see *The Concept of Law*, 102–7). It does not make sense, Raz argues (853), to say that part of that custom is to validate other customs. There is only the distinction between judicial custom and the rules and principles which judicial custom validates.

In short, Raz's sophisticated positivistic account of legal principles offers two alternatives for preserving the phenomena in positivistic terms. Seemingly unpedigreed general legal standards like 'No one shall profit from his own wrong' are either shorthand summaries of pedigreed legal rules, and so are themselves pedigreed by transitivity of pedigree; or they are independent legal standards with their own pedigree by judicial custom. In either case, the existence of general legal standards is accounted for without giving up the fundamental positivistic idea of a norm being a law only if it has a social source.

Raz's account of legal principles still leaves sophisticated positivism very close to Hart's (fairly) simple 'model of rules'. The law for Raz consists of rules plus whatever general standards are summaries of sets of such rules plus whatever general standards are independently pedigreed by judicial custom. If the point of affirming legal principles as a distinct category of legal standards is to advance the limits of law, then it might be thought that Raz does not extend those limits very far. MacCormick's sophisticated positivistic account of legal principles succeeds in advancing those limits somewhat further. 'Principles', he says, 'express the underlying purposes of detailed rules and specific institutions, in the sense that they are seen as rationalizing them in terms of consistent, coherent and desirable goals.'[42] 'The basic idea is of the legal system as a consistent and coherent body of norms whose observance secures certain valued goals which can intelligibly be pursued all together' (*Legal Reasoning and Legal Theory*, 106).

---

[42] D. N. MacCormick and Ota Weinberger, *An Institutional Theory of Law* (Boston, Mass., 1984), 73; cf. *Legal Reasoning and Legal Theory*, 152–94.

MacCormick well recognizes that consistency is a merely formal property of a set of norms. Constraints of general rationality require a set of norms to be consistent. 'Coherence' is intended by MacCormick to be 'thicker' than formal consistency. To regard the law as consisting of black-letter materials plus whatever principles organize those materials in terms of their underlying purposes and goals is to take a positivistic account of law beyond Hart's account in terms of pedigreed rules plus discretion, and beyond Raz's account in terms of pedigreed rules plus summaries thereof plus principles pedigreed by judicial custom. MacCormick's account of legal principles permits that an academic commentator, for example, may correctly assert that a certain principle is a principle of, for example, Canadian law, and be right in so saying, even though the principle is not a mere summary of black-letter law nor is there a judicial custom of regarding the principle as binding. The commentator will correctly so assert when the principle organizes a body of Canadian law rationally in terms of its underlying values.

Despite its 'thickness', MacCormick's account of legal principles in terms of narrative coherence is none the less still orthodoxly positivistic, as he himself has stressed.[43] Whatever justification for a legal decision is derived from such principles is 'a formalistic (formally rational) and relativistic sort of justification':

'Coherence' can then be satisfied by a system which does subserve what those responsible for determining its content do suppose to be values (e.g. racial purity under various elements of National Socialist law), even although from another point of view—let us say bluntly a better one—these supposed values are truly evils.[44]

MacCormick's 'narrative coherence' will permit decisions in hard cases which 'go beyond' black-letter law but will also constrain

[43] Cf. *An Institutional Theory of Law*, 74; *Legal Reasoning and Legal Theory*, 152–7, 233–40; 'Coherence in Legal Justification', in H. Schelsky, W. Krawietz, G. Winkler, and A. Schramm (eds.), *Theorie der Normen* (Berlin, 1984), 46–7. 'The rules which are rules *of law* are so in virtue of their pedigree; the principles which are principles *of law* are so because of their function in relation to those rules, that is, the function which those who use them as rationalizations of the rules thus ascribe to them' (*Legal Reasoning and Legal Theory*, 233; MacCormick's emphasis).

[44] 'Coherence', 47; cf. *Legal Reasoning and Legal Theory* and South Africa. Essentially the same point about the limitations of a positivistic notion of 'coherence' is conceded by Sartorius, 'Social Policy', 158.

such decisions. But that is as far as even a sophisticated positivism can go. For once the term 'legal principle' is extended to standards which have no roots at all in black-letter law but are non-institutionalized requirements of morality, the account of legal principles, as Dworkin well realizes, has passed beyond the limits of law, and so also the limits of positivism however sophisticated.

5.3. Discretion

The account of adjudicatory discretion attributed to simple positivism was particularly crude—the 'two-step' account that judges should attempt first to subsume the case mechanically under settled black-letter law, and when this initial step failed to dispose of the case judges should go 'outside the law' for their decision. Since this account is so crude, seeming to condone even arbitrary decision-making at the second step, it is given credence by none but the most pessimistic of legal realists in their ideological campaign against the law. There are four different ways in which sophisticated positivism goes on to develop a more plausible account of adjudicatory discretion, although these four ways have overlapping relations between them.

Before considering these four ways, let us fill out a little the notion of discretion. Raz draws a relevant distinction between 'regulated' and 'unregulated' cases or disputes:

Regulated cases are those which fall under a common law or statutory rule which does not require judicial discretion for the determination of the dispute . . . A dispute is regulated if questions of the form: 'In this case should the court decide that p' have a correct legal answer. It is un-regulated if some of these questions do not have a correct legal answer . . . no particular solution to the dispute is required by law. (*The Authority of Law*, 181)

In regulated disputes, Raz says, 'the judge can be seen in his classical image: he identifies the law, determines the facts, and applies the law to the facts' (*The Authority of Law*, 182), though this process need not be 'mechanical' and indeed is not in, for example, a complex taxation case. Compare Raz's notion of an 'unregulated dispute' with Dworkin's notion of a case where the judge has 'strong discretion'. Both focus on the fact that, where common law and statute do not determine a correct answer, the judge has discretion. Raz puts the matter by saying that the dispute is then 'unregulated'; Dworkin puts it by saying that the judge 'is simply not bound by standards set by the authority in question [sc. (I take it) the law]' (*Taking Rights Seriously*, 32). The issue here is whether these two formulations are equivalent. Does it follow from the fact that a dispute is 'unregulated' that the judge in such a case 'is simply not bound by' legal standards? Let us turn to the four ways.

1. The rhetorical power of Dworkin's argument in the passage referred to depends upon the tacit implication that positivism permits (and perhaps even endorses!) wanton decision-making in unregulated disputes. Dworkin himself, however, negates this implication, not only in that he specifies standards 'not set by the authority concerned' (and so leaving it open that there may be other kinds of relevant standards), but also in his disclaimer that 'the strong sense of discretion is not tantamount to license' (*Taking Rights Seriously*, 33). Any context of action, he acknowledges, 'makes relevant certain standards of rationality, fairness, and effectiveness'. A person exercising the strong discretion which they properly have may still be criticized for failing to observe general standards of rationality (mistakes in mathematical calculation, perhaps) or effectiveness (picking too weak a tool to do the job required). I purposely leave aside for a moment 'fairness'. These general standards of rationality and effectiveness are not peculiarly legal, but a judge like any other agent in the world of affairs is subject to them. So sophisticated positivism can repudiate any supposed endorsement of wanton decision-making and say that these standards bind the judge in the second step of adjudication—they limit the judge's discretion, or 'regulate' the dispute—without compromising the claim within legal theory that the judge is legally bound only by legal standards of the kind positivism acknowledges.

2. The idea of 'translegal' standards may be taken a little bit further, to the category of standards called 'judicial technique principles'.[45] How far positivism may embrace 'judicial technique principles' depends on how 'judging' is to be understood. Let us distinguish two different kinds of 'judging'. The first is a general

---

[45] The term 'judicial technique principles' is borrowed from Philip Soper ('Legal Theory and the Obligation of a Judge: The Hart/Dworkin Dispute', *Michigan Law Review*, 75 (1977), 484–98). His own exposition and application of the term, however, is not useful for present purposes, since he fails to observe the distinction I am about to draw between the two kinds of 'judging'.

kind, judging as done by military persons in the heat of battle, by those who award the Booker Prize, by sports umpires and referees, by politicians and their campaign managers, by . . . , . . . , *and* by persons sitting on the bench in courts of law, though not by logic professors checking simple natural deduction proofs or accountants determining whether there is an excess of revenue over expenditure in straightforward cases. The second is a specific kind, judging as carried out only by persons sitting on the bench in courts of law. Sophisticated positivism may embrace whatever 'judicial technique principles' are embodied in the first kind of judging; such principles are similar in status to general principles of rationality, as discussed in (1) above. The issue with respect to 'judicial technique principles' of the second kind is more complex. Consider the 'characteristic judicial virtues' identified by Hart in a well-known passage in *The Concept of Law*:

impartiality and neutrality in surveying the alternatives: consideration for the interest of all who will be affected; and a concern to deploy some acceptable general principle as a reasoned basis for decision. (200)

Most plausibly, such virtues and any principles associated with them are *moral* demands upon the judge as institutional official. Whether an official who ignores them is none the less still 'a judge' is a question to which positivism and its opponents will give different answers. Positivism cannot acknowledge both that such principles do necessarily limit judicial discretion and that they are extra-legal or moral principles. Positivism can only embrace 'judicial technique principles' associated with the first kind of 'judging'.

3. There are ways in which sophisticated positivism might acknowledge the propriety of references to moral values in the exercise of discretion without prejudicing the separation of law and morality.

Three possibilities can be distinguished. First, it may happen that the content of a legal norm is as a matter of fact the same or pretty well the same as the content of some moral norm. This is certainly the case with many norms concerning the sanctity of the person, of life both human and non-human, aspects of the ownership of property, of the regulation of trade, and so forth. Morality and sect. 246 of the Canadian Criminal Code alike condemn sexual assault. When therefore a court holds a defendant guilty under sect. 246, the court gives a decision which is simultaneously the application of a moral norm.

Second and third, legal philosophy has identified for us two possible cases where a permission and even an obligation to apply moral norms is an essential part of the judicial role. In some given legal system the rule of recognition itself may directly in virtue of its own provisions or indirectly via the provisions of rules that it validates permit or even require the application of moral norms. Raz (*The Authority of Law*, 149) offers a valuable analogy for understanding these cases. It might be that, in the domain of private international law, a valid provision of, say, the UK legal system directs that, in order to decide points of law or even cases of a certain kind, the relevant controlling law shall be deemed to be, say, the law of Germany. That is, the UK court is here directed by UK law to decide a UK case by applying, in whole or in part, German law. That state of affairs, however, does not make German law part of the UK legal system. It does not make what it is to be a law of Germany all or even part of what it is to be a law of the UK. So also, a provision such as sect. 7 of the Canadian Charter,[46] which refers to 'principles of fundamental justice', can be construed as likewise directing courts to go 'outside' Canadian law to 'morality' in the same way that the imagined provision directed UK courts to go 'outside' UK law to German law. A court so proceeding in a sect. 7 case will be rendering a verdict by applying a norm of morality. But that does not make the norms of fundamental justice into valid norms of the Canadian legal system. Moreover, courts may legitimately go 'outside the law' in either case only because they are antecedently authorized by law itself to do so.[47]

The third way that a judicial decision may be also the application of a moral norm is this. A given judge may perfectly well choose to exercise discretion that he or she has in some case by deciding that case on its moral merits. In so choosing, the judge will be choosing to give a verdict which is simultaneously the application of a moral norm. This class of case is differentiated

---

[46] The Canadian Charter of Rights and Freedoms, Part I of the Constitution Act 1982, being Schedule B of the Canada Act 1982 (UK), 1982 c. 11.

[47] I return to this model and its significance for a defender of the 'Weak Social Thesis', that efficacy and institutionality are sufficient for law, in Ch.12 below.

from the previous class just discussed in that, by speaking of 'discretion', we imply that the court has a permission thus to refer to morality; the court is not directed to do so. The court also has a permission not to decide by applying a norm of morality; the court may decide by employing instead norms of wealth-maximization, of utilitarian hedonism, of marxian millenarianism, of coin-tossing, or whatever. That the court is not more bound to go in any one of these directions rather than another is part of what is implied by the term 'discretion'. None the less, that the court has a discretion of this kind is determined by the institution of law itself.

4. Talk of discretion is very often accompanied by talk of 'gaps in the law'—Dworkin's 'hole in the doughnut' image feeds such talk. But the notion of 'gaps in the law' is slippery. As both Raz (*The Authority of Law*, 76–8) and Schauer (*Playing by the Rules*, 225–6) have pointed out, whether there are 'gaps in the law' in the sense that 'the law is silent' (Raz, *The Authority of Law*, 77), that there is literally no law covering the fact-situation in question, will be a function of the given municipal legal system involved. Specifically, it will be a function of the comprehensiveness of the system, and the existence and content of closure rules within the sytem. If the system does not claim to cover fact-situations of the kind in question, then its failure to do so does not create a 'gap in the law'.[48] If there is a closure rule such as, for example, the rule that whatever is not legally prohibited is legally permitted, then there will be no 'gaps in the law' where the law is silent. Legal gaps or unregulated disputes occur, Raz maintains, 'where the law speaks with an uncertain voice (simple indeterminacy) or where it speaks with many voices (unresolved conflicts)' (ibid.). These 'gaps', however, occur within the domain of what are from the positivist perspective genuinely legal [sc. properly pedigreed] standards. For Raz, indeterminacy and unresolved conflicts substantiate talk of discretion and of unregulated disputes, but quite explicitly not of uncontrolled adjudication. Raz in fact goes further and declares, 'There are no pure law-creating cases' (*The Authority of Law*, 195). He argues for a continuity between law-

---

[48] Raz believes (*Practical Reason and Norms*, 150–2), while Schauer does not (ibid.), that legal systems as such claim to be 'comprehensive', i.e. claim 'authority to regulate any kind of behaviour' (ibid. 150), though it will be a matter of social fact, for any given legal system, what issues it does as a matter of fact regulate in virtue of its claimed authority.

applying and law-making (*The Authority of Law*, 206–9). 'On most occasions, the reasoning justifying law-making decisions is similar to and continuous with decisions interpreting and applying law' (*The Authority of Law*, 208). In short, a legal system for Raz is more like a plenum than a series of atoms in a void. Yet, as long as there are uncertain voices and many voices to be heard, there is room for adjudicatory discretion.[49] The judge's possession of discretion in unregulated disputes is constrained by great masses of legal material, the same material as deprives the judge of discretion in regulated disputes. Thus sophisticated positivism repudiates totally the 'two-step' theory while defending still judicial discretion.

Hart's own explanation for why judges have discretion is unclear, and even muddled. In the space of three pages (*The Concept of Law*, 123–5) he canvasses three different accounts while seeming to regard them as all versions of the same account. On page 123 he writes:

Particular fact-situations do not await us already marked off from each other, and labelled as instances of the general rule, the application of which is in question; nor can the rule itself step forward to claim its own instances.

This remark suggests that every recognition of a case as falling under a rule is discretionary. Such a thought is more characteristic of Rule Scepticism than of Hart's own view, which rejects Rule Scepticism as much as it does Formalism and 'mechanical jurisprudence'. Second, Hart suggests there will be plain cases where the general term is clearly applicable, and that there is uncertainty only at the borderline (124–5). He speaks of general language itself as being 'open-textured'—as vivid a metaphor as

[49] The use of the term 'voice' is interesting. Radical criticism of the law frequently expresses itself by asserting that 'the law speaks in a gendered voice', or 'in a racist voice', using a favourite image of contemporary literary criticism. The fact that the concept of 'voices in the law' in exactly the same sense appears in Raz's work as a quasi-technical term within legal positivism shows, to my mind, that the conflict between positivism and, for example, Critical Legal Studies is not theoretical, but at best potentially political. It will be a matter of conflict over with what voices the law should speak, and over how morally proper it is that the law speaks with the particular voices with which it happens to speak at some point in time. The propriety of the image of the law as 'voiced' is in itself entirely compatible with legal positivism.

talk of 'gaps' and 'doughnuts', and seemingly similar in its spatial connotations. This suggestion would imply that discretion is exercisable by courts only in borderline cases, although every term will have its borderline cases. Third, he speaks in a well-known passage of 'the human predicament' and our twin 'handicaps' of 'relative ignorance of fact' and 'relative indeterminacy of aim' (125). These thoughts suggest an explanation of the having of discretion in terms of human psychology, not human language. If we were omniscient and omni-rational, then there would be no judicial discretion.[50]

Whatever is Hart's 'real' view of the reason why courts have discretion, the point to notice about the second and the third of these arguments equally is that they begin from extra-legal premises—from a feature of language itself, and from features of the human predicament itself. Thus, provided that sophisticated positivism can explain judicial discretion without prejudicing the separation between law and morality, these arguments have especial force.

The second argument is trickier, for it seems to presuppose already a positivist picture of adjudication, and the talk about discretion is amplificatory rather than justificatory. Raz too (*The Authority of Law*, ch. 4) argues for a strong connection between the Sources Thesis (that every law has a source—his version of positivism) and the existence of legal gaps. But in Raz also it is unclear whether the argument can be an independent ground for positivism. Initially, he claims that the Sources Thesis presupposes gaps in the law (recall that we have excluded gaps where the law is silent), and later that the Sources Thesis shows that gaps are inescapable. The direction of inference here is from the Sources Thesis to gaps in the law. But positivism's opponents do not deny that inference: indeed, they frolic with it.

It is important for sophisticated positivism to repudiate any implication that it condones wanton decision-making. However, it is clear from the arguments surveyed here that sophisticated positivism has many resources on which to draw for that purpose.

---

[50] And indeed *ex hypothesi* Hercules, Dworkin's ideal judge, repudiates judicial discretion—cf. *Taking Rights Seriously*, 123 ff. Schauer (*Playing by the Rules*, 35–7) also makes the point that Hart confuses penumbral uncertainty from the trouble caused by the appearance of a case not previously contemplated. As Schauer points out (ibid. 36 n. 26) 'platypus' currently has no penumbra of uncertainty, though future exploration and zoology might surprise us.

It seems hard to deny the intuition partly motivating Dworkin's attack on positivism in *Taking Rights Seriously*, ch. 2, that there is a fundamental commitment by positivism to the existence of adjudicatory discretion, even if it is some form of 'weak' discretion, rather than the 'strong' discretion of Dworkin's anti-positivist attack. None the less, any suggestion that positivism is committed to wholly unfettered discretion for judges is a mistake.

6. INTERPRETATION AND SEMANTICS

In discussing the views of simple positivism about legal interpretation, three positions were distinguished. The first argues that legal interpretation goes 'all the way down'—not only the determination of legal significance of the material facts of a case but also the determination of those facts themselves is a matter of interpretation. This view is not a version of legal positivism, but of legal realism. The second position argues the 'two-step' view that when the material facts clearly subsume a case under a settled rule, then there is necessary inference and not interpretation, and where the material facts do not subsume there is unconstrained discretionary choice. More has been said about this position in the context of discussing judicial discretion (see Ch. 2.5 above and Ch. 7 below). That legal positivism is not committed to such a simplistic view has been argued strenuously and convincingly by Hart in *The Concept of Law*[51] and elsewhere. In Hart's view, positivism can (and indeed must) acknowledge the 'open-texturedness' of the language of black-letter law. The sole consequence is that theory must then equally acknowledge the place in adjudication of a court's discretion, and the fact that judges perform a genuine rule-producing or law-making role. It is also argued, though,[52] that legal language does genuinely constrain judges and restrict discretion. 'Open-texturedness' must be seen to coexist with certainty of meaning. The third position taken by simple positivism expands upon the controls existing on the exercise of judicial discretion, controls which are demands of political morality or some other essentially non-legal source.

[51] Cf. especially ch. 7.
[52] Cf. Frederick Schauer's essay, 'Formalism', *Yale Law Journal*, 97 (1988), 509–48.

Two possible responses to positivism so construed immediately present themselves, responses that Hart himself has neatly characterized as 'the Nightmare and the Noble Dream'.[53] To the sufferers from the nightmare, the open-texturedness of black-letter law unleashes the oppressive power of the law. Law that is open-textured is law that is through and through a political instrument, and given existing structures of dominance in society becomes unavailable as a resource for the marginalized. To the Noble Dreamer, by contrast, the open-texturedness of black-letter law frees the judge who aspires to the betterment of society and to justice for the individual litigant from the shackles imposed by formalistic conceptions of the legal text. The encrusted millstone of orthodoxy and precedent is lifted from her neck. She can 'play fast and loose'[54] with the law in the name of the grand rights of political rhetoric, and trump the utilitarian inanities of black-letter law.

Sophisticated positivism is not at ease with either the free-wheeling interpretative play of the detextualizers whatever their political goal and state of mind, or the simplistic 'two-step' view of adjudication as rule plus interpretative discretion unregulated or regulated by non-source-based rule. How might one defend the simultaneous rejection of rule-formalism, nihilism, and millenarianism?

Sophisticated positivism holds that there are properly idiosyncratic standards of legal interpretation, but because and only because the specification of those standards is itself as sufficiently well pedigreed as any other part of black-letter law. Judicial decisions 'beyond' black-letter law are still constrained by a legal source because legal interpretation is constrained by the ground-rules of the judicial enterprise. More specifically, such ground-rules might be seen as having the status of secondary rules within a system of primary and secondary rules. Rupert Cross asserts the basis to be in 'a welter of judicial dicta which vary considerably in weight, age and uniformity', rather than in statute or binding decision (*Statutory Interpretation*, 42). None the less, he has little difficulty in distilling out of the dicta what rules actually are in force in the UK municipal legal system. Sophisticated positivism thus permits

---

[53] See *Essays in Jurisprudence and Philosophy* (Oxford, 1983), ch. 4.
[54] Cf. John Mackie, 'The Third Theory of Law', *Philosophy and Public Affairs*, 7 (1977–8), 15–16.

law to take an interpretative turn, as long as the legal community itself determines the rules for legal interpretation.

Simple positivism adopts a realist theory of the semantics of legal propositions. That is, it says that a legal proposition is true or false, if it is true or false, because some fact in the world—say, that the sovereign has commanded thus and so—makes it true or because no such fact does so and it is false. The allocation of propositions of law to these categories for this reason seems too simplistic for sophisticated positivism. The reasoning is as follows: a claimed parallel with literary criticism offers the initial intuitive drive.

In literary criticism, what is plainly 'in the text' allows talk of 'truth' and 'falsity' such that if a proposition in literary criticism corresponds with what is plainly in the text it is true, and if a proposition is inconsistent with what is plainly in the text it is false. But 'simple positivism' in literary criticism is unacceptable. It would devalue not only great works of literature but also great literary criticism to suppose that the intellectual stature of a literary critic had to be determined by way of whether or not what the critic said corresponded to what was 'plainly in the text'. Richer kinds of ground-rule for the literary enterprise would warrant in principle more open and imaginative modes of criticism while still remaining within a conception of literary criticism as a rational enterprise. The set of ground-rules would include both 'correspondence' rules and other rules more flexible. However, to accommodate these richer ground-rules, the semantics of literary criticism will need to be regarded as 'anti-realist'. On this conception, a proposition of criticism is acceptable, unacceptable, neither acceptable nor unacceptable, or (apparently) both acceptable and unacceptable just in case the ground-rules of the enterprise make it warrantedly assertible, warrantedly deniable, provide no warrant either way, or provide both warrants.

This model for an 'anti-realist' semantics is then transferred to the enterprise of adjudication. Judicial decisions 'beyond' black-letter law are not strongly discretionary, because judicial interpretation is constrained by the ground-rules of the judicial enterprise. One important rule is that of correspondence with institutional history as what warrants assertibility or deniability. But the customs of judicial practice underwrite in a variety of other ways the assertion or the denial of propositions of law which do not 'correspond' to black-letter law. Thus, according to sophisticated positivism, we can say that a judicial decision in a hard case (the kind where the decision is 'discretionary' or 'interstitial', the kind where the 'correspondence-sufficiency' condition is not fulfilled) has assertibility conditions none the less— the proposition of law constituting such a decision is warrantedly assertible in case it is licensed by judicial custom, whether procedurally or substantially.[55]

In short, just as literary criticism is enriched by being seen as deploying an 'anti-realist' semantics for the propositions of literary criticism, so also the enterprise of adjudication is enriched by being seen as 'anti-realist' in its semantics for propositions of law. Adjudication 'beyond' black-letter law is still subject to authoritative constraints which have a source as positivism requires.[56]

7. LAW AND THE COMMON GOOD

According to simple positivism, the theoretical separation of law and morality is total. Law may have any content and still be law. Hart has rejected simple positivism: he denies that law may have any content with his doctrine of 'the minimum content of Natural Law' (cf. *The Concept of Law*, ch. 9). Survival as an aim, he argues, is not a mere fact about the human race—as if we might have been a kind of lemming with a periodic urge to self-destruct. Rather, the goal of survival 'is reflected in whole structures of our thought and language, in terms of which we describe the world and each other' (*The Concept of Law*, 188). As I would put it, glossing Hart, we would not be the creatures that we are, with the modes of understanding we have, unless we had survival as an aim. This line of thought, however, Hart mentions only to lay aside; he goes on to pursue a different line. Even if it is a 'mere fact' that humans have survival as an aim, none the less:

[55] I do not mean to endorse here the claims by Brian Simpson ('The Common Law and Legal Theory', in id. (ed.), *Oxford Essays in Jurisprudence* (Oxford, 1973), 94) that judicial custom by itself is a sufficient ground for law, and that, *contra* Hart, no ultimate rule of recognition generally accepted is necessary. I leave unresolved this internal debate within sophisticated positivism.

[56] It may be noted that the view laid out here contains many echoes of Dworkin's reasoning in *A Matter of Principle*, part 2. I think in fact Dworkin there does come out as a positivist, and that Stanley Fish's arguments to this effect (cf. *Doing What Comes Naturally*, chs. 4, 5, 16) are sound. For my own discussion, see Ch. 8 below.

Reflection on some very obvious generalizations—indeed truisms—concerning human nature and the world in which men live, shows that as long as these hold good, there are certain rules of conduct which any social organization must contain if it is to be viable. Such rules do in fact constitute a common element in the law and conventional morality of all societies which have progressed to the point where these are distinguished as different forms of social control. (*The Concept of Law*, 188)

Law and morality as different systems of social control have been distinguished in the characteristically positivistic fashion. Now, however, the 'separation' between them is being qualified. The 'facts' are human vulnerability to physical harm from one another, approximate equality in physical and intellectual ability, limited altruism,[57] needed resources not existing in limitless abundance, and humans' limited understanding and strength of will. Given these facts, then there must be rules requiring forbearance from physical violence, rules controlling the ownership and change of ownership of resources, and sanctions to enforce observance of these rules. By 'natural necessity' (*The Concept of Law*, 195) any system of general social norms—that is, any system of morality or of law—must contain this minimum content. Therefore, it is false that law may have any content. Law must have this minimum content. By the same token, it would be false, were anyone to claim it, that morality may have any content; it too must have this minimum content. So there will always be an overlap extensionally between law and morality. None the less, what it is for a law to exist is defined by Hart in positivistic terms—laws, except for the ultimate rule of recognition, exist by being valid, that is, pedigreed. Moral standards exist as non-institutionalized social facts.

Hart in this way, contrary to simple positivism, forges a link between law and at least this minimal amount of 'common good'. But the link is not a conceptual one, and in particular the distinction is left in place between law as a system of physical coercive sanctions and morality as a system of psychological coercive sanctions (cf. *The Concept of Law*, 84, 175–6). Moreover, the normative force of law as such still has no stronger basis than the fact of its acceptance, and it is not immediately clear how social facts can produce genuine normativity.

---

[57] 'If men are not devils, neither are they angels' (*The Concept of Law*, 191).

It has in fact been argued by Gerald Postema[58] that positivism faces substantial difficulties in satisfying two constraints on the adequacy of any legal theory—that law is shown to be a social fact, and that law is a form of practical reasoning. For Hart, it may be false that 'law may have any content'; none the less, the normativity of law is crudely related to the existence of sanctions for non-compliance. Postema's sophisticated version of positivism aims to represent law's normativity as genuine, while preserving the positivistic insistence on law as a social fact. We may call his theory 'law-as-convention positivism'.

Postema's theory is set forward as a 'claim about the structure or logic of the practical reasoning implicit in [legal reasoning] and in the idea that law is characteristically a matter of public rules' (193–4). The fundamental plank of Postema's position is this—that the normativity of law is to be understood in terms of law's functioning as a *convention* in a technical sense of that term derived from David Lewis's work.[59] A convention is technically a solution to a co-ordination problem as a kind of problem of strategic interaction.

These concepts need explication. Problems of strategic interaction are characterized by the interdependence of individual decisions. Problems of strategic interaction have the following structural property:

> *Strategic Interaction*: The outcomes of the parties are jointly determined by the actions of all; so the outcome of the action of any agent depends on the actions of all the others, and the best choice for each depends on what he expects the others to do, knowing that each of the others is trying to guess what he is likely to do.

Co-ordination problems as a special case of problems of strategic interaction have three further identifying characteristics—rough coincidence of interests, mutually conditioned preferences, and ambiguity.

> *Rough Coincidence of Interests*: Each party is likely to benefit more by co-operation than by nonco-operation.[60]

---

[58] In 'Coordination and Convention at the Foundations of Law', *Journal of Legal Studies*, 11 (1982). Postema's current defence of the thought that law may be profitably construed as a convention is in rather different terms. I discuss it in Ch. 9.4 below.

[59] See D. Lewis, *Convention* (Cambridge, Mass., 1969).

[60] Eerik Lagerspitz (*A Conventionalist Theory of Institutions* (Helsinki, 1989), 41) has argued that Lewis's definition is too restrictive, and that co-ordination problems do not require coincidence of interests.

Mutually Conditional Preferences: Certain actions are preferred to others if, but only if, other parties also prefer them (or appropriately corresponding actions).

Ambiguity: There are at least two combinations of the actions of all the agents which each agent would count as 'successful' co-ordination.

A solution to a co-ordination problem requires that one of these two equally acceptable combinations of actions—the two co-ordination-equilibria—acquire the property of *saliency*. It for some reason 'jumps out at you'; it emerges from the pack of its fellow would-be solutions as the one to adopt. Saliency may of course be acquired by a given co-ordination equilibrium for utterly arbitrary reasons, or uninteresting non-arbitrary ones. An interesting non-arbitrary way of acquiring saliency is by being a *convention*. Here is Postema's definition of 'convention':

A regularity R in the behavior of persons in a population P in a recurring situation S is a convention if and only if in any instance of S

(1) it is common knowledge in P that
   (a) there is in P general conformity to R:
   (b) most members of P expect most other members of P to conform to R:
   (c) almost every member of P prefers that any individual conform rather than not conform to some regularity of behavior in S, given general conformity to that regularity:
   (d) almost every member of P prefers general conformity to some regularity rather than general non-conformity (i.e., general conformity to no regularity):
(2) part of the reason why most members of P conform to R in S is that (1a)–(1d) obtain.

The thoughts underlying this conceptual machinery can be cashed out roughly and less technically as follows. We begin with a simple picture of the individual in a situation of choice. She embarks on a preference-ranking. Sometimes these preferences can be lexically ordered neatly; sometimes they cannot, for two incompatible choices turn out to rank as equally preferable. Then, like Buridan's Ass, the chooser will be paralysed into inactivity unless one of the two equally ranked preferences emerges as salient. There is available one obvious source of saliency—a coin-toss. The choice that is correlated with the result of the coin-toss thereby acquires saliency.

Now, we begin to complicate this simple picture. First, we stipulate that among the factors to be taken into account when the individual choice is made are the intentional states of others—for example, that one course of action will upset her partner. We focus on one particular kind of intentional state of another—an expectation that the chooser will choose in one way rather than another. We complicate still further—the expectation of the other is itself partly founded in turn on an expectation about what the original chooser will do. Now, we have a problem of choice that is a problem of *strategic interaction*. It is a problem of individual preference-ranking, but not one in a vacuum. It is a problem of individual preference-ranking where the determination of the ranking is interlocked with the views of others about the result of just that same preference-ranking.

We make still further assumptions—we assume that the other with whom the chooser is interlocked has roughly the same interests—that is, the chooser has as much at stake in the satisfaction of preferences as the other with whom her choice is interlocked. We assume also that the views of the other enter into the chooser's preferences twice over—not merely is it that the other has expectations about what the chooser will choose; also, it matters to the chooser what the preferences of the other are in such a way that an alternative being preferred by the other is a reason for it being preferred by the chooser. We assume that, when all the preference-ranking is done, there are at least two alternatives that rank at the top of the list as far as the chooser is concerned. Finally, we assume that the other is in the mirror-image position with respect to the choices of the original individual chooser. To reintroduce technical terms, we have put the two persons in a situation where they have a *co-ordination problem* because they are in a situation of strategic interaction where there is more than one *co-ordination-equilibrium*. Postema proposes a case of one person flying from Chicago to Washington, and needing to be met by a friend.[61] There are two different airlines flying from Chicago to Washington, each flying from and into different airports. A *solution* to the co-ordination problem requires that one of the co-ordination-equilibria acquires *saliency*. Suppose that Midway but not O'Hare is closed by a sudden power-

---

[61] 'Coordination and Convention', 172–3.

cut; the flight from O'Hare lands at Dulles not National. Dulles now has a feature that makes it salient—it stands out as the airport for the friend in Washington to choose. Lewis's standard example is that of two people cut off during a phone call.[62] Each wants to resume the call for their own part. Each would prefer not to pick up the phone and dial if the other is about to pick up the phone and dial. It only takes either one to pick up the phone and dial to resume the call provided that the other does not pick up the phone. If you are one of the unfortunates, what do you do? Dial or wait? You have a co-ordination problem.

We complicate the situation still further. We suppose that co-ordination problems—problems with the defined structure—significantly recur over a period of time, and certain regularities of behaviour start emerging in the pattern of people's responses to these problems. Suppose also this fact becomes known. Now the regularity itself enters into the reasoning of individual choosers, because it crystallizes the reasoning in so far as it involves expectations of others' behaviour. Conformity to the regularity now becomes even more entrenched. In fact, it becomes, and the term is again being used in a technical sense, a *convention*.

The force of this conception of practical reasoning for our present jurisprudential concerns has finally emerged. The crucial feature about conventions is that just in existing they have *normative* significance. That is, when a convention is in place, the social fact of the convention existing properly enters into reasoning about preference-rankings in a new way. It would be wrong to construe the convention as merely a fact about social behaviour which produces for the individual preference-ranker a very weighty prudential reason for action—as if it were merely a sign of a great evil with which one would be visited if one did not comply with the convention. Rather, the convention introduces a reason for acting in a certain way simply because that way conforms to the convention. As Postema points out,[63] the background reasons for the normative force of conventions are standardly of two kinds—(*a*) that the convention creates expectations of behaviours, and by indicating one's acceptance of the convention one may induce others to rely on their expectations to their potential detriment;

[62] Cf. e.g. *Convention*, 36 ff.
[63] 'Coordination and Convention', 180.

that obliges one to observe the convention: (*b*) the convention may be analogous to a 'cooperative enterprise for mutual benefit' in which duties of fair play as a result obtain.

The application to law is as follows. Law as an institution has the structure of a convention, so that the normativity of individual laws derives from their status as co-ordination norms of a certain kind, conventional co-ordination norms. Laws are taken to be co-ordination norms that have emerged conventionally in the manner outlined, and have been given saliency by virtue of their acquiring positivistically understood validity via a rule of recognition. Edna Ullmann-Margalit (*The Emergence of Norms*, 96–8) suggests a distinction which will clarify the thought, even though the terminology is slightly different from Postema's. She distinguishes between conventions and decrees. Conventions are non-statutory norms, regularities of behaviour which owe either their origin or their durability to their being solutions to recurrent (or continuous) co-ordination problems. Decrees are statutory norms, issued specifically for the purpose of solving novel and acute recurrent (or continuous) co-ordination problems. Conventions, we might say, are essentially retrospective and decrees prospective. Laws are therefore most obviously thought of as decrees rather than conventions, in Ullmann-Margalit's terminology.[64] Postema's point is not lost, for to see laws as decrees in Ullmann-Margalit's sense is to see them as having normativity through being solutions to co-ordination problems. Moreover, Postema argues that laws are genuinely conventions in a deeper sense—that they emerge as statutory norms by being conventional solutions to co-ordination problems between citizen and official, and between official and official. That is, to revert to Ullmann-Margalit's terminology, laws are both decrees and conventions. With respect to first-order co-ordination problems between citizens, they are prospective decrees. But their actual enactment occurs conventionally as a solution to a second-order problem of co-ordination between citizens and officials or officials and officials.[65]

[64] Lagerspitz calls both spontaneously arising conventions and conventions imposed by authorities' 'conventions' (*A Conventionalist Theory of Institutions*, 83). This vocabulary risks blurring an important distinction.

[65] Lagerspitz defends a similar account of law as a conventionalist institution. See *A Conventionalist Theory of Institutions*, chs. 6–8. Postema's later view depends on taking these latter thoughts further than he does in the 1982 paper. See Ch. 9.4 below.

According to law-as-convention positivism,[66] then, the normativity of laws is a matter of institutionalized saliency in the face of co-ordination problems in situations of strategic interaction. As a result of law being so construed, the problem of reconciling law as normative and law as social fact is thus seemingly solved. Sophisticated positivism has shown how law can be both a matter of social fact and yet be genuinely normative—that is, create genuine demands on its norm-subjects. We thus have a richer way of denying that 'law may have any content', one that links the institutional nature itself of law to its role in serving the interests of its norm-subjects. Law as institutionalized saliency has a special role distinct from norms which are valuable merely because co-extensive with moral norms. Law is thus focused on the common good, while losing none of its status as institutional, social fact.

8. CONCLUSION

Sophisticated positivism, as much as simple positivism, is an author's creation, not a historian's discovery. Although the fact that my text contains many references to contemporary legal theorists may be taken to imply a thesis about the progress of jurisprudential thought, it is not a part of my project to assert or defend such a thesis. I am concerned with showing the structure of legal thought taking it to be a dynamic system of interacting theories, not a static system of conceptual maps. The project is therefore an a-historical project despite the fact that the interactions take place and have taken place in history—as this project itself does.

I have suggested at several places in the foregoing pages that there are various different paths sophisticated positivism takes at different points. None the less, the following is a rough summary of the claims of sophisticated positivim:

1. The law is a system of exclusionary reasons for action; it is not simply a system of good first-order reasons for action.
2. The law's connection with authority is a necessary one—it claims to pre-empt parts of our practical reasoning, subject to

[66] Note that I mean by this term a stronger theory than that defended by Coleman under the name 'law as convention positivism' in 'Negative Positivism'. Coleman's theory has been referred to in Ch. 2.4 above, n. 30.

its claims being justified by the fact that we would act in accordance with reasons that actually apply to us by obeying the law.

3. The point of view of legal theory, while indeed reproducing the internal point of view towards the law on the part of both citizens and officials, need not itself be committed to the substance of the law; legal theory may adopt a 'hermeneutic' or 'detached' point of view where the normative commitments of the law are understood and reproduced as they would be understood by one who is committed, but without being accepted by the theorist.

4. The law must be accepted in the sense that in a healthy society ordinary citizens accept the law, though the law in a 'sheep-like' society is still the law if it is passed in accordance with rules accepted by the officials of the society.

5. The judge in hard cases is indeed bound by legal principles, but legal principles are either summaries of settled law or principles which can be reasonably postulated to make coherent settled law. Thus, adjudication in hard cases is indeed discretionary, but the discretion is not 'strong'; it is guided by a variety of principles and standards which none the less do not prejudice the separation of law and morality.

6. Adjudication is not simply mechanical derivation plus discretionary choice; adjudication is genuinely interpretative. Moreover, propositions of law do have truth-values; but the semantics for propositions of law has to be anti-realist, the truth-values being based on assertibility conditions.

7. The law may be understood as a convention in the technical sense of decision theory, for then law is both a social fact and normative.

No single legal theorist has defended all of these claims. In fact it would be a project of some interest within legal theory conventionally understood to consider whether they could be consistently held, and indeed whether the result would be an overwhelmingly convincing version of legal positivism. In fact, if my interest were in finding the most convincing version of legal positivism, then I should stop here, go back to the beginning of this Part and rework it in that light. But it is not. My aim has been to show sophisticated positivism as defending the theses I have listed in order to save the positivistic enterprise from the limitations of simple positivism. In order to do that, however, sophisticated positivism has to recognize certain intuitions about law as constraints on any adequate theory of law: unless sophisticated positivism had such intuitions, no fault would have been found with simple positivism. But such fault was found. We should be able to see through such fault-finding to the genuine features of law on which the intuitions of fault were based. The description of those features will amount to that perspicuous representation of law which is the proper goal of legal theory.

The emphasis in this study on 'movement' and 'dynamics' is there, however, because I do not believe that any listing of theses held by a single variety of, let alone single instance of, legal theory is adequate for such a perspicuous representation of law. The features of law perception of which leads sophisticated positivism to say what it says are not clearly revealed by what sophisticated positivism says. We must move on to the next stage of the dynamic movement. We must consider what can be said by anti-positivism in response to the theses of sophisticated positivism. We must see how what can be said by anti-positivism has its origins in the way that sophisticated positivism responds to simple positivism. To put it paradoxically, we must see how anti-positivism is the ultimate sophisticated positivism. To show that is the task of Part III of this work, and to that task I therefore now turn.

Part III

Anti-Positivism

3

REASONS FOR ACTION

1. INTRODUCTION

At the end of Part II a theoretical position had been developed, referred to as 'sophisticated positivism'. The underlying thought for the development of the position was as follows. Part I presented 'simple positivism', seen by sophisticated positivism to be a version of positivism open to too many objections. When sophisticated positivism criticizes simple positivism for maintaining such-and-such a thesis and substitutes one of its own which is taken to be an improvement, it shows itself making certain assumptions about what are and are not acceptable claims in analytic jurisprudence. Sometimes these assumptions are explicit and articulated, sometimes not. The presumption of sophisticated positivism is that these assumptions are consistent with positivism. It is the purpose of Part III to argue that the assumptions are not so consistent. The assumptions, if given full weight, imply that positivism, even in a sophisticated form, cannot be the correct theory of law. The criticism of simple positivism by sophisticated positivism sets off movements of thought, which have as their proper resting-place, not sophisticated positivism, but anti-positivism. We will see this to be so for each of the seven issues in legal theory which are the themes of this study. We begin as before with laws as reasons for action.

The thought behind Raz's notion of 'exclusionary reason'[1] in relation to law can be put more generally. Instrumental rationality represents practical reasoning as homogeneous. One ought always, all things considered, to do whatever one ought to do on the balance of reasons.[2] Any reason is in principle capable of being weighed in the balance against any other reason, and bears upon a practical decision in logically the same way as any other reason. Raz rejects

---

[1] Cf. page 46 ff. above.
[2] Cf. *Practical Reason and Norms*, 36.

this logical homogeneity, distinguishing two different kinds of practical reasons, first-order and second-order. As he has himself recently confirmed,[3] he has two arguments for the existence of exclusionary reasons, the Functional Argument and the Phenomenological Argument.[4] The Functional Argument rests on the idea that rules, and *a fortiori* legal rules, cannot perform the function that they perform unless their role in practical reasoning is construed as that of exclusionary reasons. The Phenomenological Argument rests on the idea that aspects of the internal content of practical reasoning cannot be accounted for unless the role of rules, and *a fortiori* legal rules, in practical reasoning is construed as that of exclusionary reasons.

2. THE PHENOMENOLOGICAL ARGUMENT

Let us examine further the Phenomenological Argument. In Raz's own recent explication ('Facing Up'), it is 'an argument about features of our concepts, based on the way they function in our discourse and thought'. The features are three: we sense conflicting assessments about what we ought to do (e.g., a man who wants to spend his money on himself, but has promised to spend it on his son's education): we have the sense that it is not for us to act on the ordinary reasons which apply to the case, but that such is the task for our superiors (e.g., a private in receipt of orders from an officer): we have the sense that our hands are tied by a commitment (which is a separate element in both the above examples). Raz emphasizes that, *contra* Moore,[5] and, by implication, Flathman,[6] he does not rely on the claim that exclusionary reasons involve incommensurability. This seems autobiographically correct. The point is this. All practical reasons are homogeneous only if they are commensurable: but it does not follow that, if they are not homogeneous, they are not commensurable. Two reasons can

---

[3] 'Facing Up: A Reply', *Southern California Law Review*, 62 (1989), 1164.

[4] Chaim Gans, 'Mandatory Rules and Exclusionary Reasons', *Philosophia*, 15 (1985–6), 376–7, thinks there are four arguments; the additional 2 are best thought of as examples of exclusionary reasons, rather than arguments for the notion of exclusionary reason.

[5] Michael S. Moore, 'Authority, Law and Razian Reasons', *Southern California Law Review*, 62 (1989), 863.

[6] Richard Flatham, *The Practice of Political Authority* (Chicago, 1980), 112.

function in logically distinct ways while belonging to what is ultimately the same system of reasons.

There is an immediate and simple objection to the Phenomenological Argument. It has been urged by Flathman, Gans, Moore, Dare, Alexander, by Atiyah as regards promises,[7] and no doubt others. The psychological facts to which Raz points can be perfectly well explained by an account committed to homogeneity. The conflict of assessment we sense is a conflict of different but very close weights of reason. The sense that it is not for us to act is a sense that an order from a superior officer is a very weighty reason. The sense that our hands are tied is a sense that our commitment is a very weighty reason.

Raz seems willing to concede the Phenomenological Argument is not in itself a knockdown proof of the existence of exclusionary reasons.[8] We need not, and should not, follow him in this retreat. At the level of pre-philosophical intuition the exclusionary reason story has much plausibility. In the military, one obeys an officer's order neither out of fear of immediate reprisal nor out of awareness that it really is the best thing to do in the balance of reasons, but because it is the officer's order and that's how it goes in the military. Likewise, one visits an elderly aunt neither because one fears anyone's wrath at a broken promise nor because one senses it really is the best thing to do in the balance of reasons, but because one has promised. At this intuitive level, the simple objection fails because it rides roughshod over this plausible intuition.

The simple objection, however, can be quickly replaced by more sophisticated variants. The first deploys what Rawls calls 'the summary conception of rules'.[9] He associates it specifically with utilitarianism: such might be the paradigm case, although non-utilitarian versions of the conception are easily entertained. 'Rules are pictured as summaries of past decisions arrived at by the *direct* application of the utilitarian principle to particular cases' (Rawls's emphasis).[10] The conflict between the rule-utilitarian and

---

[7] P. S. Atiyah, *Promises, Morals, and Laws* (Oxford, 1981), ch. 4.

[8] Cf. 'Facing Up', n. 21 and accompanying text.

[9] John Rawls, 'Two Concepts of Rules', in Philippa Foot (ed.), *Theories of Ethics* (Oxford, 1967), 158–9.

[10] In fact, one of Raz's examples in *Practical Reason and Norms*, the case of Ann who will not take an investment decision because she is tired (37), seems to

Raz is that the former seeks to assimilate cases like Jeremy the private soldier and Colin the promiser (cf. *Practical Reason and Norms*, 38–9) to Ann the tired investor, while Raz seeks an assimilation in the opposite direction. We need not pursue who is right about Ann, because the conflict between the assimilation strategies is fundamental. If I am right to say that there is an important intuitive plausibility to the exclusionary reason doctrine, then rule-utilitarianism as much as the simple objection obscures the intuition.

Stephen Perry presents a more complicated alternative view.[11] Although Perry is concerned primarily with judicial reasoning from precedent cases, he presents his conceptual machinery as an alternative to Raz's account in terms of exclusionary reasons. A theory which eliminates the common law doctrine of *stare decisis* altogether would be what Raz has called a 'system of absolute discretion' (*Practical Reason and Norms*, 137 ff.)—in every case the court decides what on the balance of reasons is the best decision without regard to any previous decision in any other case. The most modest retreat from this extreme Perry calls 'the weak Burkean conception' of precedent.[12] On this view, a court could not depart from a previous decision unless it had a positive reason for doing so. A review of the balance of reasons would still have to be undertaken, but not without reference to any other case.[13] Perry himself favours, by contrast, a 'strong Burkean conception' of precedent, according to which 'a court is bound by a previous decision unless it is convinced there is a strong reason for holding otherwise'.[14] Perry has in mind that there are two different kinds

conform quite closely to this model. It is easy to suppose 'Take no investment decisions when tired' is a summary of the direct application of the utilitarian principle to particular cases.

[11] In 'Judicial Obligation, Precedent and the Common Law', *Oxford Journal of Legal Studies*, 7 (1987).

[12] 'Burkean' denotes and connotes 'a presumption of some sort in favour of previously-accepted practices'; cf. 'Judicial Obligation', 221.

[13] Something like a more general version of the 'weak Burkean conception' is defended by W. J. Waluchow in 'Hart, Legal Rules and Palm-tree Justice', *Law and Philosophy*, 4 (1985).

[14] 'Judicial Obligation', 222; Perry's emphasis. Schauer (*Playing By the Rules*, 88–93) also wants to emend Raz's account only by taking 'exclusionary' to mean a very strong presumption of exclusion. An exclusionary reason, he says (ibid. 91), is capable of override only by a particularly compelling manifestation of the very factors that the exclusion excludes—so compelling that a mere glimpse at the facts of the matter is enough to reveal its presence. If a mere glimpse is not sufficient,

of principle in practical reasoning—first-order principles which state that such-and-such a fact is a reason for such-and-such an action, and second-order principles which assign weights to first-order principles. In a later article,[15] Perry characterizes the latter as principles of 'reweighting reasons' and of 'epistemically-bounded reasons'. By this account, Perry aims to give due significance to Raz's intuition that there are two orders of practical reasons, and to the Phenomenological Argument, while denying that there are two logically different kinds of reasons. This latter denial Perry expresses by insisting that

the two modes of reason which Raz distinguishes can thus be regarded, in effect, as the two extremes of a continuum; at one end action is to be assessed on the basis of a balance of reasons in which no reason has been assigned anything other than ordinary weight, while at the other end action is to be assessed by a balance of reasons some of which have been assigned, on the basis of second-order reasons, a non-ordinary weight of zero. Between these two extremes lies an indefinitely large number of further possibilities, all of which are variations on the idea of a weighted balance of reasons. ('Judicial Obligation', 223)

Analogously, Schauer (*Playing by the Rules*, 90) uses the image of 'coarse-' and 'fine-grained' understandings of the content of the exclusionary rule, and exploits, in considering the case of Jill and her holidays, the fact that hotel prices can be ranged on a continuum from very expensive through to very cheap, and numbers assigned to points on the continuum in terms of dollars per night. Such a view is still importantly different from Raz's. Perry's reweighting and epistemically bounding reasons are determined by substantive principles, whereas for Raz the property of being an exclusionary reason is a formal property of a

the exclusion stands. Schauer seems right to say that the disagreement between him and Raz is 'ultimately an empirical and psychological one' (ibid.). How one would settle it is unclear, though. Everyone would have to be polled on whether their internal sense of military orders, for example, or of promises, corresponded to the one view or the other. It is worth noting that Schauer chooses as his test case Raz's case of Jill and her decision always to go to France for holidays. In the case of non-institutionalized norms a less restrictive account like Perry's or Schauer's may seem more plausible. It is not clear that it helps Raz's account of institutionalized normative systems to keep producing examples of non-institutionalized norms.

[15] 'Second-order Reasons, Uncertainty and Legal Theory', *Southern California Law Review*, 62 (1989), 932–45.

reason. Moreover, as noted already (Ch. 2.1 above), for Raz an exclusionary reason can only be overridden by a reason outside the scope of those it excludes: Perry's and Schauer's view contains no such limitation. A view like Perry's or Schauer's is a more powerful alternative to Raz's doctrine of exclusionary reasons, because it preserves more explicitly the intuitive basis for the Phenomenological Argument. The explanation of why the soldier simply obeys the officer is not that the soldier thinks the rule 'obey officers' is a summary of the utility of a series of past decisions, but because the soldier has accepted a second-order principle 'assign a weight of zero to first-order reasons F_1 . . . F_n when they conflict with an officer's order'. The intuitive ground of Raz's account— the sense that our hands are tied, for example—is captured by the thought that assigning a weight of zero in context eliminates the victimized reason from the reasoning.

The compatibility of these accounts with the intuitive basis for Raz's Phenomenological Argument creates a direct challenge to the doctrine of exclusionary reasons. Such accounts are sufficient to show that further support is needed if the Phenomenological Argument is to secure the doctrine of exclusionary reasons. Raz provides no such further support. Instead, he shifts the ground for his account to the other argument, the Functional Argument. We will return to the Phenomenological Argument anon. For now, let us turn to the Functional Argument and review its career.

3. THE FUNCTIONAL ARGUMENT

The basis for the Functional Argument is a particular conception of the place of rules in practical reasoning: 'They mediate between deeper-level considerations and concrete decisions. They provide an intermediate level of reasons to which one appeals in normal cases where a need for a decision arises' (*The Morality of Freedom*, 58). Rules allow people to reap the benefits of general thinking and of commitment in advance to series of actions. Raz clearly envisages a three-tier model of practical reasoning. On the top tier are basic principles. Raz's own commitment is to a plurality of these;[16] he believes the foundations of morality to

---

[16] Cf. 'Right-based Moralities', in R. G. Frey (ed.), *Utilities and Rights* (Minneapolis, 1984), 42 ff.

include rights, virtues, and goals. But some plump for only one of these categories as fundamental, others any two; some found morality elsewhere altogether, in a body of doctrine, or the deliverances of a supreme being. So at the level of principle there may be profound disagreement. On the lowest tier are judgements about particular cases. Particular cases are hugely heterogeneous; limitations of time and brain capacity, differences of background and upbringing, and the like, mean that we will not always each make the same judgement about a particular case. Many cases legitimately tolerate difference of judgement about their merits. So there will be disagreement there too. But life must go on, and indeed it does go on. On the middle tier are sets of rough moral rules and maxims—what some in the past have called 'common-sense morality'—on which people agree who would disagree deeply about the justification of principle for those maxims, and would disagree about many of the applications of the maxims in particular cases. People generally agree that stealing is as a rule wrong, even though they might disagree about whether it is wrong because God commanded that we not steal or because it is not a Pareto-optimal strategy, and about whether this auto-parts clerk who helped herself to a surplus air-filter or that elderly indigent who shoplifted a tin of pork and beans is stealing. The function of rules in practical reasoning is precisely to facilitate both talk and action by providing a focus of agreement.

From this starting-point, the Functional Argument for exclusionary reasons is disarmingly simple—rules could not perform this valuable social function unless the kind of reason for action they provide is an exclusionary reason. Take the supposed advantages of advance commitments to series of actions: an example might be Raz's Jill who makes it a rule to go to France for holidays, thus saving a great deal of tormented decision-making, money spent on writing off for tour company brochures, and time spent on deliberation.[17] The whole point of Jill's making this rule is to avoid having each year to take a decision where to go for holidays on the balance of reasons. Jill's practical reasoning can only be understood as a decision to exclude sets of reasons—for example, the price of hotels in Ibiza—from the deliberation. Jill does not deny that *ceteris paribus* the price of hotels in Ibiza is

---

[17] Cf. 'Reasons for Action, Decisions, and Norms', in id. (ed.), *Practical Reasoning* (Oxford, 1978), 141; 'Facing Up', 1156–7.

relevant to a decision as to where to go for holidays. The function of her rule is to exclude such reasons, however. The rule could only perform this function if it were in the technical sense an exclusionary reason. If it is construed merely as a very weighty reason, the internal content of Jill's reasoning would have to be represented as putting in the balance the attractions of going to France and the attractions of going to Ibiza, and the attractions of deciding by rule and the attractions of (yet again) thinking it all through, and coming out in favour of France. But *ex hypothesi* that is precisely what the internal content of Jill's practical reasoning is not.

So far, however, the Functional Argument is a general argument about one part of the structure of practical reasoning. In the context of the present discussion, however, the Functional Argument is intended to show more. Applied to the special case of legal rules, it is intended to show that legal rules cannot perform the function they perform in society unless they are construed as exclusionary reasons, and thus that legal rules are exclusionary reasons. We have to be more careful about this extension of the argument.

The thought is twofold. First, a pluralistic society will not derive collectively the kind of pay-offs in terms of co-ordination and stability that Jill derives privately from her rule about holidaying in France unless the citizens treat their legal rules as exclusionary reasons. Life will be neither nasty nor brutish nor short only so long as citizens respect the regulatory framework of their society. That means treating that framework as providing exclusionary reasons for action. Abiding by the framework out of fear of the sovereign or of the consequences of its breakdown will not ensure in the long term a stable and co-ordinated social life. Second, legal rules must not simply be agreed-upon rules; they must also be publicly ascertainable rules, if they are to yield the benefits of their co-ordinative function.[18] So the Functional Argument seems to be enough to show not merely that legal rules must be exclusionary reasons, but that they also must have whatever properties they need to have to be publicly ascertainable. The root thought here, as Raz has elsewhere shown,[19] has to do with the rule of law and

---

[18] Cf. *The Authority of Law*, 52.
[19] 'The Rule of Law and its Virtue', *The Authority of Law*, ch. 11.

the requirement that the law must be capable of guiding the behaviour of its subjects. The Functional Argument seems to show the need for laws to have their existence and content determined by a social source, for only then can they be both publicly ascertainable and capable of operating as exclusionary reasons. So we seem led inexorably from the recognition that, in order to perform their function, laws must be exclusionary reasons for action to the correctness of positivism as a legal theory.

The impression is, however, illusory. We are led certainly to law understood as positive law or human law. But the disagreement between positivism and natural law theory is not over the existence or non-existence of positive law. It is over the way that the relation of positive law to natural law enters into the analysis of the concept of law. To be an exclusionary reason for action, rather than some other kind of reason for action, is a formal property of an entity which is a reason for action: likewise, to be publicly ascertainable. Substantive debate enters in when one asks what kinds of entities are exclusionary reasons. One who construes the relation of positive law to natural law as natural law theory construes it will believe that a legal rule without the content necessary for being an exclusionary reason is a legal rule in name only. One who construes the relation of positive law to natural law as positivism construes it will believe that, provided the rule passes whatever value-free tests have to be passed for a norm to be a legal rule, it is then an exclusionary reason for action. While this disagreement may be deep and enduring, it will not be one over whether rules of positive law have the formal status of exclusionary reasons for action. That thesis is common to the two theoretical positions. Thus, while the Functional Argument may present a strong case for a theoretical account of rules of positive law as exclusionary reasons for action, it does not provide a case for the correctness of legal positivism. The soundness of the Functional Argument is compatible with the correctness of anti-positivism.

4. THE PHENOMENOLOGICAL ARGUMENT REVISITED

So far I have argued that the Phenomenological Argument provides no more reason for an account of legal rules as exclusionary reasons than it does for a 'strong Burkean conception' of legal rules. I have also argued that while the Functional Argument, presents a cogent case for an account of legal rules as exclusionary reasons, it does so in a form which is neutral as between positivism and natural law theory. Thus, while it may be true that positivism is no worse off, and may quite possibly be better off, for embracing the doctrine of exclusionary reasons, the doctrine does not serve in itself to validate positivism. There is now worse to come for positivism.

Let us return to the Phenomenological Argument. I claimed above (Chapter 3.2) that an account of legal reasoning as in part a structure of reweighting and epistemically bounding principles is as intuitively plausible as an account of legal reasoning as in part a structure of exclusionary reasons. I now want to enquire further into how our understanding of laws as reasons for action develops if we seek for arguments to 'break the tie'.

The domain of the Phenomenological Argument falls within the study of the interior content of practical reasoning. There is a difference between the *ex ante* determination of the normative significance of some fact, and the *ex post* explanation of an agent's behaviour—'*x* is a reason to *A*' and '*x* is *P*'s reason for *A*-ing'.[20] The Phenomenological Argument seems to have to do with the latter, while the claim that laws are exclusionary reasons seems to have to do with the former. But as Perry has rightly pointed out,[21] Raz assumes a symmetry here, 'that an agent always assumes that his or her subjective practical determination coincides with the objective balance of reasons'. I am content to follow Raz in this assumption. We make natural use of the interior content of practical reasoning (even, perhaps, primary use) in the explanation of behaviour. Let us consider the phenomenological aspect of exclusionary reasons as a datum in the explanation of behaviour.[22]

On one widely held view, the paradigm for the explanation of behaviour is an instrumental belief/desire explanation. Anthea's joining the golf club is explained by the facts that Anthea desires to be successful in business and that Anthea believes that joining

[20] Cf. *Practical Reason and Norms*, 18–19.

[21] 'Second-order Reasons', 922; cf. Raz, *Practical Reason and Norms*, 16–19.

[22] I appropriate here for my own use some ideas of Douglas Butler, in ways of which he might not have approved: cf. 'Character-traits in explanation', *Philosophy and Phenomenological Research*, 49 (1988). Douglas's tragic death at the age of 32 in June 1991 has deprived both the Canadian and the philosophical academy of a mind of great acuity and promise.

the golf club will help her to be successful in business. But such a view then has difficulty with commonsensically respectable explanations such as 'Shelley bought Kelly a bunch of flowers because she is thoughtful' or 'Jim lent Kim his bike because he is generous'. People who are thoughtful or generous just buy other folks flowers or lend them bikes; they don't calculate that they desire to please others and buying flowers or lending bikes is a way to please others. Douglas Butler proposes instead that this explanatory function of character traits is best illuminated by analysing character traits as involving three dispositions:

a particular sort of representational disposition, a disposition to attach what I shall call 'practical salience' to certain representations, and a desire to do certain types of things, given the contents of such representations. (220)

That is, a thoughtful person like Shelley is disposed to have representations of folks in need (a thoughtless person simply doesn't notice things such as that Kelly needs cheering up); a thoughtful person is disposed to regard a person's being in need as a reason for action (a hard-hearted or callous person notices things such as that Kelly needs cheering up but attaches no 'practical salience' to them); a thoughtful person has the desire to do such things as cheering up people who are down, given that they notice such people (a malicious person, a *Schadenfreudlicher*, would desire to maintain or worsen the condition). This pattern of explanation Butler calls the 'three-part pattern'. Traits such as courage, which seem to involve refraining from action given certain representations, have a 'two-part' analysis—a disposition to represent and a disposition not to attach practical salience.

Consider now the explanation of the behaviour of one who treats legal rules as exclusionary reasons in terms of such patterns of explanation. It would be a mistake to represent such behaviour in terms of instrumental belief/desire explanations. The bad man observes the speed limit because he desires not to attract the policeman's attention and he believes that keeping the speed limit will not attract the policeman's attention. But if one obeys the law only out of a desire to obtain a goal one believes such obedience will bring—if, that is, one looks at the law in solely instrumental terms—then one does not understand, or so sophisticated positivism has been maintaining,[23] how it is that the law is a reason for action. Do we understand any better how the law is a reason for action if we seek to explain the behaviour of one who treats legal rules as exclusionary reasons in terms of the 'three-part pattern' for explanations of behaviour?

It is very plausible to suppose that there is improvement. The person who treats the fact that an action is required by law as an exclusionary reason for performing that act (a) is disposed to have representations (the anarchist with an Ll.B., perhaps, has the representations but attaches no salience to them); (c) has a desire to do certain kinds of things, given the content of such representations (the thoroughly knowledgeable lawyer for an organized representations but attaches no salience to them); (c) has a desire to do certain kinds of things, given the content of such representtions (the thoroughly knowledgeable lawyer for an organized crime syndicate, or the revolutionary group,[24] attach practical salience to the representations in utterly different ways from the person who takes laws as exclusionary reasons). The behaviour of someone who treats the law as providing a reason for action which excludes other actions from consideration seems to be very well suited to explanation in terms of the three-part pattern. So, if to argue phenomenologically, as the Phenomenological Argument does so argue, is legitimate, then to display how the character trait of treating law as an exclusionary reason is correctly analysed on the 'three-part pattern' is to deepen our understanding of the concept of exclusionary reason.

In particular, this way of understanding the phenomenon of treating laws as exclusionary reasons enables some distance to be put between the theory of laws as exclusionary reasons and the 'strong Burkean conception' of laws as reasons for action. On the 'strong Burkean conception', law-abiding behaviour is explained by the internal correlate of a reweighting principle, a stronger general desire to do the things which fall under the description 'required by law' than to do the things which fall under the description 'what I immediately desire to do'. The 'strong Burkean conception' preserves the instrumental belief/desire pattern of explanation. But, on the three-part pattern, the tendency to

---

[23] See Ch. 2.1 above.
[24] Cf. Raz, 'Promises and Obligations', 222.

regard the law as an exclusionary reason for action is rooted in an idiosyncratic and independent disposition to attach practical salience to one representation rather than another.[25] The independence of the explanatory disposition is the correlate of the exclusionary character of the reason for action which law provides.

5. EXCLUSIONARY AND EXPRESSIVE REASONS

However, the correctness of the 'three-part pattern' of analysis for the trait of treating laws as exclusionary reasons for action is bought by positivism at a high price. I shall show what I mean.

The same three-part pattern will apply to other explanations such as, in particular, 'Johnny stood by Bonny through her ordeal because he is her friend'. 'Friendliness' as a character trait is not quite the same thing as friendship; friendliness may be shown by one person to another in all sorts of situations where the persons are not friends (between colleagues or business associates, or people seated next to each other in the theatre, for example), and even computer programs can be 'user-friendly'. Friendship as a social relation none the less is to a large degree an *Einstellung*, a 'basic stance' towards another person,[26] and this *Einstellung* is properly analysed in terms of the three-part pattern. That is, while it may be true that Johnny desires to make Bonny feel better and believes that standing by her will make her feel better, such a fact is a small part of what it is for Johnny to be Bonny's friend, and appeal to the friendship by way of explanation of behaviour is not appeal to that fact. Rather, 'because he is her friend' appeals to the fact that: (*a*) Johnny is disposed to have representations of Bonny as needing support (or as being in a considerable variety of emotional and practical conditions); (*b*) Johnny attaches practical salience to such representations (friendship is a highly interactive relationship); (*c*) Johnny has a desire to do certain things, given the content of such representations (to support her when she is under stress, rejoice with her in her successes, and so forth). If one may so put it, for Johnny to be Bonny's friend is for Johnny to

---

[25] Cf. Butler, 'Character-traits', 224.

[26] *Einstellung* does not mean 'attitude'; cf. Winch, 'Eine Einstellung Zur Seele', *Proceedings of the Aristotelian Society*, 81 (1980–1), *passim*, on the importance of avoiding this mistranslation of the word in Pt. II, sect. iv, of Wittgenstein's *Philosophical Investigations*.

treat situations affecting Bonny, or Bonny's condition generally, as reasons for action other than on the balance of reasons, as reasons excluding other reasons from practical deliberation.

Now, Raz has himself seen how friendship provides a model for a certain kind of stance which a citizen might have towards the law. Chapter 13 of *The Authority of Law* discusses 'respect for law', and, quite consistently with a commitment to positivism, insists that, while respect for law is a morally permissible state of mind, it cannot be one which we are obliged to have. Respect for law involves both cognitive and practical attitudes, a variety of affective and cognitive dispositions (*The Authority of Law*, 250–1). Respect for law then generates obligations to obey the law; that is the direction of normative significance, not the reverse. The analogy with friendship, Raz believes, is close. It is morally permissible, but not obligatory, to have friends; friendship generates obligations and not the reverse.

To describe the way that respect for law and friendship generate obligations, Raz introduces a new kind of 'reason for action'. He characterizes the kind of reasons for action that his two stances provide as 'expressive reasons'. 'Expressive reasons are so called because the actions they require express the relationship or attitude involved' (*The Authority of Law*, 255). So, it is not merely that Johnny's action in standing by Bonny is explained by the fact that he is Bonny's friend; it is also true that Johnny's being Bonny's friend gives him a reason to stand by her (and in significant cases an obligation, perhaps) which someone who is not her friend would not have. Similarly, one with respect for law has a reason to obey the law which one who does not have respect for law would not have. Johnny expresses his friendship in standing by Bonny because she is his friend and not because he needs her support to get elected, as Frieda expresses her respect for law in keeping the speed limit because it is the speed limit and not because she does not wish to attract the policeman's attention. None the less, for Raz, expressive reasons are only reasons for those with the corresponding mental states expressed by them, and the having of such states is contingent.

In the preceding paragraphs, I have attempted to establish two things. First, there is an isomorphism between the logic of explanation of behaviour via character trait and the explanation of behaviour via friendship. Second, the explanation of behaviour via character trait is an extremely plausible model for the interior content of the practical reasoning of one who regards some fact as an exclusionary reason. I shall now show that the establishment of these two points has some remarkable consequences.

The distinction between one who acts in accordance with law because she desires some goal to which acting in accordance with law is the means and one who acts in accordance with law because it is the law was given earlier as the distinction between the bad man's view of the law and the view of one who treats the law as an exclusionary reason. The same distinction is now turning up again as the distinction between the bad man's view of the law and the person for whom the fact that something accords with the law is an expressive reason.

The argument of the preceding pages thus implies a result of considerable significance for legal philosophy. The Phenomeno-logical Argument in its original form did not secure the plausibility of the exclusionary reasons account over the 'strong Burkean conception' of laws as reasons for action. If, however, the exclusionary reasons account is supplemented by a highly attractive account drawn from the philosophy of mind about how character traits function in the explanation of behaviour, then the exclusionary reasons account can be shown to be superior to the 'strong Burkean conception'. But the exclusionary reasons account supplemented by the three-part pattern of explanation turns out to be the same as the expressive reasons account of how law is a reason for action. While this fact does nothing to threaten the plausibility of the exclusionary reasons account of how laws are reasons for action, it does suggest that the price to be paid for this plausibility is the inadequacy of positivism.

The claim that laws are exclusionary reasons for action is intended to make a formal point about the role in practical reasoning of the fact that there is a law relating to such-and-such a practical matter. Formal point or not, I have argued the following about this claim. The claim that laws are exclusionary reasons for action needs some theoretical grounding to mark it off from the claim that laws are simply first-order reasons which weigh heavily in the balance of reasons. There is a highly attractive candidate for such a grounding, namely, the following. The phenomenology of the disposition to treat laws as exclusionary reasons for action conforms exactly to that of the three-part analysis for the explanation of behaviour. The 'balance of reasons' account, by contrast, can only explain law-abiding behaviour in terms of an instrumental belief/desire package, an explanation which is instantiated paradigmatically by the so-called 'bad man's' view of the law as threatening an evil with which one will be visited if one does not comply. Now, if it is a formal or conceptual point about laws that they are exclusionary reasons for action, then, supposing the argument so far to be sound, it is equally a formal or conceptual point about laws that law-abiding behaviour is best explained in terms of the three-part analysis. That is, this is not a feature contingently found in some cases of law-abiding behaviour; it belongs to the concept of law that this point holds.

Consider now the thought that laws are expressive reasons for action, a thought which states a point putatively as formal and conceptual about law as the thought that laws are exclusionary reasons for action. The phenomenology of the disposition to treat laws as expressive reasons for action is exactly the same as the phenomenology of the disposition to treat laws as exclusionary reasons for action. Thus the most plausible account of how it is that laws are exclusionary reasons for action presents laws as expressive reasons as much as exclusionary reasons. To regard laws as expressive reasons for action, however, is not to regard the existence and content of laws in factual or neutral terms. It is to regard the existence and content of laws as naturally of evaluative significance. Attention therefore to the way that the existence of laws enters into practical reasoning leads to the recognition that the existence and content of laws is naturally of evaluative significance. That will be a formal or conceptual point about laws. If that point holds, then the concept of law is not a 'content-independent' concept, and cannot be analysed in positivistic terms.

6. SOME OBJECTIONS CONSIDERED

I consider now three objections. First, it may be objected that, even if it belongs to the concept of law that the disposition to treat laws as exclusionary reasons for action is best construed in terms of the three-part analysis, it does not follow that the disposition to treat laws as expressive reasons for action belongs to the concept of law. It may be that some who treat laws as exclusionary reasons for action also treat laws as expressive reasons and some do not. That is, it may be said that it is a contingent feature of some piece of law-abiding behaviour that it may be explained in terms of a disposition to treat laws as expressive reasons for action, even if it is not a contingent feature of that piece of behaviour that it may be explained in terms of a disposition to treat laws as exclusionary reasons for action. But how is this distinction to be drawn? The primary argument for the thesis that laws are exclusionary reasons for action is the Phenomenological Argument, an argument about the interior content of the practical reasoning that treats laws as reasons for action. But there is no difference between the interior content of reasoning which treats laws as exclusionary reasons and that of reasoning which treats laws as expressive reasons. Thus the Phenomenological Argument, an argument of sophisticated positivism, itself does not permit the distinction which the above objection requires between the claim that laws are exclusionary reasons for action being a conceptual point about law and the claim that laws are expressive reasons for action being a contingent truth about some people and some laws.

Second, it may be objected that my argument, even if its premises are correct, shows only that the existence and content of law must be subjectively seen to be of evaluative significance by the norm-subjects of law. The argument does not show what it would need to show to topple positivism, that the existence and content of law really must be of evaluative significance. We must remember, however, the assumption by Raz, correctly made, of the symmetry (cf. page 112) between an agent's subjective practical determination of what there is reason to do and what objectively or in fact there is reason to do. To take care of cases where the agent makes a mistake in practical reasoning, we need to have the distinction between how it is with the agent and how it is in fact. We cannot, however, systematically prise the latter pair apart in every case of practical reasoning. The normal case is for agents to navigate themselves through the world with practical success. That fact non-contingently obtains, for otherwise there would not be such a thing as practical reasoning for Raz and others to analyse. If that is so, then this objection fails.

It may be objected, third, that this remarkable anti-positivistic rabbit so spectacularly just produced was illicitly slipped into the hat some pages ago. What was offered as an explanation in terms of the three-part pattern of the behaviour of one who treats legal rules as exclusionary reasons is in fact an explanation of behaviour in accord with law as such. It would apply as well to those whose stance towards the law is sheep-like acquiescence[27] as to those whose stance is full-blooded respect for law. A variety of different stances fit the three-part pattern. Sheep-like acquiescence is one; respect for law is another; regarding the law as providing exclusionary reasons for action is a third.[28] Which is the case for any given agent is subject to independent factual determination. But the law will remain the law through these different determinations. That fact is not merely consistent with, but implies the truth of, a content-independent account of the nature of law such as legal positivism.

The objection needs to be met. Let us consider the cases in more detail. Evidence coming out of Romania in January 1990 suggested that the average Romanian citizen's stance towards the law during the Ceausescu regime was best understood in terms of instrumental belief/desire explanations. The citizens were terrified of the consequences of breaking the law and obeyed because they desired the absence of harm such obedience would bring. But we have rejected such obedience as revelatory of the nature of law. This stance is also anything but sheep-like acquiescence; it is a lid jammed down on a boiling pot. If the concept of 'sheep-like' is to be given significant weight, it must imply some fair degree of failure to have representations of actions as required by or forbidden by law (unlike the Romanians), or some disposition not to attach practical salience to such representations but only to the barks and glares of the sheepdog, as it were; these are the representations given the content of which the subject desires to act. While sheep-like acquiescence therefore may indeed fit the three-part pattern of explanation, it does not imply a stance which contains representations of what the law requires or forbids under the description 'required/forbidden by law'. It cannot therefore be a stance which tells us anything about how the law as such is a reason for action.

[27] Cf. Hart, *The Concept of Law*, 114.

[28] Hart (*Essays on Bentham*, 256) refers to a 'standing recognition (which may be motivated by any of a variety of ultimate reasons) of a commander's words as generally constituting a content-independent peremptory reason for acting' as a 'distinctive *normative* attitude'; his emphasis.

But once we do begin with those whose stance involves a disposition to have representations of actions as required by or forbidden by law, then the variations on this stance are as adumbrated in my earlier discussion.[29] One for whom laws are exclusionary reasons may be validly contrasted with the anarchist, the psychotic, the revolutionary group, and so forth. While it may be true that there are some forms of positivism which would accept that the anarchist's or the psychotic's or the revolutionary's stance towards the law is in principle as revelatory of the nature of law as the stance of one who treats laws as exclusionary reasons or one who has respect for law, the sophisticated positivism we have been discussing here is not one of them. If it is accepted that sophisticated positivism has revealed genuine deficiencies in the way that these simpler forms of positivism represent laws as reasons for action, then the consequence of the argument here is that laws cannot be adequately represented as reasons for action in positivistic terms. The insights of sophisticated positivism lead to a non-positivistic theory of law.

[29] Cf. pages 113–14 above.

4

LAW AND AUTHORITY

1. THE INTERNAL POINT OF VIEW AS SOCIAL FACT

The sophisticated positivistic account represents law as claiming its directives to be authoritative. Suppose a case where the claim to authority is in fact accepted.[1] The positivist will emphasize that it does not follow from the fact that some group of people accept a given law as authoritative that it really is authoritative. For instance, the positivist argues, it might be that in the Ruritanian legal system, there is a statute prohibiting patients from suing doctors for malpractice. It might also be that Ruritanians in general, patients as well as doctors, regard that statute as authoritative, as justified. But, as many of us will want to argue, to enact such a statute would be a mistake. It is important that ordinary people are protected from the misuse of professional expertise, and especially so when life and health are involved. The Ruritanian legal system does not provide a remedy where, to be authoritative, law would have to provide one. In Ruritania, therefore, that law at least lacks authority, despite its being regarded as authoritative by the Ruritanians. So, provided that the claim to due allegiance is regarded as one social fact, and acceptance of the claim's legitimacy by norm-subjects as another social fact, the separation between law and morality is still preserved. Law can be defined in terms of a made and accepted claim to due allegiance, and yet the judgement of law's genuine authority will be a judgement made independently of the determination of the social fact that the law is accepted as authoritative.

That positivist argument seems a simple enough argument to put forward; it conceals, though, complications. It is all very well for

---

[1] The argument of this chapter is independent of any theory of what will count as 'acceptance'; see Chs. 2.4 and 6 for a discussion of that topic.

us to say from our point of view that this Ruritanian statute is unjust, and is therefore not authoritative. It does not seem so to the Ruritanians. If, as is *ex hypothesi* the case, it is true of them that they have the internal point of view towards that statute, then they see the claims of that statute upon them to be justified. They see it as an authoritative directive—as its claims to having authority being justified according to sophisticated positivism's 'normal justification thesis'.[2] How then is it possible for anyone else to assert that in fact the statute lacks authority, that its claims to be an authoritative directive are not justified?

The assertion that, despite the Ruritanians' acceptance of it as justified, the statute lacks authority implies, first, that there is some other point of view, one not shared by those who see the statute as authoritative, from which the claims of the statute to be authoritative seem visibly and genuinely spurious. Second, the assertion implies that this other point of view is distinctive in that from it one may genuinely see how things are. Thus, a notion of a claim genuinely being justified, and not merely of a claim believed to be justified, is in play here. We see correctly how things are in the matter of the statute's claim to authority: the Ruritanians do not.

The positivist will still not feel threatened by these remarks, for the following reason. Suppose we grant our superior moral insight to that of the Ruritanians in the matter of their non-existent malpractice statute. None the less, there is formally speaking no distinction between their position *vis-à-vis* their law and ours *vis-à-vis* our law. We also simply have certain beliefs. We accept the authority of certain laws. We have the internal point of view to certain laws. That is 'just a social fact' about us, as the corresponding fact about the Ruritanians is 'just a social fact' about them. We do not think past those laws whose authority we accept; we do not raise questions about whether the claim of those laws to have authority is justified. These facts no more show that such a claim really is justified than the corresponding failure in the case of the Ruritanians shows that their statute has authority.

[2] 'The normal way to establish that a person has authority over another person involves showing that the alleged subject is likely better to comply with reasons that apply to him (other than the alleged authoritative directives) if he accepts the directives of the alleged authority as authoritatively binding and tries to follow them, rather than by trying to follow the reasons which apply to him directly' (Raz, *The Morality of Freedom*, 53).

There is nothing here to ground the thought that law necessarily has authority. So an account of law as necessarily claiming but not necessarily having authority still seems quite correct.

2. THE INTERNAL POINT OF VIEW AS TRANSCENDENTAL CONDITION

I want to raise against positivism a difficulty with these thoughts.[3] One is only able to say that it is 'just a fact' about the Ruritanians that they accept the authority of the statute prohibiting suits for malpractice because one speaks from another point of view. That point of view, however, has the feature that acceptance of it, of certain values on one's own part, is not 'just a fact'. It is, rather, a transcendental condition of the other-directed criticism being possible. The condition of our being able in this way to criticize the positive law of another legal system for having a statute which prohibits suits for malpractice is that there are certain rules, viz., rules permitting such suits, such that if they were of our legal system then we would not know how not to see them as authoritative. We can criticize the positive law of another system as unjust only because we have certain substantive beliefs about justice and injustice. But if we do have such beliefs, we must see some other positive law to be just, for so to see it will be part of what it is to have these substantive beliefs.

Moreover, it cannot be in the same way 'just a fact' about us that we have the point of view we have, because for us to have that point of view defines or is constitutive of the kind of people that we are. We are the kind of people who have certain values; we define ourselves by the acceptance of certain values. We are the kind of people who think statutes like the one in Ruritania unjust and ones like our own just. In that case, the 'acceptance' on our part of certain values here being referred to is not as seen from our own perspective the mere 'acceptance' which would be a contingent social fact ascertainable from the external point of view. Our acknowledgement of the authority of a certain law is more deeply integrated into the fabric of our social life than the term 'acceptance' implies. It might be that some outsider—a Ruritanian,

---

[3] See also here the argument in Ch. 5 below, and the remarks about symmetry in practical reasoning in Chs. 4.4 and 4.6.

perhaps—from her point of view can say of us that we 'merely accept', but we cannot say it of ourselves. We have an *Einstellung*, a 'basic stance' towards certain values and the laws to which they seem to give authority, and this stance precludes our rejecting that authority. Call those values our 'critical morality'. Then—as it might be put—we cannot criticize our critical morality. We can only from the point of view of our critical morality criticize our and others' positive morality and positive law. We cannot criticize the critical morality of others, because, if we identify it as something they accept but we do not, then we are *ipso facto* identifying it as part of their positive morality, not their critical morality. Our critical morality we can only apply. We can from one part of it question another part of it; but we can not question it all at once. If we do, then the point of view from which this questioning takes place becomes the new critical morality, and the old critical morality becomes part of positive morality. We cannot stand to our own critical morality as we stand to the critical morality of the Ruritanians.

In any given particular case, we can perhaps imagine not having some particular law, even if we regard that law as authoritative. For example, we believe deeply in the presumption of innocence. We regard the presumption of innocence as necessary in order to protect certain individual rights and privileges. Given the appropriate adjustments elsewhere in criminal procedure, which manage to leave those rights and privileges still satisfactorily protected, the presumption of innocence is not so necessary; we might imagine a legal system which did not have it. Note, however, that the thought that certain rights and privileges of the individual must be protected in any enlightened system of criminal justice remains as a constant in each case. We would not know how to go about questioning this thought with our present concept of justice in its place.[4]

We seem to be suggesting here an argument for the anti-positivist

---

[4] I do not wish to oversimplify the issues here. As Green has shown (*The Authority of the State* (Oxford, 1988), 193–7) in his discussion of 'neo-Wittgensteinian' and idealist theories of authority, an unpleasant kind of conservative commitment to rigid social rules seems to be implied by such views. I would be as opposed to such conservatism as anyone else. But I acknowledge that the thoughts expressed here, if translated into a political theory, must be shown to allow due weight to liberty and autonomy at pain of being unacceptable. For a variety of reasons that task will not be undertaken here.

notion of a deep connection between law and morality, a connection which is obscured by the positivistic idea that law merely claims authority. If there is a significant sense in which we cannot but accept the authority of our law, then there is reason to say our law does not possess authority merely contingently, as the positivist requires. Moreover, we and our law are not idiosyncratic. We are with respect to our law in the position that anyone is with respect to their law. Thus, to the extent that it is true of us that we must see that which we see as law as authoritative, it is true of anyone that they must see that which they see as law as authoritative. But if anyone must see law as authoritative, then law must be authoritative, and the concept of law is therefore not a 'value-free' concept. The positivist imagines an Archimedean point from which absolutely all law is seen all at once as one huge social fact. But no actual person can stand at such a point.

3. A POSITIVIST RESPONSE

The positivist may reply as follows. The above thought about the protection of rights and enlightened criminal justice which we can not displace is none the less for that a moral thought. It is perfectly appropriate to say that positive law will not be authoritative despite its claims to be so unless it meets moral standards. Morality itself judges that our legal system which protects such rights makes good its claims to authority, and the Soviet or the South African legal system (the positivist might assert), when it does not protect such rights, does not make good its claims. Soviet or South African citizens who regard their law as authoritative thus are deluded, as deluded as our hypothetical Ruritanians. We, however, who regard our law as authoritative are not deluded. None the less, the relevant judgement that a particular legal system or a particular legal directive is authoritative in either case is a judgement made in accord with the normal justification thesis by morality of positive law. Law is still positive law, i.e., a matter of social fact. To say 'morality judges law' is but a fancy way of saying that we judge positive law by the standards of what law morally ought to be. The criteria for law's being authoritative are thus moral, not legal, criteria. And if they are moral criteria, then it remains true that law is not necessarily authoritative, but is authoritative only if it contingently satisfies moral constraints which are additional to its existence as law. So might the positivist argue.

4. FUNCTIONS, DEFECTS, AND NATURES

Again, this line of thought is not as straightforward and common-sensical as it appears. It needs to be demythologized. Conceptions of what X ideally ought to be like, for many cases of X, are not moral. For example, a power drill whose chuck grips the bit tight enough to cause it to rotate only at very low speeds is not what a power drill ideally ought to be like. An ear with the inner bones out of alignment so that it is useless for hearing is not what an ear ideally ought to be like. These are not, though, moral defects. It does not follow therefore that the defect in virtue of which a [system of] positive law is deemed not authoritative must be a moral defect just because it is a defect. Moreover, defects can have moral significance without themselves being moral defects. A poorly constructed electric toaster is a danger to life and health: its defects therefore have moral significance. The defects in those who knowingly manufacture and retail such a dangerous device we may properly think of as moral defects. The defects in the device itself, however, are not themselves moral defects.

The notion of 'defect' deployed here requires two background assumptions to make sense. First, we have a notion of how such a device should normally be, properly speaking. Second, this latter propriety is connected in some internal way to certain human values. Devices have *functions*, and do so in order to facilitate the achievement of certain (to varying degrees) humanly important ends. They actually do fulfil these functions by design.[5] None the

---

[5] 'By design' here does not refer to a causal and contingent relationship between a person and an artefact. A broad background of human intentionality is presupposed, in that we know the normal case to be that artefacts have the properties they have because of such causal relationships. But to speak of the design of an artefact is to speak of a structural property of it which it has intrinsically, and which we perceive it to have because of our knowledge of instrumentality. The design is internally related to the function the artefact performs. I take myself here to be using the notion of 'design' developed by Sparshott (cf. *The Theory of the Arts*, 154–6), though I do not know whether he would approve of its application here.

less, our concept of an electric toaster, for instance, is not that of an ideally perfect electric toaster approved by an immaculate and omniscient Association of Angelic Consumers. Rather, our concept of an electric toaster is the concept of the kind of thing a mundane Consumers' Association tests to sift out the best buy and condemn some others as unfit to market. Our concept of an electric toaster is the concept of a device of some kind normally performing by design a certain function. 'Normal' here means 'as *this* one functions, and not as *that* one functions'. It does not mean 'as the ideal form of Electric Toaster would function if it existed'. It may be that in the case of a defective electric toaster there are two separate judgements made, that it is an electric toaster, and that it is defective. In the case of the normally functioning electric toaster, however, there are not two judgements, 'It's an electric toaster', and 'By Golly, it does what an electric toaster is supposed to do'.[6] Rather, there is just the one judgement, 'It's an electric toaster'. An entity is an electric toaster just in case it is something that functions as a normally functioning mundane electric toaster functions.

What does all this have to do with law? Even positivists do not fight shy of acknowledging that law has or performs social functions. For example, Raz distinguishes the primary and the secondary functions of law.[7] The primary functions, he argues, are to prevent undesirable behaviour and secure desirable behaviour; to provide facilities for private arrangements between individuals; to provide services and the redistribution of goods; and to settle unregulated disputes. The secondary functions are those of determining procedures for changing the law and regulating the operation of law-applying organs. But law does not merely happen to perform certain functions; it is internal to law that law is designed to perform those functions, as much as it is internal to an electric toaster to be designed to toast. It is part of the concept of law that law normally performs these functions well. The judgement that a particular institutionalized system of norms is a system of law and the judgement that it performs certain social

---

[6] This might make sense if, for example, it were made of plastic: one would not expect a plastic electric toaster to do what an electric toaster is supposed to do.

[7] See *The Authority of Law*, 169–76, *The Morality of Freedom*, 47–52, which discusses the functions of authorities, and *The Morality of Freedom*, 58–9, on the function of authoritative rules.

functions well are as much two different versions of merely the same judgement as they are in the electric toaster example above. It is not critical morality alone that judges a particular legal system to serve well the ends of justice. It is our normal or constitutive mode of thinking (our grammar, if you like) which so judges, a mode of thinking which incorporates but is not identical to critical morality. This mode of thinking so judges in, and not additionally to, the judgement that a particular institutionalized system of norms is a legal system.

The judgement about a particular institutionalized system of norms being a legal system is like a judgement about an appliance being a toaster in being a judgement that is not in the positivistic sense empirical or factual. Such a judgement is unlike the corresponding judgement about a toaster in the following way. In the case of the toaster the judgement about some particular toaster that it fulfils well some moral purpose, for example, it reduces the inconvenience in some person's life, is a candidate judgement of critical morality different from the judgement that it functions well as a toaster or is not a defective toaster. The latter are not judgements which are in themselves candidate judgements of critical morality. On the other hand, the judgement of some system of norms that it is a legal system is at one and the same time a candidate judgement of critical morality that the system fulfils well some moral purpose. Legal systems are like toasters in that in each case it is non-contingently true that normally each performs well the function for which it is designed. The two cases differ in that in the case of a legal system the judgement that normally human flourishing is promoted by the entity's functioning in the way that it is designed is also non-contingently true, while in the case of an artefact like a toaster the analogous judgement would be if true at all contingently true. Electric toasters and hand-guns are properly functioning toasters and hand-guns when they are used for nefarious purposes like murder, whereas an institutionalized system of norms used exclusively for the coercion of the innocent just by that alone is a candidate for not being a legal system at all, or is at best a necessarily degenerate instance of a legal system.

5. IDENTIFICATION AND NATURE

We still do not have the whole story, of course. In a passage justly famous for its own majesty and authority, Hart asserts:

What surely is most needed in order to make men clear-sighted in confronting the official abuse of power, is that they should preserve the sense that the certification of something as legally valid is not conclusive of the question of obedience, and that, however great the aura of majesty or authority which the official system may have, its demands must in the end be submitted to a moral scrutiny. (*The Concept of Law*, 206)

Of course Hart is quite right. It does not follow, for any given law, that just because it is valid (i.e., is part of positive law), it is therefore authoritative. As we all know, government is the government of laws all right, but these are formulated, passed, and applied by fallible men and women. So we need to be able to tell for any putative legal requirement, permission, means of facilitation, etc., whether our belief in the existence of that requirement, etc., is a correct belief before we can begin to consider whether that requirement, etc., is justified and authoritative. We need a way of identifying unjust laws as laws, so that we can fight for their repeal or for their emasculation by distinguishing. After all, we would not want to go to the trouble of setting up an elaborate campaign to change the law on some particular issue because we deemed that law unjust, if in fact our belief that the body of settled law contained this unjust provision was a false belief.

A theory which proposes to equate law with those observable features of law that enable one to solve such problems of identification seems to offer the prospect of solving such problems of identification in the cleanest and most certain way. Positivism is such a theory. Positivism argues that we need to have a characterization of law as such, a statement of the essence of the concept of law, which is entirely value free, because otherwise the process of identification of laws cannot be non-question-beggingly carried out. Positivism offers itself as providing such a characterization, and so there is a powerful motivation here for its endorsement. It is a plain fact about human history and the contemporary world that some norms which are part of positive law are in themselves unjust laws; to act in accordance with them would be so far to do the unjust thing. It seems incoherent to say that some law which therefore as such makes a justified claim on our obedience is at the same time such that if we were to act in accordance with it we would act unjustly. So, we want to say, we have to escape that absurdity by saying that what it is for that norm to be a law must be something which is in principle as much a property of a norm which is unjust as it is a property of a norm which is just. It must be something which a norm has independently as a formal property. Being commanded by the sovereign or enacted by the Queen in Parliament is exactly the kind of thing that would meet this specification. A positivistic account of law thus seems forced upon us. But do we have to choose the card?

The positivist's mistake is to conflate criteria for the identification of a thing with an account of the nature of that thing. To see this, let us return to electric toasters. One might say in exactly the same spirit as the quote from Hart that in order to make people clear-sighted in confronting the abuse of economic power, we need to have a value-free concept of an electric toaster—'electric toaster' must mean positive electric toaster, if you like—so that we can identify an object as an electric toaster independently of discussing whether it is an acceptable electric toaster. We need a way of identifying unsafe and dangerous electric toasters as electric toasters, so that we can prevent them from being marketed.

In the case of electric toasters, this need is indeed fulfilled. Our concept of electric toaster enables us to recognize and pick out electric toasters from among other small electrical household appliances. It includes terms which refer to empirically observable features of electric toasters, which features underwrite the recognition and identification of electric toasters. Thus the concept of an electric toaster itself provides the means of solving the identification problem.

Our concept of electric toaster is none the less not an empirical and 'value-free' concept. The concept of electric toaster is not equivalent to the concept of an entity with those empirical features. One might by carefully examining the externally observable features of electric toasters assemble a summary and portable account of those externally observable features in common to all and only electric toasters (perhaps allowing for borderline cases and a penumbra of uncertainty), which account would be invaluable for those wishing to purchase electric toasters, and room for which account must be made in any adequate theory of electric toasters. But would such an account meet the need of one who wanted to know what it is to be an electric toaster? Could one know what it is to be an electric toaster by knowing exactly what and no more than one would need to know to recognize and pick out electric toasters in an appliance store?

Surely not. At some point one would have to confront what an electric toaster is for, what the function of an electric toaster is, what place it has in human social life. In so far as an unsafe or dangerous electric toaster is a defective electric toaster, it is identifiable as an electric toaster by one deploying the concept of an electric toaster. However, in so far as an unsafe and dangerous electric toaster is a *defective* electric toaster, it is not an electric toaster at all. It is a *defective electric toaster*, a rather different thing. A defective electric toaster is not a kind of electric toaster in the way that a Proctor-Silex or a four-slicer are kinds of electric toasters. It is an electric toaster, as it might be put, in name only.[8] A defective electric toaster does not do what an electric toaster normally does; it does not perform the functions an electric toaster normally performs.

Analogously, our concept of law includes terms which refer to empirically observable features of the institutions of law without the existence of which there would be no law, norm-creating, norm-changing, norm-applying, norm-enforcing institutions, and so forth. Our concept of law is one that enables us to pick out the institutions of law and their products, laws. We have a way of identifying unjust laws as laws, and that is because they conform to the criteria for the identification of laws. They are identifiable as laws by one deploying the concept of a law and making reference to observable features of laws and legal institutions. But to give the criteria for the recognition or identification of laws is not to give an account of the concept of law.

6. LAW AS AUTHORITATIVE BY NATURE

It is indeed only in virtue of positive laws having those empirical features resulting from institutionalization and formal validity that

---

[8] Cf. Aristotle, *de Anima*, 412^{b}10–25; Aristotle's examples are axes and eyes, rather than electric toasters.

positivism emphasizes that we are able to perform the socially significant feat of identifying as laws those among the body of laws that are unjust. None the less, our concept of law is not an empirical and 'value-free' concept either, any more than is the concept of an electric toaster. The concept of a legal system is the concept of an institution internally related by design to the fulfilment of certain valuable social functions, and thus internally related to the possession of authority. If some horrendously harmful consequence, whether natural or humanly contrived, will result from an action, there is excellent reason to avoid the action. So excellent is the reason that not only will the external observer find in fact few if any such actions ever performed (though accidents, wickedness, and sheer gross stupidity can occur), but also those contemplating the action may regard themselves as excluded from acting that way or pre-empted from acting that way by the altogether overpowering weight of the reason against such an action. But of course that is not what is meant by talk of a norm providing an exclusionary reason for action. Those who see the kind of reason provided against an action by the fact that it is legally prohibited as amounting to no more (though no less) than an (extremely) unpleasant consequence of so acting are held, and rightly so, to have an 'external' or 'bad man's', and so a wrong view of the law. But why? The answer is not merely that the predictive theory leaves out the role of the institutional aspects of law in relation to law's functioning as an exclusionary reason for action. Such might be a part of the positivist's response to the inadequacies of the predictive theory. Rather, a view of the law in terms of evils with which one will be visited following non-compliance obscures the fundamental fact that the law offers itself as a particular kind of exclusionary reason for action. The manner in which it does so is not reducible to an analysis in empirical institutional or positivistic terms. The law does not appeal to our desire to avoid harmful consequences; it appeals, crudely speaking, to our sense of justice and our desire to do the just thing, to live in a just world.

7. LEGITIMATE AND *DE FACTO* AUTHORITY

The distinction between legitimate authorities and *de facto* authorities is part of the positivistic project of being able to tell that a legal system exists by a value-free test. Legitimate authorities are those systems identified as claiming authority by the value-free test and which satisfy the normal justification thesis. *De facto* authorities are those systems identified as claiming authority by the value-free test and which do not satisfy the normal justification thesis. This distinction, however, is treacherous. The danger of the terminology of 'legitimate authority' and '*de facto* authority' is that authority may be seen as a genus with two species, legitimate and *de facto*. But *de facto* authority is in fact not a kind of authority at all. Compare authority here with duty. Sir David Ross was very careful when introducing the notion of 'prima facie duty' to state the following qualification on the term:

the phrase 'prima facie duty' must be apologized for, since . . . it suggests that what we are speaking of is a certain kind of duty, whereas it is in fact not a duty, but something related in a special way to duty. Strictly speaking, we want not a phrase in which duty is qualified by an adjective, but a separate noun . . . I can, however, think of no term which fully meets the case.[9]

De facto authority is similarly not a kind of authority, but something related in a special way to authority. We seem to need the notion of '*de facto* authority' to refer to systems which have all the trappings of an authoritative institutionalized normative system, but, because of the content of their norms, are not systems which ought to be obeyed. Raz remarks that 'the notion of a *de facto* authority cannot be understood except by reference to that of legitimate authority'.[10] This is both true and thoroughly misleading. It is true, because the notion of authority is that of legitimate authority. It is misleading in that what is in common to both legitimate and '*de facto*' authorities, namely, the surface appearances, the trappings of authority, pales into insignificance beside the differences between them, that '*de facto* authorities' are not

[9] W. D. Ross, *The Right and the Good* (Oxford, 1930), 20.
[10] *The Morality of Freedom*, 27; see also Leslie Green, *The Authority of the State*, 60, who makes a similar distinction in the cause of denying that 'legitimate authority' is pleonastic.

authorities at all. The expression 'a wolf in sheep's clothing' perhaps cannot be understood except by reference to the notion of a sheep. For all that, a wolf in sheep's clothing is not a kind of sheep; it is something which seems to be a sheep but is not. So also a system with the outward and visible signs of authority but a hollow or corrupt inside is something which seems to be authoritative but is not. Here too we need, not a phrase in which authority is qualified by a different adjective, but a separate noun. I can think of a term, or rather terms, which fully meet the case, viz., the notions of institutionalization and formal validity mentioned above. Institutionalization and validity are notions which play an important role in the identification of normative systems as legal systems, but there is more to the concept of a legal system than being a system with institutionalization and validity.

8. CONCLUSION

The law claims authority. That claim includes the claim that legal norms are exclusionary reasons for disregarding reasons for non-conformity, but it is more than that. The 'more' has to do with the particular appeal which the law makes to our sense of the reasons there are for action. Positivism sees correctly that the 'bad man's' view of the law is mistaken; that view cannot explain the normativity inherent to law. But to account properly for the nature of law, one must see that the law by nature 'claims authority' and does not merely 'exercise sheer power', because by nature law appeals specifically to our sense that serving the ends of justice is genuinely a reason for action, and that to act in accord with law is normally to act in accord with that reason.

The sophisticated positivistic account of the authority of law is important because it emphasizes this conceptual connection between law and [speaking pleonastically] legitimate authority. But the connection is not a mere 'social fact' about law. It is perhaps a 'social fact' that we have the conceptual scheme that we have; had we and the world we live in been very different in the way that trans-galactic aliens in an alien social world are very different, then any conceptual scheme in place would itself be very different. But in the debate over the nature of law, the expression 'social fact' as used by positivism officially identifies an entity distinct both from 'natural fact' and from 'social value'. The expression refers to contingencies in the social world the identification of which requires the making of no value judgements. To recognize both that there is an essential connection of law with authority and why that connection is there is not to indicate from the external point of view a 'social fact' in this positivistic quasi-technical sense. Rather, it is to express one's understanding from the internal point of view of the nature of law and of its place in human social life. Moreover, a normally functioning legal system is one in which the law's claim to authority is justified. To assert that law normally functions authoritatively is not to cover a 'cake' of empirical fact with an 'icing' of moral judgement.[11]

The positivist wants to preserve the separation of law and morality by insisting that the law's connection with authority is simply that law as a matter of social fact claims authority. The judgement for any given legal norm that it is an authoritative directive is supposedly a separate judgement, for an unjust law is still a law and we identify it as a law before we assess its (in)justice. First catch your norm; then acknowledge its authority. But the drive to move beyond positivism, and to break down the separation of law and morality, begins (i) with the very recognition, which even the positivist must make to distinguish law from, say, etiquette, that it is authority that law claims, and (ii) with the recognition of all that is through (i) implied about the essential and non-contingent connection between law in its natural design and functioning, and justice. Facts about the concept of law itself which sophisticated positivism is too sophisticated not to appreciate push us irresistibly away from positivistic theories of law.

[11] The image is borrowed from Julius Kovesi; see his *Moral Notions* (London, 1967), 25. In general, Kovesi's meta-ethical machinery of formal elements, material elements, and 'recognitors' would readily drive the analysis of the concept of law sketched here. The roots of both theories are Aristotelian.

5

THE POINT OF VIEW OF
LEGAL THEORY

1. DETACHED LEGAL STATEMENTS

The objection to simple positivism's conception of the point of view of legal theory was that it confined the theorist to the 'external point of view' to law, and thus could not allow the theorist to meet a constraint upon any adequate legal theory that the theory reproduce the way in which laws function in the lives of those who have the internal point of view to law. Let us call this constraint 'the reproduction demand'. Sophisticated positivism offered two devices to repair this deficiency—the notion of the 'moderate point of view' and the notion of the 'detached legal statement'. One who adopts the moderate point of view has the proper cognitive understanding of the legal system in question, and 'a full appreciation of, but no necessary sharing in, the volitional element'.[1] Such a one is therefore able to inform others of their obligations (for example) under the system: thus the point of view meets the reproduction demand. Yet such a one does not share the volitional commitment to the norms which is the mark of those who have the internal point of view. Similarly, one who can make correct detached legal statements about the obligations of others under some system of norms also meets the reproduction demand without having the same normative commitment as those who have the internal point of view. In this section, we will consider whether sophisticated positivism can indeed meet the reproduction demand by these devices.

Let us return to Raz's account of detached legal statements, and look more closely at its theoretical commitments:

---

[1] Cf. MacCormick, *H. L. A. Hart*, 38.

A detached normative statement does not carry the full normative force of an ordinary normative statement. Its utterance does not commit the speaker to the normative view it expresses. Legal scholars—and this includes ordinary practising lawyers—can use normative language when describing the law and make legal statements without thereby endorsing the law's moral authority. There is a special kind of legal statement which, though it is made by the use of ordinary normative terms, does not carry the same normative force of an ordinary legal statement. (*The Authority of Law*, 153)

The account is noteworthy because it introduces the technical concept of *force*—the idea that what distinguishes the detached legal statement from the legal statement made from the internal point of view is the force with which the statement is made. I shall show that, properly understood, the theory of 'forces' of utterances cannot be appealed to, to sustain positivism.

'Force' was introduced as a term of art into the philosophy of language by J. L. Austin.[2] He aimed to distinguish systematically between 'force' and 'sense and reference'. He characterized the term 'meaning' as 'hopelessly ambiguous'. He also introduced further technical terminology—the notions of 'locution' and 'locutionary act', 'illocution' and 'illocutionary act'. A locution is a vocable with a sense and a reference in a language, and a locutionary act the act of uttering such a vocable with that sense and reference. The illocutionary act is the act performed in uttering such a vocable with a given force. Force individuates illocutionary acts. A warning is distinguished from an announcing by the force of the utterance. Finally, Austin emphasizes that the distinction between locutionary and illocutionary act is conceptual; the former cannot be performed independently. 'To perform a locutionary act is in general . . . eo ipso to perform an *illocutionary* act.'[3]

Raz's theory says that 'statements' have 'forces'. Where in Austin's theory is there room for the notion of a 'statement'? It is not easy to see. At the beginning of *How to Do Things with Words*, Austin is very cagey about statements. The word appears as often in scare-quotes as it does without them. Page 1 suggests an

---

[2] *How to Do Things with Words* (Cambridge, Mass., 1975), 98 ff.

[3] *How to Do Things with Words*, 98, Austin's emphasis. It is not clear what the exceptions are to this general rule. Certainly, there seem none which affect the discussion here.

important distinction between the act of stating and a statement. Statements are not always used to perform acts of stating. If 'statement' is used to refer to that which is stated or said in an act of stating or saying, then 'statement' comes close in meaning to 'proposition', and the interpretation of that term is a philosophical quagmire. As early as page 3 Austin suggests the term 'constative' for a straightforward 'statement' of fact, and thereafter the term 'statement' has but a minor role in the book. The following quotation sets the tone:

One thing, however, that it will be most dangerous to do, and that we are very prone to do, is to take it that we somehow *know* that the primary or primitive use of sentences must be, because it ought to be, statemental or constative, in the philosophers' preferred sense of simply uttering something whose sole pretension is to be true or false and which is not liable to criticism in any other dimension. (*How to Do Things with Words*, 72: Austin's emphasis)

Pages 89–91 suggest that stating is a thing that one does with words, as is forecasting, endorsing, warning, asking, and so on— and (page 98) giving a description. Simply uttering something whose sole pretension is to be true or false is certainly something one does with words. But it is to be regarded as one kind of illocutionary act among others: it is not to be regarded as the primitive use of language. The locutionary act might perhaps be thought of that way, but it never occurs independently. In particular, there is no forceless act of 'making a statement' which stands by itself and to which force is added.

The point of this excursus into J. L. Austinian interpretation may be becoming clear. Despite the evocation of Austin in the terminology used, Raz in the passage cited does not use 'force' and 'statement' in the same way as Austin. Raz has not absorbed the lessons Austin was aiming to teach about meaning and language. Nor are his sophisticated positivist associates any more careful. Hart (*Essay on Bentham*, 153) simply reproduces Raz's terminology, as does MacCormick.[4] David Lyons remarks that

---

[4] Cf. *H. L. A. Hart*, 39–40, 43–4; 'Comment: The Normativity of Law', in Ruth Gavison (ed.), *Issues in Contemporary Legal Theory* (Oxford, 1987), 110–14.

we can suppose that what is common to committed and detached judgments is their identical meaning and that what distinguishes them is not part of the meaning of either. We can suppose that one who makes a committed judgment makes the same *assertion* as one who makes the corresponding detached judgment but additionally *expresses* (without asserting) the conviction that someone has a sound reason to respect the law. ('Normativity', 123; his emphasis)

These passages use confidently terms like 'meaning' and 'statement', about whose slipperiness Austin has warned us. We will see how wise Austin's warnings were.

The purpose of distinguishing committed legal statements and detached legal statements at the level of theory is to permit theory to construct a 'point of view' from which a solicitor, for example, may advise a client about his position under law—even to the extent of telling the client that he is required to or forbidden to do something by law—without on her own part accepting the bindingness of the obligation in question. We also want to show how this 'point of view' may coexist, whether within the same person or not, with a 'point of view' which does accept the bindingness of the obligation in question. We also must bear in mind that the language used, 'You ought . . .' or whatever, is typically used by the possessor of either point of view. We want, that is, to allow that (i) Able may say to Charlie 'You ought to deliver those goods' by way of advising Charlie of his strictly legal obligations while not as a matter of fact believing that Charlie really does have a broader non-legal (typically, moral) obligation to deliver the goods; (ii) Baker may say to Charlie 'You ought to deliver the goods' while in fact believing that indeed Charlie really ought—non-legally at least, and, presumably though not necessarily, legally—to deliver the goods; (iii) Charlie may say 'I ought to deliver the goods' while believing that indeed he ought—non-legally at least, and, presumably though not necessarily, legally—to deliver the goods; (iv) Able and Baker and (roughly) Charlie are 'saying the same thing'/'mean the same thing' in each case; (v) Able, Baker, and Charlie are all 'making normative statements'; (vi) Baker and Charlie have a commitment Able need not (and in the case as proposed, does not) have. Since all six demands are intuitively reasonable, there will have to be a way of securing some version of all of them together. But it remains to be seen whether such an 'all-inclusive' theory is a form of, or even compatible with, legal positivism.

The word 'statement' as it occurs in theorists' talk about 'detached legal statements' is ambiguous. It is ambiguous as between (i) the locutionary act of saying 'You ought to deliver the goods', a locution which may be uttered with one force on one occasion and with another force on another occasion, and (ii) a certain specific illocutionary act with a certain specific illocutionary force—a declaratory force, rather than, say, a minatory or exhortatory or verdictive force. 'He makes a statement' may mean either 'He utters a certain locution [sc. a piece of language, rather than a groan or scream]', or 'he states [sc. performs the speech-act of stating, not that of praising]'.[5] Expressions like 'detached legal statement' and 'ordinary/committed legal statement' in principle, therefore, might be instances of a 'statement' in either sense. If, on the one hand, the expressions 'detached legal statement' and 'ordinary legal statement' include the term 'statement' in the first sense, a vocable with a sense and a reference, then neither 'detached legal statements' nor 'ordinary legal statements' in themselves either have or lack 'normative force'; force is a feature of the illocutionary act which a speaker uses such a 'statement', such a locution, to perform. If, on the other hand, the expressions 'detached legal statement' and 'ordinary legal statement' include the term 'statement' in the second sense, a certain kind of illocutionary act, then there is something confusing and confused in the notion of a 'statement with normative force'. Such 'statements', i.e. acts with the illocutionary force of stating, *e vi termini* do not have 'normative force'. That the illocutionary act of stating does not have normative force is exactly the way in which it *qua* illocutionary act differs from such illocutionary acts as advising, ordering, approving, warning, etc. To suppose that 'what is common to committed and detached judgements is their identical meaning and that what distinguishes them is not part of the meaning of either' (cf. Lyons above) is to reaffirm an account of 'meaning' which Austin is explicitly rejecting. What is in common is the locutionary act; but that is *not* what gives the utterance of a committed or a detached judgement its distinctive

---

[5] 'He makes a statement' may also be marking the distinction between persons and parrots; I ignore that here.

character as committed or detached. What gives the distinctive character, and determines the meaning of the total speech-act, is the illocutionary force.

Although it seems that the line of argument using Raz's terminology means by 'ordinary legal statement', 'detached legal statement', etc., illocutionary acts, the resultant terminological constraints are not rigorously observed. This will turn out to be significant. Sophisticated positivism assumes that the doctrine of detached legal statements meets the demand (agreed to be legitimate), to reproduce the way in which laws function in the lives of those who have the internal point of view to law. It assumes that the doctrine does this, because: (i) those with the internal point of view to a set of legal rules accept those rules as genuinely normative and as a result utter normative statements; (ii) the theorist's utterances about the law are also normative statements, albeit detached normative statements. Thus, the claim that detached legal statements are indeed a species of normative statement is crucial to the sophisticated positivist thesis.

Sophisticated positivism now faces a dilemma. If what it is for a detached legal statement to be genuinely a statement is for it to be a specification of someone's position under the law, then, while it is perfectly true that such a statement can be made without any commitment, that is because it can be made from the external point of view, and the making of it does not in any way meet the reproduction demand. If, on the other hand, the detached legal statement is to be construed as indeed having normative force, then the making of such a statement requires the commitment which is part of the conventions for the performance of the appropriate illocutionary act. The adviser, or the theorist, who says 'You ought to deliver the goods', indeed believing that the person addressed ought to deliver the goods, indeed reproduces how it is with one who has the internal point of view to that rule, for the adviser or theorist displays the internal point of view in making the normative utterance.

The claim that the making of a genuinely normative statement requires commitment to the norm asserted amounts to the claim that the conventions for the felicitous performance of the illocutionary act of normative judgement include commitment to the norm in question. In saying 'You ought to deliver the goods', I give it to be understood that I believe that indeed you ought to deliver the goods. Without that commitment the performance, the illocutionary act, is insincere. There is a precise parallel here with factual or descriptive judgements. If I say, 'The car is in the garage', I give it to be understood that I believe the car is in the garage. If in fact I do not believe this, then my illocutionary act of informing (for example) is insincere.

It might be thought that the detached legal statement meets the reproduction demand in that, as Raz puts it (cf. page 138 above), one who utters a detached legal statement does 'use normative language'; she says, 'You *ought* to deliver the goods'. Again, an accurate understanding of Austin precludes such a claim. 'Language' in the sense of vocables with a sense and a reference—locutions—is not inherently 'normative', 'descriptive', or anything else. Locutions are just locutions, available for speakers to use to perform other kinds of speech-acts.[6] What makes a use of language 'normative' is that someone uses a given locution to perform the illocutionary act of making a normative judgement. The best sense that can be made of the expression 'normative language' (for I do not deny it seems perfectly sensible) is that certain terms—'ought', 'right', 'duty', 'should', and the like—are *standardly* or *typically* used to make normative judgements, or are *primed to* make normative judgements. So the adviser who says, 'You ought to deliver the goods', uses language (a locution) primed to make a genuine normative judgement. But it does not follow that she really is making a genuine normative judgement. Her performance will sustain the reproduction demand, however, only if she really is making one.

As has been tacitly acknowledged in the above paragraphs, talk about 'detached legal statements' is not in essence misdirected talk. Very many legal rules are not 'directly normative'. In his taxonomy of types of laws, Honoré divides laws into six kinds: existence laws, rules of inference, categorizing rules, rules of scope, position-specifying rules, and directly normative rules. In Honoré's view, the first five kinds of law, in particular position-specifying rules, are not 'directly normative' in the sense that they are not immediate 'guides to conduct' (*Making Law Bind*, 83). As a result very many of the utterances made in the course of

---

[6] Although there is nowhere outside a dictionary or thesaurus where locutions exist in such a state of readiness. They never so exist in the living of a language.

conducting the legal enterprise will not be normative illocutionary acts. There is altogether nothing wrong with saying that the enunciation or application of a position-specifying rule, for example, occurs via the making of a detached legal statement. The mistake is not to claim that there are such things as 'detached legal statements' characteristically used in the enunciation and application of position-specifying rules: it is rather in the manner of interpreting what it is for something to be a 'detached legal statement'.

The terms 'detached legal statement' and 'ordinary legal statement' refer to illocutionary acts distinguished by their force. An 'ordinary legal statement' is a use of legal language from the internal point of view with full normative force. A 'detached legal statement' is a use of legal language, the language of ordinary legal statements, without the usual normative force of the ordinary legal statement. The making of a detached legal statement is just a conventionally different kind of speech-act from the making of an ordinary legal statement, even though the locutionary act in each case may be the same—that is, the same form of words may be used. One of the differences in convention is that the making of a detached legal statement does not presuppose endorsement, but the making of an ordinary legal statement does presuppose endorsement. It is a mistake to suppose that there is one speech-act only, 'making a legal statement', which either may or may not be accompanied by a certain commitment as a contingent additional feature of any given performance of that speech-act. One is tempted to think that a detached legal statement is really a normative statement only because one interprets the paradigm case, the committed application of a norm, as the making of a detached legal statement plus something else, an endorsement. But to think that is to misunderstand the logic of the matter. There is no way in which the speech-act of making a detached legal statement carries over to and becomes a part of the speech-act of making a fully normative statement.

Sophisticated positivism sees rightly that legal theory must find a way of accommodating speech-acts such as position-specifying statements, while also distinguishing between statements about the law made from the 'bad man's' or external point of view and statements about the law made from the 'point of view of legal science', the point of view of one who is fully knowledgeable of the content of the positive law. The positivist project requires also that statements made from the 'point of view of legal science' are different from fully committed statements made from the 'internal point of view'. Sophisticated positivism attempted to find a theoretical basis for this trichotomy in the notion of the 'force' of an utterance. The 'detached legal statement' as made from the 'point of view of legal science' is 'normative'—unlike statements made from the external point of view which are merely descriptive. But the 'detached legal statement' is not made with the force of commitment. I have shown that sophisticated positivism's theoretical position is metalinguistically incoherent. The distinction within philosophy of language between 'force' and 'statement' implies that 'detached legal statements', if they do not have 'normative force', are not 'normative'. Thus the first route for sophisticated positivism to distinguish itself from simple positivism is blocked. On the other hand, if detached legal statements are 'normative', then they in some form presuppose commitment, and the other route for sophisticated positivism to distinguish itself from anti-positivism is blocked. The point of view of legal science is the point of view of a position-specifier, and in the extreme case a legal-order-specifier. But, since position-specification is only one part of the legal enterprise, to confine legal theory to the point of view of legal science is to condemn it to inadequacy.

2. COGNITIVE AND VOLITIONAL ELEMENTS

The doctrine of detached legal statements is only one device which sophisticated positivism offers to fulfil the reproduction demand. The other is the distinction between cognitive and volitional elements within the internal point of view. Let us now turn to discuss this distinction. The cognitive/volitional distinction putatively serves the following purpose. Take the case of Able, Baker, and Charlie above (page 140). The story goes like this. All three of Able, Baker, and Charlie have the cognitive understanding of the law's requirements in the relevant jurisdiction, so that all three of them know that, according to law, Charlie ought to deliver the goods. Baker and Charlie also have the internal point of view towards the law, so that they too accept that in a broader non-legal (typically, moral) sense Charlie ought to deliver the goods. Able lacks the internal point of view to the law. The difference between

Able on the one hand, and Baker and Charlie on the other—the difference which underwrites what it is for Baker and Charlie to have, and for Able not to have the internal point of view—is that in addition to the cognitive understanding of the law Baker and Charlie have a volitional commitment to the law, whereas Able does not. This story presupposes that the mind can be divided up into independent elements, and in particular that cognitive and volitional elements may be systematically distinguished. It presupposes also that understanding the nature of rules and of rule-following behaviour is in particular a state of mind without a volitional dimension. I shall argue that both these presuppositions are mistaken.

I want first to point out that MacCormick has not appreciated what hermeneutic social theory is emphasizing about the very nature of rule-following behaviour itself. MacCormick speaks as though rule-following behaviour comprised two quite distinguishable elements—(i) the designation of a certain pattern of behaviour as the behaviour in which conformity to the rule consists, and (ii) the preference that the members of the group, whose rule it is, oneself included, follow that pattern of behaviour. MacCormick's conception of a rule is 'representationalist', as it were.[7] A view of rules is 'representationalist' if it considers a statement of a rule to be a linguistic representation of a determinate pattern of behaviour.[8] Now, if representationalism is a correct account of what it is to follow a rule, the possibility of a 'moderate point of view' on the part of the theorist or observer is much more likely. But representationalism is not correct. There is a further point about rule-following behaviour as hermeneutic social theory requires us to see it—namely, that it is beyond a limit a mistake to speak of the content of the rule as being a determinate pattern of behaviour. It is of the essence of

[7] For the term 'representationalist', cf. van Roermund, 'Narrative Coherence and the Guises of Legalism', 313–23 in P. Nerhot (ed.), *Law, Interpretation and Reality* (Norwell, Mass., 1990).

[8] Gibbs's view and the Harré and Secord view (see Ch. 2.3 above) are also clearly representationalist in this sense. What it is for a group to have the rule that men do not wear hats in church is that the statement 'Men do not wear hats in church', together with other statements about answers the group give to questions about what they are doing, is true by correspondence when compared with the behaviour of the group. Despite its subtlety, and despite its quite correct criticisms of some interpretations of Wittgenstein (cf. *Playing By the Rules*, 59–60, 65–7), Schauer's account of the meaning of rules (Ibid. 55–68), relying as it does on 'semantic automony' and the notion of a 'baseline context', is ultimately also representationalist.

rule-following behaviour understood as meaningful behaviour—behaviour of agents with intentions, plans, goals, desires, etc.—that the content of the rule is necessarily subject to diachronic variation and change. The group whose rule it is cannot at a given point of time lay down for ever in the future what the content of the rule will be—what behaviour will count as conformity to the rule and what will not. Only those whose rule it is—those, that is, who accept it as normative—really know what the content of the rule is, because in an important sense *they decide* what the content of the rule is. A rule is not pointless and arbitrary. A rule has a significance which is internal to it *qua* the rule that it is. To understand the rule is to understand this internal significance, and that understanding requires the internal point of view to the rule.[9]

This point about rule-following behaviour has important consequences for what it is to understand the behaviour of a group as the following of a rule. MacCormick's earlier characterization of the 'hermeneutic point of view'—'We have to interpret the meaning of [normative] judgements from the point of view of being the person who passes judgement rather than from the point of view of one who scrutinizes behaviour from the outside' (*H. L. A. Hart*, 32)—is entirely right. Having the point of view of the person who makes normative judgements does not mean merely having the same cognitive dispositions with respect to a pattern of behaviour. It means in part and in some sense having the desires, plans, goals, intentions, preferences, etc., which go with not merely behaving in accordance with the rule but with living with the rule, maintaining the rule, reassessing the rule, adapting the rule, and so forth.[10] MacCormick speaks as though what it is to be in the position of one who passes judgement consists of three and no more than three separate elements—(*a*) the cognition that the rule says, 'In circumstances *C* do *A*'; (*b*) the cognition that here are circumstances *C*; (*c*) the will to do *A* in circumstances *C*. Looked at that way, the cognitions (*a*) and (*b*) seem eminently detachable from the volition (*c*). But that account radically and misleadingly underdescribes the position of one who passes

---

[9] Cf. R. A. Duff, 'Legal Obligation and the Moral Nature of Law', *Juridical Review* (1980), 72.

[10] Cf. here Gerald Postema, '"Protestant" Interpretation and Social Practices', *Law and Philosophy*, 6 (1987), 302–8. Postema argues that Dworkin's account of interpretation in *Law's Empire* is (in my terminology) too 'representationalist'. I express no opinion on that issue. Postema's discussion is valuable in the present context for its rich account of what it is to understand a rule.

judgement. That position involves deciding what to do when the circumstances are only fairly C-ish; when there is another rule which says, 'In C do B', and A and B conflict; when the best one can see to do is not all that A-ish; and so forth. Taking those decisions requires a sense of the goal and purpose of the rule which goes beyond the simplistic tripartite structure of *modus ponens* plus preference. The simplistic structure applies only when the rule is clear and the case in question is an easy case falling clearly under the rule—a 'core', not a 'penumbral' case.[11]

We are speaking here, not so much of what it would be to reproduce the way in which laws function in the lives of those who have the internal point of view to law, as what it is to know what to do to reproduce . . . We are speaking of what it is that one who wishes to reproduce . . . has to know or understand. The claim is the following. In order to be able to reproduce . . . the theorist must know what it is to have the internal point of view to the rule or set of rules in question. In order to do that, the theorist must understand the rule/set of rules as those with the internal point of view understand it/them. In order for that to occur, there must be some overlapping, some sharing, of concepts between the theorist and the group in question. In order to know that a certain performance is a fertility rite, for example, the theorist must certainly know that the performers themselves would understand it that way. One reason why it is a mistake (or at least highly implausible) to understand a football match as a fertility rite is that the performers will never answer, 'Performing a fertility rite', to the question, 'What are you doing?'. But this kind of argument cannot be pressed too far, for the theorist may be able to make out a good case for the accuracy of the description 'ritualized gang warfare' as applied to a football match even though no participant would describe the goings-on that way. The point I am making is a complementary one. Suppose that the performance is a fertility rite: that is, that is how the performers themselves understand what they are doing. What has to be the case for the theorist to be able to say correctly, 'That performance is a fertility rite'? The

---

[11] Schauer (cf. *Playing By the Rules*, 71) would regard any application of a rule which is at variance from what the empirical majority of members of a linguistic community would inductively infer from the existing stock of applications as a change in the rule. Just such a model of the entrenchment of a rule is being rejected here.

theorist must have grown up in a community which itself has the concept of a fertility rite. This may not require that the community actually performs fertility rites still, or even that it once did so. But it requires having the concept, and having the concept means having it from the inside.

Verifying that a performance by some group is a fertility right is much more like the philosophical activity of comparing concepts than it is like the empirical activity of verifying a hypothesis. Martin (*The Legal Philosophy of H. L. A. Hart*, 26) gives as an example of behaviour understandable from the external point of view, 'People who drive through a red light when policemen are watching are usually stopped and arrested'. He refers to this sentence as a 'low-level empirical generalization'. This is a mistake. Consider how much the observer would have to share in the way of concepts in order to know that a certain activity is 'driving', certain idiosyncratically dressed individuals are 'policemen', a certain performance is a case of 'arresting'. If a member of the target group objected, and said, 'They are not policemen; they are community wardens', subsequent discussion would have far more in common with philosophical dialogue than it would with a debate over whether in fact the cat is on the mat.

References to mutual understanding and sharing of concepts seem to conflict with an oft-mentioned ideal of social science. MacCormick mentions the social scientist who, 'in scientific abstraction from any volitional commitment of [his or her] own, seeks to understand, portray or describe human activity as it is meaningful "from the internal point of view"' ' (*H. L. A. Hart*, 43; see also *Legal Reasoning and Legal Theory*, 291). We are talking here about impartiality, and this is not the same thing as lack of endorsement. The impartiality which convention requires for the performance of the family of speech-acts which constitute scientific research is a norm within the practice of social science. This norm is neutral as between empiricist and hermeneutic accounts of social science. Here is an anthropologist of law stating this norm:

The external approach may be manifested in a number of ways. At its most extreme it takes the form of the application to the society under investigation of a theory of law formulated in the context of a different society or culture. But it may take less overt forms; an investigator after describing the social life of a people may use a criterion not recognized by the people themselves to divide the legal from the non-legal. The internal approach is adopted where an investigator, working without preconceptions, attempts to discover the classifications which members of the society use in applying normative notions to behaviour.[12]

The 'internal approach' which MacCormack here recommends seems to be exactly MacCormick's picture of proper anthropology of law. But the former contrasts it, and rightly, not with merely recording convergent patterns of behaviour, but with misapplying the hermeneutic method. One may use all the appropriately designed categories—that is, categories designed according to the norms of this 'internal approach'—and yet may fail properly to follow the hermeneutic method because one takes the categories as referring to events connected by causal laws.[13] Likewise, one may eschew any attempt merely to record convergent patterns of behaviour and make predictions. One may yet fail to produce a worthwhile theory of the law of a given society, because one pays no attention to the content of the internal point of view in that society. Thus, that this norm for social science requires a point of view we may call 'detached' does not mean that the point of view of the social scientist is 'detached' or 'external' in the technical sense built by MacCormick into his 'hermeneutic point of view'. The social scientist's 'detached', i.e. impartial, point of view is nothing other than a version of the true hermeneutic point of view itself.

3. UNDERSTANDING THE LAW

I have been arguing that the 'understanding' which is necessary in order to reproduce the way in which laws function in the lives of those who have the internal point of view to law implies some sharing of concepts with the group with the internal point of view. It will be said that sophisticated positivism has never denied that. Consider again this quote from MacCormick:

[12] G. MacCormack, 'Anthropology and Legal Theory', *Juridical Review* (1978), 216–17.
[13] Peter Winch takes Weber to task for making exactly this mistake (*The Idea of a Social Science*, 112 ff.).

the non-extreme external point of view requires (a) full sharing in the cognitive element of the internal point of view—the understanding of the pattern or patterns of behaviour as such, and (b) full appreciation of, but no necessary sharing in, the volitional element, the will or preference for conformity to the pattern as a standard. (*H. L. A. Hart*, 38)

The remarks about 'sharing in the cognitive element' and 'full appreciation of the volitional element' are intended to elucidate, not repudiate, the sharing of concepts between adviser or theorist or observer and the target person or group. But what is it to 'appreciate fully' without 'sharing' what it is to will conformity to a rule? What is it to 'appreciate fully' what is said by one who says, 'I ought to deliver the goods', when one does not oneself will conformity to such a rule about when goods should be delivered?

One has the suspicion that the facts here are being manipulated to fit a theory, rather than the reverse. In the experience of those who have the internal point of view to some rule or set of rules, their commitment to the rule is an indissoluble amalgam of cognition and volition: their understanding of the rule and what it will require of them is a subtle and continuous interplay of awareness of fact and desire for goal. I appropriate an argument of Gilbert Ryle's.[14] When we speak of someone's knowing the difference between justice and injustice, we do not distinguish two things, her knowledge of certain facts and consequences and her caring about those facts and consequences. To understand justice, to have a sense of justice, is to care. If we find that someone has ceased to care about justice and has become indifferent to justice and injustice, we do not say that she still knows very well what justice is and simply no longer has the will to do anything about it. We say she has forgotten the difference between justice and injustice.

Knowing that a set of rules are legal rules, that together they form a legal system, involves an understanding of law as a social institution. Understanding involves understanding that the enterprise of law has an essential connection with certain social values—with justice, fairness, equality, autonomy, prevention of harm, honesty, and so on. Although different municipal legal systems may differ both in the way and in the extent to which their black-letter law

[14] Cf. 'On Forgetting the Difference Between Right and Wrong', in A. I. Melden (ed.), *Essays in Moral Philosophy* (Seattle, 1958), 156.

reflects these values, law has fundamentally to do with these values and not with values like logical validity, aesthetic beauty, scientific originality, technological fertility, and so forth. Law is distinguishable from other social institutions and enterprises in that we ask in courts of law not, 'Is this a brilliant piece of engineering?', but, 'Does it infringe on patent?'; not, 'Is this statue beautiful?', but, 'Does she have a right to erect it over there?'; not, 'Is this argument valid?', but, 'Does the offering of this argument amount to fraudulent misrepresentation?'. One who understands law as a social institution must understand law's connection with these values, and therefore must understand these values, the values of legality. One cannot for legality divide the cognitive element and volitional element in the way that the story about the 'moderate point of view' requires. The person with MacCormick's 'moderate point of view' or 'non-extreme external point of view' does understand legality. She knows legal rules are in force, and *a fortiori* understands what it is for something to be a legal rule, and *a fortiori* understands legality. Her point of view is therefore not external to legality.

The preceding argument might be thought to run foul of another of the standard cases appealed to by sophisticated positivism to argue for a 'moderate' or 'non-extreme external' point of view. Consider the case, mentioned by Hart and picked up by MacCormick (*H. L. A. Hart*, 40). Hart remarks that 'one vivid way of teaching Roman law is to speak as if the system were efficacious still and to discuss the validity of particular rules and solve problems in their terms' (*The Concept of Law*, 101; his emphasis). MacCormick considers this case analogous to his case of himself knowing it full well to be a true statement of Soviet law that Soviet citizens may not hold or deal in foreign currencies, while having 'little liking for its political and legal principles'. That is, when indulging in the proposed thought-experiment, and advising a fellow student of his rights under Roman law in some hypothesized case, one is in the position of MacCormick making his true statement of Soviet law about foreign currency. But what can be meant by Hart's 'as if the system were efficacious still'? It cannot mean that it is sufficient for this procedure to be a successful way of teaching Roman law that we suppose there to be still a community somewhere in the galactic vastness where Roman law rules, but that we then go on to discuss Roman law as drily, dully, academically, non-vividly as if it were a set of statements on dusty papyri that had no relevance to ourselves. Clearly, Hart envisages that, for the purposes of the recommended teaching procedure, one becomes a citizen of Ancient Rome; one takes upon oneself the role of one whose life is conformity to and application of the rules of Roman law. That is—one seeks to understand Roman law from the internal point of view. One does appreciate the volitional element fully; one is indeed in the point of view of the person who passes such judgements; one does what one would be doing if one were the person making such judgements seriously; one takes Roman rights seriously. The Roman law case indeed shows what a hermeneutic understanding of Roman law amounts to, and how such understanding involves sensitivity to the volitional element in the form of having relevant volitional preferences.

In fact, the analogy with the position of the actor is not without merit. There is one crucial difference between the actor and the teacher/student of Roman law. The actor is (in traditional cases) following a script. That is, the plausibility of claiming that one playing Lear need not share Lear's view of the world has a lot to do with the fact that the lines in which Lear's view of the world is expressed are all there provided for the actor beforehand. Though playing Lear is more than just reciting the lines, it is at least that. The student living Roman law, however, is not just reciting lines from a prepared script: she is in some sense making them up as she goes along. To play the part well, and thus to be a candidate for 'understanding Roman law', involves a grasp of the relevant concepts in a way which is more than just 'playing a role'. The same feature appears in the case of the actor. The understanding of Lear's world-view that is necessary to being able to act Lear well goes beyond the ability to recite the lines given Lear in the play. It involves having the kind of understanding that would enable one to continue to act Lear if improvisatory scenes were added, for example. It involves, one is tempted to say, becoming Lear, making Lear's point of view one's own. It would be an exaggeration to say that in the case of law there are only improvisatory scenes, for there are the laws as inscribed rules. But understanding how to go on when the rules are in force—how to apply them, how to structure one's life and one's world by them—involves more than a cognitive grasp of patterns of behaviour.

Let us return to Honoré's classification of laws, and to his thought that very few laws are 'directly normative' (cf. page 143 above). This classification is embedded in a wider theory of law, which is set out in two other chapters in *Making Law Bind*, 'Groups, Laws and Obedience' and 'The Basic Norm'. The former represents laws as essentially laws of groups, and develops some consequences of this for legal theory. The theory is clearly a kin of Hart's view of laws as social rules, but emphases are importantly different. Honoré highlights the role in the formation and maintenance of groups of 'shared understandings' among the members of the group (cf. *Making Law Bind*, 33–8). The later chapter develops a picture of the rules of a legal system as a whole, kept together by the basic norm.[15] The basic norm is the source of normativity for the whole system of norms or rules. The thought seems to be as follows. The few and 'platitudinous' 'directly normative rules'—e.g. 'Perform contracts', 'Discharge liabilities', 'Give effect to the law', etc. (*Making Law Bind*, 88)—are directly normative because they are directly derivable from the basic norm, (in this case) the duty of co-operation. But what of the normativity of the other rules?

It is extremely plausible to regard the enunciation and application of such rules as non-normative, or descriptive, judgements. But now we can see the crucial importance of the holistic thrust of Honoré's thought. It would not make any sense to divide 'understanding of the law' into two separate compartments, a cognitive understanding of the existence and content of a vast number of rules, and a volitional commitment to a small set of platitudinous norms and a basic norm. It would not make sense, because the rules by themselves do not make sense simply as descriptions. Equally, an isolated volitional commitment to 'Abstain from torts' makes no sense in the absence of rules defining torts, rules for the adjudication of disputes in tort, the capacity to specify and grasp one's position in tort, and so forth. The insight behind the desire to see, for example, position-specifying rules and statements as in some way 'normative', even though they are plausibly not

---

[15] Honoré's proposal for the content of the basic norm is that 'members of a society have a duty to cooperate with one another' (*Making Law Bind*, 111). The matter of the content of the basic norm is not relevant to the present discussion. All I am concerned with is the formal conception of a system of norms held together by a basic norm.

normative but descriptive, is that such rules only make sense in a context of normativity, and rules that are directly normative only make sense in a context of much fuller specification. The idea that we are dealing here with a whole also blunts the edge of the standard cases which supposedly illustrate the 'moderate' or 'non-extreme external' point of view. MacCormick's non-Catholic can perhaps in isolation say, 'You ought to go to Mass'; that it is part of Catholicism to have an obligation to go to Mass is hardly esoteric, specialist knowledge. Likewise Raz's non-vegetarian, who is intelligent enough to know that vegetarians ought not to eat meat. An issue more to the point would be whether a non-Catholic could have written *Brideshead Revisited*, or whether a non-vegetarian could have written *Animal Rights*. My point is not that these are in fact impossibilities; it is that these examples point up better the nature of what is at stake when there is talk of 'full understanding without volitional commitment'. A non-Catholic who knows little more about Catholicism than that Catholics ought to go to Mass is not a candidate for 'full understanding'.

Sheer facts seem to keep intruding themselves into the discussion. It is surely just a fact that Hart and his class are not citizens of Ancient Rome. MacCormick is not a Soviet citizen, nor is he Catholic. Raz's Catholic friend is not an orthodox Jew, and his meat-eating friend not a vegetarian. So it seems absurd to try to bar these persons from any 'non-internal' point of view, if the consequence is to claim that they can understand Catholicism, for example, only by becoming a Catholic. Surely it is just a plain fact about the world that people can understand the requirements of normative systems thought binding by others without regarding the normative system as being binding upon them. Of course, it is a sheer fact, and its factuality is not in dispute. The theoretical issue concerns the appropriateness of different representations of this fact, and in particular what the fact tells us about the possibilities for the point of view of legal theory.

The positivist's account depends on the assumption that understanding of a given normative system as a whole is no more than the aggregate of iterated piecemeal instances of understanding of particular applications of norms. It can be shown that it is impossible for understanding the system as a whole to be so structured.

What is it that the qualified adviser knows? It is actually quite a complicated piece of knowledge; it contains the following four elements:

(a) P is a norm-subject of a system of norms S.
(b) Norm N is in S.
(c) N has the content 'In circumstances C do A'.
(d) P is in C.

The logical, rather than the practical, constraint on understanding of the system as a whole being iterated understanding of particular cases is that S is a computable, axiomatic system such that for any P, N, C, and A the question of whether P should do A is decidable. We have no reason to suppose that law as a social institution is a computable, axiomatic system of this type. Furthermore, we have every reason, including paradigmatically just what it is about law as a social institution that leads philosophers—and even defenders of the moderate point of view —to say that it must be understood hermeneutically, that law as a social institution is not such a system.

Lurking in the background here is the complex and technical issue of the individuation of laws. 'Laws' in the sense of individual statutes or *rationes decidendi* are not independent, self-subsistent norms. Any such 'law' will deploy terminology also deployed in many other such 'laws'. The expositor of the law will make reference to the general concepts for which such recurrent terminology stands as often as she does to a particular statute or ratio. For example,[16] the general defences of the criminal law apply to every provision of it. One can preserve the idea that each (section of each) statute is one law/norm only by postulating that the statement of these defences forms a part of each provision of the criminal code. These criminal 'laws' are thus counter-intuitively represented as vastly more complex than they really are. If one accepts the intuitively more plausible idea that 'laws' interlock and interact (that is, that they conflict with, modify, qualify, support each other in complex ways), then the possibility of understanding of the system as a whole being iterated piecemeal understanding of particular cases is undermined. Moreover, even whether a case such as the Soviet currency case or the Scots divorce law case is properly regarded as a case of the understanding of one particular law is doubtful—although I will not push that

---

[16] Cf. Raz, 'Legal Principles and the Limits of Law', 831.

here. If these points about the individuation of laws are correct, it seems much more plausible to see a municipal legal system as held together holistically by a set of principles or concepts rather than as an aggregate of individualized particular laws.

There are lines of argument here which seem to be flowing in opposite directions. No one seems willing to make the grandiose claim that, in order for the theorist or the adviser to 'understand' a legal system well enough competently to state positions under law, he or she must make a full moral commitment to each and every rule of the system. But we now have two competing suggestions of how to substitute for that grandiose claim one more modest and plausible. The first is the approach of detached legal statements, moderate points of view, and so forth. This approach severs the connection between cognition of what the rules of the system require and volitional commitment to the genuine bindingness of the rules. It awards the theorist or adviser full cognitive understanding without any volitional commitment. The second approach is to retain the interconnectedness of cognition and volition in what it is to understand a legal system, but allow as satisfying the volition requirement something much weaker than full moral commitment. Honoré takes this approach. He makes it clear (*Making Law Bind*, 36) that his required 'shared understanding' among the members of a group is not positive acceptance either in the sense of 'voluntary adhesion' (for it may be the involuntariness of conformity through fear) or adoption as part of a personal morality. In fact, 'what is needed for membership of a group is understanding minus professed rejection'; only the lone wolf who refuses to conform and leaves the pack is excluded.

Honoré's requirement is a very weak requirement. In fact it is arguably no stronger than the 'obedience for his part only' of Hart's citizens at *The Concept of Law*, 112–13, which Hart takes to be quite compatible with the external point of view. This fact is important. If we take seriously the idea that the theorist or adviser, to understand law, must eschew the [extreme] external point of view, then in fact their volitional commitment must be stronger than 'absence of professed rejection'. If we take seriously the idea of legal systems as wholes, then the volitional commitment must be to the system as a whole, and not merely to isolated laws of the system. Or rather, the more it is directed simply towards isolated laws, then, if it is to count as 'non-extreme-external', the more it must embody a commitment to more general legality values which are perceived to be instantiated by some parts of the system rather than others.

We seem to have a choice between two different claims to represent perspicuously how it is with the theorist who is to understand law and legal system well enough to reproduce the way in which laws function in the lives of those who have the internal point of view to law. Both approaches agree that the theorist does not have to share in full commitment to the bindingness of the rules in question. The first approach claims it to be enough that the theorist cognizes the existence and content of law, and appreciates what it is to be committed to the bindingness of law. The second approach argues for some weaker but still genuine volitional commitment, and does so on the grounds that in the understanding of the existence and content of law cognitive and volitional elements are inseparable. The second approach sees unobstructedly what the first only sees through the distorting prisms of positivism.

4. CONCLUSION

The truth behind the doctrines of detached legal statements and moderate or non-extreme-external points of view is that very many legal rules are descriptions of social facts—institutional facts, if you like. Since these are facts, it is unsurprising that they can be asserted to obtain without the assertion being accompanied by an evaluative judgement as regards their obtaining. We have been taking the enunciation and application of position-specifying rules as the palmary example. But to be able to assert that a given social fact exists is not what it is to understand law and legal system. The illocutionary act of position-specifying (to remain with this example) is subject to falsehood: a person's position under law may be wrongly specified. Position-specifying may also go wrong in that it may be done insincerely. The argument for that claim is as follows. The first part of the argument establishes that 'insincerity' is a legitimate dimension of assessment. This part proceeds by showing that legal discourse is to be understood, not in terms of the making of 'statements', but in terms of the performance of locutionary and illocutionary acts. The second part of the argument proceeds so. Given that systems of laws are wholes, and as part of that wholeness are intimately related to certain values, the values of legality, then the understanding of law has a volitional or affective dimension as well as a cognitive dimension. In the case of states of mind such as the understanding of law, it is a mistake in the philosophy of mind to regard these two dimensions as separable. Thus, the normal performance in legal practice is one in which commitment to law is displayed.

Legal practice has the internal point of view to law built into the logic of its practice: the internal point of view is not simply a luxury found only in healthy societies. The constraint of the theorist to reproduce the way in which laws function in the lives of those who have the internal point of view to law means that the theorist too must display the internal point of view, commitment to law. Of course some given theorist may lack the internal point of view to law, but do legal theory anyway from the external point of view. The 'bad man' lacks the internal point of view to law, but (sometimes, at least) obeys the law anyway from the external point of view. There is no more reason to suppose that we have to represent law so that the 'insincere' theorist's external point of view is dispositive of the nature of law than that we have to represent law so that the 'bad man's' external point of view is dispositive of the nature of law. Legal theory not only need not, it should not be committed to the availability of the external point of view for itself. Sophisticated positivism, by showing us so clearly why it is a mistake to take the external point of view of the 'bad man' as dispositive of the nature of law, shows us in the end why it is also a mistake to take an external point of view for legal theory as dispositive of the nature of law. The latter mistake shows why positivism cannot be the correct theory of law.

6

THE ACCEPTANCE OF LAW

1. THE 'PAYNE PROBLEM'

Sophisticated positivism argued two main theses about the acceptance of law. The first is that the minimum necessary and sufficient conditions for the existence of a legal system are satisfied in the case where no one has the internal point of view towards the primary rules of the system, and only the officials have the internal point of view towards the secondary rules. 'Have the internal point of view' is equivalent to 'accept'. The second is that 'accept' means no more than 'regard as a common standard of behaviour', and thus may be instantiated by a range of attitudes which may amount to, but which also may fall short of, full commitment to the standards as morally worthy. These two theses contain the essence of sophisticated positivism's account of the acceptance of law.

This position faces an immediate problem, which we may call, after the person who to my knowledge first urged it against Hart, the 'Payne Problem'.[1] The Payne Problem unfolds in two stages. In the first place, it is claimed, Hart's account is simply inconsistent in the treatment of primary rules. Hart is apparently committed to each of the following:

---

[1] See Michael Payne, 'Hart's Concept of a Legal System'. Rodger Beehler, 'The Concept of Law and the Obligation to Obey', *American Journal of Jurisprudence*, 23 (1978), raises essentially the same problem. His paper was published later, and so came to my attention later, than Payne's, though his n. 7, page 142, indicates it may have been written earlier. The Hodson Problem, as it were, that Hart's minimal legal system is satisfied by a cruel dictatorship (cf. John Hodson, 'Hart on the Internal Aspect of Rules') I take to be the limiting case of the Payne Problem. Roscoe Hill, 'Legal Validity and Legal Obligation', *Yale Law Journal*, 80 (1970), is working the same street. However, he represents the problem as being that the analysis of obligation-imposing rules in *The Concept of Law*, ch. 5, is irrelevant to the analysis of legal obligation on pp. 113–14, the 'minimum condition' passage. As will become clear, it is misleading to think of this passage as giving an account of 'legal obligation'—as misleading as to think of Austin (cf. Ch. 2.4 above) as giving such an account.

(a) If Rule *R* imposes an obligation then *R* is accepted [this follows from the definition of an obligation-imposing rule as presupposing the internal point of view].

(b) The primary rules in the minimal legal system are not accepted by anyone.

(c) The primary rules in the minimal legal system do impose obligations.

These three propositions form an inconsistent set. In the second place, the claim which Hart is implicitly giving up in order to become consistent deprives him of the grounds for saying his minimal legal system is not an Austinian coercive system. He cannot give up (b), for then we would no longer have a minimal legal system. That is, the minimum conditions for a legal system would be stronger than Hart's positivism seems to require (see Chapter 2.4 above). Suppose he tries giving up (a), on the grounds that, since primary rules can exist by being valid, they may thus impose obligations which no one accepts. The point is now made that the law therefore, as Hart admits, coerces its norm-subjects. The claimed difficulty with Austin's theory was that he represented the law as essentially coercive. The minimal legal system is no better. Claim (c) can be retained in the minimal legal system only if either 'obligation' is construed as Austin construed it or the acceptance of the secondary rules by the officials really is enough to create a genuine obligation to obey, and not merely a coercive reason.

We therefore need to re-examine sophisticated positivism's account of the acceptance of law. We will see that it is not possible to avoid an account of law as coercive without abandoning positivism.

2. THE 'HUGHES PROBLEM'

A theme that appears more than once in *The Concept of Law* is that there is one phenomenon to which Austin rightly draws our attention, what Hart refers to as the 'relatively passive aspect' (60, 114) of the existence of a legal system. He has in mind what he calls (ibid.) the 'acquiescence' of ordinary citizens in the results of official operations, their 'acquiescing in the rules by obeying them for [their] part only'. In an earlier paper on legal obligation, he attributed to ordinary citizens acceptance of the fundamental constitutional provisions of their society's legal framework.[2] This claim was criticized by Graham Hughes[3] on the grounds of empirical implausibility. Understanding of constitutional law is a technical matter, Hughes argued, and not normally in the ordinary person's intellectual repertoire. Hart refers in *The Concept of Law* to this criticism as 'just' (248). It thus seems that the stance of the ordinary citizen to the law is more appropriately thought of as 'passive' and acquiescent than as 'active' and accepting.

Note that there is an inverse relationship between the Hughes Problem and the Payne Problem. The more that one emphasizes the 'relatively passive' aspect of life under law, the more one represents the position of the ordinary citizen under the law as that of a coerced subject, and thus of a person external to the law. The more that one emphasizes the voluntary co-operation of the ordinary citizen in the maintenance of the system, the more one seems to be attributing to the citizen an understanding of the law which that citizen seems not to have. In order properly to understand the acceptance of law it will be important to consider whether there is a way between these two complementary obstacles.

3. HABITS OF OBEDIENCE

We have to return to the basic vocabulary of simple positivism and sophisticated positivism in their theories of the acceptance of law. I shall argue the following two theses—that Hart's discussion is infected with an unsatisfactory dualism, and that the ordinary meanings of the terms in the vocabulary are too unstable to ground a technical philosophical theory.

The *OED* defines a habit as a settled disposition or tendency to act in a certain way. Hart regards a habit as a pattern of behaviour, and the habits of a group as a convergent pattern of behaviour among the members of the group. Austin does not define 'habit', but the 'habit of obedience' which creates sovereignty is one that

[2] Cf. 'Legal and Moral Obligation', in A. I. Melden (ed.), *Essays in Moral Philosophy* (Seattle, 1958), 93.
[3] Cf. 'The Existence of a Legal System', *New York University Law Review*, 35 (1960), 1011.

must be found in 'the generality or bulk' of the members of a society, and must be 'permanent', not 'rare or transient'. Although Austin speaks of 'habits of obedience', he speaks also of laws as rules laid down for the guidance of an *intelligent* being by an *intelligent* being having power over him, and commands as wishes or desires conceived by a *rational* being, that another *rational* being shall do or forbear.[4] These three conceptions of 'habit' are not equivalent. Hart's is the odd one out, for Hart associates 'convergent pattern of behaviour' with being 'sheep-like' and with being open to description from the 'extreme external point of view' (cf. *The Concept of Law*, 87). I shall show that a concern with these details on my part is not mere obsessive pedantry.

An efficacious legal system is one in which there is conformity to the law's demands. But what does 'conformity' mean here? 'Conformity' in the most minimal sense means simply a mapping of behaviour on to a norm. That is, norm N says, 'In circumstances C do A'; some individual S is in C and does A; S thus conforms to N. This minimal characterization is much too weak to capture the conformity to law which forms part of acceptance of law.[5] Let us imagine the observer in the extreme external point of view observing behaviour. She formulates a description of a pattern of behaviour in the group. She ascertains that a certain pattern of behaviour is commanded by the sovereign.[6] She sees that the description and the command correspond. Is she now entitled to conclude that the pattern of behaviour is a habit of obedience to a command of the sovereign? No. In addition, she has to establish an appropriate kind of connection between the fact of the sovereign commanding a certain pattern of behaviour and the members of the group displaying that behaviour. The connection would have to be in some way or other causal; the counterfactual would have to be supported that if the command had not occurred the behaviour would not have occurred. It is not difficult to

---

[4] *The Province of Jurisprudence Determined*, vi. 193–6; i. 10.

[5] This minimal level of conformity is defined by Wayne Sumner to be 'conformity' as such; cf. *The Moral Foundation of Rights* (Oxford, 1987), 63, 'in order to conform to a rule I need not even know that it exists or applies to me'. There is no set of canonical meanings which rule out either his idiolect or mine as mistaken. The important thing is the identification of the phenomenon.

[6] I think in fact it is wholly implausible that an observer from the external point of view could identify a 'sovereign', or even a 'command'. But I shall not press the point here. I have written about shared conceptual schemes and their relevance to legal science in Ch. 5.5 above.

imagine how this might go. Suppose the sovereign commanded
A-ing. Was there any pattern of A-ing before the sovereign's
command? Was there such a pattern after? Did the behaviour
cease when the sovereign ceased to command it? Did A-ing
resume when the sovereign again commanded A-ing? And so
forth.

This conformity to law established by the external observer is
what one might call 'ovine conformity' in deference to Hart's
reference (*The Concept of Law*, 114) to a 'deplorably sheep-like'
society. Conformity of this kind is not as straightforward as it
seems. The ambiguities are highlighted by a well-known Gary
Larson *Far Side* cartoon. The picture shows a sheep standing on its
hind legs in the middle of a flock with its forelegs raised high and
an enthusiastic expression on its face. The caption is, 'Wait! Wait!
Listen to me . . . We don't have to be just sheep!' Sheep conform
their behaviour to the sheepdog in a sense which supposes no more
than a causal connection between the activities of the sheepdog
and their activities, of the kind discerned by the external observer
in the previous paragraph. Sheep are the paradigm of obedience
because they never display the range of behaviour which constitutes
disobedience. They do not answer back, question or debate
orders, ignore orders, make derisive gestures when the sovereign's
back is turned, and so forth. They just do what the dog says and
what their leader does. As the cartoon brings out, a society of
sheep which makes the huge leap up the chain of being to self-
consciousness and the capacity for speech and thought does not
become any the less 'sheep-like' if all the sheep do is still
obediently follow their leader.[7] But they are now metaphorically
sheep and not literally sheep. In the case of real sheep, the 'habit
of obedience' to the sheepdog and the leader is of a piece with the
honesty of Wittgenstein's dog.[8] It may presuppose intentional
states on the part of the sheep, but the nature of those intentional
states is delimited by that fundamental difference between animals
and humans Aristotle chose to mark by denying to animals
rationality.

[7] Even when he orders them not to be sheep? Well, really!

[8] 'Why can't a dog simulate pain? Is he too honest? Could one teach a dog to
simulate pain? Perhaps it is possible to teach him to howl on particular occasions as
if he were in pain, even when he is not. But the surroundings which are necessary
for this behaviour to be real simulation are missing' (*Philosophical Investigations*
(Oxford, 1958), sect. 250).

The conformity to law that exists in Hart's 'sheep-like society' cannot be construed as 'ovine conformity', nor is the conformity in the Austinian legal world 'ovine conformity'. Remember Austin's emphasis on the intelligence and rationality of sovereign and subject. Hart likewise does not suppose that the citizens of the sheep-like society have no intentional states; he does not even suppose that they have no intentional states towards the law. He supposes only that their conforming to the law is blind, automatic, uncritical—sheep-like for humans, however natural it may be for sheep.

What is the relation between 'ovine conformity' and 'Austinian conformity', the conformity to law that exists in a society where a habit of obedience has been built up by the fact that the norm-subjects will be visited with evil if they do not comply with the law's demands? Hart implies that 'Austinian conformity' is one kind of 'ovine-conformity', but there is conceptual quicksand here. In his criticism of Austin in chapter 4 of *The Concept of Law*, Hart faults Austin for leaving out the 'internal aspect' of rules, for not leaving room for the 'critical reflective attitude' towards rules which is an essential part of what it is for behaviour to be rule-governed. Hart wavers between defining the kind of obedience which lacks the internal point of view as 'obedience from any motive whatever [sc. other than the fact that there is a law on the matter]' and as the kind of conformity which is found in a 'sheep-like' society of human beings [not of sheep]. Human sheep-like conformity and human conformity 'from any motive whatever' are, however, very different notions. A morally sensitive anarchist will never obey the law just because it is the law. On the other hand, she might often conform to the law, on those occasions where she is satisfied that it is right to do *A* in circumstances *C* when the law requires its norm-subjects to do *A* in *C*. Her reasons for doing *A* in *C* will be fundamentally unconnected, or at best indirectly connected, with the fact that the law requires its norm-subjects to do *A* in *C*. She is on the other hand far from being sheep-like. She conforms to law from some quite specific and articulate motive. The sensitive anarchist exhibits 'indirect moralistic conformity', as it might be called—the conformity to law which involves on each occasion doing what the law requires because one judges such behaviour as morally required independently of whether the law requires it. That is to be distinguished in its turn from 'direct moralistic conformity', where one judges, for whatever reason, that to obey the law as such is the morally right thing to do.

The notion of 'obedience' is in fact doing three quite different jobs in *The Concept of Law*, and Hart does not keep them firmly apart. First, 'obey' and cognates, as pages 19–20 make clear, are terms of art, code-words, for what I am calling 'Austinian conformity', the conformity to law which results from being coerced by threats. Second, 'obey' and cognates are used to refer to 'outward' behaviour describable without remainder from the external point of view, which contains no implication about the intentionality of the entity exhibiting the behaviour. Hart implies this sense when he distinguishes between a 'habit of obedience' as simply a pattern of behaviour and rule-governed behaviour as a pattern of behaviour plus some 'inner' mental accompaniments (cf. pp. 54–60). Third, 'obey' and cognates are used to refer to a pattern of behaviour which may be performed as an expression of a variety of attitudes, while the referrer prescinds from investigation of or reference to the actual attitude accompanying the behaviour. Hart's discourse exemplifies this sense when he speaks about obedience 'from any motive whatever' and obedience 'for his part only' (cf. pp. 113–14). Consider again the anarchist who none the less conforms to some subset of the law's demands because she believes they represent genuine moral duties, and performs the required actions under that description. She does not 'obey' the law in the first sense, since she does not obey out of fear of the consequences and is not coerced. Equally, it is a controversial philosophical hypothesis which would analyse the anarchist's behaviour as 'colourless movement' plus 'inner state'; the truth of such a hypothesis does not follow from the accuracy of the description 'she obeyed the law out of moral respect for its demands as such, and not because the law commanded her'.

Hart also deploys two different conceptions of 'habit'. First, to refer to someone as habitually behaving in a certain way refers to the observable externalities of her behaviour, making no reference at all to the inner mental events that are accompanying the behaviour. It is compatible with behaviour being in this sense 'habitual' that there are no accompanying mental events at all, or at least none of any humanly intentional kind—sheep have 'habits of behaviour' in this sense. Second, to refer to someone as habitually behaving in a certain way refers simply to the fact that she regularly behaves that way; nothing is implied about her reasons for behaving that way. For any given habit, there might be a variety of different reasons for behaving that way, but the reference prescinds from investigation into them.

Confusion occurs because Hart maps these two sets of distinctions on to one another in the wrong way. He interprets the 'obedience' of Austinian conformity as a 'habit of obedience' in the first sense of 'habit', when he claims that part of the difficulty with the doctrine of 'habits of obedience' is that it leaves law-conforming behaviour comprehensible without remainder from the external point of view. But this interpretation is a mistake. Recall the external observer who establishes a causal connection between the occurrence of behaviour and the commands of a sovereign. A causal connection of that brute kind could as well be established between the occurrence of a pattern of behaviour and the sovereign riding around on her Harley-Davidson. But Austin's references to the intelligence and rationality of subject and sovereign show that he does not have such a relationship in mind as the relation between the sovereign and the subjects which creates law. The way that Hart distinguishes between 'habit' as convergent pattern of behaviour and rule-following behaviour implies that both the person with the external point of view and the habit of obedience, and the person with the internal point of view to the rules display the same pattern of behaviour. This fact can be acknowledged. But it is wrong to represent the fact as saying that, while both persons 'obey' or conform to the law, the first person merely 'obeys', whereas the second person 'obeys' and has the internal point of view to her obeying. For if 'obedience' is a code-word for Austinian conformity, then it is just false that the person with the internal point of view displays Austinian conformity and in addition has some other 'mental accompaniments'. Austinian conformity is a habit of conscious conformity to the commands of the sovereign under that description. It is not 'mere external behaviour', although and moreover it is incompatible with possession of the internal point of view.[9]

---

[9] Sumner is guilty of the same confusion. In addition to 'conformity' (see n. 3 above), he defines 'compliance' as conformity to a rule at least in part because of one's awareness of it (*The Moral Foundation of Rights*, 63). The inclusion of the previous term in the definition of the latter term is deliberate; the test for

Only the influence of philosophical dualism produces the thought of habits of obedience and convergent patterns of behaviour as 'merely external' or observable without remainder from the external point of view. The dualistic picture seems forced upon us by the simple fact that we have to make room for the case of 'outward' conformity to law accompanied by 'inward' repudiation. Bishop Bramhall has a good turn of phrase here. In the context of the religious struggles in England in the seventeenth century, where the pressure to make public religious observances was great even if one was a dissenter, Bramhall is at pains to block the inference from public observance to genuine belief. He writes: 'They confound obedience of acquiescence with obedience of conformity'.[10] The public 'obedience' is the same in each case; the private 'acquiescence' or 'mere conformity' is what makes the difference. We have 'external behaviour' plus one set of 'mental accompaniments' rather than another set of 'mental accompaniments'. But we have to realize that when we speak in such terms of 'habits of obedience' and the like, we are performing an abstraction from the actual intentional behaviour of persons; we

compliance entails the test for conformity but not vice versa (ibid.). But how can a test based on self-conscious behaviour 'entail' or include a test based on behaviour that need not at all be self-conscious? The two tests do not stand to each other in entailment relationships. They are simply two quite different and independent tests. The temptation to see the tests related as Sumner sees them arises only because self-conscious behaviour is construed as 'mere' behaviour or 'colourless movement' plus some inner thing else.

[10] *A Just Vindication of the Church of England* (Dublin, 1674), ii. 56. A note about 'acquiescence' in Hart. On page 197 in *The Concept of Law* he treats 'acquiescence' as equivalent to 'obedience' (in his technical sense). On page 114 he refers to the ordinary citizen in the minimal legal system as 'acquiescing in the rules by obeying them for his part alone'. It is not clear whether this sentence makes the two terms equivalent or not. On page 60 Hart writes that the ordinary citizen 'manifests his acceptance largely by acquiescence'. This is equivocal. If 'acquiescence' is equivalent to 'obedience', and 'obedience' is incompatible with 'acceptance', then the remark on page 60 is nonsensical. On the other hand, if the remark on page 60 is legitimate, and 'sheep-like acquiescence' is a form of acceptance from the internal point of view, then it becomes even less clear how Austin so sadly failed in characterizing the nature of law. The *OED* in fact lists as senses of 'acquiesce' and cognates both ones which connote acknowledgement of authority, thus coming close to Hart's 'acceptance', and ones which connote silent or 'mere outward' conformity, thus coming close to Hart's 'obedience'. Thus Hart's slides in the use of 'acquiescence' seem faithfully to reflect ambiguities in the term itself. Hart is using ordinary fuzzy-edged and imprecise terms as if they were hard-edged technical terms, yet without clarifying the hard-edged technical meaning, and this causes difficulty with this part of his theory.

are not referring directly to the actual non-intentional behaviour of non-persons, or of a part of a person.

Wittgenstein considers two cases where we 'speak of a man's angry voice, meaning that he was angry, and again of his angry voice, not meaning that he was angry'.[11] He imagines someone saying that 'in the first case the meaning of the description of his voice was much further reaching than in the second case'. That is, the description in the first case 'reaches under the surface' whereas the description in the second case remains on the surface. The first reaches beyond the surface expression to the real anger beneath, whereas the second reaches only to the surface anger. He goes on to say that the difference corresponds to a *picture*, not to two genuinely different usages of the expressions in the descriptions. We have a picture of an inner state lying behind overt behaviour; but it does not follow that legitimate usages of terms correspond to the picture. 'We naturally use this picture to express the distinction between "on the surface" and "below the surface" . . . But we misapply the picture if we ask whether both cases are or aren't on the surface.' We use the picture naturally to distinguish the 'obedience of conformity' and the 'obedience of acquiescence' or acceptance. But it does not follow that 'conformity' is simply the 'surface' part of 'acceptance'/'acquiescence as acceptance'. If we were to think in those terms, the picture would have taken over. It would have developed a life of its own, and forced our thinking into its pattern. The picture would have become our master, not our servant.

There are two quite different continua of cases here. The first continuum runs from blind, unthinking ('sheep-like', if you insist) conformity at one end to highly self-conscious and articulate conformity at the other end. The second continuum runs from sheer fear of the physical sanction at one end to full commitment to moral worthiness at the other. That these continua are different is shown by the fact that the external point of view may be found anywhere on the first continuum—both the anarchist and the revolutionary self-consciously and articulately repudiate the authority of law. On the other hand, the point of the second continuum is to show that at some stage one passes from the

---

[11] 'Notes for Lectures on "Private Experience" and "Sense-Data"', *Philosophical Review*, 77 (1968), 303–4.

external point of view to the internal point of view as one progresses along the continuum. Hart's complaint about Austin may be seen as the complaint that Austin locates the intentional stance which helps to create law far too near the beginning of the second continuum. Hart's anti-positivistic opponent will say that the same is true of Hart himself. Note though that, *contra* Hart and Sumner, there is *no* continuum which runs from mere convergent patterns of behaviour or, in Sumner's sense, mere 'conformity' at one end to convergent pattern of behaviour plus full commitment to moral worthiness at the other. Hart construes his disagreement with Austin as being where to locate the existence of law on that putative but illusory continuum only because of his thinking of the mind in dualistic terms. The 'picture' of Wittgenstein's discussion has taken over.

We are now in a position to see why it is important to move out from under the shadow cast by philosophical dualism when thinking about the acceptance of law. The notion of a habit as a settled disposition or tendency to act in a certain way is at face value a pre-philosophical or pre-analytic notion. 'Disposition' here does not have to be the technical term of philosophical behaviourism, but merely a reference to the logic of the notion. Now, Hart's vulnerability to the stresses of the Payne Problem and the Hughes Problem is a consequence of his desire to give full weight to the 'relatively passive aspect' of everyday life under the law. I have claimed that the way to a satisfactory account of the acceptance of law will be one which avoids those stresses. I have now shown that Hart's construal of the 'relatively passive aspect' is infected with philosophical dualism. It is tempting now to diagnose that the infection is causing the vulnerability. Perhaps if we cease to think about the 'relatively passive aspect' in dualistic terms, we may be able to construe that aspect in a way which avoids the two Problems, and which thus leads to a more plausible account of the acceptance of law. The price will of course be that such a more plausible theory will be a form of anti-positivism.

4. THE RULE OF RECOGNITION

The coincidence of the two Problems obtains primarily with respect to the Ultimate Rule of Recognition, that secondary rule which is the source of validity for all the other rules of the system. The ultimate rule of recognition, Hart says,

exists only as a complex, but normally concordant, practice of the courts, officials, and private persons in identifying the law by reference to certain criteria. (*The Concept of Law*, 107)

It is clear that appreciation of technical questions of constitutional law is reserved for professionals, and thus that whatever stance the ordinary citizen has towards the ultimate rule of recognition it is unlikely to be the full internal point of view. Thus it seems most plausible to represent the stance towards the ultimate rule of recognition of the ordinary citizen as one which requires little in the way of specific mental accompaniments. The price to be paid, and Hart clearly thinks it worth paying, is that the citizen then merely 'obeys' the law, like an Austinian subject.

Let us look more closely at the characterization of the ultimate rule of recognition above. As previous discussion has indicated (page 167), whatever intentional stance towards the law we regard as necessary to create law, it has to be one in which the law goes under the description 'the law'. The ultimate rule of recognition is a normally concordant practice of *identification*. What does this mean? Even if we restrict attention momentarily to the officials, the 'practice' does not refer merely to explicit verdicts relating (in Canada) to cases involving the documents specified in sect. 52(2) of the Constitution Act 1982.[12] A court which unhesitatingly rejects an act by a corporation or person on the ground that it infringes a controlling statute is as much participating in the 'concordant practice' of identification as the Supreme Court in a Charter case. That is, the Supreme Court displays its acceptance of the ultimate rule of recognition explicitly, by acknowledging a decision as required by the Charter. The other court does so

[12] These documents are the Canada Act 1982, a statute of the Westminster Parliament, which includes the Constitution Act containing the Charter of Rights and Freedoms; 30 other Acts and orders which are schedules to the Constitution Act; and any subsequent amendments to the foregoing. As Peter Hogg points out (*Constitutional Law of Canada* (2nd edn., Toronto, 1985), 6–7), the wording of sect. 52(2) says merely that the Constitution of Canada 'includes' these documents. There are a number of other plausibly constitutional documents, including, e.g., the Supreme Court Act, which are not on the schedule. There are also those conventions of government which 'are not contained in any authoritative written instrument'.

implicitly, by applying a rule which is valid by the requirements of the Constitution of Canada. So the practice is misleadingly described as one of 'identification'. It would only be in the rare case that the issue before a court would be resolved by a decision which *identified* a norm as a valid rule. The concordant practice is far more one of the *use* or *application* of certain rules rather than others, rules with the proper 'pedigree'. The participants in the practice all agree that a norm is a valid legal rule just in case it has a certain pedigree, and they agree on what that pedigree is. 'Valid legal rule' here means that the rule is properly applied in, for example, the adjudication of disputes or in the specification of legal position. The norm is one such that understanding of it is properly an essential element in the possession of 'legal expertise'.

We seem now though to have simply shifted the problem, by substituting 'use' for 'identification'. Hart (*The Concept of Law*, 114, 117) uses the expression 'accept and use', almost as if this was a hendiadys. He also (*The Concept of Law*, 59–60) distinguishes legislators making law within their powers, courts applying laws in adjudication, and experts advising under law from the ordinary citizen who keeps the law, makes claims, and exercises power under it, thus manifesting his or her acceptance largely by acquiescing. A variety of different cases need to be here distinguished. There is certainly a sense in which the officials of the system actively 'use' both the secondary rules which regulate their official duties and the primary rules which they apply in their daily execution of their professional duties. There is a sense in which every citizen in everyday life makes use of private law—in using public transport of civic or private ownership, in making purchases at stores, and so forth. The citizen driver also makes use of a particular regulatory framework. Even though we may not every day write a cheque or make a deposit or buy or sell an investment, our money is every day subject to and (usually) protected by law. Moreover, every citizen benefits from the existence of set and enforceable procedures for the undertaking of voluntary obligations, even though that diffuse benefit is distinct from the particular benefit gained from embarking on a particular undertaking. Some parts of private law are highly specialized, and only those in certain positions will make use of it—immigration law, the law of libel, copyright law, etc. Every citizen 'uses' in the sense of 'benefits from' 'public good' laws such as laws imposing licensing standards, pollution regulations, safety standards, and so forth. In these cases, it is not the citizen who 'uses' the law in the sense of immediately abiding by the law—that will be the manufacturer, the lawyer, doctor, innkeeper, etc. But the laws daily affect our lives.[13] Every citizen (or the vast majority of citizens) 'uses' the criminal law in a different sense from the regulatory framework. For any who do not break the criminal law abide by it. Only the milk manufacturer abides by milk-purity regulations, though many people benefit from this abiding. But all who do not steal abide by the law against stealing, and so in a sense 'use' it.

In short, the problem is not that the term 'use' is too opaque to describe clearly how citizens stand to the legal system. The problem is rather that citizens stand to the system in many different ways, and this variety is concealed by the deployment of a single term like 'use'. This is, though, a significant result. For, while Hart and Hughes have rightly pointed out that the officials' and the citizens' stances to the law cannot be reduced to one model, Hart has adopted none the less one model of what it is to 'accept' the law, the one he finds in the officials as they daily enact their official duties. 'Acceptance' as a state of mind is one determined to exist as a straightforward function of episodes of interaction. Furthermore, the notion of 'habit', with which 'accept' is contrasted, is also ambiguous. Two quite different cases may be distinguished. The first is the case of some personal mannerism of which the person might not at all be aware, such as walking with one's hands joined behind one's back, or (as I'm told I behave) smoothing the hair forward while lecturing. 'Habitual' behaviour in this sense can certainly be 'sheep-like' in the sense of 'mindless'. But when Aristotle in *Nicomachean Ethics*, ii. 6 and elsewhere argued that virtues should be regarded as *hexeis* or 'dispositions', and that a virtue is a disposition to choose according to the mean, he did not mean to urge the moral value of a sheep-like existence. Instead, he meant to depict the virtuous person as the person who

---

[13] Soper misleadingly talks of the 'involuntary, passive stance' of those who benefit from public good regulations (*A Theory of Law*, 72). I think the remark is misleading, because our stance towards such regulations when we simply live in an environment which they regulate is neither 'active' (unlike the manufacturer or the environmental activist) nor 'passive' (unlike the residents of the company town who put up with pollution for the sake of jobs).

had developed the capacity to do the good thing without thinking, who had internalized virtuous behaviour to the point where it had become (as we say) 'second nature'. This second sense of 'habitual', so far from being incompatible with the internal point of view, in fact presupposes it. Hart, however, concentrates only on the first paradigm of 'habit'. It is at least possible that, by his concentration on one paradigm of both 'accept' and 'habit', Hart has presented a false picture of the acceptance of law. I shall now argue that such is indeed the case.

5. INTERACTING WITH THE LEGAL SYSTEM

It is not difficult to see how the concentration on one paradigm might have arisen. I surveyed above different ways of construing the notion of 'using' a legal system. If we think of 'using' as 'directly interacting' (in some sense), then it is easy for the officials' participation and certain instances of citizens' participation to be the paradigms of 'using'. Being served with a writ, suing for breach of contract, being arrested, voting on a bill, hearing a Charter of Rights case, being given a parking ticket, and so forth, will all be instances of directly interacting with the legal system. If this is the model for 'using' the legal system, then it is clearly so that officials of the system 'use' it far more than do ordinary citizens. Moreover, if 'use' is at all closely connected with 'accept', then it is very easy to assume that the system will function only if acceptance of law is found in officials, and that acceptance of law is therefore not required of citizens. For 'use' in this sense of 'direct interaction' with the legal system does not imply 'acceptance' for many activities that citizens might undertake. A black person in South Africa, for instance, may hire a lawyer to pursue such lawful avenues as exist for getting detainees released from prison, while altogether repudiating the internal point of view towards a legal system based on apartheid.

As we saw above, the Hughes Problem forced Hart to reconsider his optimism about citizens' 'acceptance', and to prefer the Payne Problem as the lesser of two evils. He did not take this option arbitrarily. Assume *arguendo* that Austin did indeed set jurisprudence going in the wrong direction by emphasizing habits of obedience to a sovereign, commands backed by threats, and so forth. Austin, we might say, obscured the difference between conformity which is 'sheep-like' or 'for any reason whatever', on the one hand, and conformity from the internal point of view on the other. All the same, Austin was not obtuse. There is, as Hart remarks, a 'vital difference' (*The Concept of Law*, 112) between the behaviour of officials in relation to the law and the behaviour of ordinary citizens in relation to the law. This difference is such that to say that the latter 'obey' the law is pretty much the truth, whereas to say that the officials when carrying out their official duties 'obey' the law distorts enormously the nature of rule-making, -identifying, -applying, and -enforcing. Austin was very well aware of that difference, even if he thought that legal rules were commands. Moreover, to say that legal rules are commands of superiors to inferiors is not at all a bad way of marking that difference. Hart tried to combine Austin's insight with his own by thinking of the behaviour of the officials in relation to the law as essentially 'active' and the behaviour of the ordinary citizens in relation to the law as essentially 'passive'. The combination works as follows. One can indeed obey a rule passively/acquiescently, so that Austin's insight can be preserved; it is rules that can be obeyed passively, so Hart's own insight can be preserved. However, acceptance and the internal point of view are clearly incompatible with passive obedience. Therefore, it seems extremely plausible to say that only the active officials really accept the legal system.

6. THE DISPOSITION TO ACCEPT THE LAW

Let us review so far the discussion of the acceptance of a legal system. The Hughes Problem is a real problem. True, genuine acceptance of the law implies more than mere conformity of external behaviour to the law: it requires some intentional element. None the less, it is counter-intuitive to represent the ordinary citizen as interacting with the law in just the way that the official of the system interacts with the law. The citizen's mental stance towards the law cannot be represented as embodying the knowledge of the professional. On the other hand, if it is a mistake to represent the law as a system of coercive commands, then the Payne Problem is a real problem too. One cannot pay the price for avoiding the Hughes Problem that one leaves the citizen as conforming to law only through sheep-like acquiescence or a fear of being visited with evil. Justice is not thereby done to the demand for an adequate account of the internal point of view to law. We need a way of understanding how citizens accept the law which none the less preserves the real difference between the role of citizen and the role of official. We need a conception of how the ordinary citizen interacts with the law that manifests acceptance, while acknowledging that this acceptance is not manifested in the way that the officals' daily and continuous intentional operation of the system in accord with its secondary rules manifests their acceptance of those rules.

Let us return to the philosophy of mind and its bearing on the question of the acceptance of a legal system. I have quoted already Wittgenstein's claim that surroundings are necessary to make a particular piece of behaviour an expression of a mental state (cf. page 164 above). Here is a passage from Wittgenstein's *Brown Book*, which makes a similar claim about the idea of voluntary action:

Acting voluntarily (or involuntarily) is, in many cases, characterized as such by a multitude of circumstances under which the action takes place rather than by an experience which we should call characteristic of voluntary action.[14]

Wittgenstein in this passage is primarily concerned to talk about the nature of understanding, and this remark about voluntary action is thrown in by the way. There are in fact two points to be made and this is only one of them. The other is implicit in his discussion of grief in Part II of the *Philosophical Investigations* (pp. 174, 187), where Wittgenstein says things like 'Why does it sound queer to say: "For a second he felt deep grief"? Only because it so seldom happens?' When one is dealing with a mental state like grief, or understanding, or, I want to say, the acceptance of a legal system, not only is one dealing with a state whose logic is that of a disposition existing over time, not that of an episode; one is also dealing with a state whose existence is criterially linked to a certain context. These points are independent though collaborative

[14] L. Wittgenstein, *Generally Known as the Blue and Brown Books* (New York, 1965), 157.

in the following way. It is true that, for example, a particular
episode in a person's life is the expression of grief—tears come to
his eyes and he falls silent. But what makes that episode the
expression of grief—rather than, for example, dismay or tearful
anger—is in part the context in which the episode occurs. A loved
one has been lost, there are other similar episodes around the
same time, and, most importantly, he is in a culture where grief is
expressed thus. Even though tears and silences are stronger
candidates for 'natural reactions' than the wearing of black
armbands and the closing of businesses, they are still culturally
conditioned. Thus, to grieve is to be disposed to certain reactions,
and to be so disposed in a certain cultural context.

Concentration on the cases where a person directly interacts
with the legal system in constructing the paradigm for 'acceptance'
selects as the paradigm an act which is a dateable episode. As a
paradigm for the acceptance of a legal system, however, the
signing of a contract or the making of an arrest is liable to mislead
in two ways—first, these events are episodes rather than dispositions, whereas accepting the law is a dispositional stance, not a
dateable episode: second, a genuine signing of a contract, despite
what the liberal paradigm takes it to be, is not a mere episode; it
requires a cultural context, in the form of an understood set of
rules—not any signature on a piece of paper is a signing of a
contract. I want to suggest now how construing acceptance as
primarily a long-term disposition in a social context provides a
more satisfactory picture of the 'relatively passive aspect' of law,
the everyday stance of citizens towards the law.

Let us look again at some remarks of Hart himself. On page 60
of *The Concept of Law* he remarks that the ordinary citizen
manifests his acceptance of law largely by acquiescence in the
results of the officials' activities. Let us call the episodes which
count for purposes of determining acceptance 'manifestations' of
acceptance, where 'manifesting' means weakly 'giving evidence',
not strongly 'giving conclusive evidence'. This comment about
acquiescence Hart then glosses as the fact that the citizen 'keeps
the law which is made and identified in this way, and also makes
claims and exercises powers conferred by it'. Pages 98 and 107
concede to 'private persons' as well as to officials the ability to
identify laws and to use them. Hart also on page 99 refers to the
use of legal language in a certain way as being evidence for

acceptance, for example, the use of expressions of the form 'It is the law that . . .'. Finally, on pages 136–7 he makes clearly the point that acceptance, or possession of the internal point of view, is quite compatible with the occurrence of law-conforming behaviour being on some given occasions quite thoughtless and instinctive. Let us apply these points to the case of the ordinary citizen and the law.

One must certainly count in while assessing the acceptance of law by ordinary citizens the occasions when they overtly make claims and exercise powers. My argument is an argument against views which count in only such episodes. We must also take seriously as genuine manifestations of acceptance the use of normative language and the keeping of the law. Granting the fact that my view of what the law is does not have the status that my lawyer's does, and that each of those does not have the status that Bora Laskin's or Brian Dickson's did, and especially when they sat as Chief Justice, none the less I see no reason not to and every reason to count informal use of normative language as part of the episodes which contribute to the acceptance of law by ordinary citizens. After all, Hart mentions as part of the evidence for a system of rules existing that deviations are regarded as open to criticism, threatened deviations meet with pressure for conformity, and criticism is regarded as legitimate. It is extremely difficult to see how all that could go on without the use of normative legal language.

However, the proposed criterion that really interests me is that of 'keeping the law'. I think Hart is quite right about this, and that he overlooks its significance. I manifest, i.e. give evidence of, my acceptance of criminal statutes every time I do *not* murder, do *not* steal, do *not* assault a policeman in the execution of his duty, do *not* commit contempt of court, and so forth. As Schauer has rightly observed, the number of times when a person explicitly seeks legal advice 'is dwarfed by the number of times that the law guides behaviour without any intervention whatsoever' by officials of the system ('Easy Cases', 413). Schauer points out that any case where behaviour is otherwise than it would have been but for the law qualifies as a 'legal event', and claims, again rightly, that 'it is only because of the frequency with which the law is followed that the significance of this commonplace phenomenon is ignored' (ibid.). In fact, one may go further. For an unthinking observance of law to be a 'legal event' it is not necessary that the counterfactual 'if there had not been a law, he would have behaved differently' is true. Every failure to commit incest is a legal event even if it is true that we are 'hard-wired', or deterministically 'soft-wired' by culture, not to commit incest. The same point may be made for any so-called *mala in se*.

Here we need to remember the distinction between legal duties and legal prohibitions. When I have a legal duty of care towards my neighbour, I manifest my acceptance of that duty by taking such care—warning her I am mixing explosive chemicals, doing it far from the property line, and so forth. But where the law prohibits something, I manifest my acceptance of that prohibition, not by acting, but by omitting to act. To put out one's hand towards the cookie jar and withdraw it, or to turn down the offer to cut one in on a good caper that one just received in a pub are certainly among kinds of action that manifest acceptance. But there is no good reason for a prejudice in favour of commissions over omissions. Turning offers down and the like are not dissimilar to criticizing, pressing charges, suing for damages, marrying before witnesses, because they are 'active'. But suppose one simply never steals. The 'passive' nature of that by comparison should not blind us to the fact that *not* stealing, raping, driving while impaired, etc., is in fact *actively* to lead a law-abiding life. If the constraint is that acceptance must be inferred chiefly from what people 'actively' do, it is perverse to count a failure to steal as activity of the relevant kind only if it is accompanied by something like turning down a proposal in a pub.

Likewise, active episodes in relation to public good regulations may be confined to those who bring suit if the regulations are broken or who campaign for tightening or relaxing the regulations. But there is no more reason to deny the attribution to me of acceptance of milk purity regulations, e.g. when all I do is buy milk, than there is to deny the sleeping virtuous person his or her virtue. Although there is room for episodes in the analysis of virtue, their role is more complex than directly to provide the evidence for the possession of virtue. Aristotle distinguishes two aspects in the performance of virtuous acts—the development of the disposition to act virtuously, and the exercise of that disposition on some given occasion by performing a virtuous act.[15]

[15] Cf. *Nicomechean Ethics*, i. 8, ii. 1; *de Anima*, ii. 1.

The virtuous person is still virtuous while asleep,[16] and a virtuous act is only centrally so when done by the virtuous person. Precisely the same act done by one learning to be or feigning to be virtuous is 'virtuous' in some derivative (though easily comprehensible) sense.

What makes the sleeping virtuous person virtuous is the truth of a variety of counterfactuals—if she were awake and in such-and-such circumstances, she would act thus and so. The truth to the talk of the 'relatively passive aspect' of the legal system is this—that for most ordinary citizens the occasions on which they directly interact with the legal system are relatively few. I make this concession, though I have given some reasons above for thinking it none the less to be a mistake (cf. pages 178–9). But as long as the attribution of the acceptance of law can be supported by the truth of counterfactuals, there is no reason to regard the 'relatively passive aspect' of law as evidence of sheep-like acquiescence. The surrounding cultural context is very different from that of the sheep paddock.

I distinguished above (pages 116–7) two different senses of 'habit', a sense which was compatible with the behaviour of animals being called 'habitual', and one which was not. An episode in which a gunman points a gun and says, 'Your money or your life', is not in itself evidence of a 'habit of obedience'. Part of the reason why Austin emphasized 'habits of obedience' was his awareness of the twofold generality of law. Laws differ from the commands of a gunman in being both commands of classes of acts, and commands addressed to classes of people. Law is also continuous and persistent, not occasional. These facts seem to imply a greater degree of conscious complicity on the part of the law-abiding than the simple model of commands backed by threats allows. Hart's proposal, to include in the analysis of law the internal point of view to law, but to say that law, to be law, may be obeyed 'for any motive whatever' is an attempt to include complicity, but to have it still as a formal notion. The price is an essentially coercive model of law, and moreover one that seems to depend on a separation of mind and body of an implausibly dualistic kind. The view being presented here is one that in a sense reinstates the notion of 'habit' as a way of understanding law-abiding behaviour. The importance

[16] The truth of this remark is not confined to those specialized occasions where being asleep is the virtuous thing.

of construing the 'habit' as the developed disposition of an intelligent being is that its 'passivity' implies a 'thick' notion of complicity, one that involves acceptance of the legitimacy of the law's demands. It becomes, as it might be put, 'second nature' to us to obey the law. 'Second nature' might be distinguishable from 'first nature'—let us suppose that non-humans only have 'first nature'—but none the less for that 'second nature' is 'nature'.

Here it is necessary to investigate seriously what it is to take the internal point of view to law. It is not simply a matter of producing episodes which manifest the internal point of view. It is a matter of a stable, long-term disposition to produce such episodes. I have been arguing that, once this claim is granted, the major motive for, and the major reason for, interpreting the 'relatively passive aspect' of everyday life under the law as a mode of 'sheep-like acquiescence' disappears. None the less, some account is needed of why it might be 'second nature' to obey the law, other than the account which has been ruled out of obedience coerced by threat. Antony Duff has argued that

we can explain what it is to accept a legal rule, and what the significance of such acceptance, by officials or citizens, is within a legal system, only if we explicate the kinds of significance or value which are internal to this, as to any, kind of rule . . . . ('Legal Obligation', 79)

He quotes Aquinas on law as an ordinance of reason for the common good and says that (82) 'if law is essentially a rational enterprise of this kind, a legal system . . . must be justified to [its citizens] by an appeal which refers to some conception of the common good'. In other words, it is true that simple positivism errs through omitting reference to the internal point of view, and to the acceptance of law. But sophisticated positivism, in deeming law to exist even in the minimal legal system where the internal point of view is confined to the officials, in fact no more than simple positivism takes the internal point of view seriously. By construing the internal point of view to law as a matter of the successive production of episodes of interaction, sophisticated positivism omits to take into account what sort of enterprise law is. Law addresses itself to the citizen as much as to the official. It addresses itself to the citizen *qua* rational agent, not *qua* manipulable sheep. It claims to earn acceptance by standards of reason, justice, and the common good. But if a stable and functioning legal system exists, and the system is not a coercive system, then it follows that the system must be accepted. And if a normative system is not a legal system unless it is not coercive, then a normative system is not a legal system unless it is accepted. To point to a largely non-coercive and efficacious legal system is therefore to point to an entity which is paradigmatically a legal system, not merely a healthy example of something which is just as much a legal system even if coercive and not 'healthy'.

7. CONCLUSION

The most simple, and perhaps most simplistic, account of the acceptance of a legal system is one which reduces acceptance to passive conformity. But if we take seriously the differences between humans and sheep, then we see that there is something deeply misleading about looking at human conformity to law as 'sheep-like'. We also have the sense that to represent the normativity of law as purely coercive is to distort law. It is to imply, what is not the case, that we would have the concepts of law and legality that we have even though history contained nothing but repressive regimes.

However, if we start to take seriously the intentional element in acceptance of law, and we interpret the intentional element in terms of the knowledge of and stance towards the technicalities of law found among officials, it remains hard to see how citizens can accept the law. On the other hand, if citizens do not accept the law but merely conform to its demands, then law remains from the point of view of its citizens a coercive order.

Theory now faces a dilemma. On the one hand, acceptance by citizens cannot be the same as acceptance by officials; on the other hand, acceptance by citizens has to be genuine acceptance. I have suggested that the obstructive force of this dilemma derives from assuming an episodic model for acceptance and consent. If acceptance is construed in terms of a disposition to display law-abiding behaviour, then there is no bar to finding that the ordinary citizen accepts the law. The ordinary law-abiding citizen's inter-action with the law is as deliberate and complicitous and as enduring as that of the professional official.

Then we have to ask the question of whether it is plausible to construe such acceptance as simply contingent. Is it purely a matter of historical accident whether a legal system is 'healthy' or 'sheep-like'? If it is a perversion of law that the legal order is a coercive order, then it cannot be contingent that law is accepted. But if that is true, then the merit of law is not separate from its existence. And if that is true, then positivistic or content-independent accounts of law cannot be correct as theories of law.

The insight that legal theory needed to take into account the point of view of those who accepted the law arose within the positivistic tradition. It arose in connection with the insight that to represent law as a system of commands backed by threats is to misrepresent law. But if those insights are valid insights, then legal theory is impelled irresistibly away from legal positivism.

7

PRINCIPLE AND DISCRETION

1. ADJUDICATION AND JUSTIFICATION

The transition from simple positivism to sophisticated positivism with respect to discretion and principle is the transition from a crude, 'two-step' view of adjudication to a more complex analysis. Sophisticated positivism rejects both parts of the 'two-step' view. It rejects the thesis that, once the state of settled or black-letter law has been established, the discretion the court has to 'go beyond' settled law is 'strong' and untrammelled. It also rejects the thesis that settled law exercises a control over the legal decision which cannot be modified. It favours instead a more subtle model of the relation between settled law and other factors, a model which permits some degree of mutual accommodation. Of course, sophisticated positivism is still positivistic in that it equates law with settled law, and analyses 'legal principle' in ways that do not allow materials other than settled law to be part of 'the law'. But none the less sophisticated positivism acknowledges the legitimate influence of factors other than settled, positive law strictly conceived on the judicial decision.

These theoretical moves rest on some intuitive insight about the nature of law. We must consider whether this insight can ever be fully articulated in a positivistic theory. There seem to be two thoughts underlying the rejection of the 'two-step' view. The first is that formal justice or consistency of treatment is important to the rule of law. Were that not so, then there would be no desire to take the first of the two steps. The distinction between a system of absolute discretion and a legal system is fundamental. The second thought, by contrast, is that some legitimate goal of law is well served by enriching the nature of the legal materials available to the court beyond settled law narrowly conceived.

The first thought is important because, as has been acknowledged already,[1] it is a pre-philosophical datum that a legal system is an *institutionalized* normative system. Positivism draws strength from arguments by anti-positivism that, to be law, law should conform to some moral ideal. Such an argument seems to repudiate the institutional nature of law, and yet law is unmistakably institutional. The first thought, however, wants law to conform to some distinctively *legal* ideal. It is an ideal *of law*, not of morality, that adjudication should be formally consistent. We should treat the second thought in the same way. The point is not that law will serve some moral purpose central to the good of the community if the legal materials available to the court are enriched. Rather, the point is that law will serve some purpose internal to law if the legal materials available to the court are enriched.

One single thought underlies both of the above, a thought which has been well expressed as 'getting *this case* just right'.[2] The ideal of getting the particular case just right is an ideal of justice in law. 'Getting just *this* case right' as an ideal of justice has much to do with a particular set of traditions in political morality. Litigants before a court are thought of primarily as individual persons, as individual members of the kingdom of ends. They, and so the circumstances in which they come before the court, are unique. They have a basic right to an individualized decision suited to the special nature of their particular case. To do justice by such individuals is to give a decision which gets *their* case just right. Decisions made according to inevitably over- or under-inclusive rules which do not respect the circumstances of a person's individual case thus easily appear unjust. The ideal of consistency of treatment is another ideal of law, and ultimately has the same roots. For if it is just to treat individual *A* a certain way, and individual *B* is in exactly the same circumstances, then it is necessary, to do justice to *B*, to treat *B* in the same way as *A*.

The thought underlying both has to do with the same issue as we raised in Chapter 1.6 above—the rejection of 'palm-tree justice', adjudication which consists of giving a decision about a particular

---

[1] In the Introduction, sect. 2.
[2] Frederick Schauer, 'The Jurisprudence of Reasons', *Michigan Law Review*, 85 (1987), 847; his italics. Cf. also *Playing By the Rules*, 137: 'We equate Solomon's wisdom with justice . . . because he came up with exactly the right solution for the case.'

case quite independently of any other particular case. Our question is, what does it tell us about the nature of law if intuitively we require adjudication to be consistent and judicial decisions to be 'just right'? If it were not necessary that a judicial decision be backed up by the kind of reasoning which could constitute a justification for the decision, then there would be no need to be afraid of absolutely discretionary judicial decision-making. It is internal to the nature of law that judicial decisions are *justified*.

What is it for a legal decision to be justified? Here are two contrasting responses. According to the first, the adjudicatory obligation of a judge is to apply settled law to the material facts of the case before them, and to give that verdict which settled law requires. The judge is an official of a social institution. The institution has its own rules. The obligation of the judge is to adjudicate in all and only the ways required by the rules of the legal system. When and only when a judge fulfils that requirement is the judge's decision justified. According to the rival theory,[3] the fact that a particular decision is required by the institutional rules of the legal system has nothing at all to do with whether the decision is justified. Whether a decision required by the rules of an institution is justified depends on considerations quite other than the matter of requirement by the rules of an institution. The latter is a requirement of 'derivability'. The 'derivability' of one statement from another statement is an issue of formal logic, and as such quite different from the 'defensibility' of the derived statement. A derived statement is defensible when it is derived from morally sound premisses. Justification has to do with 'defensibility'. 'Justified' means 'morally justified'; the decision is the morally right decision to take. That is a quite general point about what 'justification' means; the present issue about the adjudicatory obligations of a judge is but a special application of the general point.

Stated in those extreme terms, neither of these views seems plausible. In easy cases, a legal rule states unambiguously that a certain set of material facts have a certain legal significance; there

[3] Something very close to this theory is defended by David Lyons in recent writings; see 'Justification and Judicial Responsibility', *California Law Review*, 72 (1984), and 'Derivability, Defensibility and the Justification of Judicial Decisions', *Monist*, 68 (1985). See also William Conklin, 'Clear Cases', *University of Toronto Law Journal*, 31 (1981), 247; Jeffrey Goldsworthy, 'The Self-Destruction of Legal Positivism', 456–7.

is no other relevant controlling rule; those material facts unambiguously obtain. In such a case the judge is then uncontroversially required to give the decision the rule dictates. But in hard cases, the rule is not unambiguous, or more than one rule is relevant, and conflicting results each seem plausible. To require the judge in a hard case straightforwardly to apply the law seems unrealistic. Any acceptable version of the former theory must say something about the adjudicatory obligations of judges in hard cases. Moreover, the second theory makes a mockery of the notion of law as a social institution. If applied *au pied de la lettre*, it would license a judge to disregard all authority and arguments of counsel and simply to decide on the basis of what he or she decided, after however conscientious a deliberation, was the morally correct decision in the case.[4] But judges are not *qua* judges purely and simply moral agents and deliberators. It may be right to say by way of consciousness-raising that judges should be aware of the way in which whether to decide as the law requires may be a moral issue; it is surely right to say that to put on the wig and robes does not require taking off morality, and that in extreme cases a judge would act the better for refusing to apply the law, or resigning his or her appointment. None the less, a judge is a judge. Here too realism may be lacking; to require judges to be prepared continually to suspend their institutional obligations for independent moral assessment is unrealistic. Any acceptable version of the second theory must say something about the adjudicatory obligations of judges *qua* officials of the law as a social institution.

I propose not to prejudge the development of an acceptable theory of legal justification by calling only one kind of proposed justification 'justification'. Let us adapt some recent terminology[5]

---

[4] Cf. F. Schauer, 'Exceptions', *University of Chicago Law Review*, 58 (1991), 895: 'If there is a power to create exceptions in the name of purpose, and to apply those exceptions immediately, then the exception-creating power is identical to the power to apply the purpose rather than the rule, or to take the purpose as being in fact the rule. . . . The power to create an exception to a rule when required by justice is equivalent to the power to do justice *simpliciter*'; cf. also *Playing By the Rules*, 83: 'continuously malleable rules of unlimited specificity may be rules only in form and not in effect.'

[5] See Aleksandr Peczenik, *On Law and Reason* (Dordrecht, 1989), 156–7. Peczenik speaks of 'contextually sufficient legal justification' and 'deep (fundamental) justification'. His extremely complex theory shows an acute awareness of the manifold parameters of legal justification. It seems to me he is unduly optimistic about the possibility of combining them in one total and meaningful theory; but I cannot pursue that here.

and speak of 'contextual' and 'deep' justification. 'Contextual justifications' are those provided for decisions when the rules of the legal institution unambiguously require a particular decision. 'Deep justifications' are those that begin with fundamental principles of morality. Our task here might be thought of as concerning the relation between contextual and deep justifications, and in particular how far the judge should as such be concerned with deep justifications. The key issue concerns whether sophisticated positivism offers a satisfactorily 'deep' account of the justifications internal to law.

There is a serious question here. The law is constituted exactly by its institutional independence and neutrality (impersonality, even). The deep justification of law as a social institution depends heavily on being able to justify the features of law which make possible the ambivalence of law—that blind application of the law can produce both justice and injustice. Although it may seem a weakness of formalism that blind application of the law can produce injustice, it is misleading to think that it is a strength of formalism that blind application of the law can produce justice. Reasoning in law comprehends more than reasoning according to rule. That means that even cases of reasoning according to rule must not be considered as a special case of this wider context.[6]

2. THE FANTASY OF HERCULES

Dworkin's superhuman judge Hercules plays an important role in the rhetoric of analytical jurisprudence.[7] Hercules is the idealization of mundane adjudication. Hercules is good science fiction, telling us something about our selves and our world: he is not some bizarre freak whose description tells us nothing about anything except the ingenuity of its creator. It is not clear whether Hercules suffers from the well-known twin handicaps of relative ignorance of fact and relative indeterminacy of aim (cf. Hart, *The Concept of Law*,

[6] The nature of decision-making according to rule, and the reasons for tolerating, and even requiring, decision-making according to rule, are important topics in their own right, and only sketchily discussed here. For a full and illuminating discussion, see Schauer, *Playing by the Rules, passim.*

[7] I refer here to the Hercules of *Taking Rights Seriously*, ch. 4, 'Hard Cases'. Hercules the defender of law as integrity in *Law's Empire*, first, is not the same character, and, second, raises different philosophical issues. See Ch. 12.3 below.

125). Such handicaps restrict those with a concern for the empirical. Hercules by contrast concentrates on the theoretical, and his special skills reveal this—he has 'superhuman skill, learning, patience and acumen' (*Taking Rights Seriously*, 105). He has whatever is needed to work out theories to the full, when we mundane folk are too readily limited by finite intellects and a desire to sit on committees or watch sports. The fantasy of Hercules models at its idealized limit judicial concern with consistency and with justification as they bear on determining the proper decision in the instant case, that individualized decision to which every litigant has a basic right. When Hercules has his theory fully worked out, every decision will be consistent with every other decision—that is what it is for the theory to be fully worked out.[8] Every decision will also be justified, for it will have its place in the theory. Hercules 'gets this case just right' *every time*. His fully worked-out theory ensures that each decision does justice to the facts of the particular case (gets *it* 'just right'), is consistent with every other decision, and is justified. It is clear that the first of this trio is connected with the other two. But how is the second connected with the third?

3. PROPERTIES OF LEGAL SYSTEM

3.1. Closedness and completeness

Formalism can be a vice only because it enjoins a restricted conception of adjudication. The restriction is, however, underwritten by the finiteness of the body of rules in an institutionalized normative system like a legal system. This finiteness may be expressed as the thought that legal systems are *closed*. A normative system would be 'open' if in fact there were no restrictions of the kind found in legal systems on what could count as a norm of the system.[9] This 'closedness' of legal systems seems

---

[8] That Hercules requires a theory of mistakes (cf. *Taking Rights Seriously*, 121–2) with which to deal with settled law is proof of this claim, not an objection to it. If the settledness of settled law were irrelevant to theorizing, there would be no need of a *theory* of mistakes as part of the grand theory. The putatively recalcitrant data would be accommodated into the theory.

[9] In the same passage of *Practical Reason and Norms*, Raz offers as a third characteristic of legal systems as a distinctive kind of institutionalized normative system 'openness'. He means by this however a different property from the one we

to conflict with the connected properties attributed to legal systems by Raz of being 'comprehensive' and claiming to be 'supreme' (cf. *Practical Reason and Norms*, 150–2). By 'comprehensive' is meant that a legal system 'claim[s] authority to regulate any kind of behaviour', though of course whether the system actually has such authority is subject to separate determination. The claim to supremacy means that 'every legal system claims authority to regulate the setting up and application of other institutionalized systems by its subject community (*Practical Reason and Norms*, 151). It seems extraordinarily presumptuous to claim authority to regulate any kind of behaviour from a basis of a finite set of norms: formalism seems a vice of exactly such presumptuousness.

The real conflict, however, which invites talk of presumptuousness is that between comprehensiveness and *completeness*. That is, law which is comprehensive must also be law which is complete, law that has no 'gaps'. The notion of a 'gap in the law' is metaphorical; it needs interpretation before it can be of use in legal theory. Raz (*The Authority of Law*, ch. 4) has distinguished carefully two different notions of a 'gap in the law'.[10] The first kind of gap occurs when the claim that there is a legal requirement to perform an action of a certain kind is neither true nor false and the claim that there is a legal permission to omit that same action is neither true nor false. The second kind of gap occurs when it is not the case that there is a legal requirement to perform a certain action and it is not the case that there is a legal permission to omit that action (*The Authority of Law*, 71). Shortly after (77), Raz more colloquially and memorably characterizes the second gap as occurring when 'the law is silent', as opposed to cases where the law speaks with an uncertain voice or where it speaks with many voices. The point on which Raz wishes to insist is that simple indeterminacy in the law (through ambiguity of language, for instance) or unresolved conflicts between rules are cases where the law speaks with an uncertain voice or with many voices. Such cases

are considering here—'a normative system is open to the extent that it contains norms the purpose of which is to give binding force within the system to norms which do not belong to it' (152–3). I do not discuss this sense of 'openness'. Schauer ('Formalism', 522–3) shows that 'closedness' as here defined is not the same as 'mechanical deducibility'; either may exist without the other.

[10] I put into plain English what Raz expresses in symbolic notation.

exemplify gaps in the law of the first kind. Law would be problematically incomplete only if there were gaps of the second kind, where the law was silent. However, as long as there are in the legal system, as indeed there typically are, closure rules such as the rule that whatever is not legally prohibited is legally permitted and vice versa, then there can be no gaps of the second, problematic kind. Thus it is quite compatible with the comprehensiveness of law that it secures its completeness by closure rules.[11] One way to 'get this case just right' is to acknowledge that there is clearly no law prohibiting the defendant from doing what he or she is doing, and therefore that there is no cause of action against the defendant.

If, however, a legal system may be complete as a result of closure rules, then its closedness ceases to be a threat to its comprehensiveness. This result is to be expected, given the understanding we are deploying of the vice of formalism. That is, recall, to fail to make use of a 'rule-avoiding reason' when the system makes such a reason available. Formalism *qua* vice is not the following of rules as such. Therefore, the facts that a legal system is a complete system and a closed system are not in themselves what makes formalism in adjudication a vice.

It is tempting to think that Hercules with his superhuman qualities can save judicial reasoning from incompleteness. This thought would be a mistake. Hercules saves us from identifying prematurely gaps in the law of the kind which result from unresolved conflicts, and from indeterminacy in so far as ambiguities may be removed by a consideration of areas of settled law remote from the instant case. Hercules will also save us from thinking that a closure rule is dispositive of a case when in fact there is a relevant substantive rule. But sophisticated positivism is sufficient to save us from thinking that the law is incomplete when it is not.

3.2. *Consistency and categoricity*

I mention completeness and closedness only to identify them as properties of legal systems separately from the discussion of two further properties of legal systems, properties which are much more central to the present discussion—consistency and categoricity. Let us deal with consistency first.

[11] See also the discussion on pp. 84–5 ff. above.

In contemporary philosophy there are two popular models for justification. According to the first model, one justifies a judgement in a particular case by showing that it is deductively derivable from a fundamental principle or principles, the soundness of such principles being taken for granted in the immediate context. In the second model, the concept is laid aside of justification via derivability from principles antecedently and independently accepted as sound. It is replaced by justification via consistency with antecedent principles without assuming the independent soundness of those principles. Because the independent soundness of the principles is not at issue, permission is given to achieve the consistency of principle and particular judgement as much by altering or discarding judgements of principle to make them consistent with particular judgements as by altering or discarding particular judgements to make them consistent with judgements of principle. The goal of the justificatory enterprise is no less and no more than an equilibrium between judgements of principle and judgements about particular cases, regardless of how the consistency or equilibrium is achieved.[12] The motivation for the second model is not hard to understand. The deductivist model of course raises the question of the origin or the criterion of the soundness of the principles. A lower-level judgement is not going to be proved sound (that is, justified) simply by being shown derivable from higher-level principles unless those principles are in fact sound principles. Without a proof of the soundness of the principles, derivability from them does not seem a very significant property. Notoriously, however, it is difficult to find an independent proof of the soundness of fundamental principles.

The two models differ in their treatment of soundness. According to the first model, the soundness of judgements both particular and of principle is ultimately a matter of correspondence with some independent reality. In the second model, soundness is simply a matter of internal coherence between the total set of judgements. Simple consistency within a set of sentences is

---

[12] John Rawls speaks of a 'reflective equilibrium' between principles and 'considered judgments duly pruned and adjusted' (*A Theory of Justice* (Cambridge, Mass., 1971), 20). See also *A Theory of Justice*, 46–50, and Rawls's essay 'The Independence of Moral Theory', *Proceedings and Addresses of the American Philosophical Association*, 47 (1974–5). For more on Rawls and method see Ch. 8.3.3 below.

substituted for the derivability of one set of sentences from another set of sentences, and such consistency is held to be an adequate replacement for soundness of fundamental principles as a standard of justification.

Despite these fundamental differences, a certain formal ideal of rationality is in common to both the first model requiring derivability from independently established principles and the second more fluid model of 'justification' via attainment of equilibrium. This common formal ideal is shown most clearly in the second model, because the second model consists of nothing more than this formal ideal—the ideal of formal consistency. As long as one prescinds from the distinction between truth by correspondence and truth by coherence for both principles and particular judgements, there is an important common core to the models in terms of the requirement of consistency.[13]

The two models also share the formal property of categoricity. By speaking of the formal ideal of 'categoricity', I mean something like the following—a justificatory theory is categorical just in case for any particular judgement within the domain of the theory submitted to the theory for justification, the question whether the judgement is justified is decidable. There is, if you like, in some form a determinate answer to every question. Categoricity so understood is an ersatz version of categoricity as a formal property of formal systems. Clearly, assuming soundness and completeness of principles, the first model implies categoricity. It is important to realize that the second model may well imply categoricity too. The second model is pragmatic and non-eschatological. That is, it does not suppose that any present state of equilibrium from which justification would flow is deceptive and temporary, pending some final day of judgement when perfect equilibrium is achieved. Rather, it supposes that, though any present equilibrium is revisable and so a hostage to fortune, it does generate justification

---

[13] I do not mean to be bypassing here legitimate questions raised by legal theorists about the precise nature of formal relationships between judicial decisions and legal principle. Barry Hoffmaster, for example, in 'A Holistic Approach to Judicial Justification', *Erkenntnis*, 15 (1980), has presented a formal analysis of a holistic approach to justification which deploys more than deductive relationships strictly conceived. Peczenik's account in *On Law and Reason* is similarly non-deductively holistic. The analysis offered here is neutral across different formalizations of consistency. I discuss the deductive case only because that is the most straightforward, and the most favoured.

as long as it persists. So it may well be that the structure of
principle and particular judgement obtained by freezing a set of
beliefs at a point in time has the property of categoricity, and that
the property will persist through revisions in the structure. It
would be a question-begging repudiation of pragmatism to say that
such categoricity 'on the fly' was not categoricity.

However, the difference between the two models shows that, if
we are to take seriously 'deep' justifications for legal decisions, we
cannot rest content with the second model, and thus that
consistency and categoricity cannot be the only relevant properties
of legal system.

In the first place, formal consistency is bi-directional, and thus
yields a bi-directional conception of justification. Formal consistency
in itself would yield no less reason to think that the principle is
justified because of its consistency with the particular judgement
than to think that the particular judgement is justified because of
its consistency with the principle. Herculean justification, however, is 'top down'. Herculean justification consists of not merely
the consistency of the set of sentences giving the description of the
proposed decision with the sentence describing the principle, for
that gives no priority to either set of sentences. Herculean
justification assumes that, given as a necessary condition the
formal consistency of principle and particular judgement, the
principle is of a more privileged status than the particular
decisions. There must be something about the principles which
gives them a privileged status. The vice of formalism is evaded by a
rule-avoiding reason. But if there was as much force to the thought
that the facts of the case justified the reason as that the reason
justified a decision in the case, then the distinction required to
escape formalism between the rule to be avoided and the rule-
avoiding reason could not be drawn, for both the rule and the
reason are consistent with the facts of the case.

Moreover, if the principles did not have antecedent and
independent justificatory force, the notion of 'principled adjudication' would not have the appeal which it undoubtedly and rightly
has and which is expressed in the fantasy of Hercules. By making
adjudication 'principled', a court is supposed to avoid formalism
and improve its decision-making. But this could not be possible if
being 'principled' simply meant achieving a formal consistency
between principle and particular judgement with either one

vulnerable to rejection in the cause of achieving consistency. There must be in some sense of the term a commitment to the priority of principles in any adequate theory of legal justification. The focus is not so much on the thought that every question has a right answer as on what it is for an answer to be a right answer.

4. BACKGROUND POLITICAL MORALITY

I have argued so far that the ideal of legal decisions as justified requires a commitment to principles as of independent justificatory force. First, the Herculean ideal is committed at least to coherence/consistency and categoricity—purely formal properties. This is perfectly proper, for we do indeed expect law to be coherent. That expectation is akin to the intuitive rejection of the legal irrationality of 'palm-tree justice', for that is a mechanism for adjudication which permits a series of individual verdicts not bearing any logical relationship to each other. We expect more of mundane adjudication than this *ad hoc*-ery. Quite clearly, however, and second, there is more to the appeal of the Herculean fantasy than an appeal simply to the desirability of these formal features. Herculean adjudication is 'principled' not merely because the Herculean schema is formally consistent and categorical; not merely because it is also a schema of 'top-down' justification; but also because it provides a mechanism for rooting adjudication in background political morality. We must consider whether the notion of 'principled adjudication' is a 'content-independent' notion, or whether there is a 'content-dependent' constraint on what will count as a Herculean justification—that is, a justification is Herculean only if the values it imports have a certain content. I shall try to show that this constraint does apply.

Hercules is not a superhuman Rawlsian moral agent; his task is not the production of the perfect moral theory. He is a judge in some representative jurisdiction. The Herculean fantasy is relevant to 'the *present* structure of the institution of adjudication'.[14] The mundane judge is faced with the facts of institutional history; that's part of what it is to be a mundane judge. It would be an enormous cosmic fluke, however, if every single provision of

---

[14] Cf. Dworkin, *Taking Rights Seriously*, 123; my italics.

existing, historically conditioned, settled law mapped perfectly on to an ideal, a-historical Herculean schema. Hercules in his relationship to settled law must therefore be prepared to have a 'theory of mistakes'—he must be prepared to deem certain parts of settled law mistaken just because they do not map on to the schema (cf. *Taking Rights Seriously*, 118 ff.). He must though be prepared to determine mistakes in a principled way; he cannot 'make impudent use' of his theory of mistakes (cf. *Taking Rights Seriously*, 121) and the licence that he has to disregard parts of settled law.

Dworkin himself is confused when he tries to state why Hercules cannot make impudent use of his theory of mistakes. Dworkin's reason is that 'if [Hercules] were free to take any incompatible piece of institutional history as a mistake, with no further consequences for his general theory, then the requirement of consistency would be no genuine requirement at all' (ibid.). Dworkin's remark shows that the requirement of consistency is not a merely formal requirement, though it is at least that. In a purely formal sense, the formal requirement of consistency would be meaningless if Hercules could decide at will whether some given sentence expressing a legal verdict is or is not consistent with the rest of the set of sentences that constitute the Herculean schema. We have to have in place some notion of consistency as *truth related*.

Truth-relatedness can be understood quite abstractly. Suppose that (i) p and q are rules or decisions in settled law, (ii) R is a principle instinct in settled law, and (iii) p, q, and R are inconsistent in that they cannot all be true. The formal truth-relatedness of p, q, and R amounts to no more than this: if p and q are deemed true R must go, and if p and R are deemed true q must go, and if q and R are deemed true p must go.[15] This relationship is purely formal, in that it does not tell us which of p, q, and R Hercules (or for that matter anyone else) does deem true, and therefore which of p, q, and R have to be rejected. The relationship places limits on what else Hercules can do, given some initial truth-value assignment and certain syntactical relations

---

[15] To be able to say, for example, that if p is true, q and R must go would require more information about the relations between p, q, and R than simply that they form an inconsistent set.

between the sentences. It says nothing about the initial truth-value assignment.

Dworkin confuses this way of 'having further consequences for the general theory' with a related but distinguishable notion. If Hercules were quite willing antecedently to regard any principle of background political morality as vulnerable in the light of decisions or rules in settled law, then the formal truth-related requirement of consistency would not in itself prevent him from taking any piece of institutional history he liked as mistaken. Only substantial views on Hercules' part as to the priority of certain principles over others could so prevent him. Hercules could maintain perfect consistency with the aim of attaining reflective equilibrium even in this abstract truth-related way by being as much prepared to abandon the principle which purported to justify that piece of history as to abandon that piece of institutional history itself. The whole Herculean project is powerful, as indeed it is powerful, only because independently of the justificatory procedure he adopts Hercules also favours certain substantial values over others.[16] The appeal of the Herculean fantasy as an account of principled adjudication is rooted not merely in the fact that Herculean theory conforms to the formal ideals of consistency and categoricity. It lies in part also in the fact that Hercules is expected to show in his schema the consistency of legal decisions with background political morality. The requirement of consistency is a genuinely powerful engine for instilling values in settled law only because *ex hypothesi* some initial assignment, some unbudgeable initial assignment, of truth-values has already been made. That is to say, consistency is important, not as truth-related in some formal sense, but as *truth preserving*. That is the role of the acceptance by a given society of its own principles of background political morality, to which principles Hercules defers and with which he seeks to put settled law in equilibrium.

The next question we must ask concerns where the assignment of these initial truth-values comes from. Content-independence

[16] Cf. Schauer, 'Exceptions', 886: 'Given the ability to draw a theoretical distinction, any doctrinal rule reflecting that distinction would have to be considered principled, for there is nothing to the idea of a principled distinction other than the willingness to adhere to the previously drawn distinction.' This disparagement by Schauer of the thought that historically conditioned black-letter law inherently contains certain 'principles' shows by refraction how strong is the commitment of the Herculean project to a-historical principles.

for the concept of law can be preserved only by supposing a relativistic account of this assignment of initial truth-values.[17] That is, the initial assignment could be understood as merely the social fact of the acceptance by any given society of its own principles of background political morality, and the social fact of the settled law in that society having as its 'spirit' the particular values that it has. A statement asserting such social facts would be a value-neutral statement. However, such a relativistic account must be inadequate to cash out the appeal of the notion of 'principled adjudication'. For, given everything I have said so far, it is perfectly possible for an iniquitous legal system in a country with an iniquitous background political morality—we may, for example, wish to cast Kuwait, or Iraq, or Romania, in this role—to have its own Hercules working out in advance all the correct ways to apply laws for the execution of quislings and adulterers, laws for compulsory procreation, or whatever, and for the country to expect of its judges that they aspire to mimic this iniquitously Herculean scheme. The notion, central to the Herculean enterprise, of the 'character of the game' (cf. *Taking Rights Seriously*, 101–5), despite the way that it is in *Taking Rights Seriously* presented, is a purely formal notion. The claim, which it is surely plausible to make, that under the present regime an Iraqi Hercules is a contradiction in terms cannot make sense unless it is part of the very judicial ideal that Hercules represents—that is, part of the character of the judicial game— that he operates a schema based on certain values rather than on others.

Thus the Herculean ideal represents a commitment to substantial value that cannot be captured by the formality of a social relativism. The Herculean ideal is only satisfied by a schema which, allowing for non-impudent use of a theory of mistakes, leaves settled law in equilibrium with a theory in background political morality which has to be defined substantially. It has to be a theory of background political morality based (broadly and crudely speaking) on equality and justice. The Herculean ideal uses derivations from just such a background theory and no other to provide adjudication in new hard cases which is properly 'principled'. 'Principled' means not the purely formal notion of deductive derivability, but the

---

[17] We saw in Ch. 2.5 that this fact was explicitly recognized by MacCormick in his doctrine of legal justification by coherence. Peczenik's coherence theory of legal justification in *On Law and Reason* is equally relativistic.

substantial notion of deductive derivability from some principles rather than others, the 'some' being picked out by criteria which relate to the substantial content of the principles concerned, and one particular substantial content at that. The rationality of law is substantive.

If all of these claims are true, then of course the Herculean fantasy, if understood as a fantasy about the very concept of law itself, implies a deep connection between law and substantial value that any content-independent analysis of law such as legal positivism is unable to capture.[18] Hercules indeed is the embodiment of what we expect from norm-applying officials of a municipal legal system, an expectation we may summarize as 'principled adjudication'. What it is for adjudication to be in this sense 'principled', as given by the Herculean fantasy seen as an idealization of this expectation, is not a purely formal—that is, evaluatively neutral—ideal. It includes, all right, the formal notions of consistency and categoricity. These are given point, however, by and only by their association with some given background political morality. Moreover, this cannot be just any old background political morality; it must be specifically a background political morality based on values such as equality and justice. Otherwise, the formal properties remain at best formal and at worst destructive elements, destructive because generative of injustice. The formal properties cannot in themselves underwrite any Herculean aspirations, aspirations which are a deep part and a non-positivistic part of our concept of law.

5. CONCLUSION

We recognize a sense of 'formalism' as a 'Bad Thing' in judicial reasoning. The vice of formalism occurs when a court chooses to follow precedent or interpret a statute, or to do either narrowly, when it need not have done so. The modality here is legal: the system itself provided the resources for distinguishing the case, or for interpreting it more widely. An example might help. One

---

[18] The claim that law *must* involve the attempt to reach the best result in individual cases . . . cannot start from positivist conceptions of law' (Schauer, 'Rules and the Rule of Law', *Harvard Journal of Law and Public Policy*, 14 (1991), 663).

long-standing rule of the common law is the so-called exclusionary rule that the recovery of pure economic loss will be precluded in negligence when it is consequent upon an injury to the person or property of a third party.[19] The rule in some form goes back to 1875.[20] However, it seems possible to track in the decided cases a gradual loosening up of the rule. Lord Atkin's well-known 'neighbour' principle is commodious,[21] as is Lord Macmillan's equally well-known dictum from the same case that 'the categories of negligence are never closed' (at 619). More specifically, economic loss consequent upon negligent misstatement has been recognized as recoverable;[22] the economic loss of a frustrated beneficiary has been recognized as recoverable from a negligent solicitor;[23] there was some loosening of the immunity of public authorities when exercising statutory powers;[24] the rule itself has been denied to be absolute.[25] All these decisions, and other case-law not referred to here, made quite comprehensible the House of Lords' decision in *Junior Books*,[26] which allowed recovery for purely economic loss in an action brought by a factory owner against a subcontractor with which they had no contractual relationship. *Junior Books* thus seemed to open up the whole field of recovery for purely economic loss.

In subsequent UK decisions, however, the door has been firmly

---

[19] I borrow this formulation from Bruce Feldthusen, *Economic Negligence* (2nd edn., Toronto, 1989), 200, who in turn acknowledges earlier writers. Feldthusen's book should be consulted for a thorough analysis of the issues and cases alluded to here.

[20] *Cattle* v. *Stockton Waterworks Co.* (1875) LR 10 QB 453.

[21] *Donoghue* v. *Stevenson* [1932] AC 562, at 580, that a duty of care is owed to 'persons who are so closely and directly affected by my act that I ought reasonably to have them in contemplation as being so affected when I am directing my mind to the acts or omissions which are called in question'.

[22] *Hedley Byrne and Co. Ltd.* v. *Heller and Partners Ltd.* [1963] 2 All ER 575 (HL).

[23] *Ross* v. *Caunters (a firm)* [1979] 3 All ER 580 (ChD).

[24] *Home Office* v. *Dorset Yacht Co. Ltd.* [1970] 2 All ER 294; *Anns and others* v. *London Borough of Merton* [1977] 2 All ER 492 (HL). In the latter case, Lord Salmon caps Lord Macmillan's dictum with 'and there are now a great many of them' (513).

[25] *Caltex Oil (Aust) Pty Ltd.* v. *The Dredge 'Willemstad'* (1976) 11 ALR 227 (HC): *Canadian National Railway Co.* v. *Norsk Pacific Steamship Co. Ltd. et al* 65 DLR 4th (1990) 321 (FCA). Wilson J. also characterizes recovery for economic loss under certain conditions as 'accomplish[ing] a number of worthy objectives', *City of Kamloops* v. *Nielsen et al* 10 DLR (4th) 641 (SCC), at 681.

[26] *Junior Books Ltd.* v. *Veitchi Co. Ltd.* [1982] 3 All ER 201 (HL).

closed. *The Aliakmon*[27] emphasized the crucial role of particular circumstances, and limited recovery for economic loss to cases where damage to a third-party's property or person caused by the defendant's negligence resulted in the third party being unable to fulfil a contract with the plaintiff. *Candlewood* affirmed that limitation.[28] *Muirhead*[29] held *Junior Books* to require 'very close proximity' for an entitlement to recovery, a relationship which did not exist between a wholesale fish merchant and the manufacturer of the pumps in their storage tanks. In *Pilkington Glass (No. 2)*,[30] the relationship between a main contractor and a supplier of materials to a subcontractor was not held to be close enough. Moreover, Dillon LJ strenuously repudiates *Junior Books*: *Books*:

The case cannot now be regarded as a useful pointer to any development of the law . . . Indeed I find it difficult to see that future citation from *Junior Books* can ever serve any useful purpose. (at 805)

In *D. & F. Estates Ltd.*[31] recovery was denied for the purely economic loss of repairing a defect discovered before it had caused injury; the set of facts was very close to those in *Junior Books*. Oliver LJ again pushed *Junior Books* to the background: 'I do not think the latter is of any help in the present context' (at 1013). *Junior Books* has thus been interpreted to stand only for the very specific facts which it exemplifies, and not to underwrite any more broad incursion into the exclusionary rule.

It has been suggested that *Junior Books* has been as a result 'constructively overruled', and that the House of Lords should put the case out of its misery by deploying the House's powers under the 1966 Practice Statement and actually overrule *Junior Books*.[32] However, the door to recovery for purely economic loss still seems

---

[27] *Leigh and Sillivan Ltd.* v. *Aliakmon Shipping Co. Ltd.* [1985] 2 All ER 44 (CA).
[28] *Candlewood Navigation Corp. Ltd.* v. *Mitsui OSK Lines Ltd. and another* [1985] 2 All ER 935 (PC), at 945 per Fraser LJ.
[29] *Muirhead* v. *Industrial Tank Specialities Ltd. and others* [1985] 3 All ER 705 (CA).
[30] *Simaan General Contracting Co.* v. *Pilkington Glass Ltd. (No. 2)* [1988] 1 All ER 791 (CA).
[31] *D. & F. Estates Ltd. and others* v. *Church Commissioners for England and others* [1988] 2 All ER 992.
[32] Peter Cane, 'Economic Loss in Tort', *Modern Law Review*, 52 (1989) (HL). 203.

not yet shut and bolted. *Banque Financière*[33] contemplates the possibility of 'rare' cases where recovery is justified. In *Reid*[34] the idea of narrowing grounds for recovery for economic loss to those contemplated in *Hedley Byrne* is rejected by Ralph Gibson LJ. In Canada the door is more than ajar. MacGuigan JA in *Norsk* argues that there is no exclusionary rule in Canada, and that where there is no physical danger to a plaintiff's property, there is no presumption against proximity of the required kind, but rather 'neutrality as to possible conclusions'; other factors may give rise to a conclusion of proximity (at 357, 360).

The House of Lords in *Junior Books* was faced with a relatively clear rule, and a number of other legal materials which could be taken to argue for an extension, if not even a rejection, of the rule. They did not decide formalistically, in that they opened the door to considerable change in the law. But they also made possible the emasculation of *Junior Books* by the technique of distinguishing precedents. The courts who took this latter option could be said to have argued formalistically. Rule-avoiding reasons in the form of the decision in *Junior Books* and the decisions which lay behind it were available to the courts in *The Aliakmon* and its successors. The courts chose not to follow those reasons, and to revalorize the exclusionary rule.

One can imagine other ways to cash out formalism as the refusal to follow a rule-avoiding reason. A constitutional document like the Canadian *Charter of Rights and Freedoms* contains many references to broad values of political morality, such as the references in sect. 7 to the 'right to life, liberty and security of the person' and 'the right not to be deprived thereof except in accordance with the principles of fundamental justice'. One might take the view that the content of 'fundamental principles of justice' and other such phrases is to be determined by and only by how courts have in the past interpreted that and other similar phrases. In a recent article, for example, Donna C. Morgan argues that demands for judicial review under sect. 7 of prosecutorial decisions should be possible at least on the grounds of procedural fairness and bad faith/improper purpose. Her discussion articulates these terms, however, by reference to 'general principles of

---

[33] *Banque Financière de la Cité SA* v. *Westgate Insurance Co. Ltd.* [1989] 2 All ER 952 (CA), at 1009.
[34] *Reid* v. *Rush & Tompkins Group plc* [1989] 3 All ER 228 (CA).

administrative law', rather than any concepts 'outside' the law.[35] Even in sect. 7 cases, it may then be argued, the court has no permission to go 'outside' black-letter law. Such a view qualifies to count as a 'narrow' or 'constructivist' view of constitutional interpretation. As such, it is a controversial, and indeed much rejected, view of constitutional interpretation. The point being made here, however, requires merely that a constitutional provision such as sect. 7 could be interpreted as mandating a court to take a far broader view of a citizen's rights and to depart from settled law as a result.

Note that the rule-avoiding reasons of which the House of Lords in *Junior Books* did avail itself and the courts in *The Aliakmon* and its successors did not are reasons within the common law. In some plain sense, legal doctrine authorized the avoidance of legal rule, as it might be put. The same could be said of cases where a court hearing a Charter case placed a broad interpretation on the Charter, and postulated a citizen's right for which there was scant other basis in settled law. Wilson J. argued in *Morgentaler*[36] that sect. 7 protects the decision of a woman to terminate her pregnancy and thus that sect. 251 of the Criminal Code restricting abortion is contrary to the Charter. Many persons, whether they agree with the moral ideal behind her argument or not, regard her claim as within the above category of cases.

The following objection may be raised. I have spoken approvingly of the extension of liability for economic loss in *Junior Books* and the extension of women's sect. 7 rights in Wilson J.'s opinion in *Morgentaler*. I have attributed the vice of formalism to the courts which isolated *Junior Books* from the mainstream of legal discourse, and to commentators who argue for a narrow ground for interpretation of sect. 7 of the Canadian Charter. Are these remarks on my part anything more than expressions of my personal values? Can they contribute anything to analytical jurisprudence? I do not deny that my remarks express value judgements, and ones with which many disagree for many reasons. It is important to realize the point cuts both ways. Courts have to choose between rule-following and rule-avoiding reasons. Formalism is a vice just in case the rule-avoiding reasons are stronger, and a

---

[35] See 'Controlling Prosecutorial Powers', *Criminal Law Quarterly*, 29 (1986–7), esp. 56–65.

[36] *Morgentaler, Smolling and Scott* v. *R.* (1988) 31 CRR 1 (SCC); see esp. 80–8.

virtue just in case the rule-following reasons are stronger. We show thereby that the ideal internal to law of 'getting *this* case just right' cannot make sense unless the standards of justification for legal decisions are not purely formal. To show that is to show the limitations of positivism as a theory of law.

Schauer recounts a less grand case which raises precisely the same issues. In *Hunter*,[37] Hunter, an incumbent Vermont state senator seeking re-election, missed by three minutes the statutory deadline for filing his nomination papers, and the County Clerk Ms Norman refused to accept them. Hunter filed an action in equity for extraordinary relief, to appear on the ballot. He argued that he had the papers ready in the morning, that he had been informed erroneously by Ms Norman's office that he needed to appear in person, and that he would have filed the papers by courier in good time but for this erroneous advice. He also cited *Ryshpan*,[38] a case where on very similar facts the Vermont Supreme Court had ruled in favour of the plaintiff and granted relief. Now, as Schauer points out (517), any legal system is replete with *Ryshpan* equivalents—provisions which allow the avoidance of some rule. But (cf. 518) the court could have decided to 'create' *Ryshpan* in its absence—that is, to decide in equity for Hunter in any case. The court would in all likelihood not simply press a button and vote for Hunter, but would present argument 'by reference to general principles that lurk in various corners of the legal system', as Schauer vividly puts it (518), an established principle, for example, that parties are stopped from relying on laws whose contents they have misstated to the disadvantage of another.[39]

---

[37] *Hunter* v. *Norman* No. S197-86-WrC (Vt. July 28, 1986); otherwise unreported. Cf. Schauer, 'Formalism', 515–16.

[38] *Ryshpan* v. *Cashman* 326 A 2d 169 (1974).

[39] Comparable cases in the United Kingdom might be the following. Sect. 33(1) of the Limitation Act 1980 (replacing sect. 2D of the 1939 Limitation Act, as inserted by the Limitation Act 1975, sect. 1) gives to courts an 'unfettered' discretion 'to override the [3-year] time-limit [for bringing personal injury claims] where it is fair and just to do so' (*Firman* v. *Ellis* [1978] 2 All ER 851 (CA), per Denning MR at 859, 863). Subsequent cases have confirmed this unfettered discretion, and that sect. 33(3) 'focus[es] the attention of the court on matters which are likely to call for evaluation in the exercise of discretion and which must be taken into consideration by the judge'; the subsection 'is not intended to place a fetter on the discretion given by sub-section (1)' (*Donovan* v. *Gwentoys Ltd.* [1990] 1 All ER 1018 (HL), per Griffiths LJ at 1023; see also *Thompson* v. *Brown Construction (Ebbw Vale) Ltd. and others* [1981] 2 All ER 296 (HL), *Hartley* v.

Schauer goes on to develop three different models for the availability of such 'ameliorative principles', as he calls them. In the first model,

> the existing escape routes in the system represent an incomplete list of principles to ameliorate the rigidity of rules, and the judge may add to this list where amelioration is indicated but no applicable ameliorative principle exists. In such instances, the judge might discuss justice or fairness or some other general value . . . ('Formalism', 519)

Unsurprisingly, Schauer associates this model with Dworkin. In the second model, the stock of ameliorative principles within the system is regarded as more or less complete, and an escape route always available through them. This model is associated with Llewellyn. In the third model, the stock of rule-avoiding norms is both incomplete and closed. The third model seems to invite charges of 'formalism', but this would be misleading in so far as the closedness deprived the judge of a real choice.

The three models present valuable contrasts, but it can be argued that their implications are obscured. The first of the three models presents the real challenge to positivism. As we have seen in Chapter 2.5, sophisticated positivism amounts to presenting different versions of the second model. Simple positivism, perhaps, represents the third model. Positivism can readily agree that any decision which conforms to the second model is justified, even though it involves the rejection of a locally applicable rule and the deployment of rule-avoiding reasons. The challenge of the first model is this. The restriction of available rule-avoiding reasons to principles which the legal system itself makes available is at best arbitrary and at worst an exhibition of the vice of formalism. To put the point at its most sharp, let us suppose that, when Hunter challenged the non-acceptance of his papers, not only was there no *Ryshpan*; there were also within the system no principles of estoppel or reliance; and so forth. Would it not *still* evince the vice of formalism to deny Hunter relief? Would not Hunter's argument be *just as strong* even if the rule-avoiding reasons lay 'without' the system? Would not the decision to find for Hunter be genuinely

Birmingham City Council, The Independent Law Reports, 16 Aug. 1991 (CA)). Although there is clear statutory authority for the exercise of equitable discretion, one can again imagine that a court might have 'created' *Firman* without such authority.

and deeply *justified*? What is true is that, if the rule-avoiding reasons selected by the court were that Hunter had blue eyes, or a golf handicap of scratch, we would repudiate such reasoning. But it does not follow from the fact that reference to justice and fairness is acceptable and reference to skill at golf is not, that the second model has to be the correct model for legal justification.

Sophisticated positivism has acknowledged that, to give a proper picture of judicial discretion and the role of principles in legal justification, it is necessary to acknowledge that the court's discretion in a hard case is not 'strong', but is circumscribed by a variety of factors. It is also necessary to acknowledge that there may be legal principles, standards to which the judge properly appeals, which underwrite the avoidance of rules, and so of the vice of formalism. I have argued that these acknowledgements rest on the underlying goal of 'getting *this* case just right', of doing justice to the particular claims before the court. I have argued that principles of formal rationality cannot suffice to account for 'getting *this* case just right', and that we must understand the goal as a substantial one. I have elucidated the powerful fantasy of Hercules the superhuman judge as an articulation of this legitimate goal for mundane adjudication. I have argued that the notion of the justification of a legal decision which resonates with the goal is one which must admit justifications beginning from principles not necessarily 'within the law'. If all these claims are correct, then a positivistic account of discretion and principle must be mistaken. And it has been shown to be mistaken on the basis of claims about discretion and principle made by sophisticated positivism itself.

8

INTERPRETATION AND SEMANTICS

1. SOME PRELIMINARY DISTINCTIONS

Sophisticated positivism as it was presented in Chapter 2.6 above replaced a realist account of the semantics for propositions of law with an anti-realist account, and also took what has been called the interpretative turn. It made these moves because of a sense that simple positivism made too attractive a formalist approach to legal language. Simple positivism did not forbid the court to 'go beyond' settled law: rather, simple positivism provided no way of constraining such vagaries by any legal standards. Sophisticated positivism saw anti-realism and the interpretative turn as underwriting the permission to 'go beyond' settled law while remaining bound by constraints internal to the judicial enterprise. We must now investigate the viability of such a theoretical position. We will see that the price to be paid for escaping a simple positivistic view of interpretation and semantics in relation to law is one that can be paid only in anti-positivistic currency.

Not even the most extreme form of anti-positivism claims that law and morality are identical as normative systems, however close it may think the relationships may be. Since there is intuitively some distinction between law and morality, the task of giving an account of the semantics for propositions of law will be distinct from the task of giving an account of the semantics for propositions of morality. We need also to make distinctions between: a theory of law which makes necessary or central to law some relationship between propositions of law and an independent moral order (leaving that term right now very unspecific); a theory of law which makes necessary or central to law some relationship between propositions of law and independent social facts; and a theory of law which makes necessary or central to law some relationship to morality where law and morality are conceived of as part of the same order, or as on the same dimension. For instance, traditional natural law theory might be an example of the first kind of theory; traditional positivism might be an example of the second kind of theory; traditional legal realism might be an example of the third kind of theory.

Putting these two sets of distinctions together gives us the following six-fold taxonomy of legal theories:

(1) A theory which believes that propositions of law are understood by knowing the independent facts in virtue of which they are true or false, believes the same about propositions of morality, and takes propositions of law to be true or false in virtue of an independent moral order.

(2) A theory which believes that propositions of law are understood by knowing the independent facts in virtue of which they are true or false, believes that propositions of morality are understood by knowing the conditions that warrant their assertion, and takes propositions of law to be true or false in virtue of an independent moral order.

(3) A theory which believes that propositions of law are understood by knowing the conditions that warrant their assertion, may believe that propositions of morality are understood either in terms of truth-conditions or in terms of conditions for warranted assertion, and takes propositions of law to be in part warrantedly assertible in virtue of rules which connect propositions of law with propositions of morality.

(4) A theory which believes that propositions of law are understood by knowing the independent facts in virtue of which they are true or false, takes propositions of law to be true or false in virtue of independent social fact, and has no views (or no relevant views) on the semantics for propositions of morality.

(5) A theory which believes that propositions of morality are understood by knowing the independent facts in virtue of which they are true or false, and gives to propositions of law no independent status.

(6) A theory which believes that propositions of morality are understood by knowing the conditions that warrant their assertion, and gives to propositions of law no independent status.

The first two theories would both count as versions of natural law theory. Among modern writers, for example, it is clear that both Michael Moore[1] and David Brink[2] sponsor versions of (1). They argue both that propositions of law map semantically on to propositions of morality, and that propositions of morality are to be given a realist semantics. Beyleveld and Brownsword, on the other hand, argue (*Law As a Moral Judgment*, 152–6) that natural law theory is quite compatible with moral relativism. According to their theory of law, Alan Gewirth's Principle of Generic Consistency[3] grounds a structure of moral reasoning on to which law as a structure of practical reasoning must map; but the status of the structure of moral reasoning may be left indeterminate. (3) seems to be the position defended by Dworkin in recent writings,[4] and which will be discussed anon. (4) I understand to be exemplified by a positivism such as Raz's Sources Thesis.[5] By (5) and (6), I understand different possible versions of Legal Realism or Critical Legal Studies. Joseph Singer, for example,[6] holds to a version of (6), but Marxism-inspired critiques of legal doctrine would count as versions of (5).

Philosophers have a tendency to value taxonomies for their own sake. There is a purpose to my taxonomy here. (1)/(5) differ from (2)/(6) in their views on the semantics for propositions of morality. Many moral theorists believe that a realist account of the semantics for propositions of morality cannot be correct, for there are no 'independent moral facts' such that the meaning of propositions of morality can be given by stating the conditions under which propositions of morality are true by virtue of

[1] See, for example, 'The Semantics of Judging', *Southern California Law Review*, 54 (1981), 'Moral Reality', *Wisconsin Law Review* (1982), 'A Natural Law Theory of Interpretation', *Southern California Law Review*, 58 (1985), 'Metaphysics, Epistemology and Legal Theory', *Southern California Law Review*, 60 (1987), 'The Interpretive Turn', *Stanford Law Review*, 41 (1989), and numerous other articles identified in the footnotes to the foregoing.

[2] *Moral Realism and the Foundations of Ethics* (Cambridge, 1989), 'Legal Theory; Judicial Review', *Philosophy and Public Affairs*, 17 (1988); 'Semantics and Legal Interpretation', *Canadian Journal of Law and Jurisprudence*, 2 (1989).

[3] Cf. his *Reason and Morality* (Chicago, 1978), esp. pt. 3. The PGC reads, 'Act in accord with the generic rights of your recipients as well as of yourself' (*Reason and Morality*, 135).

[4] Cf. *A Matter of Principle*, pt. 2; *Law's Empire*, chs. 1–7.

[5] Cf. *The Authority of Law*, ch. 3.

[6] 'The Player and the Cards', *Yale Law Journal*, 94 (1984); cf. esp. 8–9, 'law and morality have no rational foundation', a fact which liberates us to embrace passionate commitments in both fields.

correspondence with those facts. Whether such theorists are right is not an issue in this book. The difference between (1) or (2) and (3) is an issue in this book, but it is independent of any debate within moral theory about the difference between (1)/(5) and (2)/(6). The supposed reasons for preferring (2) to (1) or (6) to (5) from the point of view of moral philosophy, even if cogent reasons, are nevertheless *not* reasons for preferring (3) to (2) or to (1) from the point of view of legal philosophy. Variants of (4) will be discussed anon.

2. POSITIVISM AND SEMANTIC REALISM

The line of argument attributed to sophisticated positivism in Chapter 2.6 substituted an anti-realist semantics for the realist semantics of simple, or version (4), positivism; it also construed adjudication as interpretation, instead of construing it as description plus evaluation/discretion, as in simple positivism. The first step in the argument of this chapter is to criticize sophisticated positivism's picture of simple positivism. I shall show that it is not in any straightforward sense true to say that simple positivism's mistake is to propose a realist semantics for propositions of law.

Positivism is represented as saying that a proposition of law will be 'assertible as true' (cf. Dworkin, *A Matter of Principle*, 134) only if (for example) the sovereign has issued a command of the appropriate sort, and 'deniable as false' only if the sovereign has commanded the contrary proposition. The putative point is that it is a mistake to regard with the positivist a proposition of law as acceptable, whether by correspondence or by warranted assertibility, just in case it bears some appropriate relation to a social fact or some social fact obtains.

The thought here is confused. First, the expression 'assertible as true', on the standardly accepted vocabulary, is ill-formed. 'Truth' or 'falsity' are properties propositions have just in case the meaning of such propositions is determined by a realist semantics. 'Warrantedly assertibility/deniability' are properties possessed by propositions just in case a realist semantics is not available, and the meaning of such propositions is determined by rules for the applicability of the propositions under given circumstances. 'Assertible as true' is an impossible hybrid formed from the vocabulary of two incompatible theories. Second, there are two different ways of construing legal positivism and the semantics for propositions of law it subtends. The thought that simple positivism is mistaken just in adopting a realist semantics for propositions of law relies on conflating these two construals. On the first of them, simple positivism can be construed as adopting a realist semantics for propositions of law. However, the proposed alternative view, if one applies to it the same criteria for such an adoption, will turn out to be equally realist and equally positivist. If the alternative view is superior, as it may be, that will not be because it abandons a realist semantics for propositions of law. On the second construal, we can draw a significant distinction between a theory which is realist and a theory which is anti-realist about the semantics for propositions of law. However, both sophisticated positivism and the proposed alternative view are anti-realist on this construal. Either way, there is no room for an anti-positivist theory which is superior to positivism just in virtue of repudiating a realist semantics for propositions of law. I shall show what I mean.

1. Positivism says that, if a proposition of law is true, that is because some fact in the world makes it true; if a proposition of law is false, that is because no such fact obtains. The facts in question are facts about whether the sovereign has commanded the proposition in question, and so forth. Note that such a realist account could apply to propositions of law of the form 'A is mandatory', 'A is prohibited', and 'A is permissible', whether the latter is grounded in an actual legal source or the use of a closure rule. These three propositions would be true just in case the sovereign has commanded that A is mandatory, that A is prohibited, and either that A is permitted or neither that A is mandatory nor that A is prohibited. Positivism so construed is realist in its view of the semantics for legal propositions. Positivism so construed, however, does leave indeterminate some actual legal questions as they fall to be answered by courts: these are cases where facts about what the sovereign has commanded (for instance) will make the law speak with an uncertain voice or with many voices.[7] The indeterminacy is epistemological. The law speaks with an uncertain voice because the statute or ratio or

[7] Cf. here Raz's distinction between the two kinds of gaps in the law, and the non-existence of gaps where the law is silent (*The Authority of Law*, 70–7; also see Ch. 2.5 and Ch. 7.3.1 above).

constitutional clause was formulated many years ago when the possibility of the fact situation before the court could not have been contemplated. The law speaks with many voices because, for example, it took the ingenuity of the counsel in the instant case to juxtapose two diverse parts of the law and reveal the tension. The court does not, at first sight,[8] know how to decide the case. Positivist talk about adjudicative discretion arises from this epistemological indeterminacy. The indeterminacy need not be in the semantics; rather, the statement of the truth-condition is itself indeterminate and this indeterminacy is naturally transferred (under the semantic theory) to the proposition of law.

Dworkin finds the positivist doctrine of judicial discretion objectionable. He believes that the indeterminacy implied by the doctrine of judicial discretion is not merely epistemological. If a court has positivistic 'strong' discretion in, say, a contracts case, then it must be that the sovereign has not commanded a proposition which entails the validity of the contract at issue and that the sovereign has not commanded a proposition which entails the invalidity of the contract at issue. If so, then 'This contract is valid' will be neither true nor false. Thus the positivist doctrine of strong discretion is incompatible with its semantic realism. Suppose that we do not want to follow the route, which seems opened up by the failure of semantic realism, of rule-scepticism; we want to deny judicial discretion. We also have to give up a realist semantics as construed by positivism, for that commits us (in Dworkin's view) to the erroneous claim that positive law has already determined the answer to every legal question. It seems very tempting to claim then the following. Rules for when we are warranted in asserting given propositions of law constrain the court towards one view or another of, say, the validity of a contract. Thus the court does not have discretion, even though there is no fact in the world which makes 'This contract is valid' true, and also none which would make 'This contract is invalid' true.

Such a line of argument presents reasons for abandoning a realist semantics for propositions of law and adopting instead an anti-realist semantics. But does it present a set of reasons for abandoning positivism in favour of anti-positivism? Dworkin does

---

[8] And perhaps not at nth sight, though it will have to come to some decision.

not put his anti-positivist criticism in precisely the terms of the foregoing argument. He claims that positivism has a 'naïve' notion of 'fact'; positivism thinks that only 'hard facts' are facts.[9] However, according to Dworkin, deploying a parallel with literary criticism, there are also such things as facts of narrative consistency. For example, that David Copperfield had a homosexual affair with Steerforth is not a 'hard fact' in the novel *David Copperfield*, for the text is entirely silent on the matter explicitly. But perhaps to say David Copperfield did have such an affair provides a better fitting, more coherent narrative, and therefore the interpreter may still speak truly when claiming that David Copperfield had a homosexual affair with Steerforth.[10] The interpreter may speak truly, because she states a 'fact of narrative consistency'. The judge likewise when taking a decision on the basis of 'best fit' may not be exercising discretion in some interstice between 'hard facts', but may be uttering a proposition of law which has a truth-value, one determined by a legal 'fact of narrative consistency'. Or so the argument goes.

Now, it may or may not be right to say that there is no judicial discretion in hard cases. It is not relevant here either to refute or assert such a claim.[11] My point now is that the proposed interpretivist alternative, if phrased in terms of the concept of 'facts', may present just as much as the impugned positivism a realist construal of the semantics for propositions of law. Propositions of law still have truth-values, and have them because and only because they bear a certain relationship to real facts. The novelty of the 'narrative consistency' proposal is simply to extend the range of facts supplying truth-conditions for propositions of law within a realist semantic theory.

Here is an example. In a recent case,[12] a tender by the plaintiff

---

[9] *A Matter of Principle*, 138 ff., 167–8.

[10] It may be said that Dworkin has chosen a remarkably unhelpful example of an interpretative issue in literary criticism, one which is about as enlightening as the number of Lady Macbeth's children. Most worthwhile literary criticism has to do with richer and subtler issues—for instance, the quality and depth of the emotional relationship between Copperfield and Steerforth. But, unless one is to beg the question against Dworkin from the outset by saying that these richer and subtler matters are not 'factual', the logic of what he says remains unaffected by a change to a more plausible example.

[11] See Ch. 7 above for a discussion of the issues.

[12] *Blackpool and Fylde Aero Club* v. *Blackpool Borough Council* [1990] 3 All ER 25 (CA); see the discussion of the case by John Adams and Roger Brownsword, 'More in Expectation than in Hope', *Modern Law Review*, 54 (1991).

for a concession to be granted by the defendant was placed by the plaintiff in good time in the defendant's mailbox. The box was not emptied as it was supposed to be. The plaintiff's tender was marked as received late and not considered. The plaintiff brought an action alleging a breach on the part of the defendant of a warranty to the effect that if a tender were received by the deadline it would be considered along with other conforming tenders. The UK Court of Appeal unanimously held that there had been a breach of contract. Let us express the court's decision as a determination that, as a fact of narrative consistency, to hold that there had been a breach of contract in the circumstances specified would be more consistent with established standards to do with reasonable expectations, reasonable reliance, commercial practice, and the like (not to mention whatever wider principles of political morality may or may not be legitimately referred to) than would be the holding that there had been no breach.[13] *Ex hypothesi* there could be no claim that already there was a 'hard fact' in positive law which would make true the proposition 'defendant had in the fact or situation specified breached their contract with plaintiff as tenderers', since that particular fact situation had never previously come before any court nor had it been referred to explicitly in legislation. None the less, the court's claim that a decision should be given for the plaintiff, on the 'facts of narrative consistency' account, is true, if it is, because there is a fact of narrative consistency which makes it true.

The disagreement between positivism and this position taken by Dworkin can be expressed as a conflict between these two views:

(4a) A theory which is realist about the semantics for propositions of law, takes propositions of law to be true or false in virtue of independent social facts, limits social facts of the required kind to 'hard facts', and has no views (or no relevant views) on the semantics for propositions of morality.

(4b) A theory which is realist about the semantics for propositions of law, takes propositions of law to be true or false in

---

[13] Bingham LJ observes of the contention made by the defendant that their acts amounted to a warrant only that conforming tenders might be considered: 'This is a conclusion I cannot accept, and if it were accepted there would in my view be an unacceptable discrepancy between the law of contract and the confident assumptions of commercial parties' (ibid., at 30).

virtue of independent social facts, permits both 'hard facts' and 'facts of narrative consistency' to be social facts of the required kind, and has no views (or no relevant views) on the semantics for propositions of morality.

It is thus a disagreement *within positivism*, a disagreement perhaps between a sophisticated positivism and a simple positivism. It is not the disagreement Dworkin conceives it to be between positivism and some form of anti-positivism. It may be true that (4b) is a more satisfactory legal theory than (4a), because it subtends a better account of judicial discretion. But, even if that is true, it does not follow that positivism is wrong in claiming a realist semantics for propositions of law. The superiority of (4b) is perfectly compatible with a realist semantics for propositions of law.

2. Why is one tempted to think that the alternative 'interpretative' position is anti-realist, not realist? Well, what makes the claim about David Copperfield and Steerforth true, if it is true, is that its assertion is warranted by the rules of the literary enterprise—the claim does not correspond to anything that is really in the black-letter text, and so is not really a 'fact in the world'. Any theory of criticism, in order to represent criticism perspicuously, must allow for propositions of criticism to have meaning even though they are not true or false by correspondence to facts in the text. A theory assigning meaning to propositions of criticism must therefore be based on rules for when the assertion of such propositions is warranted. One such rule may be that the assertion of a proposition of criticism is warranted if what that proposition asserts corresponds to, or is clearly implied by, some proposition(s) of the relevant literary text. There are also other rules having to do with assertion being warranted when a greater narrative consistency is achieved by that assertion over some other available assertion. Anti-realism for propositions of criticism is motivated by the thought that a literary text is an artificial construct. If the text is silent on some point, it is absurd to suppose there is a 'truth of the matter' awaiting discovery. The indeterminacies in literary texts are not merely epistemological. The genuine meaningfulness of propositions of criticism must therefore be underwritten by conditions which warrant assertibility.

Again, however, a refutation of positivism cannot be built on this basis. A positivist may also view law as in this respect exactly like literary criticism. Positivism may be seen as denying that legal facts are really 'facts in the world'—rather, they are social constructs. The Blackpool Borough Council's contractual obligation to consider the Blackpool and Fylde Aero Club's tender exists, if it does, not naturally or in itself, but only because there are conditions which warrant the assertion that the obligation to consider the tender exists. These rules have a social source. The assertion of the Council's contractual obligation, according to the positivist, is an applied legal statement, which is, if it is, warranted by the 'ground-rules' of the legal enterprise. Positivism so construed is thus as 'anti-realist' as the interpretative theory, the theory which is supposedly superior just in being anti-realist. There is still a genuine dispute between the alternative theory and the positivist about the extent of the discretion actually permitted to judges by the ground-rules of the legal enterprise. But, if it is a Good Thing to be anti-realist about the semantics for propositions of law, then, on this second way of construing what it is to be realist about propositions of law, positivism can be represented as anti-realist in just the same way that the theory of law as interpretation is anti-realist.

In short, if any facts can underwrite a realist semantics for propositions of law, 'facts of narrative consistency' could in principle be as much the kind of social facts which underwrite in a realist way a positivist account of propositions of law as the original 'hard facts'. It would be an internal debate between rival realist accounts of the semantics for propositions of law whether there were semantic relations to 'facts of narrative consistency' or not. If simple, 'hard fact' positivism is wrong, as indeed it might be, the mistake would not be in semantic theory, but in semantic content. The dispute between 'hard fact' positivism and 'facts of narrative consistency' positivism would be the dispute between (4a) and (4b) above (page 214). On the other hand, suppose we acknowledge that to root the meaning of propositions of law in conditions for warranted assertibility rather than correspondence with facts is to be 'anti-realist'. We reject, that is, 'realism' about the semantics for propositions of law. A sophisticated positivism may then have common cause with Dworkin's interpretative theory in this rejection. If such a sophisticated positivism is wrong, as it might be, that is because it has wrong the warranted-assertibility conditions, the ground-rules. The dispute between a sophisticated positivism and an anti-positivism which alleged such a mistake on the part of the sophisticated positivism about the conditions for warranted assertibility of propositions of law would be the dispute between

> (3) A theory which believes that propositions of law are understood by knowing the conditions that warrant their assertion, may believe that propositions of morality are understood either in terms of truth-conditions or in terms of conditions for warranted assertion, and takes propositions of law to be in part warrantedly assertible in virtue of rules which connect propositions of law with propositions of morality.

and a form of positivist theory

> (4c) A theory which is anti-realist about the semantics for propositions of law, takes propositions of law to be warrantedly assertible by and only rules which have a social source, and has no views (or no relevant views) on the semantics for propositions of morality.

Positivism and natural law theory are on one side of a dispute about whether propositions of law can have determinate meaning (whether because they have truth-conditions or conditions for warranted assertibility). The parties on the other side are those versions of Legal Realism and Critical Legal Studies which stress radical indeterminacy in the law, the impossibility of legal doctrine, and so forth. There can be serious disagreements between the supporters of determinate meaning and acceptability for propositions of law. Are determinacy and acceptability to be construed in terms of 'truth' taken as 'correspondence with reality', or are they to be construed in terms of 'warranted by conventions of assertibility'? This disagreement is independent of another disagreement, also potentially serious, over what is the relevant part of 'reality', or what are the relevant conventions of assertibility. Some theorists think that the reality is a moral order, or that the conventions are moral conventions; call them 'natural law theorists'. Other theorists think that the reality is a realm of social fact, or that the conventions are social conventions; call them 'positivists'. Those who take some given one of the variety of available positions naturally think that those who take the others are mistaken. There is however no way in which the mistake of positivism as such is to adopt a realist semantics for propositions of law. The mistake, if there is one, is either to be realist, or to be positivist, or to be both, and quite different kinds of arguments would be required for each of the three variants. It is not possible to reject simple positivism merely by repudiating its commitment to a realist semantics for propositions of law.

3. DOING WITHOUT SEMANTICS

The theory attributed to sophisticated positivism in this chapter so far has drawn on ideas sketched out by Dworkin. That may seem counter-intuitive, since Dworkin has deservedly made a reputation as an opponent of positivism. I shall show in Chapter 12 below that there are reasons for treating carefully Dworkin's claims that his views are not positivistic. However, at the present time I am simply allowing sophisticated positivism to gather potentially useful arguments where it may. In such a spirit, let us continue to consider Dworkin's views on law, interpretation, and semantics.

3.1. *The semantic sting*

In the first three chapters of *Law's Empire*, his latest expressed views on semantics and legal philosophy, Dworkin seems to be expressing a view different from the one I have been discussing. He wants to defend the radical originality of his new theory of law as integrity by distinguishing it from all three of positivism, natural law, and realism. All of these traditional theories are victims of what he calls 'the semantic sting'; his theory 'pulls the semantic sting'. That is, the three traditional theories each in their own way think that semantics is relevant to legal philosophy. Dworkin now thinks that to hold that semantics is relevant to legal philosophy is the big mistake, rather than, as he thought in *A Matter of Principle*, that the big mistake was to have the wrong semantics. The language of his exposition, familiarly, is suggestive and metaphorical. 'The semantic sting' is said to be the idea that lawyers cannot meaningfully disagree about the core meaning of legal terms, or (another formulation), cannot meaningfully disagree about what are the pivotal cases of certain legal concepts. This belief about the impossibility of disagreement is said to be 'semantic', because the rules in which the modality is embodied are semantic rules. Terms like 'offer' or 'acceptance', so the traditional theories of law supposedly maintain, have determinate meanings which are underwritten either by a theory which generates the truth-conditions for sentences containing these terms or by a theory yielding the conditions for warranted assertibility of such sentences. These conditions are exemplified in the pivotal cases of such terms. Dworkin talks of 'rules' rather than conditions, and his new theory 'pulls the semantic sting' because it denies the existence of any such fixed meaning-rules. If law is an interpretative practice, then at any time the agreement which is the ground of law is, as he puts it, contingent and local. It cannot be said that 'offer' just by virtue of its determinate meaning picks out the kind of thing this plaintiff did. Rather, we can only say that this particular group of people at this particular time regard such an action as a clear case of an offer. The point of 'pulling the semantic sting' is to free politicians and judges and citizens to look beyond actual legal practices at any given point of time and place, and to think deeply about what the practice might become if it is to be the best instance of that practice, goals of fundamental importance to Dworkin's project in the book.

I shall show that it is perfectly possible to make sense of the thought that legal theory can 'do without semantics'. However, I shall also show that the possibility does nothing to help sophisticated positivism in any campaign against simple positivism.

3.2. Rawls and the independence of moral theory

The key to understanding Dworkin's views on the present topic lies in a continuing interest on his part with views expressed by John Rawls.[14] In his 1975 paper, 'The Independence of Moral Theory', Rawls distinguishes systematically and stipulatively between 'moral philosophy' and 'moral theory'. Moral philosophy includes such things as epistemology, ontology, and philosophy of mind as they relate to morality. Moral theory is 'the study of substantive moral conceptions, that is, the study of how the basic notions of the right, the good and moral worth may be arranged to form different moral structures' (5). The theme of Rawls's paper is that the two are independent. Moral theory does not suppose either

---

[14] Since I do not wish beyond a certain point to focus on intellectual biography, it may lie in their both being heirs of a common US tradition of pragmatism.

that the results of such theorizing are assertions of objective truth, or that they are not.

The point of Dworkin's calling law as integrity an 'interpretive' theory seems precisely to be to exhibit it as 'legal theory', and thus independent of 'legal philosophy', in the sense of Rawls's 'theory'/ 'philosophy' distinction. In order to see whether Rawls's view would underwrite Dworkin's, it will be necessary first to discuss further Rawls's views in their own right.

Rawls is here carrying forward methodological ideas embodied in the earlier *A Theory of Justice* (1971). In his earliest attempt to formulate a methodology for moral philosophy,[15] Rawls aimed to present 'a reasonable method for validating or invalidating . . . moral rules and . . . decisions' (177) by defining, first, 'a class of competent moral judges' (178–81) and, second, 'the class of considered moral judgments' (1813). These definitions are complex, and make no reference to the content of such judgements. The preferred device for validating and invalidating moral rules and decisions will be given by a set of principles that systematically define the interrelations between the set of judgements in question (184). As has been remarked,[16] this early conception of method in ethics takes a (scientific, not legal) positivist conception of science as its model. Observation (considered judgement of competent judge) is clearly distinguished from theory (explication by principles). The job of theory is to codify independent observations. This quasi-scientific positivism has, however, gone by the time of *A Theory of Justice*. Instead (cf. *A Theory of Justice*, 48), Rawls makes it quite clear that, as he sees things in that book, initial conviction and proposed general conception have no innate priority one over the other. On page 20 of *A Theory of Justice*, he writes that in the process of balancing considered judgements against principles 'we work from both ends'. When there are discrepancies between our judgements of principle and our considered particular convictions 'we have a choice. We can either modify the account of the initial situation or we can revise our existing judgments'. By 'going back and forth' in this way we arrive at a 'reflective equilibrium' in which our principles 'match our considered judgments duly pruned and adjusted'. Theoretically,

---

[15] 'Outline for a Decision Procedure in Ethics', *Philosophical Review*, 60 (1951).
[16] By C. F. Delaney, 'Rawls on Method', in Kai Nielsen and Roger A. Shiner (eds.), *New Essays on Contract Theory* (Guelph, Ont., 1977), 158.

either may give way in the search for reflective equilibrium. Later the state of having arrived at a theory of justice is said to be 'one reached after a person has weighed various proposed conceptions and he has either revised his judgments to accord with one of them or held fast to his initial convictions (and the corresponding conception)' (48).

Rawls's desertion of a model which owed something to positivism in philosophy of science is not coincidental. This impression is reinforced by key footnotes acknowledging the influence on his methodological views of Goodman's (*A Theory of Justice*, 20 n. 7) and Quine's (*A Theory of Justice*, 579 n. 33) opposition to a positivism in science which privileges observational protocols.[17] Quine, in fact, is specifically echoed when Rawls remarks 'there are no judgments on any level of generality that are in principle immune to revisions' ('Independence', 8). The classic statement of the relevant methodology is found in Goodman:

> Rules and particular inferences alike are justified by being brought into agreement with one another. *A rule is amended if it yields an inference we are unwilling to accept; an inference is rejected if it violates a rule we are unwilling to amend.* The process of justification is the delicate one of making mutual adjustments between rules and accepted inferences.[18]

Compare that quotation with this passage from Rawls's 1980 Dewey Lectures on Kantian Constructivism:

> The parties in the original position do not agree on what the moral facts are, as if there were already such facts. It is not that, being situated impartially, they have a clear and undistorted view of a prior and

---

[17] Note that Rawls himself seems to be unclear about the relation between *A Theory of Justice* and the 1951 paper. *A Theory of Justice*, 579 n. 33, implies no change in view. It is of course appealing to dissolve the unclarity by saying that between the 2 writings Rawls's views of both science and morality have changed in lockstep. But *A Theory of Justice*, 49, implies a difference between them in that, whereas we cannot change the motions of the heavenly bodies, there is nothing analogously immune from change in morality. For a valuable discussion of problems in the way both Rawls and Dworkin treat the analogy between moral/political theories and scientific theories, see Marsha Hanen, 'Justification as Coherence', in M. A. Stewart (ed.), *Law, Morality, and Rights* (Boston, Mass., 1983), *passim*. See also my 'The Metaphysics of Taking Rights Seriously', *Philosophia*, 13 (1982), 234–9.

[18] Nelson Goodman, *Fact, Fiction and Forecast* (New York, 1965), 64; Goodman's italics.

independent moral order. Rather (for constructivism) there is no such order, and therefore no such facts apart from the procedure of construction as a whole; the facts are identified by the principles which result.[19]

Despite all the claims about the independence of moral theory, Rawls has both an implicit epistemology and an implicit ontology. The epistemology is coherentist and the ontology nominalist. Rawls is after a form of justification, which is spelt out as 'a matter of the mutual support of many considerations, of everything fitting together in one coherent view' (*A Theory of Justice*, 579; cf. generally 577–82). Without the claims about revisability and justification, we would have pure moral theory. But with them, we do have moral *philosophy* in the technical sense Rawls employs. It is true that it takes the form of saying that moral philosophy is irrelevant to moral theory, but this does not prevent it from being a moral philosophy. The passage quoted from the Dewey Lectures makes the point clear. It is couched in quite explicitly 'philosophical' terms. Rawls may say, 'I do not know whether there are independent moral facts or not. But I do not have to know. For I consider moral claims sufficiently justified if they nest with each other appropriately in a theory in reflective equilibrium.' But that is not a remark in moral theory; it is a remark in moral philosophy about the justification of moral theories.

3.3. *Hercules and the independence of legal theory*

Let us now see how ideas such as Rawls's were applied by Dworkin to law. In an important paper which preceded (at least, in terms of date of publication) the introduction of Hercules in 'Hard Cases' (*Taking Rights Seriously*, ch. 4), Dworkin elaborated upon Rawls's conception of reflective equilibrium in an interesting way ('Justice and Rights', *Taking Rights Seriously*, ch. 6), and implicitly invited its application to law. 'We have,' he says, 'a choice between two general models that define coherence and explain why it is required' (*Taking Rights Seriously*, 160). One of these he calls a 'natural' model, and the other a 'constructive' model. On the natural model, the significance of coherence in a moral theory or a Herculean theory of law is instrumental. Such a

---

[19] 'Kantian Constructivism Moral Theory', *Journal of Philosophy*, 77 (1980), 568.

theory, according to this model, putatively describes an objective moral reality. The theory is related to particular intuitions of this reality as a physical theory is related to observation statements. 'Moral reasoning or philosophy is a process of reconstructing the fundamental principles by assembling concrete judgments in the right order, as a natural historian reconstructs the shape of the whole animal from the fragments of its bones that he has found' (ibid.). The 'constructive' model, on the other hand, 'treats intuitions of justice not as clues to the existence of independent principles, but rather as stipulated features of a general theory to be constructed as if a sculptor set himself to carve the animal that best fits a pile of bones he happened to find together . . . It does not assume that the animal it matches to the bones actually exists' (ibid.). Dworkin goes on to state his own clear preference for the 'constructive' model, and I believe we are meant to take it as the model for adjudicative deliberation. Applied to the problem of adjudication specifically, the constructive model yields the recipe that a judge faced with a novel claim accepts existing precedents 'as specifications for a principle that he must construct, out of a sense of responsibility for consistency with what has gone before' (161).

Dworkin takes the constructive model to be metaphysically unambitious. It does not, he says, 'deny, any more than it affirms, the objective standing of any of' the convictions that men and women who reason within the model hold sincerely and bring to it. 'It is therefore consistent with, though as a model of reasoning it does not require, the moral ontology that the natural model presupposes' (*Taking Rights Seriously*, 162). In this claim he is marching in parallel with Rawls in 'The Independence of Moral Theory'. The issue of whether the constructive model can be transferred to adjudicative deliberation is a great deal more complicated than Dworkin acknowledges.

In the first place, note the difference between the following theses about legal justification:

(A) In the complete scheme constructed by Hercules, his judgments about particular cases are justified if and only if they cohere with the principles of background political morality he uses, and the principles of background political morality he uses are justified if and only if they cohere with his judgments about the particular cases.

(*B*) Particular mundane judicial decisions are justified if and only if they cohere with legal principles, and legal principles are justified if and only if they cohere with particular mundane judicial decisions.

(*A*) represents the construal of Herculean theorizing in constructivist terms. (*B*) represents the construal of mundane legal justification in constructivist terms. These two construals are distinct and independent.

It is important to draw these distinctions for two reasons. First, (*B*), as a candidate theory of mundane legal justification, on the face of it makes no reference to any Herculean scheme. In order to defend (*B*) as a model of mundane adjudicative deliberation, there is no need at all to postulate a judge of superhuman skill, learning, patience, and acumen who represents the idealization of the model. (*B*) stands or falls on its own feet as a theory of mundane legal justification. Second, if we suppose that 'legal principle' is given a reading consistent with a content-independent theory of law—e.g., 'abbreviated reference to a number of legal rules', as in Chapter 2.5 above—then (*B*) is the kind of coherence theory of mundane legal justification defended by MacCormick (cf. Chapter 2.5). As such, (*B*) is not strong enough to support the 'noble dream' of fully 'defensible' and 'deeply justified' judicial decisions. For the latter purpose, some 'thicker', content-dependent notion of 'principle' is required, such as, for example, Dworkin's in his original paper 'The Model of Rules': a 'principle' is a 'standard to be observed . . . because it is a requirement of justice or fairness or some other dimension of morality' (*Taking Rights Seriously*, 23).

The purpose of Herculean theorizing is not merely to reach an equilibrium in which as a matter of fact the principles that happen to have occurred to Hercules and the particular cases that happen to have occurred to him are stably coherent. That would not differentiate Hercules from any moderately reflective and experienced mundane judge. Hercules is superhuman because every candidate principle and every possible particular case has occurred to him, and his coherent scheme results from pruning and adjusting among all of these. Hercules is granted the capacity to 'work out [his] entire scheme in advance, so that he would be ready to confront litigants with an entire theory of law should this be necessary to justify any particular decision' (*Taking Rights Seriously*, 117). But, if every possible particular case—every possible fact situation that might come before a court—has occurred to Hercules, and he has found a place coherent with fundamental principle for each and every one, then the fact that this equilibrium was arrived at by searching Goodmanesquely for coherence drops out as irrelevant. It does so for two reasons.

The first I have discussed in Chapter 7. Formally, a coherent scheme and a deductively sound scheme, if both are complete and categorical, are equally consistent and coherent. The justificatory work is done by presumably sound principles. Justification by coherence has been abandoned in favour of justification by derivability from sound principle. Hercules has become the supreme exponent of 'mechanical jurisprudence'. Mechanical jurisprudence is the spectre that it is in the context of mundane adjudication because and only because one knows that the mundane judge not only will be working from a limited set of principles but also will be limited in his or her ability to make deductively sound applications of those principles to particular cases. Hercules *ex hypothesi* is not so lacking. Herculean mechanical jurisprudence is the painless version of something which in its mundane form is all too painful. Moreover, even the fact that Hercules has a scheme involving principles as well as judgments about particular cases drops out as irrelevant. As long as Hercules does have the right answer about every particular case, the process by which he arrived at that answer is of merely anecdotal interest. Hercules is not merely the perfect philosophically articulate mundane judge; he is also the perfect Herbert, the judge who lives and dies by the application of rules and the exercise of discretion. Hercules has also become the perfect Hero, the exponent of palm-tree justice for political ends.[20] Or, best of all, at the infinite Herculean point these three sharply contrasting techniques of mundane adjudication will non-asymptotically converge.

The second reason is this. Suppose we take seriously the distinction between (*A*) and (*B*) above. Our interest is in Hercules as a conceit for interpreting mundane adjudicative deliberation. The existence of a Herculean theory is supposed to show how it is

[20] 'Hero' is Harris's Ungerian counterweight to Hercules; see 'Legal Doctrine and Interests in Land', in J. Eekelaar and J. Bell (eds), *Oxford Essays in Jurisprudence*, iii (Oxford, 1987), 194 ff., 'Unger's Critique of Formalism in Legal Reasoning', *Modern Law Review*, 52 (1989), 46 ff. Harris's third character Humdrum seems remarkably like Dworkin's 'Herbert'.

that when judges 'go beyond' settled law, they do not float free in a space beyond semantics. The fantasy of Hercules does generate a theory of justification for the mundane judicial decision. Such a theory, however, is not a constructivist theory of mundane adjudication. We may suppose, for example, that Hercules has already considered as a hypothetical possibility the very particular type of fact situation which constitutes *Junior Books*,[21] and figured out its legal significance. He has found that either a verdict for the plaintiff or a verdict for the defendant is that singular verdict which will make *Junior Books* consistent with the rest of his scheme. He is prepared to face litigant or judge with his views on *Junior Books* when that case or one identical to it actually comes before the bar. When the House of Lords found itself in 1982 asked to adjudicate *Junior Books*, it was committed as it were to ringing Hercules up and requesting his answer to the question of how *Junior Books* should be decided. Or, to bring the image up to date, it might be that the Herculean scheme is on-line via Herculexis; the court's duty is to type in the fact situation, and adjudicate by reproducing the answer that comes up on the screen. The mundane judicial decision in some particular case is justified if and only if it is that decision which corresponds to the decision on the fact situation of that case in the Herculean scheme. I emphasize 'correspond' to focus on the nature of the mode of justification embodied in the 'Herculexis' model. The justificatory theory embodied in the model is non-coherentist and non-relativist. It is in fact a thoroughly modern version of the Holmesian 'brooding omni-presence'.[22] The propositions of law which constitute judicial verdicts map directly on to the Herculean scheme to find their truth-conditions. Hercules' scheme is, from the point of view of a mundane judge, an 'independent moral order'. One who insists that from *Hercules'* point of view his scheme is *not* a description of 'independent moral order', but something Hercules has *constructed* is simply insisting on the truth of a theory of type (2) in our initial taxonomy, as opposed to a theory of type (1). He or she is not defending a theory of type (3) which conceives of propositions of law as having meaning through conditions for warranted assertibility. However metaphysically unambitious and Goodmanian Hercules

---

[21] *Junior Books Ltd.* v. *Veitchi Co. Ltd.* [1982] 3 All ER 201.
[22] *Southern Pacific Company* v. *Jensen*, 244 US 205 (1917), at 222.

is, as long as his deliverances define for mundane judges the correct verdict, then the adjudicative activity of mundane judges is not *itself* being interpreted constructively; nor is there any lack of metaphysical ambition on the part of the interpreter. Once again, while we have produced a theory different from simple positivism, it is as much as simple positivism a theory which proposes a realist semantics for propositions of law. We have thus still failed to 'draw the semantic sting'.[23]

3.4. 'Political, not metaphysical'

Let me briefly review the argument of this chapter so far. Sophisticated positivism's thought (in Chapter 2.6) was that a richer and more plausible positivistic theory of the semantics for propositions of law could be devised by taking interpretation seriously and giving an anti-realist account of that semantics. This claim by sophisticated positivism was simply laid out in Chapter 2.6; it was not evaluated. I have argued here first (Chapter 8.2) that, although the possibility exists for serious disagreement between realist and anti-realist accounts of the semantics for propositions of law, the difference between realist and anti-realist accounts does not at all map on to the opposition of simple and sophisticated positivism, nor on to the opposition of positivism and anti-positivism. I argued second (Chapter 8.3) that the insistence on the constructive character of a 'Herculean theory' of law as the basis for the correctness of mundane propositions of law does not produce a theory of mundane law which 'does without semantics'. In fact, a 'Herculean theory' implies a realist account of the semantics for propositions of *law*. The result of this discussion is that we have not yet given a clear sense to the claim by sophisticated positivism to improve upon simple positivism by abandoning realist semantics and taking the interpretative turn.

There is a further development yet in the project of 'doing without semantics' in Rawls's most recent work, beginning with the revealingly titled paper 'Justice as Fairness: Political not Metaphysical'.[24] This work does indeed secure the independence

---

[23] Cf. Schauer, *Playing By the Rules*, 217: 'The realist programme works only if the semantic theory on which it is based incorporates a theory of optimal particularistic decision-making.' My remarks here assert the complementary conditional. The Herculean project, as 'a theory of optimal particularistic decision-making', requires a realist semantic theory.

[24] *Philosophy and Public Affairs*, 14 (1985); also 'The Idea of an Overlapping

of moral theory, and so we may enquire whether it will underwrite talk of 'pulling the semantic sting' in legal philosophy and doing without semantics. In this work, the primary thrust is on the instrumental importance of using moral reflection to achieve an 'overlapping consensus' on a given political conception of justice, in order to produce a stable democracy given the fact of moral pluralism. An 'overlapping consensus' is to be contrasted with a mere 'modus vivendi', an agreement as might be reached in labour negotiations—a 'Hobbesian' solution which no one likes but is agreed on just so that life can continue. This conception of justice as fairness is indeed 'political', not 'metaphysical'. Its justification lies in its instrumental value, not in its resulting from a process of pruning and adjusting among principles and considered judgements. The only 'metaphysical' commitment being made is to the fact of moral pluralism. But that is no 'metaphysical' commitment at all. The thought does not have to be that people who believe that there is moral truth and that they know it are mistaken. It merely has to be that, like it or not, they have to get on in a democratic society with people who think differently, and therefore that, if the society is to be stable, they all have to develop a consensus on which they can agree despite other fundamental disagreements. The point in the present context is that, since this political conception of justice as fairness eschews metaphysics, its cogency as a political conception has no metaphysical significance. Its cogency presents no arguments either for or against any given view of the semantics for propositions of morality, politics, or law.

We thus can make sense of the idea of 'doing without semantics' in political or moral or legal theorizing. We construe a given theoretical project as being simply the matter of developing a political or moral or legal conception of some kind, either for its own sake, or, more plausibly, for the sake of some goal we believe the development of such a conception will serve. Such a project can well be done without making specific reference to semantics. But there is a price. The satisfactory completion of such a project does nothing to show that any given semantic theory about the

Consensus', *Oxford Journal of Legal Studies*, 7 (1987), 'The Domain of the Political and Overlapping Consensus', *New York University Law Review*, 64 (1989). For a thorough analysis and criticism, see Jean Hampton's 'Should Political Philosophy Be Done Without Metaphysics?', *Ethics*, 99 (1989); see also my 'Consensus as Foundation', in Carole Stewart (ed.), *Moral Relativism* (Toronto, 1992).

propositions occurring in such a project is mistaken. I have argued that prior to the last few years Rawls's own work was not purely 'political'; it had a 'metaphysical' element in it. Moreover, this element was crucial to the project as Rawls conceived it. He was concerned to show how a particular conception would be *justified*, not merely necessary for political stability. Justification, however, is an issue of 'metaphysics', not 'politics'. Thus Rawls took a stance on issues in 'metaphysics' to the extent that he defended a constructivist account of justification. He no longer takes such a stance, since the public justification for a given conception of justice is 'political, not metaphysical'. The frame of reference for the project has been changed. The project of defending a certain conception of justice as necessary for political stability in a pluralistic world is not a project abstract enough to raise issues of semantics. Semantics is not 'done without' in a way which implies errors on the part of other theories which 'do semantics'. Rather, issues of semantics simply do not arise at the level at which the project operates.

As noted, Dworkin sees his project in *Law's Empire* as 'doing without semantics'. It is in fact possible to see his concerns in the same kind of light as Rawls's recent work, as 'political, not metaphysical'. Even in *Taking Rights Seriously*, there are elements of a 'political' motivation for the requirement of 'articulate consistency' and the emphasis on justification by coherence. The constructive model for reflective equilibrium does not require a metaphysically ambitious ontology, because, Dworkin claims, 'its requirements are independent of it' (*Taking Rights Seriously*, 162). 'The constructive model requires coherence for independent reasons of political morality' (*Taking Rights Seriously*, 163), namely, that 'it is unfair for officials to act except on the basis of a general public theory that will constrain them to consistency, provide a public standard for testing or debating or predicting what they do, and not allow appeals to unique intuitions that might mask prejudice or self-interest in particular cases' (*Taking Rights Seriously*, 162–3). Consider also the important notion in *Taking Rights Seriously* of 'articulate consistency'. Judges, Dworkin says (*Taking Rights Seriously*, 87), are subject to the doctrine of political responsibility. 'This doctrine states, in its most general form, that political officials must make only such political decisions as they can justify within a political theory that also justifies the other decisions they propose to make' (ibid.). The doctrine of political responsibility demands 'articulate consistency' (*Taking Rights Seriously*, 88), the articulation of a consistent set of coherent justificatory principles.[25] Hercules appears later on as the paradigm of articulate consistency. The project of law as integrity in *Law's Empire* also has a clear political dimension to it. In chapters 8–10, Dworkin shows how Hercules, the arch-exponent of law as integrity, would go about deciding centrally important cases. The point of the discussion is to show law as integrity at work in substantive adjudication.[26]

If in fact the reasoning in the early part of *Law's Empire* was that the theory of law as integrity 'pulls the semantic sting' because it does legal theory in a purely political fashion, then we could understand the project as 'political, not metaphysical' on the model of Rawls and the overlapping consensus. But that is not Dworkin's argument. He links his position to the same metaphysical issues in philosophy of science as he did in *Taking Rights Seriously* and that Rawls did in *A Theory of Justice*—the well-known 'constructivist' image from Otto Neurath of rebuilding the ship while at sea is invoked (*Law's Empire*, 111). But, as I have shown, constructivism does not 'do without semantics' and eschew metaphysics. It is one particular theory in these domains, a theory of an anti-realist and ontologically indiscriminate kind.

Dworkin thus has a fundamental choice to make. Several reviewers of *Law's Empire* have claimed that Dworkin's eschewal of semantics is self-deceptive; he in fact has a semantic theory.[27] It

[25] MacCormick also defends the requirement of adjudicative coherence for reasons of political morality; cf., e.g., *Legal Reasoning and Legal Theory*, 187. Coherentist anti-positivism differs from coherentist positivism in the account of what must all cohere, not in the demand for coherence as such. See also Ch. 2.5 above.

[26] Cf. however Denise Réaume's convincing argument in her essasy on *Law's Empire* that as a political project law as integrity suffers from deep conceptual flaws: 'Is Integrity a Virtue?', *University of Toronto Law Journal*, 39 (1989).

[27] John Finnis, 'On Reason and Authority in Law's Empire', *Law and Philosophy*, 6 (1987), 367, quoting *Law's Empire*, 91; Steven Burton, 'Ronald Dworkin and Legal Positivism', *Iowa Law Review*, 73 (1987), quoting *Law's Empire*, 91, and also the discussion of evil legal systems and internal v. external scepticism (*Law's Empire*, 76–86, 101–8); Réaume, 'Is Integrity a Virtue?', 381–2, arguing that Dworkin's theory is committed to propositions of law having truth-values. She does not quote a passage, but the following will surely do: 'According to law as integrity, propositions of law are true if they figure in or follow from the principles of justice, fairness, and procedural due process that provide the best constructive interpretation of the community's legal practice' (*Law's Empire*, 225).

is not necessary for my argument that they are right, although as a matter of fact I think they are. Rather, my argument is dilemmatic (and see Ch. 12.3 below for a further dilemmatic argument against Dworkin). Dworkin's argument against the three traditional theories of positivism, natural law theory, and legal realism cannot be that those theories have a semantics for propositions of law and law as integrity does not. It can only be that the semantic theory of law as integrity is a better semantic theory than the others. If the mistake of positivism, for instance, is in its semantics, then a better theory can only be better by having a better semantics. If on the other hand law as integrity and as constructive interpretation (*Law's Empire*, 52) is 'political, not metaphysical', then indeed it can 'do without semantics'. But it pays the price then of in no way cutting against those theories of law which discuss the semantics for propositions of law such as positivism. In fact, the avowedly political and extra-foundational nature of the enterprise has led many theorists sympathetic to Critical Legal Studies to claim that Dworkin owes us an explanation of why his view is any different from theirs.[28] There is no coherent third way of 'pulling the semantic sting' by showing, without doing metaphysics, that the metaphysical mistake is to do metaphysics; of showing without doing semantic theory that the semantic theorist's mistake is to do semantic theory.

4. THE RIGHTS THESIS

The original motivation for sophisticated positivism's move away from a realist semantics for propositions of law lay in distrust of a theory which licenses formalistic reasoning and unfettered discretion. But why have those concerns? Such a theory is of type (4) in our initial taxonomy (see page 208 above). Why think that such a theory is inadequate? The explanation must be that such a semantics would be too restrictive. It would not admit into the set of considerations relevant to the meaning of legal propositions some rules which should be admitted. It is in some sense unjust or

---

[28] See Allan Hutchinson and John Wakefield, 'A Hard Look at "Hard Cases"', *Oxford Journal of Legal Studies*, 2 (1982); Allan Hutchinson, 'Indiana Dworkin and Law's Empire', *Yale Law Journal*, 96 (1987); Andrew Altman, 'Legal Realism', *Philosophy and Public Affairs*, 15 (1985–6); J. M. Balkin, 'Taking Ideology Seriously', *UMKC Law Review*, 55 (1987).

unfair to litigants not to allow courts that degree of freedom in interpreting propositions of law. The discussion in the preceding sections has shown that simple positivism's mistake, if there is one, cannot be remedied by abandoning a realist for an anti-realist semantics, nor can it be remedied by abandoning semantics, period. The supposed mistake is independent of realism and anti-realism as those positions might characterize types (1)–(3) of the taxonomy. The reason is not hard to see—the mistake is one about the range or scope of propositions of law with truth-values prior to the decision in the relevant legal case.

The strongest version in recent legal thought of the view that the claim of law asserted by a litigant has in principle a truth-value prior to the decision is, of course, Dworkin's 'Rights Thesis', the claim that 'judicial decisions enforce existing political rights' (*Taking Rights Seriously*, 87), and its corollary, that even in hard cases it is the judge's duty to discover what the rights of the parties are, and not to invent new rights retrospectively (*Taking Rights Seriously*, 81). The Rights Thesis is roundly anti-positivistic. I shall argue, though, that adoption of the Thesis, or some legal theory of similar metaphysical ambition, is the only alternative to simple positivism's views on interpretation and semantics.

It is an important part of the theory of law as an interpretative enterprise that adjudication in hard cases is not discretionary, but is constrained by authoritative non-source-based rules. The thesis that aims to differentiate law-as-interpretation from simple positivism is the Rights Thesis. The law–literature analogy is introduced to show how there can still be right answers to legal questions even though the standard of rightness is not to be explained in narrow descriptivist or realist terms. That is, an adjudicative decision in a hard case may indeed be in principle correct, but not because the dispositive proposition of law enunciated in giving the decision maps on to an independently existing fact of some kind. The decision in a hard case will rather be correct because the decision is a proper interpretation of the relevant law, according to some antecedently existing standards of propriety in interpretation. The Rights Thesis asserts that behind even a hard case there exist antecedent entitlements which allow us to speak of a decision as correct in case it enforces these entitlements. Thus the Rights Thesis seems fully 'realistic' in its underlying semantics. On the other hand, the move from description to interpretation is to be seen as a move from 'realism' to 'anti-realism'. That is, the point of moving from correctness of description to correctness of interpretation is to move from a realist standard of correctness which is unpacked in terms of a semantic relation to some independent fact (in the case of positivism, for example, some 'social fact' and of natural law some 'natural' fact) to an interpretivist standard of correctness which is unpacked in terms of 'correct because warrantedly assertible'. Anti-realism and 'warranted assertibility' are therefore being used both to underwrite the adjudicative enforcement of antecedently existing entitlements in accordance with the Rights Thesis and to avoid the difficulties of a realist semantics for statements of law.

This combination makes no sense. Consider literature. A novel or other work of literature is the product of an artist. The world of the work may in various ways map on to or be like our world. But it is in one very fundamental way different from our world. It has in it only what its creator has put there. So there can be aspects of that world about which the text of the work is silent—say, about David Copperfield's blood-type or on whether David had a homosexual affair with Steerforth. Were David one of us, then, while we might not know which of the relevant propositions is true, we do know that either David had such an affair or that he did not have such an affair or that one of a variety of ambiguous borderline cases occurred depending on how 'affair' is defined. Our ignorance about the literary David Copperfield is of a different order. If we wanted to find out the truth about a David in our world, we could hire a private detective. No private detective would help us in the case of Dickens's David, or only the kind of private detective who discovers authors' diaries and discarded drafts in attic trunks.

All this of course yields for the enterprise of literary criticism a significant difference between a narrow set of ground-rules excluding and a wider and more flexible set of ground-rules including such interpretivist considerations as 'best fit' or 'narrative coherence'. Under the narrow set, literary interpretation would indeed be a boring business; the narrow set would also devalue great works of literature and their creators. It makes much more sense to adopt some more flexible set of ground-rules as the ground-rules for the enterprise of literary interpretation just because the world of the work is created in a particular way, and literary criticism from the empirical point of view would thus be narrowly constrained by purely descriptive ground-rules.

Now, is the legal world—that world of which the true propositions of law are supposedly a description—like our natural world or like the world of a novel?

It might be said that in one way the legal world is very like the world of a novel. It is like the world of a novel in that the characters in it only have the properties they have—duties, rights, liberties, immunities, powers, etc.—because some creator—a legislature, a sovereign, a court—has given the characters those properties. Just as it is only true-in-the-world-of-David Copperfield that David had an aunt called Peg, so it is only true-in-the-world-of-legal-system-LS_1 that in a certain fact situation George has grounds for divorce from Georgina. If the settled law of LS_1 does not say either way whether in certain circumstances George has grounds for divorce from Georgina, then but for the deployment of closure rules we would have no more reason to say that George does have grounds for divorce from Georgina than we have to say in the face of Dickens's silence on the subject that David had type A blood or had a homosexual affair with Steerforth.

Such a story is of course a quite familiar story about the nature of the legal order. However, it is *simple positivism*'s story. As such, the story promotes no parallel between interpretation in law and interpretation in literature which will appeal to simple positivism's opponents. The acknowledgement that the judge faced with the task of interpreting created legal texts is facing a task analogous to that facing the interpreter of a literary text in that both are dealing with created worlds is *de facto* an acknowledgement that positivism is importantly right about the nature of law.

On the other hand, if one rejects the law–literature analogy and takes seriously the thought that the legal world is like the natural world, not the world of a work of literature, and that our uncertainty about what properties we have in the legal world is on a par with our uncertainty about the possession or otherwise of a property by a real person, then the Rights Thesis indeed has real point to it. So, moreover, does the injunction to require a dimension of fit additional to fit with settled law—namely, fit with the best justification in background political morality of settled law. The Rights Thesis tells a particular litigant that he or she may well have a certain legal right even though an initial inspection of settled law leaves it uncertain whether he or she does or not. It is most important to require judges to respect those rights. The judge under a duty to carry out the required detective work in the form of pursuing the second dimension of fit will, if she carries out the work properly, discover either that the right exists or that it does not, and thus will be able to adjudicate correctly.

However, the result of in this way taking rights seriously is that a 'realistic' commitment in some form to rights given independently of judges' interpretative activities becomes inevitable. The Rights Thesis is a metaphysically ambitious thesis in the sense that it makes a commitment to an ontology for propositions of law. It requires for propositions of law a truth-theoretical semantics by virtue of a relationship to a moral order which is just so far independent of the legal order, whether or not it is 'independent' in the strong sense associated with moral realism.[29] Positivistic social or institutional facts about what is required by the black-letter law of the jurisdiction are indeed not enough to ground either antecedently existing political rights or a judicial duty to enforce such rights.

The Rights Thesis cannot have it both ways. If the Thesis wants to regard adjudication even in hard cases as the enforcement of rights litigants already actually have, then it is committed to propositions of law as uttered by judges being true realistically—being true just in case antecedently existing political rights make them true, where these rights are such that in the determination of their existence and content judicial interpretation plays no role. Suppose the Rights Thesis argues instead that law is like literature, and a judge's assertion of right is true just in case the interpretative rules of the legal enterprise warrant its assertion. The jurisprudential field has then essentially been conceded to simple positivism and the denial of the Rights Thesis. The law–literature analogy and the anti-realist semantics for propositions of law and of morality which accompanies it therefore blocks rather than facilitates defence of the challenging claim that judicial decisions enforce antecedently existing political rights.

---

[29] Cf. again the difference between (1) and (2) in the original taxonomy (page 208 above).

5. CONCLUSION

It is time to bring this discussion to an end. We began at a point where we have been before in this Part (cf. Chapter 7), with simple positivism's conception of adjudication as either strict inference from settled law or the exercise of 'strong' discretion. Sophisticated positivism aimed to find an alternative to such a view on the one hand and a full commitment to legal decisions as being justified only by some relationship to an 'independent moral order'. In this chapter, we have been examining the contribution to the problem of the discourses of 'anti-realist semantics', 'interpretative practices', and like terminology. The thought behind sophisticated positivism's recourse to these notions is, first, that 'interpretation' seems not only a proper alternative to 'description' and 'evaluation', but in fact precisely the right term for what judges actually often do in adjudication: second, that to construe judicial decisions as justified because 'warrantedly assertible by the ground-rules of the judicial enterprise' seems both to provide the needed further resources for justification and to avoid the problematic commitment to an 'independent moral order'.

I have argued that this attempt to stake out a middle ground fails. In the first place, the relevant philosophical issues are greatly over-simplified by the thought that simple positivism's simple mistake is to be realist about the semantics for propositions of law. Second, I have discussed the thought that the way to avoid a 'realistic' commitment to an 'independent moral order' is to do without semantics. I showed that the initial plausibility for this thought derives from constructivist methodology as found in the pragmatist tradition, and I considered in this context Rawls's claims about the independence of moral theory. I argued for three claims in this section: first, that to defend a constructivist account of the justification for moral or legal decisions is not to eschew semantics but to have a semantics of a particular kind; second, that, even if Herculean theorizing is taken to be a constructive enterprise, the role that it plays in the justification of mundane judicial decisions makes that justification itself anything but constructivist; third, that one may indeed make sense of a moral or legal theory as independent of semantics, by taking the theory to be 'political, not metaphysical' in the sense in which Rawls now understands his current work, but that on such an account legal theory turns out to be as legal realism or Critical Legal Studies takes it to be, not as positivism takes it to be. I then turned to the Rights Thesis, that judicial decisions enforce existing political rights, as being the thesis which motivates sophisticated positivism's rejection of simple positivism, and considered how far the Thesis is compatible with an anti-realist semantics for propositions of law and law construed as interpretation. I argued that the Thesis is gutted of all its force if it is construed in such terms. This claim I reinforced in the last section by a further discussion of the putative analogy between legal and literary interpretation.

The message of the discussion is clear. If it is acknowledged, as it is indeed acknowledged by sophisticated positivism, that adjudication is more than formalism plus strong discretion, then only an anti-positivist theory can give full significance to the acknowledgement. If a simple positivist account of the correctness of judicial decisions in terms of a relationship to social fact is inadequate, then only an account in terms of a relationship to a moral order independent of the legal order, whatever the semantics and the ontology of that moral order considered in its own right, will be adequate. If a simple positivist account of the adjudicatory obligations of judges in terms of strong discretion is inadequate, then an account of adjudication as constrained by institutional history, or by the conventions of a caste of officials,[30] or by the rules of a professional grammar,[31] or by communities of interpreters,[32] or by the rules of the legal enterprise, is just as inadequate. Call adjudication 'interpretative' if you will, but the term will carry no freight unless it is strengthened by an anti-positivist and realist semantics for propositions of law.

[30] Brian Simpson characterizes the common law as 'a customary system of law in this sense, that it consists of a body of practices observed and ideas received by a caste of lawyers . . . These ideas and practices exist only in the sense that they are accepted and acted on within the legal profession . . . Formulations of the law are to be conceived of as similar to grammarians' rules' ('The Common Law and Legal Theory', 94).

[31] According to Owen Fiss, legal interpretation is objective because the interpreter is constrained by a set of 'disciplinary rules' which have their 'authority' conferred by 'an interpretative community'; the rules are 'a professional grammar' ('Objectivity and Interpretation', *Stanford Law Review*, 34 (1982), 744–5).

[32] Stanley Fish argues in the theory of literary criticism and of legal interpretation alike that interpretations are constrained by and only by the conventions of interpretative communities. See his *Is there a Text in this Class?* (Cambridge, Mass., 1980) and most of the essays reprinted in *Doing What Comes Naturally*.

9

LAW AND THE COMMON GOOD

1. THE NORMATIVITY OF CONVENTIONS

Sophisticated positivism's complaint about simple positivism was that, by separating law so severely from morality, no proper account could be given of the normativity of law. Sophisticated positivism set itself the task of respecting the Normativity Thesis—explaining how law could be normative—while also respecting the Social Thesis—showing law to be a social fact. The solution proposed was law-as-convention positivism—the thesis that law is a convention, and thus normative in the way that conventions are normative.

Let us consider first how it is that conventions are normative. Lewis's own answer is illuminating. In the first place, what gives a convention its normative power is fundamentally its saliency. Saliency, Lewis insists, is evaluatively neutral; one co-ordination-equilibrium can as well be salient by being uniquely bad as by being uniquely good.[1] Schelling proposes a matrix in which there are four co-ordination-equilibria, three with a pay-off of 10 and one of 9, and suggests that the latter will be salient.[2] Now 10 and 9 are pretty close. But imagine a case where the relative difference between the pay-offs is rather wider. In the second place, Lewis draws (*Convention*, 88 ff.) an important distinction between a convention and a social contract:

For convention, we require that each agent prefer general conformity to conformity by all but himself, ignoring his preferences regarding states of general nonconformity. For social contract, we require that each agent prefer general conformity to a certain state of general nonconformity, ignoring his preferences regarding conformity by all but himself. (*Convention*, 90)

---

[1] Lewis, *Convention*, 35.
[2] Thomas Schelling, *The Strategy of Conflict* (Oxford, 1960), 295–6.

Conventions, that is to say, as opposed to social contracts, are not designed to deal with would-be defectors from conformity.[3] There is already a standing preference for conformity on the part of each agent; the need is for a rational way to achieve it. It therefore follows almost by definition that any given agent has reason to believe that conforming to the convention would answer to her own preferences, and to the preferences of most other agents involved in the co-ordination problem. We presume, Lewis continues, that, other things being equal, one ought to conform to one's own preferences, and that, other things being equal, one ought to conform to the preferences of others (*Convention*, 98). Thus conformity to a convention, by virtue of the kind of thing a convention is, necessarily has the rationality of conformity to preference, and thus necessarily has whatever normative force attaches to conformity to preference.

'Preference', however, is here a very 'thin', even formal, term. It has little more content than that of a subjective ordinal ranking of states of affairs revealed in conduct. It is 'formal' in that the identification of a preference prescinds from enquiry into the reasons for the preference. In some given person's case, a particular preference might be a strong moral preference, but it does not enter into decision theory under that description. The thought is not that the content of any relevant preference must in fact be 'thin', but rather that it must be treated as so for the purpose of decision theory. Preference so construed does not have the 'thickness', the substantiality, required for the genuine normativity of law. Suppose that I rank very highly my preference for not being visited with evil, and thus comply with the coercive commands of a wicked dictator. I have acted in accord with the minimal demand of rationality that one conforms to one's highest-ranked preferences. But I have not thereby shown that this system of coercive commands is a legal system, nor have I thereby shown that the system is genuinely normative. The normativity of a

[3] Lewis plausibly suggests (*Convention*, 103) that the criminal law is best thought of as a social contract rather than a convention. He also points out a variety of other rules which are not strictly conventions, and which have their analogues in law. Any cogent version of a law-as-convention theory must take account of this multifariousness. See also Gerald Postema, 'Bentham on the Public Character of Law', *Utilitas*, 1 (1989), 49–56, for more on the distinction between different game-theoretic problems. Postema also suggests that, while the wrongness of crimes may not be conventional if crimes are *mala in se*, the law's task in formulating strategies for response to crime has a strong co-ordinative element (59).

system of co-ordinated revealed preferences is no more than a set of reasons for actions which people *believe themselves to have*, and the criticism of Hart which was laid out in Chapter 2.7 above excludes such a system from being an adequate model for law.

2. LAW-AS-CONVENTION POSITIVISM

The intuitive appeal of law-as-convention positivism is two-fold[4]—that, ideally at least, some legal system is better than no legal system, and that there is none the less no unique set of norms which would provide the resultant benefits. This intuitive appeal, though, does not by itself underwrite law-as-convention positivism. Law claims a particular status in society: it claims to be salient in a particular way—to be *authoritative*. Suppose we acknowledge by way of deference to positivism that to claim authority is not the same as to have authority, and thus we do not argue that law necessarily has authority. Still, even the positivistic thesis marks a connection of the concept of law with the concept of authority which must be respected. To claim authority is not the same thing as to claim saliency. Law-as-convention positivism represents law as being that feature of society which injects saliency and thus a solution into social co-ordination problems. The crucial question is whether full weight is thereby given to that quality of law marked in the recognition that it is in the nature of law to claim *authority*.

The answer to that crucial question is negative.[5] Law-as-convention positivism reduces authority to saliency; its theory of law as a convention says that the authority of law when its claim to authority is justified is nothing more than its saliency with respect to a co-ordination problem. The reduction cannot be justified, for saliency is neither necessary nor sufficient for authority. First, the

---

[4] Cf. Leslie Green 'Law, Co-ordination and the Common Good', *Oxford Journal of Legal Studies*, 3 (1983), 322.

[5] Green, *The Authority of the State*, 111 ff.; 'Co-ordination', 315–20. Postema, 'Public Character', 50 ff., argues that one can in fact explain the role of sanctions while thinking of law in game-theoretic terms. Social life must be seen as a complex of prisoner's dilemma, assurance, and co-ordination problems, and the sanctions of law are needed for law to solve problems of the first two kinds. Whatever the intuitive attractiveness of this picture of social life, the comment strengthens, rather than mitigates, the present difficulty with law-as-convention positivism.

solution of a co-ordination problem is not sufficient for authority. Authority provides a reason for action of a different kind from the reason provided by the weight of first-order reasons: authorities are exclusionary reasons for action. A co-ordination problem, however, may be solved by an utterance, for example, which has neither exclusionary nor binding force, and which instead works by altering the balance of first-order reasons. Orders given loudly and confidently during the evacuation of a ship may solve a co-ordination problem without emanating from an authority. Second, the solution of a co-ordination problem is not necessary for authority, since authority is sometimes properly exercised to destabilize or even prevent conventional solutions to co-ordination problems, as in anti-trust and anti-cartel legislation.

Lagerspitz (*A Conventionalist Theory of Institutions*, 82–4) defends a conventionalist view of authority. He would claim, if I understand him aright, that, in a case like mine, the person uttering the subsequently obeyed orders becomes thereby an authority; thus the case is no counterexample. There are difficulties with this response.[6] We have to bear in mind that even conventions that arise spontaneously are not like forest fires. The group among which they arise are thinking persons. Any plausible account psychologically of how the convention arises will make reference to beliefs, intentions, expectations, and so forth. Those beliefs, expectations, and so on will be held because they will be to some degree grounded. That will only be so because already in the group there will be some commitment to 'co-operative virtues', as they may be called. Lagerspitz recognizes this to the extent that he talks about conventions arising only in an efficacious normative order (cf. ibid. 83). But he misses the significance. The convention arises as an expression of the normative order, the commitment to co-operation, and not the reverse. Thus the saliency some convention has pre-supposes a prior willingness to solving co-operatively co-ordination problems, from whence the convention derives its authority.

The positivist might claim that the reduction of authority to saliency is justified because only the authority of law provides

[6] I rely here on Govert den Hartogh's forthcoming critical review of Lagerspitz's book, 'Rehabilitating Legal Conventionalism', *Law and Philosophy*, 11 (1992), and on an unpublished paper 'A Conventionalist Theory of Obligation'. I am grateful to Govert for permitting me to see his paper before publication.

'real' saliency. Only if what makes one of the co-ordination-equilibria stand out is that the equilibrium is authoritative can that equilibrium be regarded as genuinely salient. But consider what conditions a reason for that claim would have to meet. It would have to be a reason that took some account of what it was for an equilibrium to be authoritative, and moreover an account of that which went beyond the mere fact that the solution was conventional. If the only reason that made a particular *legal* solution authoritative was that it was conventionally authoritative—it was the convention we happened to evolve to adopt, on the basis of regularity of behaviour—that would not show that the solution was really authoritative. Postema ('Coordination and Convention', 179–82) has suggested a 'thicker' account of the normativity of conventions, which would, if true, say something about why conventions are authoritative. He offers the alternatives of either construing conventions as imposing obligations to conform to avoid detrimental reliance, or as imposing obligations of fair play in co-operative enterprises. But the case of cartels exposes the difficulty. We may say that a cartel imposes local obligations of conformity on its members—Saudi Arabia may be criticized locally by other OPEC members for unilaterally raising production levels—without supposing that from the global point of view these obligations are legitimate or genuinely normative.

In short, whether a convention is genuinely normative depends ultimately on the content of the convention. The dilemma for law-as-convention positivism, therefore, is neatly expressed by Green —'Citizens who treat the law as authoritative cannot validly view it as merely conventional; those who treat it as conventional are wrong to view it as authoritative' (*The Authority of the State*, 121). Note again that we are still speaking in 'subjective' mode—we are talking about the constraints imposed by the mere facts that law claims authority, and that it must be experienced by the citizens as having authority. Even these facts about law, law-as-convention positivism cannot explain.

Here is an apparent reason for reinstating law-as-convention positivism. One of the defining conditions for a co-ordination problem is that the choosers see themselves as deriving benefits from co-operation between each other. So therefore the choosers must have some background values in terms of which they are conducting their preference-rankings. Cannot therefore the authority of law be presented in terms of its unique ability to secure these background values? Now, law may well be salient because as a matter of fact it promotes important social values that cannot be promoted by any other means. Moreover, law might be regarded as authoritative for exactly the same reason, for uniquely promoting important social values. But note that such circumstances, were they to obtain, would not show authority reducible to salience. Rather, the value-free notion of salience is thereby most plausibly explained in terms of the value-laden notion of authority, and law's status as a convention drops out. This putative argument for law-as-convention positivism, that is, represents the first horn of Green's dilemma. If a citizen experiences law as authoritative just in case she experiences it as uniquely promoting important social values, then the citizen is not seeing law as merely a valuable convention in the sense of having just that value and no more that conventions have—the value of solving co-ordination problems. The citizen is locating the authority of law in some value law serves —a value which, it is true, law serves by being conventional, but a value which is not itself merely the value that conventions have. Law's authority is thus entirely a derivative authority, derived from its happening to promote certain values. Any other scheme which promoted those values to the same degree would do just as well, and one that promoted them to a greater degree would do better. There is nothing here to ground the idea that law is authoritative in some unique way such that to base a theory of law on such a property of law is to state what it is that distinguishes law from other normative systems.

3. LAW-AS-CONVENTION-FOR-THE-COMMON-GOOD POSITIVISM

Aquinas comes as near as he ever comes to a definition of law in the claim that 'Law is nothing else than an ordinance of reason for the common good, made by him who has the care of the community, and promulgated'.[7] This general definition is followed by a distinction between the three kinds of law—eternal, natural, and human. Now, it might seem that on its own Aquinas's

---

[7] St Thomas Aquinas, *On Law, Morality and Politics* (Indianapolis, 1988), Q. 90 A. 4.

characterization as applied to the specific case of human law would produce a basically positivistic view of human law. We can clearly understand God as having care of the ideal community, and as promulgating ordinances of reason for the common good of that community. We can make sense of the thought (even if we reject it) that 'Nature' similarly works for the 'common good' of purely 'natural' things—a standardly teleological theory of biology might claim something like that. But, it may be said, the obvious way to understand the definition in the case of human law is in terms of a ruler, or whoever is designated as lawmaker by the rule of recognition, promulgating laws in terms of the lawmaker's perception of the good of the community. As Aquinas said, 'human laws should be proportionate to the common good' (Q. 96 A. 1). Moreover, it may be argued, if we assume a democracy of some kind, in which there is substance to the idea that the people are the lawmakers, do we not then have a case where the people make laws in terms of their own subjective perceptions of the common good? And, furthermore, if that is the case, then is it not very tempting to look at the resultant laws in very much the same kind of terms as those of law-as-convention positivism—namely, as solutions to co-ordination problems? Only one minor adjustment has to be made to the basic model of law-as-convention introduced above—namely, that the choosers from whose choices the conventions emerge be concerned not merely with their own private good, but also, and even predominantly, with the common good. That adjustment is given by the interpretation of even human law as an ordinance of reason, for it is rational to seek the common good. Thus we seemingly have a new way of satisfactorily respecting both the Normativity Thesis and the Social Thesis, one which builds on the thought that to solve co-ordination problems is to contribute to the common good, and moreover a way which avoids the reduction of authority to salience, since it restricts the grounds for salience to the promotion of the common good. We simply add as a constraint on people's subjective preferences as they enter into the emergence of the convention which constitutes legal system that the preferences, and thus the resultant convention, are to a significant degree aimed affirmatively at the common good, and not simply at the avoidance of private disutility.

This is a very attractive line of argument. It has in fact attracted

Finnis.[8] The role of positive law in Finnis's scheme of natural law and natural rights is exactly to be a solution of this particular kind to a co-ordination problem—a conventional solution for the common good. In that way, Finnis seeks to combine the machinery of contemporary game-theory with a very traditional understanding of law. Despite the blessing of its authorizer, however, the union is doomed to instability. It will be instructive to see why.

One kind of objection one might have to Finnis's position would be that to ground the normativity of law in law's serving the common good is to show how that an action is required or forbidden by law provides a reason for action by altering the weight of first-order reasons rather than by presenting an exclusionary reason. Thus, even if Finnis were correct in showing that we therefore always have a reason to obey the law, he would have failed to show law to be authoritative, and for that reason his theory cannot stand. Since my topic here is not the authority of law, I shall not discuss this possible objection further.[9] A different kind of objection would be that a convention-for-the-common-good is a peculiar sort of convention, if one at all; that the reason it provides for action is not the kind of reason for action a convention is. I shall urge that objection, and show the philosophical consequences of its putative success.

Finnis brings a certain wide conception of the common good to bear on his argument. He characterizes it as follows:

'The common good' refer[s] to the factor or set of factors (whether a value, a concrete operational objective, or the conditions for realizing a value or attaining an objective) which, as considerations in someone's practical reasoning, would make sense of or give reason for his collaboration with others and would likewise, from their point of view, give reason for their collaboration with each other and with him. (*Natural Law and Natural Rights*, 154)

This is glossed as 'a set of conditions which enables the members of a community to attain for themselves reasonable objectives, or to realize reasonably for themselves the value(s), for the sake of which they have reason to collaborate with each other (positively

---

[8] Cf. *Natural Law and Natural Rights*, chs. 9–10.
[9] But see Chs. 3, 4 above.

and/or negatively) in a community' (*Natural Law and Natural Rights*, 155).

The thought seems to be this. For Finnis, there are seven basic forms of human good—life, knowledge, play, aesthetic experience, friendship, practical reasonableness, and 'religion'. These are all independent values, not mutually reducible, and they thus allow for considerable legitimate variation in life-plans from individual to individual. However, that very diversity gives rise to a co-ordination problem—the need for a set of framework conditions within which individuals can choose and realize their own life-plans. The 'common good' is the goal of maximal realization of such objectives. Law *qua* 'ordinance of reason for the common good' is to be construed as the set of conventions which emerge as the framework conditions required.

How successful is the theory of law as a convention for the common good in combining coherently the Social Thesis and the Normativity Thesis?

The difficulty found with law-as-convention positivism was that it did not, despite its pretence to do so, satisfactorily respect the Normativity Thesis. Finnis's theory does not appear to fail in that way. His construal of his basic thesis about the common good is 'realistic'. He distinguishes three kinds of legal statements—S_1 statements: claims made from the point of view of acceptance of the cogency of the claim both for the speaker and others; S_2 statements: the sociologist's or external observer's claim that some people find an S_1 claim cogent; S_3 statements: claims about how things are from an S_1 point of view but without thereby endorsing or rejecting the S_1 claims, a 'detached' or 'professional' viewpoint (*Natural Law and Natural Rights*, 234–5). Finnis's claim about the nature of the common good is officially an S_1-type claim. But we must consider carefully none the less how far he departs from the subjective normativity of law-as-convention positivism.

Classical game-theory regards co-ordination problems as problems of reasoning *ex hypothesi* 'disconnected from the objective situation' (Schelling, *The Strategy of Conflict*, 93). The notion of rationality involved prescinds from questions of substantive rationality. It presents a formal theory of the rational thing to do, given that one has nothing more to work with than ordinally ranked subjective preferences. Clearly, however, the notion of rationality embodied in Finnis's foundational concept of practical reasonableness is vastly 'thicker' than any such concept. Not only are the eight requirements of practical reasonableness themselves not every one formal requirements; they include respect for basic values, coherence, and structuring by practical reasonableness (itself a non-formal concept). Also, they are given point only by their role in the facilitation cf the attainment of the basic human goods, the status of which is not open to debate.

Now the instability of Finnis's position is becoming evident. He wants to define a role for positive law as a set of conventions providing solutions to co-ordination problems, against a background of legitimate diversity of individual interests based on individual choice of life-plans. This is his tactic for respecting the Social Thesis as far as he wants to respect it: that the desires and life-plans of individuals have the diversity they have is a social fact. The tactic seems none the less to fit well with Finnis's basic natural-law approach, despite its individualism, because one can preserve the basic structure of formal rationality (or so it seems) while introducing out of deference to natural law the concept of the common good. If we are to take seriously, however, the notion of the 'common good' as an indispensable part of any adequate theory of law, then the common good must bear on the matter in its own right. The common good must have independent normative force; its normative force cannot be simply identified with whatever intrinsic normative force is possessed by law understood as law-as-convention positivism understands it.

This point has two corollaries. First, the common good then cannot be understood as merely the result of processing individual goods through some aggregating function. Finnis, note, accepts this corollary. The theory of the common good is individualistic—it defines the common good in terms of the good of individuals. It is also, because of the incommensurability of the basic values, non-aggregative: aggregative conceptions of the common good, such as utilitarian conceptions, are roundly rejected as 'senseless' (*Natural Law and Natural Rights*, 113). However, as a second corollary, *contra* Finnis, a conception of the common good as having independent normative force cannot be purely individualistic either. Individuals may make their own choices of life-plans from the legitimate diversity of life-plans, and so far the conception can be individualistic. But the individuals do not choose the parameters which define the limits of this legitimate diversity. The limits are set by the basic human goods; the latter constrain the individual's choice of life-plans.

To type Finnis's view accurately, we need to make a distinction between a 'weakly individualistic' and a 'strongly individualistic' conception of the common good. A conception of the common good is *weakly individualistic* if, though not making individual good entirely subservient to the common good, it none the less deploys a conception of the content of the common good to delimit the legitimate diversity of individual life-plans. A conception of the common good is *strongly individualistic* if it defines the common good, whether aggregatively or not, in terms of individual subjectively perceived benefit and flourishing. One might say that a weakly individualistic conception of the common good is not really very individualistic at all, and a strongly individualistic conception of the common good is not really a conception of the common good at all. Finnis's theory is in the above sense weakly individualistic, in that the common good is only good in so far as it promotes the choices of those whose life-plans are devoted to the basic human values.

The model of rationality embodied in game theory, even in that part of it which defines the structure for the solution of co-ordination problems, is purely formal. The model cannot generate from its own private resources anything other than a strongly individualistic notion of the common good. The notion may be in addition either aggregative or non-aggregative. Many versions of utilitarianism are purely aggregative, since it is consistent with such theories that there are individual losers provided that there are enough individual winners to improve the aggregate or average utility. A theory which accepts the Pareto principle will be non-aggregative.[10] The principle sets a threshhold constraint that no one will be a loser, and thus is concerned separately with the good of each individual. As David Gauthier has shown in his work,[11] one can by developing a strongly individualistic and non-aggregative theory of formal rationality come interestingly close to

[10] A strategy for collective action is Pareto-optimizing when it aims for a state in which any further action makes no one better off and at least one person worse off. A step in the execution of this strategy is Pareto-rational when it makes at least one person better off while making no one worse off. Thus aiming for a Pareto-optimal goal by Pareto-rational steps does not countenance creating losers in order to make winners.

[11] Cf. primarily *Morals By Agreement*.

capturing the content of a substantial and fundamentally non-individualistic (or at least weakly individualistic) theory of the common good. But such an approach is fuelled by our independent acknowledgement of the validity of the substantial and non-individualistic conception. The approach therefore cannot prove that our conception of the common good really is reducible to the formal and strongly individualistic conception, without abandoning as a resource the non-formal and non-individualistic conception of which it is supposed to be the model.

Finnis is, however, if I understand each of them aright, engaged on a different project from Gauthier. He is not merely trying to reconstruct in the terms of formal rationality a substantial conception of the common good. He is claiming that law understood as law-as-convention positivism understands it—law, that is to say, understood formally and strongly individualistically —does the job that an anti-positivist theory of law demands of law, namely, that law be shown as such to serve the common good. But, given that the anti-positivist notion of the common good is an ineluctably substantial notion, Finnis demands the impossible.

If one has a conception of the common good that is beyond the reach of formal rationality, it then becomes unclear how far it is a useful conception for an analysis of all law in law-as-convention terms. The law-as-convention model has point only for the project of defining a formal and strongly individualistic conception of the common good. Once we acknowledge that the agenda for a theory of law is set by the requirement that a set of norms, to be law, must be for the common good, then we must go beyond any conception of laws as mere co-ordination norms, as conventional solutions to co-ordination problems. A theory which requires law to be for the common good may say that law is for the common good because it is a conventional solution to a co-ordination problem. But as long as the theory begins with the common good, and not with individuals' subjective preferences, the theory is motivated by quite different goals from those of law-as-convention positivism. On the other hand, if the claim is that law construed as a convention defined formally is essentially an instrument for an independently defined common good, then the claim is no more than the claim of law-as-convention positivism. There can be no content-independent conception of law-as-convention which is not just so far a positivistic conception.

A content-dependent theory of law as a convention is, of course, Finnis's real view. He puts it clearly at the end of a more recent article—'it is the values of the Rule of Law that give the legal system its distinctive entitlement to be treated as the source of authoritative solutions'.[12] These values cannot be defined by 'the emaciated and instrumental rationality of game-theoretical postulates'.[13] So why did Finnis, as Green shows in 'Coordination', toy with just such postulates? I have suggested (page 244 above) a set of reasons why.

4. CONSTRUCTIVE CONVENTIONALISM

The point of the two preceding paragraphs is not to be unpleasantly *ad hominem* and polemical towards Finnis. In fact, issues of considerable importance for understanding the relation between law, convention, and the common good are at stake, as I shall now show. For the moment, I will lay Finnis on one side. I want first in this section to discuss more fully Postema's more recent writings on law and co-ordination.[14] Postema develops in a different direction ideas that were present in 'Coordination and Convention' with some other import. In the latter paper, Postema distinguished three levels of interaction contributing to the 'conventional' character of modern law—interaction between citizens, between citizen and official, and between officials. He sketched there some not entirely convincing arguments for construing all three kinds of interaction as having the structure of a co-ordination problem in the game-theoretic sense. This view he no longer believes to be correct.

Postema wants to take Bentham's objections to the common law tradition and parlay them into a deeper understanding of what might be meant by seeing law as 'conventional'.[15] He finds in

---

[12] 'The Authority of Law in the Predicament of Contemporary Social Theory', *Notre Dame Journal of Law, Ethics and Public Policy*' (1984), 136.

[13] Ibid. 129 n. 38.

[14] In addition to 'Public Character', I have in mind *Bentham and the Common Law Tradition* (Oxford, 1986), 'The Normativity of Law', in Ruth Gavison (ed.), *Issues in Contemporary Legal Philosophy* (Oxford, 1987), '"Protestant" Interpretation', and 'In Defence of "French Nonsense"', in Neil McCormick and Zenon Bankowski (eds.), *Enlightenment, Rights and Revolution* (Aberdeen, 1989).

[15] Cf. *Bentham and the Common Law Tradition*, ch. 5; 'Public Character', *passim*; '"French Nonsense"', *passim*.

Bentham's objection to the theory of law as a discrete series of monadic judgements by legal officials and legislators a more accurate account of that which, in his (Postema's) (later) view, the theory of law as a convention is aiming to bring out. Bentham's emphasis is on law as:

the realm in which agents, who are and will probably remain strangers, nevertheless interact, whose actions and decisions are interdependent in important ways, who thus exchange evaluations and criticism of those actions and decisions, and who often deliberate and act together. ('Public Character', 44)

The element of explicit mutual interaction is lacking in cases of Lewisian conventions such as the phone-call example.[16] The 'co-operation' that arises from the development and maintenance of the convention arises without explicit debate and discourse. The rules of a modern legal system never so arise, except possibly genuinely customary law. Any adequate theory of law must take into account the level of interactive discourse 'above' the bare social facts about the content of settled law at any point in time.

For this reason, a solid objection against (at least, simple) positivism may be urged. Again the argument begins by standing on Hart's shoulders to see further than he could. Passages in *The Concept of Law* suggest a view according to which the reasons why norm-subjects acknowledge laws as imposing obligations are no part of the province of jurisprudence; it is sufficient for law that acknowledgement occurs.[17] Postema calls this the 'simple convergence thesis'. It is rejected by both the strict conventionalist[18] and the natural law theorist. The former adds the additional requirement that the convergence come about through strategic

---

[16] See page 95 above.

[17] I am deliberately putting the point without using any of the standard terminology here—conformity, efficacy, obedience, acceptance, internal point of view, acquiescence, etc. I hope that Chs. 5 and 6 above have shown how treacherous this terminology is. Since I regard the argument of each section in Part III as standing alongside, rather than building on, the argument of other sections, I want to say what I say here as far as possible in philosophically uninterpreted language. 'Acknowledgement' is intended here to be philosophically uninterpreted. The other terms already have so many philosophical encrustations that use of them would be counter-productive.

[18] Postema does not say whether his earlier theory in 'Coordination and Convention' is a version of 'strict conventionalism'. It seems to me that it is, and that therefore the newer version represents a change of mind.

interaction, and the latter that acceptance on each person's part must be for the right kind of reasons, a justified perception of authoritativeness. But, argues Postema ingeniously, we now have a problem. If the strict conventionalist's requirement of strategic interaction is correct, then natural law theory fails to meet the requirement; it cannot explain the 'enriched convergence' on the right reasons when that occurs. However, if natural law theory is correct in saying that not just any reason for acceptance will do, then strict conventionalism is inadequate; it does not enquire into the reasons for accepting the convention provided that the convention is in place. We need a theory which does justice to the valid points in strict conventionalism and natural law theory which avoids the deficiencies in each. 'Constructive conventionalism' is the answer:

On this view, officials recognize. and are committed by their actions and arguments to recognize, that their joint acceptance of the criteria of validity must be linked to more general moral-political concerns . . . But they also realize that *an essential part* of the case to be made for the criteria rests on the fact that they jointly accept the criteria, or *could come to accept them* after reflection and participation in a forum in which reasoned and principled arguments are exchanged amongst equals. ('Normativity', 104; Postema's emphasis)

The thought here is related to the earlier talk in 'Coordination and Convention' about the reasons which lie behind the development of the convention, but the emphasis is importantly different. I do not think it is unfair[19] to say that Postema's strict conventionalist remains at the level of 'rule', while his 'constructive conventionalist' takes into account a level of 'principle', in something like the sense of Dworkin's familiar distinction between those notions. What I mean is this. Bentham's original objection is to treating the law as a series of discrete cases and statutes: an important level of public and rational deliberation about and justification for the law is omitted. This objection has a surface similarity to the criticism that seeing law as a system of rules and ignoring the role of legal principles omits an important level of public and rational deliberation about and justification for the law.

---

[19] I am content to be judged by what is expressed in the quote from 'Public Character' a few paragraphs above.

I argued above, in section 2 of this chapter, that an account which related law and the background values promoted by it to each other instrumentally did not do justice to the Normativity Thesis, however much it might have respected the Social Thesis. That argument gives us a benchmark for the present discussion. The minimal expansion of strict conventionalism might be a theory like Honoré's,[20] which emphasized the role of 'shared under-standings' in defining what is law in a social group. Such a 'shared understanding' might, very minimally, mean no more than a shared notion of the 'ruledness' of the rules. It would more plausibly be a shared understanding of the rules together with the purposes of the rules. The minimal interpretation again of such a 'shared understanding' is relativistic and inter-subjective.[21] That is, we enrich the idea of law as a 'convention' to the point where we say that it is not merely a co-ordinated set of beliefs and actions, but that it includes beliefs that there are not merely regularities of behaviour but rules,[22] beliefs that there are principles and purposes behind the rules, and beliefs as to the content of those principles and purposes. But we still interpret 'convention' in this enriched sense as relative to the beliefs of the group whose convention it is. As such, if it is a legitimate demand that an explanation must be given of the 'enriched convergence' on the right reasons when that occurs, then we still do not have such an explanation. One might object to law-as-convention positivism in the spirit of Postema's discussion in 'Public Character' (49–56) that social life includes many different kinds of game-theoretic problems, and that law should be construed so as to reflect this fact: law-as-convention positivism focuses too narrowly on only one such kind of problem, problems of co-ordination. The point about 'principles and purposes' is a separate point. But even if we enrich our notion of 'convention' by combining the two points, we still have not explained 'enriched convergence' on the right reasons.

Postema's 'constructive conventionalism' is *yet another* enrich-ment of the notion of convention; hence its subtlety and importance. Postema draws attention to the distinction between a Lewisian convention and a co-ordination problem on the so-called

---

[20] *Making Law Bind*, ch. 2; see Ch. 5.5 above.

[21] I have discussed the adequacy of such an interpretation in Ch. 5.5 above.

[22] Lewis's definition of 'convention' is in terms of regularities; cf. *Convention*, 78.

'battle of the sexes' model.[23] In the case of a convention, what matters is simply that there be a solution to the co-ordination problem; there are no embedded views about the form a solution might take. In the phone-call case, as long as at least and at most one person calls back, it is immaterial which person does. The 'battle of the sexes' model forces convergence on what each side can accept in terms of antecedent commitments. Unlike the convention model, it does not 'give too much weight to the role of consensus at the expense of the equally important ideal element'.[24] Postema praises Bentham[25] for having incorporated into the analysis of law the power of law to realize concretely an antecedent willingness on the part of all (or all but the immovably recalcitrant) citizens to forge schemes of co-operation.

However, having milked Bentham of all the good points which he has seen and others have missed about the public character of law, Postema argues that there is still one thing even Bentham has missed.[26] Bentham makes one specific objection to rights talk. Rights talk is, for Bentham, inherently indeterminate. This indeterminacy means that it cannot be public in the way that his commitment to the public character of law requires. To be public, law must be determinate and demonstrable. Postema calls this the demonstrability thesis.[27] Postema's advance over Bentham is to reject the demonstrability thesis. It is not merely compatible with, but required by, Postema's view that law is essentially interactive and public that the thesis be rejected:

Legal arrangements and their histories provide a lens through which potentially divergent ideals of justice and the common good can be focused on the concrete present and future, and thus provide a common world or body of common experience from which we can explore paths of resolution of differences. Law provides a language within which members

[23] 'A man and a woman each have two choices for an evening's entertainment. Each can either go to a prize fight or a ballet. Following the usual cultural stereotype, the man much prefers the fight and the woman the ballet; however, to both it is more important that they go out together than that each see the preferred entertainment' (R. Duncan Luce and Howard Raiffa, *Games and Decisions* (New York, 1957)).

[24] Postema, 'Public Character', 55.

[25] Ibid. 56 ff.

[26] Cf. '"Protestant" Interpretation', 313–19; 'Public Character', 59–61; '"French Nonsense"', 121–7.

[27] '"French Nonsense"', 119.

of a community can justify to each other their common institutions and their own decisions and actions taken within them. This is an aspect of the public character of law that Bentham's account entirely ignores.

. . . The legal practice of our day, as that of Bentham's, is a practice of asserting, defending, interpreting, and revising propositions of law, which are used to give public justification for decisions of officials and lay citizens alike. A jurisprudential theory which focuses solely on the (temporary) product of this practice, and treats the process and practice from which it issues, and to which it is responsive, as external to it, gives us a narrow and misleading picture of law. It obscures the resources the law provides for the continued solution of problems of cooperative action. ('Public Character', 61)

The attractive vision being presented here is that of a democratic polity with a strong convergence on a set of underlying ideas which form the constitutive myths and traditions of the polity, and a strong tradition of vigorous public discussion of the interpretation of that tradition and those myths. Who would not want to live in such a polity?

Is the account of this polity, however, an account of the concept of law? Why is it not simply a normative recommendation to those people who do not live in such a polity to fix things up so that they do? What meaning does it have to those citizens in what is ostensibly such a polity who find that the dominant tradition, and the dominant interpretations of the tradition, marginalizingly patriarchal, capitalist, and racist? I ask these questions, not because I have any particular interest here in one answer or another,[28] but to indicate a difficulty with Postema's view. The dilemma is straightforward. Either (i) the requirement of reference

[28] Though I might well have elsewhere. In his Introduction to a recent book of legal theory by Canadians (Bayefsky (ed.), *Legal Theory Meets Legal Practice* (Edmonton, AB, 1988), 1–3), the distinguished Canadian jurist Allen Linden rejects assimilation to any US tradition of jurisprudence: Canadians, '(and hence our jurisprudence which reflects those features) [have] respect for authority, pluralism, compromise and compassion. Canadians respect law, order, hierarchy. Contrary to the revolutionary zeal of the [US] Americans, Canadians maintained a Family Compact in Upper Canada and the Seigneurs of early Quebec . . . It is no accident that the British North America Act spoke of "peace, order, and good government", rather than "liberty, equality and fraternity" or "all men are created equal". It was an expression of our Canadianism' (1). Several speakers in the audience when Postema gave ' "French Nonsense" ' as an invited address to the World Congress of Philosophy of Law in Edinburgh in 1989 expressed similar disquiet at the 'partisan' nature of the theory of law being presented.

to a tradition, to interpretation of the tradition, to public debate and discussion, and so forth, is construed as a reference to a series of mental states and acts independently of their content and intentional objects. In that case, for the purposes of our theoretical goals here, the theory is subject still to the same objections as brought against Hart that we do not have an account of the normativity of law: we have a theory which is as strictly positivistic as strict conventionalism or any of the putatively unsatisfactory theories supposedly replaced. This option is clearly available, since one could imagine traditions in which a practice of public debate existed with respect to a set of ideals that are in their content quite reprehensible.[29] Or (ii) we take seriously the idea of foregrounding convergence on the *right* ideas, and thus do not count as a tradition of the relevant kind one that is reprehensible in its content—in which case we have left far behind any positivistic theory of law, though we have quite satisfactorily explained the normativity of law. (iii) We could, of course, recommend the tradition of political interaction and debate as a worthy social ideal, and put a concept of law instrumentally to work in the service of that ideal. But then we would be doing something different than either positivism, 'constructive conventionalism', or natural law theory take themselves to be doing. We would not be participating at all in the theoretical debate going on in this chapter about the concept of law.

Let us now recall Finnis, and the supposed instability in his theory in *Natural Law and Natural Rights*. As indicated above, he resolves the instability by opting for a full content-dependent theory of law. As Postema rightly notes,[30] Finnis uses the notion of 'co-ordination problem' in a broader and non-technical way, so that prisoner's dilemma problems, assurance problems, and co-ordination problems in the strict sense all count as 'co-ordination problems'.[31] Postema implies that such a broad use suits Finnis's jurisprudential purposes, although cutting him off (in Postema's view) from the debate to which Postema is contributing. The broad use suits Finnis's purposes, because in the end what matters

---

[29] Such in fact would be the view of the US taken by those of its citizens who think that, to put it crudely, what is needed is a whole lot less debate by white, male politicians and a whole lot more action in remedy of social ills.

[30] 'Public Character', 51 n. 25.

[31] Cf. *Natural Law and Natural Rights*, 255; 'Law and Authority', 133.

is not social facts of social interaction of whatever kind, but an independently defined notion of 'common good' at which all social action and interaction, and *a fortiori* legal action and interaction, must aim. Thus technical distinctions between kinds of social interaction are irrelevant to the real theory of law being defended. My argument against Postema might be summed up by saying it is an argument of exactly the same form. That is, Postema's real goal seems to be either to expose the nature of a particular constitutional and political tradition to those whose tradition it is and who may seem to have lost sight of it (or, perhaps, simply to participate in the interactive determination of the content of that tradition); or to recommend that tradition to those who do not as yet share it. But if that is so, then technical distinctions between kinds of social interaction are just as irrelevant to the real theory being defended. The difference is that Finnis really does defend a theory of law as such, whereas Postema's project, however humane and humanly important, and of course it is both, seems tangential to theory of law in the form which the project has now taken.

5. ANTI-POSITIVISM AND THE COMMON GOOD

There are still unresolved problems for anti-positivism's views about co-ordination and the common good. Postema suggests that natural law theory cannot give a proper account of the need for strategic interaction. He writes:

The naturalist, after all, must regard convergence of conviction regarding the proper criteria of validity in a system of law to be a necessary condition of the existence of law while at the same time insisting that this convergence is, *from the point of view of participants*, nothing more than a happy accident. There is nothing logically contradictory in this, but it is implausible.[32]

Of course it is implausible; but I do not see why natural law theory is so committed. The 'accident' idea seems to arise as follows. Take any arbitrary participant X in some legal system. Natural law theory must say: X's reasons for thinking the norms binding must have to do with a justification in political morality—say, that the norms reflect

---

[32] 'Normativity', 102; Postema's emphasis.

proper standards of justice and equality. That they do, for X, is
something X figures out for him/herself. Now, X happens to meet
Y, and discovers that Y thinks the same thing of the norms, and
for the same reasons. For natural law theory, this convergence has
to be just like discovering that the person next to one in the bus
queue [in Edmonton!] is also a fan of Australian Rules Football,
or Balinese gamelin music, etc. Such a view omits the necessary
element of interdependence which the conventionalist properly
emphasizes.

If we consider traditional forms of natural law theory, they
contain the material for denying this apparent commitment to
accidental convergence. Aquinas, for example, despite acknowledging the difference between speculative and practical reason in
terms of universality, says that 'truth or rectitude is the same for all
and is equally known by all'.[33] He quotes approvingly Augustine's
claim that 'knowledge of the eternal law is imprinted on us',[34] and
says that the natural law is promulgated by the very fact that God
instilled it in men's minds so as to be known by them naturally.[35]
All this talk implies that the commonality of response is not at all
contingent, but is a manifestation of the natural law itself. The
talk, however, seems to incorporate an awful lot of debatable
'supernatural' baggage. Is it possible to 'demythologize' the talk
and to forge a reply in plain language?

Let us agree that morality is not going to have the content it has
unless there is widespread agreement as to that content. It does
not at all follow that morality must be 'conventional' in the sense
of the product of strategic interaction. The point about 'widespread agreement' implies that the morality of a society, even its
critical morality, cannot be rejected wholesale by its citizens as a
permanent and pervasive feature of the social life of that society. If
there were moral views which were permanently and pervasively
rejected, then we would not say that they formed part of the
morality of the group who rejected them. Say if you like that any
given participant 'assumes' without checking it out that other
participants share a similar view. Given what it is for a certain set
of principles to constitute a morality, the participant cannot but be
fully justified in so assuming. This marks the difference between

[33] *ST* I-II, Q. 94 A. 4 (*On Law, Morality and Politics*, 51).
[34] Q. 93 A. 2 (*On Law, Morality and Politics*, 35).
[35] Q. 90 A. 4 (*On Law, Morality and Politics*, 17).

the case of morality and the case of taste in music of a certain kind.

Natural law theory regards convergence of criteria as necessary for the following reason. If only acceptance for certain reasons will count as acceptance of the law, and there is acceptance of the law, then trivially there will be a convergence on those reasons—otherwise we would not have law, and *ex hypothesi* we do have law. So—while it is true that without such a convergence there would not be law, that fact follows from the way law is defined. For natural law theory, the 'not just any reasons' demand and the 'convergence' demand are not independent of one another, as they are for even 'constructive conventionalism'; they are deeply connected. What must not be ignored here is the fundamentally 'organic' nature of the perspective of Natural Law Theory. To borrow a distinction from Wittgenstein,[36] there is a difference between 'agreement in opinion' and 'agreement in judgement'. The agreement reached by an explicit process of strategic interaction is an 'agreement in opinion'—the product of separate action by atomistic individuals—as would be a common content to a set of judgements reached quite independently, as when every judge at a skating competition awards the same mark. The thought behind 'agreement in judgement' is that we cannot but agree in our judgements about how things are, for otherwise there would be no 'we' either to agree or disagree. Agreement in judgement is a transcendental implication of there being our human life at all. In short, if natural law theory is permitted only the resources of methodological individualism, then perhaps it is true that it cannot explain convergence of conviction regarding the proper criteria of validity. But so to restrict natural law theory is to fail to see how central it is to natural law theory to repudiate such a methodology. Natural law is a communitarian theory metaphysically.

6. CONCLUSION

We posed at the beginning a certain problem for Austin's and Hart's analyses of law as social fact, and for any form of positivism thereby. The problem was that law-as-social-fact seemed to be law without genuine normative force, and law essentially has genuine

---

[36] *Philosophical Investigations*, sect. 240–2.

normative force. The proposed solution was law-as-convention positivism. But law-as-convention positivism itself ran into difficulty. Law is not merely normative; it is, or claims to be, authoritatively normative. But law-as-convention positivism cannot explain the authority-claiming aspect of law. It might then be supposed that what one may call law-as-convention-for-the-common-good positivism could so explain the normativity of law. However, to make sense of such a theory, a story is needed about the common good. One might try to explain the common good in conventional terms. If so, then law-as-convention-for-the-common-good positivism reduces to law-as-convention positivism, and thereby fails in its task of explaining law's particular normativity, its authority-claiming aspect. Law-as-convention-for-the-common-good positivism succeeds only when the notion of the common good is given some substantial and non-individualistic characterization—that is to say, when law-as-convention-for-the-common-good positivism ceases to be a form of positivism, and regards the concept of law as in part a content-dependent concept. We considered a number of different variants on the notion of 'convention', and argued that precisely the same difficulty would be found with each.

Positivism requires a formal conception of the inherent rationality of law. Even law as claiming authority, and not solely as having authority, requires a substantial conception of legal rationality. If the normativity of law is linked to its character as the promoter of the common good, then a positivistic theory of law must be inadequate. The Social Thesis and the Normativity Thesis so interpreted cannot be reconciled in the way that positivism demands. If both theses represent valid constraints on a theory of law, then positivism cannot be the correct theory of law. The move towards convention and the common good began within positivism, because of sophisticated positivism's own dissatisfaction with standard positivistic accounts of the normativity of law, and its own ingenuity in the search for alternative accounts. Unlike many arguments for the falsity of positivism, the argument of this chapter begins with premisses promoted by positivism itself.

10

ANTI-POSITIVISM'S CONCLUSIONS

In the preceding chapters of Part III we have developed the outlines of an anti-positivistic theory of law. The theory sketched is anti-positivistic in the sense that it abjures the systematic conceptual separation of law and value. It claims that the concept of law is not properly understood unless law is seen as having some essential, or internal, conceptual connection with human value. I have deliberately used the unspecific term 'anti-positivistic', rather than the specific term 'natural law theory'. The reason is that the term 'natural law theory' is associated with a particular historical tradition, and a particular way of understanding the connection between law and value. Natural law theory as traditionally understood is an example of anti-positivism. But I do not wish to argue that those philosophers within the natural law tradition in fact hold all of the views, or produce all of the arguments offered in this Part.

I should like to think, even, that many of the arguments offered in this Part against positivism and for anti-positivism are original. It is necessary for my purposes in this study that the anti-positivistic theory developed in this Part has some intrinsic plausibility and attractiveness.[1] I hope that goal has been achieved. Furthermore, one of the important claims made here about the anti-positivism presented is that the motivation for believing it, and the fundamental premisses for its defence, are found in positivism itself. I shall now summarize the theory as presented.

---

[1] As we shall see in Part IV, it is not necessary that it actually be the *correct* theory of law. See also the Introduction.

1. REASONS FOR ACTION

Simple positivism represented law as a reason for action on the balance of reasons. Sophisticated positivism regarded simple positivism as inadequate for that reason, claiming that so to regard law did not allow for differentiation between the 'bad man's' view of the law—or law seen from the external point of view—and the point of view of those for whom law was not merely coercive. The best alternative account suggested by sophisticated positivism is to construe law as an exclusionary reason for action, an account which is an explicit alternative to a 'balance of reasons' account. Sophisticated positivism therefore criticizes simple positivism on the basis of the inadequacy of an account of law which leaves law as coercive. Sophisticated positivism, however, needs to argue for the exclusionary reason account. Two main arguments are offered, the Functional Argument and the Phenomenological Argument. The latter has to bear the argumentative weight. We understand law properly when we understand how it is mentally with those who see law as an exclusionary reason for action.

A plausible way to explore the notion of how it is mentally with those who see law as an exclusionary reason for action is to examine the notion in the light of theories about the role of character traits in the explanation of behaviour. A highly plausible such theory is the so-called 'three-part analysis', which analyses character traits as a particular sort of representational disposition, a disposition to attach practical salience to certain representations, and a desire to do certain types of things, given the contents of such representations. This analysis explicates explanations of the form 'P did x out of C', where C is some character trait. In the cases at issue, we explain law-abiding behaviour by appeal to the trait of taking law to be an exclusionary reason for action, the trait to which the Phenomenological Argument points. Sophisticated positivism's objection to simple positivism can be expressed in terms of the 'three-part analysis'. Simple positivism's account of law as a reason for action is satisfied by 'sheep-like', acquiescent conformity to law. Sheep-like acquiescence therefore may indeed fit the three-part pattern of explanation, but it does not imply a stance which contains specifically representations of what the law requires or forbids under the description 'required/forbidden by law'. It cannot therefore be a stance which tells us anything about how the law as such is a reason for action in the way that sophisticated positivism requires.

Once we do begin with those whose stance involves a disposition to have representations of actions as required by or forbidden by law, those for whom laws are exclusionary reasons may be validly contrasted with the anarchist, the psychotic, the revolutionary group, and so forth, as possessors of the external point of view. The contrast is underwritten, however, by the fact that in conforming to law, those for whom laws are exclusionary reasons are in fact *expressing* their character. Their reasons for conforming to law are 'expressive reasons'. But if law is properly understood only if it is seen to provide an expressive reason for action, then law is only properly understood when seen as having whatever value it has to have to provide an expressive reason. If it is accepted that sophisticated positivism has revealed genuine deficiencies in the way that these simpler forms of positivism represent laws as reasons for action, then laws cannot be adequately represented as reasons for action in positivistic terms. Laws must be represented as expressive reasons for action, in which case laws necessarily deserve respect. The insights of sophisticated positivism lead to a non-positivistic theory of law.

2. AUTHORITY

Sophisticated positivism wants to preserve the separation of law and morality by insisting that the law's connection with authority is simply that law as a matter of social fact claims authority. The judgement for any given legal norm that it is an authoritative directive is supposedly a separate judgement, for an unjust law is still a law and we identify it as a law before we assess its (in)justice. Sophisticated positivism, however, does think that the connection of law and authority is essential. Law is not understood aright— not understood in the way that permits, for example, the distinguishing of law as a normative system from etiquette, or fashion—unless it is argued that law's distinctiveness as a normative system lies in claiming *authority*. That theoretical claim, however, turns out to imply a view about the essential and non-contingent connection between law in its natural design and functioning, and justice. No such non-contingent connection is compatible with positivism. Facts about the concept of law itself which sophisticated positivism is too sophisticated not to appreciate push us irresistibly away from positivistic theories of law.

3. THE INTERNAL POINT OF VIEW TO LAW

Simple positivism not only thinks that a legal theory may be complete without mentioning the internal point of view to law. It also thinks that legal theory itself may be properly practised from the external point of view. Sophisticated positivism rejects the first of these claims, but continues to maintain the latter. It rejects the first claim, because it accepts as a constraint on any adequate legal theory that the theory reproduce the way in which laws function in the lives of those who have the internal point of view to law. However, these reasons as reasons for rejecting the first claim of simple positivism are in fact reasons for rejecting simple positivism's second claim as well. Legal practice has the internal point of view to law built into the logic of its practice: the internal point of view is not simply a luxury found only in healthy societies. The constraint of the theorist to reproduce the way in which laws function in the lives of those who have the internal point of view to law means that the theorist too must in the normal case display the internal point of view, commitment to law. Of course some given theorist may lack the internal point of view to law, but do legal theory anyway from the external point of view. There is no more reason to suppose that we have to represent law so that a theorist's external point of view is dispositive of the nature of law than that we have to represent law so that the 'bad man's' external point of view is dispositive of the nature of law. Legal theory not only need not, it should not be committed to the availability of the external point of view for itself. Sophisticated positivism, by showing us so clearly why the latter is a mistake, shows us in the end why the former is too, and thus why positivism cannot be the correct theory of law.

4. THE ACCEPTANCE OF LAW

The most simple, and perhaps most simplistic, account of the acceptance of a legal system is one which reduces acceptance to passive conformity. But if we acknowledge the differences between humans and sheep, then we see that there is something deeply misleading about looking at human conformity to law as 'sheep-like'. We also have the sense that to represent the normativity of law as purely coercive is to distort law. However, if we start to take seriously the intentional element in acceptance of law, and we interpret the intentional element in terms of the knowledge of and stance towards the technicalities of law found among officials, it remains hard to see how citizens can accept the law. On the other hand, if citizens do not accept the law but merely conform to its demands, then law remains from the point of view of its citizens a coercive order.

Theory now faces a dilemma. On the one hand, acceptance by citizens cannot be the same as acceptance by officials; on the other hand, acceptance by citizens has to be genuine acceptance. The obstructive force of this dilemma derives from assuming an episodic model for acceptance and consent. If acceptance is construed in terms of a disposition to display law-abiding behaviour, then there is no bar to finding that the ordinary citizen accepts the law. The ordinary law-abiding citizen's interaction with the law is as deliberate and complicitous and as enduring as that of the professional official. Then we have to ask the question of whether it is plausible to construe such acceptance as simply contingent. Is it purely a matter of historical accident whether a legal system is 'healthy' or 'sheep-like'? If it is a perversion of law that the legal order is a coercive order, then it cannot be contingent that law is accepted. But if that is true, then the merit of law is not separate from its existence. And if that is true, then positivistic or content-independent accounts of law cannot be correct as theories of law.

The insight that legal theory needed to take into account the point of view of those who accepted the law arose within the positivistic tradition. It arose in connection with the insight that to represent law as a system of commands backed by threats is to misrepresent law. But if those insights are valid insights, then legal theory is impelled irresistibly away from legal positivism.

5. DISCRETION AND PRINCIPLE

Sophisticated positivism has acknowledged that, to give a proper picture of judicial discretion and the role of principles in legal justification, it is necessary to acknowledge that the court's discretion in a hard case is not 'strong', but is circumscribed by a variety of factors. It is also necessary to acknowledge that there may be legal principles, standards to which the judge properly appeals, which underwrite the avoidance of rules, and so of the vice of formalism. These acknowledgements rest on the underlying goal of 'getting this case just right', of doing justice to the particular claims before the court. Principles of formal rationality cannot suffice to account for 'getting *this* case just right', and so we must understand the goal as a substantial one. The notion of the justification of a legal decision which resonates with the goal of 'getting *this* case just right' is one which must admit justifications beginning from principles not necessarily 'within the law'. If all these claims are correct, then a positivistic account of discretion and principle must be mistaken. And it has been shown to be mistaken on the basis of claims about discretion and principle made by sophisticated positivism itself.

6. INTERPRETATION AND SEMANTICS

Simple positivism presents a straightforward account of the semantics for propositions of law in terms of a relationship to social fact. It also presents adjudication as a discretionary and evaluative choice of a verdict after the determination of the appropriate social facts. Sophisticated positivism argues that such a view is too simple because of its commitment to a realist semantics for propositions of law. Rather, the semantics for propositions of law must be construed as anti-realist. Adjudication can then be construed as interpretation, and the judge as constrained by the ground-rules of the interpretative enterprise.

However, institutional history in the form of the accepted ground-rules of the legal enterprise, as sources of constraints on the adjudicator, are as much social facts as the 'commands of a sovereign'. To construe the semantics of propositions of law in terms of a relation to such social facts is as much to construe the semantics realistically as does simple positivism. To constrain the judge by such social facts is to interpret adjudication as formalistically as does simple positivism.

Therefore, if a simple account of the correctness of judicial decisions in terms of a relation to social fact is inadequate, then only an account in terms of a relationship to a moral order independent of the legal order, whatever the semantics of that order considered in its own right, will be adequate. If it is acknowledged, as it is indeed acknowledged by sophisticated positivism, that adjudication is more than formalism plus strong discretion, then only an anti-positivist theory can give full significance to the acknowledgement. Call adjudication 'interpretive' if you will, but the term will carry no freight unless it is strengthened by an anti-positivist semantics for propositions of law. The error of simple positivism is not to be realist about the semantics for propositions of law, but to construe such semantics in terms of a relation to social fact, rather than a moral order. The error of simple positivism is to be formalist about adjudication. Only a non-positivistic theory avoids the error of formalism.

7. LAW AND THE COMMON GOOD

The problem for the analysis of law as social fact, and for any form of simple positivism thereby, is that law-as-social-fact seemed to be law without genuine normative force, and law essentially has genuine normative force. Sophisticated positivism's proposed solution was law-as-convention positivism. But law-as-convention positivism itself ran into difficulty. Law is not merely normative; it is, or claims to be, authoritatively normative. Law-as-convention positivism cannot explain the authority-claiming aspect of law.

It might then be supposed that what one may call law-as-convention-for-the-common-good positivism could so explain the normativity of law. However, to make sense of such a theory, a story is needed about the common good. One might try to explain the common good in conventional terms. If so, then law-as-convention-for-the-common-good positivism reduces to law-as-convention positivism, and thereby fails in its task of explaining law's particular normativity, its authority-claiming aspect. Law-as-convention-for-the-common-good positivism succeeds only when the notion of the common good is given some substantial and non-individualistic characterization—that is to say, when law-as-convention-for-the-common-good positivism ceases to be a form of positivism, and regards the concept of law as in part a content-dependent concept.

Other variants on the notion of 'convention' have been offered —'constructive conventionalism', or a conventionalism based on taking seriously the public and interactive character of law. Analogous difficulties are found with each variant. Either the convention is still no more than a social fact, and thus cannot have the salience of authority. Or, if authoritativeness is a prerequisite for being a convention of the desired thought, the theory is fully anti-positivistic. A third possibility, just hinted at, is that the theory is a fully normative account of how to design a constitution, in which case the theory no longer belongs to the project of analytical jurisprudence.

Positivism requires a formal conception of the inherent rationality of law. Even law as claiming authority, and not solely as having authority, requires a substantial conception of legal rationality. If the normativity of law is linked to its character as the promoter of the common good, then a positivistic theory of law must be inadequate. The Social Thesis and the Normativity Thesis so interpreted cannot be reconciled in the way that positivism demands. If both theses represent valid constraints on a theory of law, then positivism cannot be the correct theory of law. The move towards convention and the common good began within positivism, because of sophisticated positivism's own dissatisfaction with standard positivistic accounts of the normativity of law, and its own ingenuity in the search for alternative accounts.

As in Parts I and II, we may try to summarize anti-positivism in terms of seven theses, complementary to those of simple positivism and sophisticated positivism:

1. Law provides expressive reasons for actions, which implies that law must be worthy of respect.
2. The authority of law derives from standards internal to law, through the essential and non-contingent connection between law in its natural design and functioning, and justice.
3. The constraint of the theorist to reproduce the way in which laws function in the lives of those who have the internal point

of view to law means that the theorist too must in the normal case display the internal point of view, commitment to law.

4. Since it is a perversion of law that the legal order is a coercive order, then it cannot be contingent that law is accepted.
5. The anti-formalist goal of adjudication to judge cases correctly requires reference to principles not necessarily contained within black-letter law, and such principles will limit judicial discretion.
6. The semantics for propositions of law, and legal interpretation, must be construed realistically and to include a relationship to an independent order of value.
7. The normativity of law is linked to its promotion of the common good, where that receives an account independent of the preferences of lawmakers and citizens.

As with simple positivism and sophisticated positivism, my claim is not that any particular legal theorist has held all of these theses in one theory. Some, no one but the implied narrator of Part III has held. None the less the theses represent an intuitively plausible response by anti-positivism to the views of sophisticated positivism. The theses draw their strength, as I have tried to show, from beliefs held by sophisticated positivism itself. Thus the argument against positivism begins from within positivism, from views which sophisticated positivism holds about the inadequacy of simple positivism, and demands which sophisticated positivism itself holds it proper for legal theory to attempt to meet.

Part IV

Beyond Positivism and Anti-Positivism

11

THE MOVEMENTS OF LEGAL THOUGHT

1. IDENTIFYING LEGAL NORMS

This book could have ended with Part III, with the articulation of an anti-positivist theory of law. But such a book would not express what this book aims to express, the theory of law of its author. As I indicated in the Introduction (pages 2–3), this book takes seriously notion of 'movement'. To pass from simple positivism through sophisticated positivism to anti-positivism constitutes a movement of thought. To rest content with anti-positivism constitutes stasis. This book repudiates stasis, so the movement of legal thought must continue. The argument of Part III followed the principle that anti-positivism relied for support on claims made by positivism. If the movement of legal thought is to continue, we should now expect a reply by positivism to the case for anti-positivism. The claim of this book that movement of legal thought is inevitable will be most plausible, if the positivist's reply can be grounded in claims made by anti-positivism. Let us consider whether that is so.

Both positivists and anti-positivists alike often claim, and rightly, that an obsession with whether 'an unjust law is still a law' disguises and obscures central issues at stake in the theoretical debate about the nature of law. As Schauer has recently and plausibly said, 'positivism is about the ability to identify a normative domain that is smaller than and distinguishable from the entire normative universe'.[1] Members of the normative universe include norms of many different kinds. There are for instance nutritional norms about the value of eating tomatoes, and horticultural norms about procedures of growing tomatoes. It is intuitively implausible to claim that these norms are part of the legal system, and are extensionally within the set of legal norms.

[1] 'Is the Common Law Law?', *California Law Review*, 77 (1989), 460.

The issue of whether an unjust law is still a law is simply another example of the extensional issue. The underlying reason for thinking that horticultural norms are not within the set of legal norms is exactly the same reason as the reason for thinking that a norm is still a legal norm even if from the moral point of view what the norm enjoins are unjust acts. The thought is that legal norms are a specific subset of the total normative universe. It never follows simply from the fact that a proposition states a norm that it states a legal norm; it never follows simply from the fact that a norm is a legal norm that it is also a norm of some other subset of the total normative universe, or that it has the same content as some other such norm. However, nothing said so far bars a given norm from being a member of more than one subset, more than one normative domain.

We must distinguish between 'extensional divergence' and 'extensional uniqueness'. One set of norms is extensionally divergent from another set just in case at least one norm is a member of one set but not the other set. It is a commonplace that positive law and morality are extensionally divergent. Societies acknowledge moral requirements that they do not back up with the force of law. They also often for purely regulatory and co-ordinative purposes make legally mandatory acts to which in themselves morality is indifferent. The thesis that positive law and morality are extensionally divergent is a thesis with which anti-positivism can comfortably agree.

The notion of 'extensional uniqueness' is different. A set of norms is extensionally unique just in case no norm which is a member of that set is a member of any other set of norms. Commonsensically, it might seem implausible that there are any such sets of norms. Suppose what might seem the best kind of case, the norms of an artificially created and highly structured activity like a game—bridge, for example. Even here, there are general norms of card-playing strategy in partnership trick-taking games which are not peculiar to bridge. In any game there apply broad strategies of goal-directed behaviour which apply also to many contexts outside games. Despite common sense, however, the claim to extensional uniqueness surfaces in technical legal theory.

Consider the following claim:

It is a feature of the concept of law that it makes the content of law recursively dependent on legal practices. The concept of law determines what counts as legal practice in part through determining that, within the constraints imposed by the concept, any practice is a legal practice if given this character by another legal practice.[2]

The notion of 'recursive dependence' is not the same as Schauer's notion of 'extensional divergence': it amounts in fact to a claim of extensional uniqueness. To claim that legal norms are necessarily a particular subset of the total normative universe is not to claim that norms become members of the subset through some recursive definition. The 'recursive definition' criterion would, though, absent duplicate norms, and ensure that the norms for a domain such that membership in it is defined recursively would be members only of that domain. Thus, as Schauer rightly indicates, the 'extensional divergence' claim leads to positivism, because positivism provides a way of securing the 'extensional divergence' claim along with extensional uniqueness. Raz's 'recursive dependence' claim *is* positivism. Anti-positivistic theories of law can be happy with the 'extensional divergence' claim, but they cannot accept the 'extensional uniqueness' claim or the 'recursive dependence' claim.

It may seem, however, that it cannot be right to tie positivism to the extensional uniqueness thesis. It has also been claimed by positivism that legal systems are *comprehensive*; that is, that they 'claim authority to regulate any kind of behaviour'.[3] Even if it is[4] true that actual mundane legal systems in fact do leave kinds of behaviour unregulated, the positivistic thought is that such a fact is contingent, not conceptually necessary. So let us suppose a grimly unhealthy society in which the legal system really does exercise its claims to the full and regulate all kinds of behaviour. Is the set of legal norms in that society extensionally divergent, let alone extensionally unique?

It is not clear that legal theory knows how to go about answering that question, and I am not now going to try to answer it. The following point is clear. The question can be answered, once we

---

[2] Joseph Raz, 'Dworkin: A New Link in the Chain', *California Law Review*, 74 (1986), 1114.
[3] Raz, *Practical Reason and Norms*, 150.
[4] Fortunately, almost always, and even always.

take a firm stance on how it is that norms become members of the set(s) of norms to which they belong. If it is by purely procedural criteria, such as the notion of 'recursive dependence' embodies, then comprehensiveness and extensional uniqueness are perfectly compatible. If it is in some way by their content, then comprehensiveness and extensional uniqueness are not compatible. However, whether the criteria of membership in the set of legal norms are wholly formal and procedural, or are in some way and to some degree substantive is not an issue that can be decided independently of the opposition between positivism and anti-positivism. It is a central issue at stake in that opposition.

It would, however, be less satisfactory for the overall thesis of this book if positivism could respond to anti-positivism only with claims anti-positivism is committed to rejecting. If positivism and anti-positivism had no common ground, then the fact of their continued appeal and opposition would in a deep sense be wholly unexplained. However plausible it might be to claim, therefore, that the theses of recursive dependence and extensional unique-ness define positivism, these theses cannot constitute the expository basis here for positivism's response to anti-positivism. That basis must lie in a thesis that anti-positivism itself accepts, the thesis of extensional divergence.

2. A POSITIVIST REPLY

We can now see how positivism will exploit the 'extensional divergence' claim in responding to the seven theses of anti-positivism.

1. It will be argued that not every norm of respect-worthiness is a norm of legal respect-worthiness, that not every expressive reason for action is a reason expressive of respect for law. We therefore need some criterion independent of respect-worthiness as such for identifying a norm of legal respect-worthiness. Any such criterion will result in the separation of law and morality/ value in the form which positivism demands. Moreover, even if it is true that law in the normal case must have something to do with expressive reasons for action, the most that the argument of Chapter 3 can show is that, for stable law-abiding behaviour to be explained, laws must be believed to be expressive reasons for

action. Law and value would be linked only if laws are shown necessarily to be expressive reasons, not necessarily to be believed to be such reasons.

2. It will be argued, first, that, while it may be true that the authority of law derives from the functions law performs in a society, none the less the judgement that law should perform those functions is a judgement made of one normative system, law, from the point of view of a different normative system, morality. Moreover, even if there are standards of justice internal to law, to equate those standards with standards of justice in background political morality is to ignore the independence of law as a subset of the total normative universe. Not every standard in background political morality is a candidate for being a standard internal to law. Reference will have to be made to a separately identified normative system to discover which are the relevantly internal standards.

3. It will be argued that, if the internal point of view is a matter of approval of, or commitment to, legal norms from some point of view other than the strictly legal, then the extensional divergence of the legal from the non-legal is not being respected. The internal point of view is, as it were, inside citizens' and officials' heads. Those norms which are the 'targets' of the internal point of view will have to be identified separately from the facts that there is towards them this internal point of view.

4. It will be argued that in, for example, countries like Poland, or East Germany, or Romania, there was law before the recent political changes even though there was no, or at best very little, acceptance of the law before those changes. The fact of extensional divergence between the set of legal norms and whatever set of norms it was that citizens genuinely did accept is needed to explain why there was law without acceptance. Moreover, even if we regard cases like the ones just mentioned as in some way derivative or degenerate cases of legal systems, in those paradigm cases where the law is accepted, 'accepted' only refers to a state of mind on the part of citizens. It does not refer to an objective acceptability, and thereby create a conceptual link between law and standards of acceptability.

5. It will be argued that, while it may be true that respect for certain principles of political morality may result in a set of legal norms more coherent with background political morality than

would otherwise be the case, none the less an inventory of such principles will not be an inventory of a part of the law, and the theory of such principles will not be a part of legal theory. The principles in question remain part of a separate normative domain from the legal domain unless they are incorporated into the legal domain by the appropriate procedure. Any sense a person might have that an iniquitous legal system cannot just for that reason be coherent expresses that person's moral sense, not a part of the analysis of the concept of law.

6. It will analogously be claimed that the following argument is sound. On the one hand, if the realm that gives propositions of law truth-values is the extensionally separate domain of institutional fact, then the task of elaborating a theory of the conditions under which propositions of law have truth-values is properly a part of legal theory. Likewise, if the choice of certain materials with a view to the task of elaborating standards of interpretation for those materials is constrained by appropriate procedures, then the task of elaborating those standards is properly a part of legal theory. On the other hand, if the realm that gives propositions of law truth-values is conceived of as some extensionally distinct domain, such as an independent moral order, then the task of elaborating a theory of the conditions under which propositions of law have truth-values in terms of such an independent normative order will not be a part of legal theory, but will be a part of political theory, moral theory, social psychology, or whatever. Furthermore, if the choice of certain materials with a view to the task of elaborating standards of interpretation for those materials is not constrained by appropriate procedures, then the task of elaborating those standards is not properly a part of legal theory, but will be a part of political theory, moral theory, social psychology.

7. It will, finally, be argued that, while the goal of having the set of legal norms serve the common good is a worthy goal, to be a legal norm and to have the normativity of a legal norm is to be a part of one normative domain, and to be a norm which serves the common good is to be a part of another normative domain. It cannot therefore be in the nature of law to serve the common good.

As an exponent of anti-positivism, Aquinas acknowledges the extensional divergence of the legal from the non-legal, in so far as he explicitly defends the category of 'human law'.[5] His position draws on two very different sets of resources. First, in accord with Aristotelian doctrine, Aquinas says that only the general principles of the natural law are known naturally; their particular applications to actual situations have to be worked out by human reason, and the products of such reasonings are human laws. Second, in accord with a theological demand to account for human fallibility, Aquinas appeals to the humanity of human law to explain why there may be in some cases divergences of human law from what natural and divine law ideally demand.

For the positivist, of course, legal theory is the theory of human law. Theory of divine law or of natural law is moral, or political, or some other sort of normative theory. Legal theory for anti-positivism turns out to be a branch of, or a special application of, political or moral or social theory in a general sense. The positivist's claim is not that to apply political or moral or social theory in a general sense to law is a mistake: in fact, such activities can be of immense social significance. The claim is simply that, in not respecting the extensional divergence of legal norms from the rest of the total normative universe, the construction and investigation of such theories is not legal theory. The price that anti-positivism pays for its rejection of the extensional separation of law and morality is to remove itself from the domain of theory of law. We noted at the very beginning of this study in the Introduction that in a sense positivism cannot be wrong about the nature of law, for positivism asserts truisms. We noted also that anti-positivism cannot be right, and we now see the reason why— anti-positivism ends up by subsuming legal theory under some wider kind of theorizing, in violation of the truth of truisms. The movement of legal thought which takes it from simple positivism through sophisticated positivism to anti-positivism is a movement which takes it to the point where the resultant theory is not a theory *of law*, but of politics, of society, of human character and virtue; where the theory can give only an instrumental place, not a conceptual place, to those features which uniquely identify legal systems as a particular kind of institutionalized normative system.

---

[5] *ST* I–II. Q. 91 A. 3 (*On Law, Morality and Politics*, 21–2).

3. LEGAL THEORY AT AN IMPASSE

We have now, however, reached, not a solution to a conflict between positivism and anti-positivism, but an impasse. The emphasis on the extensional divergence of legal norms from the rest of the total normative universe is nothing more than the reiteration of what was earlier called simple positivism. We can see this as follows.

1.* The most straightforward way of distinguishing legal norms and non-legal norms as different kinds of reason for action is to treat them as extensionally different domains on a single level plane of reasons. But to do that is to adopt simple positivism's view of the way that laws are reasons for action. It was, however, sophisticated positivism's dissatisfaction with simple positivism on this issue that led us to the anti-positivism here being impugned.

2.* To create a separately identifiable normative system with its own internal standards of authority, and to emphasize beliefs about authority at the expense of actual authority, is to evade the issue of the authority of law. The most straightforward way of not evading the issue consistent with separate identification and emphasis on belief is to find the authority of law in citizens' beliefs about standards external to law. But to do that is to adopt simple positivism's view of the way that law has authority. It was, however, sophisticated positivism's dissatisfaction with simple positivism on this issue that led us to the anti-positivism here being impugned.

3.* The most straightforward way to create a separately identifiable normative system which is equally separately identifiable from the point of view which the norm-subjects have to the system is to create a system fully identifiable and understandable from the external point of view. But to do that is to adopt simple positivism's view of the external point of view to law. It was, however, sophisticated positivism's dissatisfaction with simple positivism on this issue that led us to the anti-positivism here being impugned.

4.* The most straightforward way to explain how it is possible that a normative system may be genuinely a legal system even though it is accepted by few, or even at most one, of its norm-subjects is to regard the level of acceptance of a legal system as a wholly contingent feature of the system. But to do that is to adopt simple positivism's view of the acceptance of law. It was, however, sophisticated positivism's dissatisfaction with simple positivism on this issue that led us to the anti-positivism here being impugned.

5.* The most straightforward way of restricting membership in the domain of legal norms to those which are incorporated by an appropriate procedure, and of repudiating the claims of principles of background political morality to be legal principles, is to regard the law as consisting of statutes and common-law rules only, and of regarding judicial discretion in hard cases as strong discretion. But to do that is to adopt simple positivism's view of discretion and principle. It was, however, sophisticated positivism's dissatisfaction with simple positivism on this issue that led us to the anti-positivism here being impugned.

6.* The most straightforward way of keeping the elaboration of semantical rules and interpretative standards for propositions of law within the strictly legal domain is to define the truth-conditions for propositions of law in terms of social facts, and to eliminate special standards of interpretation. But to do that is to adopt simple positivism's view of semantics and interpretation. It was, however, sophisticated positivism's dissatisfaction with simple positivism on this issue that led us to the anti-positivism here being impugned.

7.* The most straightforward way of denying that it is in the nature of law to serve the common good is to regard the extent to which any system of positive law serves the common good as a contingent feature of that system. But to do that is to adopt simple positivism's view of law and the common good. It was, however, sophisticated positivism's dissatisfaction with simple positivism on this issue that led us to the anti-positivism here being impugned.

My claim here is not that simple positivism provides the most plausible way of responding to perceived difficulties with anti-positivism. My claim is that it is the most straightforward way, the most 'simple' way. The argument for the endless movement of legal thought relies on three claims: first, that sophisticated positivism follows from positivism's difficulties with simple posit-ivism; second, that anti-positivism follows from sophisticated positivism's difficulties with simple positivism; third, that simple positivism follows from positivism's difficulties with anti-positivism. The thought that the preceding paragraphs (1*–7*) are mistakes because sophisticated positivism is the *best* response to anti-positivism misses the point. Of course sophisticated positivism is the best response positivism can give to anti-positivism. But why is it the best? Because simple positivism as the most straightforward form of positivism is not an adequate response to anti-positivism, although it is the most direct response. Sophisticated positivism emerges from simple positivism as the most plausible response to anti-positivism. The claim that 'anti-positivism leads to simple positivism' is not historical, but conceptual. That actual positivistic legal theory passes through the stage of simple positivism in a flash, as it were, is a claim I neither need to nor do deny. My concern in this book is with conceptual, not historical, movements.

The story of the pages which have intervened between the Introduction and the present page is the story of legal theory's dissatisfaction with simple positivism—and not just anti-positivistic legal theory, but positivistic legal theory as well. If the point of legal theory is to gain a perspicuous representation of the nature of law, then simple positivism has failed to advance the enterprise. The richer, non-truistic theories, however, led from simple positivism through sophisticated positivism to anti-positivism. Once legal theory took on board the task of finding some point outside the straightforwardness of simple positivism from which to aim to represent law perspicuously, legal theory was driven to leave positivism behind. But, the positivist has argued, in so doing, anti-positivistic legal theory leaves *the law* behind, and so cannot develop a perspicuous representation of the nature of *law*. Simple positivism is unacceptable as a theory of law. But the logic of the reasons for its unacceptability have led to something which is not so much an unacceptable theory of law as not a theory of law at all.

Legal theory begins with philosophical perplexity about the nature of law. Philosophical perplexity does not begin with ignorance of the truistic and the familiar, but is rather provoked by the truistic and the familiar. Thus simple reaffirmation of the truistic and the familiar cannot help. Positivism seems restricted by the fact that it relies so heavily on the truth of truisms. Anti-positivism, on the other hand, moves so far away from the strictly legal in the development of its theories that it too is of no help to those who are perplexed about the nature of *law*. To be told that law is not law but something else does not help those who know full well that law is law, and are none the less puzzled by what it is for law to be law.

Legal theory thus seems to have reached an impasse. Legal theory is either inadequate or not legal theory. We will confront this impasse directly in the last chapter of this Part. First, however, we must consider another possibility. The methodology of this study is orthodox in the sense that it represents legal theory as a perennial conflict between positivism and anti-positivism. But some recent writers have argued that precisely that is the central mistake of existing legal theory. They have taken seriously the possibility of a 'Third Theory of Law',[6] a theory which takes from positivism and anti-positivism what is correct in each, leaves behind what is incorrect, and thereby constructs the right theory, a middle-ground theory. Some of these writers have addressed specifically Dworkin's critique of positivism, and have argued that everything Dworkin says is compatible with positivism. Others have defended the view that it is compatible with positivism to make the existence and content of some laws depend on moral argument. I therefore give the general name of 'compatibilism' to this attempt to construct a middle-ground theory. It is clearly crucial to the present study, with its emphasis on the necessary movement of legal thought, that a stable 'compatibilist' middle ground is not available. The conclusions of the examination of compatibilism in the next chapter are therefore important.

[6] The echo of the title of John Mackie's well-known article is deliberate. Mackie considers the attempt of Dworkin to develop an alternative to positivism and natural law theory a failure. I will consider Dworkin myself shortly, 12–3 below.

12

COMPATIBILISM

1. HERCULEAN POSITIVISM

Dworkin's original challenge to legal positivism in his 1967 paper 'Is Law a System of Rules?'[1] claimed that positivism could not account for the obligation on the part of courts in appropriate circumstances and ways to adjudicate by inference from principles which were morally, rather than legally, authoritative. Much time and ink has been expended on the attempt to identify the precise details of the premises and inferences which constituted the challenge. I am going to bypass all that discussion here, and limit myself to what are, I hope, minimally controversial interpretative claims. The availability of 'extra-legal' principles binding on judges, if it obtains, challenges positivism, according to Dworkin (*Taking Rights Seriously*, 44), in three ways. (i) The law of a community can no longer be identified by any single test of recognition, or 'pedigree'. (ii) Judges do not have 'strong' discretion to adjudicate in certain cases without guidance from authority. (iii) Legal obligation might well be wider than strictly rule-related obligation.

In Chapter 2.5 above, I developed a response by sophisticated positivism to supposed weaknesses in simple positivism's understanding of legal principle and judicial discretion. The response tried to offer as rich an understanding of principle and discretion as possible while remaining firmly within a positivistic theory. As the critique by anti-positivism in Chapter 7 indicated, sophisticated positivism fell some way short of anti-positivism's ideal of acknowledging the adjudicative discretion of courts to be bound by moral principle and of ultimately marginalizing the requirement of pedigree. It will be noted that these latter remarks on my part

---

[1] Reprinted as ch. 2 of *Taking Rights Seriously* under the title 'The Model of Rules I'.

depend for their sense and plausibility on the deployment of spatial metaphors. Implicit in the remarks seems to be a picture of a continuum with simple positivism at one end, anti-positivism at the other, sophisticated positivism some way down the continuum from simple positivism towards anti-positivism, but not too far down. Thus we have the image of a space on the continuum between sophisticated positivism and anti-positivism, which, it is attractive to suppose, may be filled by a theory which does more to meet anti-positivism's legitimate demands than sophisticated positivism, without committing itself to being a full-blown version of anti-positivism.

The first form of compatibilism I shall consider aspires to be such a theory. Sophisticated positivism's concept of 'legal principle' is regarded by anti-positivism as inadequate because its roots are still too deep in settled or black-letter law. That the principle may be 'moral' in the sense that the form of words used to enunciate it could also be used to enunciate a principle of morality is not enough. The content of the legal principle is still subject to constraint by institutional history, and principles of morality are subject to no such constraint. It is felt to be important that principles of morality bear, if they bear, on legal cases without such constraint. One aim of Dworkin's theory important to him is clearly to permit, and even encourage, courts to reform the law— that is, to use moral principles to upgrade black-letter law; to pursue the path of righteousness when black-letter law is insufficiently righteous. To allow the content of legal principles to be determined by institutional history would severely constrict, and perhaps prevent, such reform. Compatibilism takes up the challenge of assigning to courts a permission, and even a duty, to apply principles of morality in full unrestricted form.

Much of course turns on how the theoretical commitments of legal positivism are to be understood. Jules Coleman defines what he calls 'negative positivism'.[2] Coleman's 'separability thesis' says that 'there exists at least one conceivable rule of recognition (and therefore one possible legal system) that does not specify truth as a moral principle among the truth conditions for any proposition of law' (141). Negative positivism claims no more than the separability thesis. It is perfectly obvious that Dworkin's challenge, if valid,

---

[2] 'Negative and Positive Positivism', *Journal of Legal Studies*, 11 (1982), 140 ff.

would defeat negative positivism. But it is also obvious that there is in principle a lot of 'space' between negative positivism and the possible anti-positivistic position that 'there is no possible legal theory that does not specify truth as a moral principle among the truth conditions for any proposition of law'. Theories in this middle ground might be called forms of 'positive positivism'. Coleman himself considers two such versions and defends the second of them—'hard fact positivism' and 'law-as-convention positivism'.[3] These are both versions of sophisticated positivism as understood in this study, and I shall not discuss them further. Another kind of positive positivism claims that 'there is at least one possible legal theory that specifies truth as a moral principle among the truth conditions for some proposition of law'. The theories we are considering here are instances of this kind.

Remember that the crucial distinction is between a principle whose content is subject to restriction by institutional history and a principle whose content is not so restricted. The focus is on principles of morality which are unrestrictedly part of the law. So we might state precisely the form of positive positivism being considered here as the claim that 'there is at least one possible legal theory that specifies truth as a moral principle unrestricted by institutional history among the truth conditions for some proposition of law'. Rolf Sartorius, for example, thinks that a legal system may contain as part of the law broad constitutional principles or statements of policy 'recursively characterized as those established, exemplified, or implied by "first-order" standards, either directly or indirectly'.[4] The 'established by' is the significant point, for 'exemplified' and 'implied' amount to content restrictions by institutional history; 'established by' implies no such restriction. Philip Soper considers first what he calls a 'simplified equity system with the rule of recognition that whatever Rex enacts is law, and the single enactment by Rex that 'all disputes are to be settled as justice requires'.[5] Such a system puts no restrictions of institutional history on the content of the concept of justice. He then supports Sartorius in proposing that the form of such a simplified system is

[3] In his sense of this term. I have made some remarks about his views in Ch. 2.4 and Ch. 2.7 above.

[4] 'Social Policy and Judicial Legislation', *American Philosophy Quarterly*, 8 (1971), 155–6

[5] 'Legal Theory', 509 ff.

not lost when the system acquires the complexity of a mature contemporary municipal legal system. David Lyons thinks that 'the criteria of validity of a legal system may, but need not, incorporate a moral test';[6] that there is nothing in the notion of 'pedigree' which implies that only rules and not principles can be 'pedigreed' (422); that constitutions and other such documents may incorporate moral notions into adjudication in such a way that courts cannot interpret such documents without engaging in moral reasoning (425).

The fullest attempt to argue for a 'Herculean positivism', and the strongest resulting version, is in Wilfrid Waluchow's paper of that name. Waluchow declares himself ready, in the first place (187–8), to grant to Dworkin: (*a*) that judges can be as bound to take into account Dworkinian principles as they are rules; (*b*) that judges have an obligation, not to adjudicate *ad hoc*, but to develop a theory about the principled roots of the decisions they take, and, if necessary, to regard the theory as decisive; (*c*) that the legal rights of litigants may ultimately be for such a theory to decide. He responds to other arguments of Dworkin's by showing: (1) that not only principles, but rule-like valid legal standards may need to be weighed, and may be overridden; (2) that a rule of recognition may as a matter of contingent social fact contain moral require-ments; (3) that even for a positivist law may not have to have maximal stability and certainty; (4) that courts may have only weak discretion, and may not exercise any discretion at all.[7] This theory is clearly 'Herculean' in its concessions to Dworkin. If it is to be positivism, some fine-tuning is needed. (4) and (*a*) must be interpreted in the light of (2). That is, the principles which bind and limit discretion must be recursively identified by the rule of recognition. (*c*) must be subject to a similar condition. But with these refinements, we have an intuitively powerful version of Herculean positivism.

The significant features of all four—Sartorius, Soper, Lyons, Waluchow—of these accounts, however, is that their sponsors are not willing to hand in their credentials and resign their position as

---

[6] 'Principles, Positivism and Legal Theory', *Yale Law Journal*, 87 (1977), 418.

[7] For Waluchow's distinction between 'having' and 'exercising' discretion, see Ch. 1.5 above. Sartorius in 'Social Policy' without articulating the distinction argues in fact as part of his position that courts should never exercise discretion even if they might on a rare occasion have discretion. Cf. 157–8.

positivists. These are Herculean *positivisms*. It is true that, to use Sartorius's terminology, the content of the principles that are among the binding legal standards in some system is not restricted in the way that it would be if the content had to be 'exemplified' or 'implied' by institutional history. But the presence of any given principle among the standards that bind courts in some system is 'established' by institutional history. It is, as Waluchow puts it,[8] 'a matter of contingent social fact'. If Raz[9] and Sartorius are right in thinking that recursive characterization of legal materials is an essential feature of legal positivism, then Herculean positivism respects the requirement of recursive characterization.

I do not wish to deny that there may be attractive features of Herculean positivism. When discussing Neil MacCormick's concept of 'narrative coherence' in Chapter 2.5 above, we noted his acknowledgement of its 'relativistic' character. If we suppose a jurisdiction in which references in the black-letter law to 'equality', for example, are thin on the ground and feeble in their implications, then even to grant to courts the power to seek 'narrative coherence' with such materials will not extend by much the resources for the pursuit of equality. If on the other hand we suppose that there is now introduced a Charter like the Canadian *Charter of Rights and Freedoms*, with the strong regard for equality rights expressed in its sect. 15, then the resources for the pursuit of equality are much extended. Such indeed is one standard argument for the introduction of documents such as Bills of Rights and Charters of Rights and Freedoms. Note, however, that the dispute between friends and foes of such documents cuts across the dispute between positivism and anti-positivism. Herculean positivism says that unrestricted principles of morality are binding on judges only if they are incorporated in some way by a rule of recognition. But if they are, then they are fully part of the law.

Anti-positivism may be loosely characterized as (in part) the view that (appropriate) moral principles are binding upon judges independently of their being pedigreed by some recursive procedure. The appearance of advance on the part of Herculean positivism over forms of positivism that do not allow for the pedigreeing of principles at all is exaggerated through the comparison with a very

---

[8] 'Herculean Positivism', *Oxford Journal of Legal Studies*, 5 (1985), 195.
[9] 'Link in the Chain', 1114.

strong form of anti-positivism. If positivism is thought of as the theory that there is no conceivable legal system in which principles of morality are pedigreed, and anti-positivism as the theory that there is no conceivable legal system in which principles of morality are not pedigreed, then Herculean positivism seems an attractive alternative. It says, quite reasonably, that there are conceivable legal systems in which principles of morality are pedigreed, and conceivable legal systems in which principles of morality are not pedigreed, and for any given legal system it will be a matter of contingent social fact which it is. On this construal of the issue, there seems lots of space between the extremes for a more reasonable theory. But suppose the issue between legal positivism and anti-positivism is presented differently. Suppose it is presented as follows. Positivism says that there is no conceivable legal system in which principles of morality are part of binding legal materials unless they are pedigreed by a rule of recognition. Anti-positivism says that there is at least one conceivable legal system in which principles of morality are part of binding legal materials even though they are not pedigreed by a rule of recognition. Is there now 'space' between positivism and anti-positivism for some third, more reasonable theory such as Herculean positivism? The answer is clearly negative. Without wishing to settle, or even raise, the question of intellectual biography whether Dworkin himself meant his challenge this way, anti-positivism as just expressed does present a severe challenge even to Herculean positivism, for it strikes at the heart of positivism, the requirement of recursive delineation of binding legal materials.

Coleman remarks that his 'negative positivism' is a weak theory —'there is at least one conceivable legal system in which the rule of recognition does not specify being a principle of morality among the truth conditions for any proposition of law'. But the complementary thesis of anti-positivism—'there is at least one conceivable legal system in which a principle of morality is among the truth conditions for some proposition of law without being specified by the rule of recognition'—is not at all a weak thesis. If the aim of the form of compatibilism being considered here, Herculean positivism, is to incorporate some of what is believed by anti-positivism compatibly with remaining positivist, then the compatibility with positivism is certainly achieved. But if the anti-positivistic thesis just mentioned sets the minimum for incorporation of anti-positivist theses, and I believe that it does, then not even Herculean positivism achieves such incorporation.

2. THE WEAK SOCIAL THESIS

I did acknowledge in the previous section that Herculean positivism differed from some other possible versions of positivism in one important respect—principles of morality were incorporated in such a way that their binding content was unrestricted by institutional history, even though the fact of their incorporation was so restricted. I have suggested that in fact, from the perspective of anti-positivism, this difference does not seem significant. It does to the proponents of Herculean positivism, of course. We should consider why this is so, and whether a significant challenge to anti-positivism can be reinstated.

Much of the motivation for thinking that Herculean positivism and kindred theses are important new versions of positivism, especially so in Waluchow's case, comes from responding to arguments in Raz's essay 'Legal Positivism and the Sources of Law' (*The Authority of Law*, ch. 3). Raz defines first what he calls the *Strong Social Thesis*:

A jurisprudential theory is acceptable only if its tests for identifying the content of law and determining its existence depend exclusively on facts of human behaviour capable of being described in value-neutral terms, and applied without resort to moral argument.[10]

He then distinguishes the strong social thesis from the *Weak Social Thesis*. The weak social thesis holds simply that institutionality and efficacy are necessary and sufficient for the social foundation of law.[11] The weak social thesis, moreover, Raz says,

is compatible with

(*a*) Sometimes the identification of some laws turns on moral arguments,

but also with

[10] *The Authority of Law*, 39–40. Raz acknowledges that 'this formulation is less clear than it might be'.
[11] The strong social thesis does not regard either institutionality or efficacy as either necessary or sufficient conditions for law; cf. *The Authority of Law*, 46.

(*b*) In all legal systems the identification of some laws turns on moral argument. (*The Authority of Law*, 47)

For this reason, Raz claims, the weak social thesis is 'insufficient to characterize legal positivism'. (*a*) 'depends on the contingent existence of source-based law making moral considerations into the criteria of validity in certain cases'. (*a*) 'is on the borderline of positivism and may or may not be thought consistent with it'. (*b*), however, 'asserts a conceptual necessity of testing law by moral argument and is clearly on the natural law side of the historical positivist/natural law divide'. The strong social thesis, which Raz defends, excludes both (*a*) and (*b*), for, as noted, it says that the existence and content of laws must depend on *sources*.[12]

A law has a source if its contents and existence can be determined without using moral arguments (but allowing for arguments about people's moral views and intentions, which are necessary for interpretation, for example).[13]

Raz gives as an example a legal system in which the law requires that unregulated disputes be determined on the basis of moral considerations (*The Authority of Law*, 45–6). As Waluchow demonstrates,[14] cases of (to use his term) 'Charter societies', societies which have 'at some point adopted a constitutionally entrenched charter of rights setting out certain moral rights the infringement of which by legislation or judicial decision renders the latter legally invalid',[15] are equally paradigmatic and historically more frequent examples of societies seemingly based on (*a*) and thus seemingly not conforming to the strong social thesis. A court, in determining, for instance, whether a particular statutory employment arrangement infringes a right to equal protection and benefit of the law without discrimination based on sex, seems to have to determine the validity of such a statute by deploying moral

---

[12] Raz henceforth refers to the strong social thesis as 'the sources thesis', but we will remain with the longer name.

[13] This and the preceding quotes are from *The Authority of Law*, 47. Note that my anti-positivism at the end of sect. 1 quantifies existentially over legal systems, whereas Raz's (*b*) quantifies universally over legal systems and existentially over laws within legal systems. This is not a relevant difference.

[14] 'The Weak Social Thesis', *Oxford Journal of Legal Studies*, 9 (1989), 34–7, 49–55; 'Charter Challenges', *Osgoode Hall Law Journal*, 29 (1991), *passim*.

[15] 'Weak Social Thesis', 28.

considerations concerning the meaning and extent of such a charter or constitutional right.

In the present context we need not concern ourselves with legal theories that defend (*b*) or something stronger, for our concern here is not with paradigmatic anti-positivistic theories. Our focus must be on (*a*) and the implications of it. Two things are to be noted about Raz's remarks. First, he does acknowledge that thesis (*a*), which is compatible with the weak social thesis, depends on the *contingent* existence of source-based law making moral considerations into the criteria of validity in certain cases, thus acknowledging a point our discussion of Herculean positivism has shown to be relevant. Second, he none the less claims that only the strong social thesis properly characterizes positivism; the weak social thesis does not. Waluchow's interest in 'Weak Social Thesis' and 'Charter Challenges' is in arguing that the weak social thesis in fact does represent a genuine form of positivism, and one that has the advantage over the strong social thesis of subtending a positivist account of charter societies and of maintaining the advantages of Herculean positivism over the regular kind.

The case for the claim that the weak social thesis represents a genuine form of positivism relies on the contingency referred to and the consequent respect for the recursive nature of the characterization of legal materials. The case for the weak social thesis as the only proper form of positivism relies on the following line of reasoning. The strong social thesis says that courts cannot determine the existence and content of laws by means of moral arguments; a court in deciding a Charter case clearly determines the existence and content of valid law by means of moral argument;[16] Charter adjudication therefore refutes the strong social thesis.

Things, however, cannot be this simple. To some extent, Raz does load the discussion in his favour by picking unregulated, rather than constitutional/Charter, cases as his examples. This is clear from his first implied response to defenders of the weak social thesis. He dismisses the forms of compatibilism he refers to,[17] by saying that a criterion is needed to distinguish between when resorting to moral considerations amounts to the application

---

[16] Cf. here Waluchow's discussion of *Andrews* v. *Law Society of B.C.* [1986] 4 WWR 242 (BCCA) at 'Charter Challenges', 192–9.

[17] Lyons and Soper, *The Authority of Law*, 47 n. 8.

)f pre-existing law and when it amounts to discretionary changing)f the law, and no such criterion has been supplied. If Charter :ases are taken as the paradigm, then a criterion is easily available —does the case indeed fall within the domain of the Charter? A ,econd possible response does not avail Raz much either. As noted ibove, he permits within the extension of his technical term source' empirical arguments about people's views and intentions vhich may be necessary for interpretation. So, for instance, if it is)ermitted to refer to Hansard or the Congressional Record in letermining the meaning of a clause of a statute, to find out what he legislators intended the clause to mean, then such a reference s still a reference to a 'source'. But Raz could bring all Charter ınd constitutional cases under this heading only at the cost of ıdopting a dubious theory of constitutional interpretation, that vhat the words mean is what historically the legislators intended hem to mean. Raz in fact explicitly rejects this route. *The Authority of Law*, page 46 n. 7 distinguishes 'morality' and 'social norality', 'the customs, habits and common views of a community'. The issue between the strong social thesis and the weak social thesis s the issue of the deployment of considerations of *morality*, not ,ocial morality, in adjudication (*The Authority of Law*, 46).

The issue now becomes more subtly joined. It would be a nistake to interpret Raz as making a factual error, as thinking that :ertain kinds of performances by courts—resorting to moral :onsiderations to decide cases—do not occur when in fact they lo.[18] Raz makes it quite clear in *The Authority of Law*, page 46, hat the question is one of how best to account for such cases at the evel of theory, not one of factual occurrence. In fact, he gives us a ,tory about how the strong social thesis will have to interpret the :ind of case whose interpretation is at issue. The strong social hesis cannot accept as a description of what occurs that 'moral :onsiderations have become part of the law of the land'. Rather,

o conform to the strong thesis we will have to say that while the rule ·eferring to morality is indeed law (it is determined by its sources) the norality to which it refers is not thereby incorporated into law. The rule is ınalogous to a 'conflict of law' rule imposing a duty to apply a foreign ,ystem which remains independent and outside of the municipal law.

[18] The mistake would be analogous to that discussed in Ch. 2.5 above as regards)workin and legal principles.

What Raz has in mind is this. In Illyria, there is a need for widget-doctors. So would-be immigrants who are widget-doctors are exempted from certain requirements of the application process. An immigration tribunal is hearing an appeal from someone not exempted from these requirements. She, a Ruritanian, says she is entitled to exemption because she is a qualified widget-doctor; the Immigration Office said she was not so qualified. The tribunal says, We'll let the issue be settled by looking at the official Ruritanian definition of 'widget-doctor'. So they look, and decide (R), 'This person is a qualified widget-doctor'. Now (R) is the relevant proposition of Illyrian law whose existence and content is at issue. The strong social thesis says, '(R) satisfies the condition that its existence and content are fully determined by social sources. It exists, because it is an *intra vires* ruling by an authorized tribunal; it has the content that it has because the tribunal looked where a source-based norm said they should look'. Reference to the appropriate sources determines the truth of the pure proposition of Ruritanian law, (C) 'To satisfy criteria $C_1 \ldots C_n$ is to be a qualified Ruritanian widget-doctor', and the truth of that claim (C) is dispositive for the case, the disposition of which results in (R) being a valid applied proposition of Ruritanian law.

So, let us again suppose the case of an employment statute which is a candidate for being in conflict with the equality rights section, sect. 15, of the Canadian *Charter*. In order to decide the case, the court has to resort to moral argument to determine the truth of the moral claim that the statute discriminates against women, for instance. The conclusion of the argument is a moral judgement (C^*) that 'To satisfy criteria $C_1 \ldots C_n$ is to be objectionably discriminatory from the moral point of view'; this judgement occupies the same slot as (C) in the immigration example. The court then uses that piece of information about how things are with morality to make the ruling (R^*) that in law the statute is in conflict with sect. 15. This ruling corresponds to (R). (R^*), despite its dependence on (C^*), the strong social thesis claims, is none the less a normative proposition whose existence and content are fully determined by social sources. Note that the strong social thesis does not claim that, in determining that (C^*) is true as a proposition of morality the court is exercising a discretion which sect. 15 of the *Charter* authorizes it to exercise.[19] The court

[19] If I understand him aright, Waluchow so misinterprets the strong social thesis in 'Charter Challenges', 199.

is as bound by what Ruritanian law says, or what morality says, as it is by what Illyrian law says, or what the Queen in Parliament says. Thus the court is determining what the rights of the litigants already are, or what the constitutionality of the statute already is: the court is not deciding those rights, or that constitutionality, retroactively by the exercise of discretion.

The issue is not whether the strong social thesis and the weak social thesis have different stories to tell about Charter adjudication and like cases. It is clear that they do. The weak social thesis, at least as defended by Waluchow, claims that in such cases courts resort to moral argument to determine legal issues in a way that is in conflict with the requirements of the strong social thesis that the existence and content of every law is fully determined by social sources. The strong social thesis, as I have interpreted its deployment of and reliance on the 'foreign law' analogy, denies that in such cases courts resort to moral argument to determine legal issues in a way that is in conflict with said requirement about sources. But if that is where the issue is joined between the two theses, then the issue is misrepresented if it is put thus: that the weak social thesis acknowledges what the strong social thesis denies, that courts resort to non-source-based moral considerations in deciding Charter cases.[20] For the strong social thesis claims that: just as the Illyrian and Ruritanian legal systems remain separate, with the latter not 'incorporated' into the former despite their linkage through Illyrian provisions concerning the conflict of laws; so also a given municipal legal system in a 'Charter society' and morality remain separate, with the latter not 'incorporated' into the former despite their linkage through the constitutional provisions of the Charter society.

I do not have a view to offer about how to decide between the strong social thesis's story and the weak social thesis's story. Clearly, if we had a secure and issue-independent grip on what it was for one normative system in whole or in part to be 'incorporated' into another normative system, then we might be able to decide whether the strong social thesis was correct in denying that its 'foreign law' model condoned the 'incorporation' of morality into law. Given the heavily metaphorical nature of the language, I am not hopeful. But I have no stake in the outcome of the search for the most plausible form of positivism. My concern

---

[20] Again, if I understand him aright, Waluchow does in both 'Weak Social Thesis' and 'Charter Challenges' so put the issue.

here is compatibilism, the idea that a 'third theory of law' may be found which preserves the insights and avoids the mistakes of paradigm positivism and anti-positivism. The issue between positivism and anti-positivism gets joined over whether and in what sense standards which are not part of positive law—moral standards, for instance—are 'part of the law' in a way which makes them binding on courts, for instance. Positivism says: since 'law' equals 'positive law', such standards cannot be 'part of the law' *e vi termini*. Anti-positivism says: 'Agreed, they are not part of positive law; but law is not just positive law'—or, 'We don't understand positive law fully unless we see it as a putative determination of the natural law'. A theory which thinks that 'moral standards' are 'part of the law' even though they do not have a source is not a form of positivism. On the other hand, if the standards in question have a source and are 'part of the law', then we have a form of positivism, but we no longer have non-source-based moral standards. So if the weak social thesis differs from the strong social thesis in rejecting the 'foreign law' model, and says that moral standards are 'part of the law' even though they are not source based, then indeed there is a substantial difference between the weak social thesis and the strong social thesis. But that is the difference between a positivistic theory and an anti-positivistic theory. On the other hand, if the weak social thesis puts great weight on contingency and recursive delineation of legal materials, then it has not yet shown that its story about Charter challenges and like cases is superior to the 'foreign law' model of the strong social thesis. We have not yet defined a 'third theory' which is different from the strong social thesis and like anti-positivism in acknowledging that non-source-based moral considerations are binding upon judges, and yet is like the strong social thesis and unlike anti-positivism in thinking it an error to claim that moral considerations are as such binding on judges.

3. LAW AS INTEGRITY

The previous two sections have argued against different attempts to construct a 'third theory of law'.[21] My argument in this chapter

---

[21] I also argue against Philip Soper's candidate 'third theory' in my review of *A Theory of Law*, in *Ratio Juris*, 2 (1989).

against compatibilism would be the better if a transcendental argument could be found to supplement the piecemeal ones. As noted above (Chapter 11.3), the term 'third theory of law' was originally applied by Mackie to Dworkin. I have made various references at different points in this study to the latter's views, but have not attempted so far to confront them directly. I do so now. I believe Mackie's characterization of the *Taking Rights Seriously* theory as a 'third theory' may not necessarily be correct.[22] The recent theory of Law As Integrity is explicitly intended to be a 'third theory'.[23] I shall therefore consider it here as such, as a sophisticated form of compatibilism. I believe that it will give me the required transcendental argument.

I will sketch the theory too briefly to do justice to the length and richness of detail in its exposition in *Law's Empire*.[24] The enterprise of law is an essentially interpretative enterprise. It is possible to distinguish a pre-interpretative stage of simply identifying commonsensically legal materials from the interpretative stage, crucial to adjudication, of settling on a general justification for the main elements of the identified practice (65–6). There is also the post-interpretative stage of reforming the practice in the light of the interpretative judgements. But it is the interpretative stage which holds the attention of legal theory. There are two dimensions which constrain the judge at the interpretative stage— the dimension of fit with existing institutional history, and the dimension of justification (230 ff.). In the latter, the judge must seek to develop a theory, drawing on principles of political morality, which would make institutional history the best it could be. A judge's convictions about fit provide a 'rough threshold requirement' (255), but the requirement is not an absolute constraint. In the end, the judge must come to 'an overall judgment that trades off an interpretation's success on one type of standard against its failure on another' (239). Neither dimension has lexical priority over the other. Hercules reappears as 'an imaginary judge of superhuman intellectual power and patience

---

[22] The argument of Ch. 8 above implies that the Rights Thesis only makes sense as a strongly anti-positivistic theory. In so far as the 'old' Dworkin was a defender of the Rights Thesis, then the theory subtending the Rights Thesis will not be a 'third theory'.

[23] Cf. *Law's Empire*, ch. 3, ch. 7.

[24] Page references in parentheses are to the book.

who accepts law as integrity' (ibid.), and who may be assumed to display his powers in finding a coherent integration of the two dimensions of interpretation as they apply to any given instant case.[25]

This theory falls out as compatibilist in the following way. Positivism might be thought of as the theory which champions fit with institutional history. Anti-positivism might be thought of as the theory which champions justification in terms of principles of political morality. The theory of law as integrity does not sponsor either of the two dimensions exclusively. Rather, it represents the goal of adjudication as the proper balance of the two different elements, as the reconciliation of the claims of institutional history and the claims of moral principle. The notion of law as an interpretative enterprise is meant to highlight the fact that a legal decision even, and perhaps especially, in a hard case is not simply an assertion of a pre-existing order. Nor is it a declaration of how things shall in the future be unconstrained by how they have been in the past. Rather it is an interpretation of the past in the light of the ideals embedded in the past.

But is the theory of law as integrity, with its emphasis on the coherence of the two dimensions of interpretation, itself coherent as a theory of law?

One thing worth noting about the forms of compatibilism considered so far is that the compatibilizing drift is all in one direction. The defenders of Herculean positivism want to show that positivism can take on board elements of anti-positivism. The weak social thesis aims to admit elements of anti-positivism which the strong social thesis excludes. If the arguments of Part III of this study are correct, then this drift is no coincidence. Positivism's commitment to positivism is not incompatible with sensitivity to the insights of anti-positivism. Dworkin, however, has to move in the opposite direction. The Rights Thesis in its original form and the parading of requirements of moral principle as binding on judges in themselves would place a theory firmly in the anti-positivist camp. But, as Chapter 11 indicated,[26] full-blown anti-positivism is problematic. It does not give enough weight to the undoubted status of a legal system as an institutionalized normative

---

[25] Chs. 8–10 of the book display Dworkin's own powers as a 'Herculean' adjudicator, and reveal him as a prime candidate for the short list.
[26] And for that matter the Introduction.

system. Dworkin's original theory made room for institutional support,[27] in the story about the bindingness of principles. In the *Law's Empire* version, institutional fit is given equal place with justification from principle in the search for an integrated, coherent interpretation. Such a construal of the interpretative enterprise, of course, is required to underwrite the thought that Hercules is a superhuman *judge*. A judge is not purely and simply a moral agent, working out what it would be best from the moral point of view to do in some situation. A judge is an official of an institution and must therefore apply and conform to the rules of the institution to the extent appropriate for one in her position. So it is not difficult to see why fit with institutional history is a constraint.

The result of imposing on Hercules the constraint of respect for settled law, however, is to diminish severely the appropriateness of the emphasis on coherence in legal interpretation. As we saw above in Chapter 7, the model of justification by coherence relies on there being no foundationalist commitments to entrenched judgements or principles. But, if Hercules is to take seriously the dimension of fit with institutional history, then Hercules is no longer able to prune and adjust at will, any more than is a mundane judge able to ignore at will a statute or precedent he or she happens to find disagreeable.[28]

The thesis of law as integrity wants us to believe that the second interpretative dimension, the requirement of coherence with legal principle, sufficiently frees the judge from the restrictions imposed by coherence with settled law to make coherence overall a proper model for legal interpretation. The impression is illusory. The sponsor of the coherence model still faces a troublesome dilemma. Either coherence with settled law is a genuine requirement, in

---

[27] Cf. *Taking Rights Seriously*, 40.

[28] One theme running through Stanley Fish's well-argued critique of Dworkin in several papers collected together in *Doing What Comes Naturally* is that Dworkin, despite his emphasis on interpretation, coherence, and the like, has a thoroughly foundationalist commitment to the reality of the text to be interpreted. See e.g. 95, 105 ff., 360. Note that I am not entering into the merits of the Dworkin/Fish controversy. I am only affirming Fish's claim that Dworkin has not rid himself of foundationalist commitments. In fact, there are serious difficulties at the level of philosophical aesthetics with Fish's own views about interpretation and interpretative communities; cf. here Annette Barnes, *On Interpretation* (Oxford, 1988), ch.6, and my review essay on *Doing What Comes Naturally*, in *Journal of Aesthetics and Art Criticism*, 49 (1991).

which case the content of the law becomes determined relativistically, iniquitous pseudo-Hercules arise, and the 'nobility' of the model's 'dream' disappears. Or coherence with settled law is not a genuine requirement, in which case the judge is being licensed to 'play fast and loose' with settled law, and is thus no longer a judge.[29] Neither does the concession to Hercules of a 'theory of mistakes'[30] help matters. For we need to know the source of the constraints that will forbid its 'impudent use'. Existing legal practice contains rules about when lower courts may regard decisions of higher courts as taken *per incuriam*, for instance, and rules about when highest tribunals may overrule their own past decisions. As Raz has argued (cf. *The Authority of Law*, 183–9), even that much-vaunted source of creativity in the law, the process of following and distinguishing precedents, implies much more than the power, as it might be put, impudently to distinguish cases. Is Hercules to be bound by just these rules, or may he determine for himself what counts as 'impudent use of the theory of mistakes'? The choice presents the same dilemma. Either Hercules is bound by the rules of a given jurisdiction, in which case he cannot ward off any iniquities those rules compel. Or he is not bound by those rules, and thus is no longer a judge of that jurisdiction.

Now, it might be said that I am here being deliberately perverse, and am missing the whole point of the way that the theory in *Law's Empire* is 'interpretative'. The point of the insistence on the two dimensions is that a judge does not become a mechanical slave

---

[29] The 'relativism' point and the 'fast and loose' point are not in themselves original points. The 'relativism' argument directed against the *Taking Rights Seriously* version of Dworkin's theory may be found in Sartorius, 'Social Policy', and is cited with approval by C.L. Ten in 'The Soundest Theory of Law', *Mind*, 88 (1979). The argument is offered as grounds for saying Dworkin has not said anything inconsistent with legal positivism. There also seems to be a version of it in S. Lewis, 'Taking Adjudication Seriously', *Australasian Journal of Philosophy*, 58 (1980), 377–87. The canonical source for the 'fast and loose' argument is the late John Mackie's 'The Third Theory of Law', *Philosophy and Public Affairs*, 7 (1977–8), 14–16. It is repeated by Ten, 534–5. Ten clearly sees that, to follow this route consistently, Dworkin must make a commitment to natural law (536–7). But he does not argue dilemmatically. The original claim I make here is that Dworkin faces both of these 2 putative counter-arguments as a dilemma. Either institutional support is a side-constraint on mundane judges, and then Dworkin is committed to relativism; or institutional support is not a side-constraint on mundane judges, in which case Dworkin is committed to 'playing fast and loose' with settled law.

[30] A feature of the earlier view which survives into *Law's Empire*; cf. 247.

either to institutional history or to noble dreams. The judge who is a slave in the first way is incompetent; the judge who is a slave in the second way is barely a judge. There is a quite legitimate adjudicatory obligation to make the community's law the best it can be. The judge should push to its limits whatever capacity to be deeply justified is possessed by the settled law of his or her jurisdiction. Settled law and institutional history represent an inertial mass which will slow down progress towards a legal system fulfilling the Herculean ideal of a perfect equilibrium between settled law and sound political morality. But the ideal remains as a legitimate ideal for adjudication. In that case, the value is not diminished of the normative recommendation to judges to search for that interpretation of institutional history which best preserves the coherence of settled law with background political morality. The constraint imposed by the need to respect settled law limits how much any one judge can do in any one case. Progress towards the ideal will be incremental. But it will not be impossible. Such a conception of judicial obligation, surely, it may be said, is faithful to institutional history and to the demands of justice.[31]

I want to suggest that even this argument, plausible though it is, does not deliver the theoretical goods it purports to deliver. Indeed, settled law must, by virtue of the particular social institution that law is, play a distinctive and indispensable role in adjudication. Hercules is bound by institutional history not to make impudent use of his theory of mistakes, just because institutional history and settled law are integral to the social institution that is law, as opposed to non-institutionalized practices such as etiquette or honour among gentlepersons. Moreover, exactly this fact about law is exploited in the familiar argument that law serves human flourishing by providing a certain and stable framework for producing and acting out life-plans. Law also, if it is to respect the demands of justice, must be sensitive to criticism of its institutional aspect as constricting, and to the need for flexibility in the achievement of justice.

[31] Something very like this line of argument may be found in Roberto Unger's exposition of 'internal development' as a part of his proposed 'expanded version of legal doctrine'. See 'The Critical Legal Studies Movement', *Harvard Law Review*, 96 (1983), at 576–83, esp. 579–80. Given the affinities of the 'nightmare' and the 'noble dream' it is not perhaps surprising that similar arguments are found in Unger and in Dworkin. For serious criticism of whether law-as-integrity does represent a coherent moral ideal, see Denise Réaume, 'Is Integrity a Virtue?', *passim*.

From this ambivalence emerges a sound, and platitudinously familiar, conception of judicial virtue—a good judge is one who is able to keep a right balance between the institutionalized claims of settled law and the claims of background political morality. The theory of law as integrity cannot be faulted as a statement of such a truisim, for truisms are true. Such a conception, however, does not leave us with what it purported to deliver, a systematic theory of legal interpretation which avoided the mistakes of both positivism and anti-positivism, a legitimate and compatibilist 'third theory of law'.

It seems tempting to suppose that Herculean adjudication combined with justification by coherence, by idealizing the above conception of judicial virtue, does produce such a desired systematic theory. That seems so, however, only because the idealizing extrapolation is understood on the following model. We know what makes one goalkeeper better than another—he or she doesn't drop centres, let shots trickle under the body, hang back from challenging opponents for through balls, and so forth. But we know that even the best mundane goalkeeper sometimes does these things. None the less, even though we do not expect of a mundane goalkeeper that he or she be perfect, we can easily construct a notion of a 'Herculean goalkeeper'. A 'Herculean goalkeeper' is one who never once makes the kind of mistake that even the best mundane goalkeeper sometimes makes and the less good ones make indecently often. Analogously, we recognize the fallibility of even the best mundane judge; we therefore see Hercules as one who never does what even the best mundane judges unfortunately sometimes do and the worst ones do with depressing regularity—namely, fail to discern that interpretation of institutional history which helps make the community's legal record the best it can be.[32]

This seemingly attractive parallel with the goalkeeping case is, however, thoroughly misleading. The Herculean goalkeeper *ex hypothesi* is ideal because he overcomes the characteristically human deficiencies of will and intellect which result in goal-keeping fallibility. But Hercules, working out his 'full interpretation of all his community's law at once' (*Law's Empire*, 245), with or without a theory of mistakes, would not merely be overcoming

---

[32] For more on the platitude, see Ch. 13 below.

those human deficiencies of will and intellect which result in adjudicatory fallibility. He would be overcoming one special 'deficiency' of a human or mundane judge—the 'deficiency' of being bound by institutional history and settled law. That, however, is not a 'deficiency'. Exactly what it is to be a judge (as we understand the term) is to be part of a social institution integral to which is the historically conditioned fact of settled law.

In a recent essay on coherence in legal reasoning, S. L. Hurley has clearly made distinctions which are relevant here. She proposes, first, a broad notion of 'settled case' which connotes simply that its resolution is or would be clear to the relevant decision-maker(s).[33] This characterization allows both actual and hypothetical cases to be 'settled'. She distinguishes, second (ibid. 239–41), between two coherence requirements with respect to settled cases in the sense given. The 'weaker' requirement is simply that of formal consistency with settled cases. The 'stronger' requirement privileges actual settled cases over hypothetical settled cases by according weight to the mere fact that decisions have occurred. A case changing its status to actually settled from hypothetically settled on the weaker requirement does not, but on the stronger requirement does affect the set of cases with which a pending decision must cohere. The question now to put to the theory of law as integrity is this—does the theory sponsor Hurley's weaker requirement or her stronger requirement? If the point of a 'third theory' is to ackowledge positivism by giving to institutional history the kind of weight it has in a positivistic theory, then a 'third theory' will have to sponsor the stronger requirement. But law as integrity, as laid out by its proponent, sponsors only the weaker requirement. It cannot therefore be a 'third theory', but must be some version of anti-positivism. On the other hand, if law as integrity does sponsor the stronger requirement, then it is still not a 'third theory', for it is then a version of positivism. There is no middle ground between the two requirements for a 'third theory'.[34]

[33] 'Coherence, Hypothetical Cases, and Precedent', *Oxford Journal of Legal Studies*, 10 (1990), 223.

[34] Compare here the extremely elaborate coherence theory of law developed by Peczenik in *On Law and Reason*. His theory balances requirements of institutional history, moral, and other substantive practical requirements, and, influenced by Robert Alexy (see *Theory of Legal Argumentation* (Oxford, 1989)), principles of rational practical discourse. A principle of precedent corresponding to Hurley's

To understand the pull of the Herculean fantasy requires appreciating how institutional history is a given and constrains mundane adjudication. The Herculean fantasy depends for its power on postulating as the end of Herculean interpretation a state of affairs in which settled law is in perfect equilibrium with the demands of background political morality. But in such a case, the settledness of settled law, as it might be put, drops out as a relevant feature of it.[35] The very notion of mundane judicial virtue, of which Hercules is supposed to be the idealization, is that of a person who has to balance the claims of settled law against the claims of principle. If what it is for Hercules to be superhuman is for him to break the bounds of *that* constraint, then he is not a superhuman judge at all, as we understand the term 'judge' to apply to one of us.

André Gombay has suggested that the 'goalkeeper' analogy as just presented is tendentious:[36]

For the goalie, standards of excellence depend on the rules of the game . . . Not so with Dworkinian superadjudication. Here the standard is set *absolutely*, by the principles of justice; the actual rules (positive law, among them) under which the judge operates make that ideal more or less difficult of attainment . . . it is as though the superperformer were still expected to make the fantastic leaps . . . but under some rules of the game lead weights were tied to the legs; under others, the performer was made to wear a blindfold; and so on. (Gombay's emphasis)

This revision of the analogy is entirely faithful to what the law-as-integrity theory implies about the nature of the judicial role. That theory implies that, were judges not bound by institutional history, and perhaps by other human imperfections and maybe even

strong requirement is, for Peczenik, justified only to the extent that it serves valid moral or economic goals (see *On Law and Reason*, 333–40). Aulis Aarnio in his Introduction to *On Law and Reason* wisely refers to Peczenik's theory as 'neo-realist': 'neo-realism is constructive, and not, as classical Legal realism, destructive' (*On Law and Reason*, 1) of high-level legal theory. None the less, neo-realism is clearly not a 'third theory of law'.

[35] Or, as it might more fancifully be put, the principled judgements of Hercules and the 'palm-tree' judgements of a perfect Herbert at infinity coincide. See also Ch. 8.3.3 and Ch. 8.4.

[36] In a comment on an earlier version of my remarks—Shiner, 'Adjudication, Coherence, and Moral Value', in Bayefsky (ed.), *Legal Theory Meets Legal Practice*; Gombay, 'Commentary', *Legal Theory Meets Legal Practice*, 116.

relative ignorance of fact and relative indeterminacy of aim, they could judge perfectly. But, since they are, the best that can be hoped for is some proper accommodation of the 'weights on the legs' and the ideals. The judge is expected to do the best she can, given that she is (regretfully) shackled by the rules.

It is worth recalling how naturally the metaphors of 'binding', 'shackling', 'fettering', and so forth come to the mind and the lips when reflection occurs on features of the operation of a legal system. One famous expression of legal realism is the remark by C. K. Allen, discussing the doctrine of *stare decisis*, that

The superior court does not place fetters on [the judge]; he places the fetters on his own hand . . . the humblest judicial official has to decide for himself whether he is or is not bound, in the particular circumstances, by any given decision of the House of Lords.[37]

I do not think we should underestimate the capacity of adjudicators to be self-deceptively captivated by their own myths and fantasies. The fantasy of Hercules appeals to all those who feel, 'If only I did not have to follow precedent/follow the rules, how much justice would I then do!' The case is rather like this: a referee in a game might think, 'If only I did not have to referee according to the rules, what a splendid game of football I could orchestrate'. A splendid spectacle, quite possibly, but not a game of football. In this sense, law is like a game. To be bound to adjudicate disputes by the rules is an internal feature of the judge's task. The doctrine of *stare decisis* is an interesting example. It is a commonplace that the doctrine is followed with more rigour in some common law jurisdictions than in others, and that it scarcely has a place in civil law jurisdictions at all. So a judge in a jurisdiction where the doctrine is rigorous can dream wistfully of being a judge in a jurisdiction where it is less rigorous, and perhaps of reforming the doctrine in her own jurisdiction. But deference to institutional history in the broad sense being here considered does not stand in the same relationship to 'noble dreams'. Failure to be bound by institutional history is not the limiting case of diminishing degrees of rigour in *stare decisis*: it is the limit of repudiation of the nature of law as an institutionalized normative system.

[37] C. K. Allen, *Law in the Making* (7th edn., Oxford, 1964), 290.

4. NO 'THIRD THEORY OF LAW'

The impossibility of a 'third theory of law' which combines the best of positivism and anti-positivism should now be clear. The strength of legal positivism lies in the prominence it gives to the institutionalized aspects of law, and a legal system is indeed an institutionalized normative system. The strength of anti-positivism lies in the prominence it gives to the non-institutionalized aspects of law. It is internal to law that the normal functioning of a legal system is to serve the ends of justice, and that legal systems which do not so serve, to the extent that they do not so serve, are degenerate cases of legal systems. These strengths, however, pull in opposite directions, and the dividing line between the grand theories they sustain is sharp. If a legal system is an institutionalized normative system, then it is *always* going to be impossible for the decision-maker every time to take that very decision which is as just a decision as the decision the ideal moral agent would take in the same situation.[38] That this is so is not an unfortunate contingent fact; it follows with transcendental necessity[39] from the very concept of an institutionalized normative system. In so far as anti-positivistic theories of law constantly encourage the decision-maker to break away from institutional constraints, then their incompatibility with positivist theories is complete.

The idea of a 'third theory of law' amounts to this. We have to suppose a theory which gives the same kind of weight to institutional history as does a positivist theory although, to avoid the errors of a positivist theory, not to the same degree; and the same kind of weight to the ideals of justice as an anti-positivist theory, although, to avoid the errors of an anti-positivist theory, not to the same degree. The supposition is incoherent, because precisely what distinguishes positivist and anti-positivist theories is not the degree of weight that each gives to the institutional aspects of law, but the kind of weight. To say that 'the existence of law is

---

[38] 'Rules [are] necessarily *suboptimal*. . . . A system committed to rule-based decision-making attains the benefits brought by rules only by relinquishing its aspirations for ideal decision-making. . . . Although there will be occasions on which the rule-indicated results will be inferior to the justification-indicated result, there will be *no* occasions on which the rule-indicated result will be *superior* to the justification-indicated result', Schauer, *Playing by the Rules*, 100, his emphasis. See also ibid., *passim*.

[39] 'Grammatically', if you like.

one thing, its merit or demerit another', is to give a kind of weight to the institutional aspects of law, not a degree of weight. To say that *lex injusta non est lex* is to give a kind of weight to the moral quality of law, not a degree of weight.[40] Two different kinds of weight cannot be commensurable on the same metric of weight.

I shall turn in the next and final chapter to a discussion of the consequences for theory of law of the arguments presented to this point in the study. At the end of the chapter I shall keep the promise to state the theory of law presented in this study.

[40] It should be clear by this point in the present study that I do not believe either of these slogans to be either accurate or useful characterizations of serious claims made by positivist and anti-positivist legal theories. None the less, I am here speaking about such theories in the broadest sense, and so one may hope that broad characterizations are legitimate.

13

THE CONCEPT OF LAW

1. PLATITUDES

So far during this study we have collected as assay samples two different philosophical platitudes, or trivialities, or truisms. The first is the claim that a legal system is an institutionalized normative system; the second is the claim that a good judge is one who is able to keep a right balance between the institutionalized claims of settled law and the claims of background political morality.

Let us first consider further the former platitude. In the Introduction (page 10), I made a large and promissory claim about how it is that legal positivism has no inner resources of its own, nothing on which to draw in order to provide that illumination from a source external to the practices of law which a deeper understanding of law requires. We are now in a position to see what all that means. It is central to positivism to claim that the characterization of legal materials must be recursive. But then the philosophical task of searching for a perspicuous analysis of the concept of law faces a dilemma. Only a characterization of law in terms of entities or expressions already acknowledged to be legal will be faithful to law's recursive character. Yet no such characterization will shed light on what it is about law so conceived that causes philosophical puzzlement. The thought that legal positivism has no inner resources of its own expresses this dilemma.

As for the second platitude, again, positivists such as Raz have emphasized[1] the 'closedness' or 'systemic isolation'[2] of a legal system as positivism envisages it. The character of a legal system as an institutionalized normative system must in the nature of the case isolate law from other normative systems. Thus, precisely

---

[1] Cf. here e.g. Raz's essay on 'gaps in the law', ch. 4 of *The Authority of Law*.
[2] The expression is Schauer's; see 'Formalism', 522.

what defines law also hampers law from its own successful pursuit of ideals internal to itself. An institutionalized normative system, as a system operating with entrenched norms or rules, renders the background justifications for the norms or rules inaccessible to a degree to the rule-guided decision-maker.[3] Such a decision-maker is in the nature of the case barred on occasion from reaching back to the justification. Yet the ideals such background justifications represent are the ideals of legality itself, the ideals internal to law. Stanley Fish rails against the theory of law as integrity as being 'superfluous': '"law as integrity" [is] an unnecessary (and empty) addition to a system of practice that already displays what it would provide' (*Doing What Comes Naturally*, 371). The criticism is in one sense unfair, for truisms, as we shall shortly see, may play a role in philosophical debate. But the criticism is not unfair in so far as the proponent of law as integrity thinks that a new and challenging theory is being enunciated by the proffering of a platitude.[4]

The problem with platitudes and truisms is that, *natura sua*, we already know the truth of what it is the platitude has to tell. The only true remarks philosophers ever make occur when they remind us of the familiar. Yet we turn to philosophy precisely when we lose our way and become strangers amid the familiar, when we need to reinherit the familiar. There are dangers, however, in the method of restating the familiar by stating platitudes. Wittgenstein has remarked that

there is no common sense answer to a philosophical problem. One can defend common sense against the attacks of philosophers only by solving their puzzles, i.e., by curing them of the temptation to attack common sense, not by restating the views of common sense. (*The Blue and Brown Books*, 58)

The difficulty for legal theory is that here positivism in one way, and in another way law as integrity in so far as it represents the second platitude, represent common sense about law and about adjudication. These theories are therefore of course inherently appealing, for there is nothing so appealing as things we already

---

[3] Cf. Schauer, *Playing By the Rules*, chs. 3–5 *passim*.
[4] Fish himself does not avoid the problem of platitudes: see my review essay on *Doing What Comes Naturally*.

310   BEYOND POSITIVISM AND ANTI-POSITIVISM

know. Positivism, however, cannot soothe disquiet concerning positivism itself as a solution to philosophical puzzles about law, puzzles which focus on the content-independent character of positivism's account of law. Law as integrity, likewise, cannot soothe disquiet about philosophical puzzlement concerning law's character as procedural institution and substantive form, for all it achieves is to remind us of the duality which puzzles us.[5]

The preceding chapters in this study have been the story of the duality of law—that, on the one hand, a legal system is *qua* institutionalized normative system a social fact; and on the other hand that ideals of justice are internal to the concept of law, and a legal system derives its normative power from the normality of its service of those ideals. The tension the two parts of the story produce is not straightforwardly resolvable. It may seem to legal positivism that it is, because positivism has a prepared account of the duality in terms of the notions of 'law' and 'morality'. But even these notions are less theoretically aseptic than they might seem.

The root problem is caused by a certain picture of how law and morality relate to each other. This picture I shall call the 'concentric circles' picture. The picture is as follows. The concept of law is the concept of a bounded and finite system. A legal system is an institutionalized normative system bounded at its outer limit by a rule of recognition, a rule which gives that criterion, satisfaction of which makes a norm a legal norm. This system exists as a circle within the wider domain of social life. Outside this circle, between the limits of law and the limits of understanding, lies morality. The limits of morality, but not those of law, are co-terminous with the limits of human social understanding. A judgement of critical morality about positive law is made therefore from a point of view within that band of morality which is external to law. There is some common content to law and morality, where the circle of law is superimposed upon the circle of morality. Morality, however, goes beyond law, and fills the sphere of social life. Not merely may the question of the legitimate authority of some given particular valid legal norm be subjected to

---

[5] I again exempt here from this criticism chs. 8–10 of *Law's Empire*, which display considerable 'intellectual power and patience', and display political reasoning about cases at (somewhere near) its best. My criticisms are directed only at the futility of the attempt in the rest of the book to *say* at length, and proffer as constituting a theory of law, what it is these chapters *show*.

determination by morality. Because law is a limited institution within the domain of morality, the whole of a legal system at once may be subjected to the judgement of morality on its legitimacy and authoritativeness. To accept the moral authority of a system of law as such is always no more than an option. One may legitimately stand in a place external to law and from the point of view embodied in such an option judge all law, all legal system.

These remarks are an accurate depiction of a set of assumptions about the relationship between law and morality accepted by legal positivism. The reason, of course, why the 'concentric circles' picture appeals to positivism is that by virtue of being an institutionalized normative system, positive law is identifiable by a content-independent test. Precisely in being so identifiable it is distinguishable from morality. Moreover, we do judge positive law from a point of view 'outside' positive law.

Anti-positivism raises a fundamental challenge to this standard picture. Let us take some time to elaborate how this challenge comes about.

2. JUSTICE IN THE GARDEN OF EDEN

Legal philosophers[6] have made use in various ways of the technique of armchair legal palaeontology—the technique of imagining some early world lacking various features of modern society in order to shed light on the nature of law in our world, mundane law. Both Finnis (*Natural Law and Natural Rights*, 267) and Raz (*Practical Reason and Norms*, 159) consider whether there could be any need for law in a society of perfect beings. Hart in chapter 5 of *The Concept of Law* is preoccupied with the transition from primitive actual societies to modern legally sophisticated societies. The relevant issue here is this: why does the presence of a certain feature—namely, being an institutionalized procedure for dispute-settlement—count for a system's being a legal system? One obvious answer is that the prima-facie case for a system of institutionalized dispute-settlement in a society of angels being a legal system is made out just in that the system is an

---

[6] The following 3 paragraphs summarize an argument given at greater length in my paper 'Justice in the Garden of Eden', *Philosophy*, 63 (1988), 301–9.

institutionalized system of dispute-settlement. However, such a doctrine would already presuppose a positivist theory of law. The positivist will focus on the transition from a non-institutionalized 'society of angels' to an institutionalized 'society of angels', and argue that this is the crucial transition for legal theory. Anti-positivism will focus instead on the role of dispute-settlement in Finnis's and Raz's intuition that the 'society of angels' they envisage has (in some form) a legal system.

The difference between an aggregate of atomic individuals and a social group is important; we see the difference in a pure form if we make the contrast in a pre-lapsarian context. The Garden of Eden became a social group not merely by the creation of Eve, but by some form of union between Adam and Eve. Why are Adam and Eve a social group and not a mere aggregate? There are two factors which define a social group—acceptance of norms, and reciprocal acknowledgement. Within a social group, the conception of a certain procedure as one of dispute-*settlement* presupposes two factors over and above mere termination of a dispute. It presupposes a background of mutually accepted norms and concepts both of the propriety of applying such norms to the issue over which there is variance, and of how such norms are properly to be applied to such an issue. Recognition of fellow membership of a group brings along with it recognition of equality among members, and of each as having dignity, being worthy of respect. Recognition of oneself as a member of a group implies recognizing the reciprocity embodied in this equality of status.

None the less, with the move to a social grouping comes pluralism. The possibility of dissonant opinion and judgement within a fundamental agreement of judgement is exactly what a society of individuals embodies. The norms accepted even in the prelapsarian social group will in part be norms for the interpersonal settlement of what may now be called 'disputes'. The concept of an independent and definitive settlement is not purely formal. To agree to submit a dispute to independent settlement is in one respect to agree to a formal procedure—one agrees to accept the outcome of the procedure whatever the outcome. But although such a procedure is so far 'formal', in another way it is not at all formal. Over time, not just any procedure defined formally and independently of the decisions it produces will stand as a candidate procedure for dispute-settlement. The choice of a procedure presupposes views on the kind of result to be expected from the procedure. A procedure will be found wanting to the extent that it substantially fails to produce the desired and expected kind of result. A certain procedure is accepted as a proper procedure for dispute-settlement because and only because there are already in place norms and values both before which the original debate takes place and which carry over their influence to the choice of a certain procedure as a proper procedure for settling disputes. All this one may sum up (stipulatively and hand-wavingly so from the point of view of substantial political theory) by saying that any social group must have as such a sense of justice, and that an authoritative non-institutional dispute-settler's judgements must accord with the social group's sense of justice. This notion of a 'sense of justice' is substantive. It is none the less offered here, despite its substance, as something whose existence is a transcendental condition for the possibility of any social group at all.

Hart describes in chapter 5 of *The Concept of Law* first of all (89) a society which consists of a structure simply of primary rules of obligation. He then points out (90–1) that in any except highly unlikely historical circumstances there will be defects in such a structure—the system will be uncertain, static, and inefficient. These defects are to be remedied by the institution of secondary rules of, respectively, recognition, change, and adjudication (91–3). The details are well known and will not be rehearsed here. Hart constructs his fable of a transition from the pre-legal to the legal world in order to explicate and support a fundamentally positivistic story about the nature of law. It is thus extremely important for Hart's project that fulfilment of the felt need for socially authoritative determinations coincides with the introduction of just those entities which are the characteristic institutions of a developed legal system and with which legal positivism identifies law. If, however, the myth of the prelapsarian social groups is persuasive, then positivism faces a double obstacle. In the first place, the conceptual foundations of law arguably are laid in the form of a source for independent and authoritative dispute-settlement, long before anything that looks like a legal institution as positivism would understand it is in place. That in itself is not a hugely powerful point. Hart himself acknowledges the possibility of various kinds of system with to varying degrees the trappings of a fully-fledged legal system and thus to various degrees meriting the title of 'legal system' (cf. *The Concept of Law*, 114–20). Hart, therefore, could easily acknowledge that the prelapsarian society with its custom-based procedures for dispute-settlement is one of these intermediate cases. Far more significant, however, is the second obstacle.

Legal theory has been conditioned by centuries of 'possessive individualism'[7] to seek the justification and meaning of law in the avoidance of free-rider problems and in the task of promoting human flourishing in the face of human selfishness and greed. Hobbes set a precedent that legal theory has felt bound to follow. To achieve such goals is admittedly one function of a modern legal system. However, if the origin of law lies in the need to have under certain circumstances independent and authoritative dispute-settlement, then the need for dispute-settlement can meaningfully arise in circumstances other than a possessive-individualist hell. Such a need can arise also in a prelapsarian communitarian paradise. The need for authoritative dispute-settlement may coherently be both felt and met without the introduction of legal institutions as positivistically defined. Moreover, the existence of a 'sense of justice' is presupposed by the very stating of such a need for dispute-settlement.

Why are the defects Hart identifies in his primitive society defects—or, rather, how shall we understand the presuppositions of the fact that these defects are, as they indeed are, defects? The problems which produce defects such as inefficiency and uncertainty do not exist as problems in a normative vacuum. There is not one absolute standard of certainty which any norm just *qua* norm must embody or any one standard of efficiency just *qua* standard of efficiency in the pursuit of goals. Whether a norm or an instruction is uncertain depends not only on the context but also on the background values which inform action in that context. The time taken or precision embodied in a process or result may in one context be inefficient and in another not. Thus, in order to judge a particular procedure for dispute-settlement 'inefficient', or a particular set of norms or normative deliverances 'uncertain', there must already be in place a conception of a goal to be reached, or purpose found, and of what are to count as standards

[7] Cf. C. B. Macpherson, *The Political Theory of Possessive Individualism* (London, 1962).

of success for reaching efficiency and certainty in relation to that goal or purpose. The same is true for the static character of a particular set of norms. As Hart points out (*The Concept of Law*, 89–90), in anything other than a society stable and highly unified through isolation, it will be necessary for some provision to be made for change of norms. But a provision of changing norms by evolution is none the less a procedure for change. Therefore, it is always a choice made by a group (whether deliberately or by the invisible hand of evolution) to change or not to change a norm in the face of altering circumstances. For a group to be able to conceptualize such a change, or to be able to accept on a standing basis the results of leaving change to gradual evolution, the group must be supposed to accept certain background values, as a presupposition of any such choice being rational.

Of course, after the Fall, when men cease to be angels but become, in Hart's famous phrase, neither devils nor angels (*The Concept of Law*, 191), the need for coercion of the recalcitrant comes into being. As a result the notions of uncertainty, a static character, and inefficiency as defects take on a whole new dimension. The very idea of primary rules of obligation presupposes a postlapsarian society. In the prelapsarian world there are no duties or obligations; there are merely expressions of respect and acknowledgements of value and worth. Hart for his part begins in the postlapsarian world, a world containing malefactors and recalcitrants. Hart therefore begins in a world where a customary system will have exactly those particular versions of his defects which will require for their remedy the legal institutions beloved of positivism. This fact disguises from Hart the role played by a background scheme of values before which the development of independent and authoritative dispute-settlement takes place. Independent and authoritative dispute-settlement arises out of a need to promote the expression of values—values, moreover, such that the acceptance of those values is constitutive of the existence of the relevant social group. These values will include the flourishing of the different members of the group, but will none the less be far from values resultant from a Hobbesian war of self-aggrandizement between atomistic individuals. Law as an institution characterized by secondary rules of recognition, change, and adjudication is certainly needed in our complex contemporary world. It is needed, however, not because of deficiencies in a customary system of dispute-settlement *per se*, but rather because of deficiencies in such a system relative to certain circumstances. These are that men are neither devils nor angels; they are vulnerable to physical harm in the way that they are; they live in a world of limited resources; they are roughly equal in strength; and so forth—exactly those very general facts of nature which Hart identifies in chapter 9 of *The Concept of Law* as forming by 'natural necessity' the minimum content of any normative system.

These thoughts open up the way to a powerful and anti-positivistic thesis about the nature of law. It can be claimed that the non-institutionalized source of authoritative dispute-settlement which can exist in a prelapsarian social group is a prefiguring of law as much because of its connection with justice as because of its connection with dispute-settlement in any formal sense. If that is so, then we have reason to expect that it will be wrong to regard the concept of law as a content-independent concept. Armchair legal palaeontology has thus been deployed to develop the foundations for an anti-positivist theory of law.

3. 'CONCENTRIC CIRCLES' AGAIN

If the myth of the Garden of Eden is coherent and plausible, then we seem to have raised a real difficulty with positivism's 'concentric circle' model of the relation between law and morality. Law cannot be represented as a 'circle' within morality, for concepts fundamental to the understanding of law are in place before morality begins. The difficulty is not only apparent; it is real. But it is a difficulty not only for positivism.

The anti-positivist's case against positivism is that positivism makes an illegitimate assumption. It assumes illegitimately that the concept of 'morality' is available to describe features of the prelapsarian social group. As the story of such groups has been told, that concept, the argument goes, is not available. It is true that there is either an embryonic or no 'law' in the prelapsarian society, even after the development of a form of socially authoritative dispute-settlement. But, the anti-positivist argues, because there is no law in that society, then there is no morality either. Our concept of law requires as a foil the concept of morality. Hart spells out in chapter 8 of *The Concept of Law* some features in virtue of which we distinguish in contemporary society between law and morality—importance, liability to deliberate change, involuntary character of (some) offences, form of pressure to conform (cf. *The Concept of Law*, 169–76). These features our law has and our morality does not have by virtue of law being a system of institutionalized norms, and exactly these features are, of course, the features of law on which positivism concentrates. However, this seeming dependence of the concept of law on the concept of morality is not just one way. It is in fact an interdependence. Just as we understand law only as an 'institution-alized' normative system in contrast with morality which is 'not institutionalized', so we understand morality as 'not institution-alized' only by comparison with law which is 'institutionalized'. When and only when a concept of law is in place is a concept of 'morality' in place also. The prelapsarian social group in the myth *ex hypothesi* has no law. Therefore, it has no morality either.

We who have the concepts of law and of morality easily and naturally apply those concepts to a prelapsarian social group. We speak of their norms for interpersonal behaviour as moral norms. This fact does not of course secure the further fact that members of the group themselves could so describe their norms. In fact, the group cannot themselves describe their norms as 'moral', nor for that matter as 'legal' either. *Ex hypothesi* the separation of law and morality has not yet taken place. That the group cannot so describe their norms tells us something about how fundamental are the notions of 'law' and 'morality' in our ways of understanding ourselves. It tells us that these concepts are *not* fundamental. They both, in so far as they are opposed in the way that positivism opposes them, are products of a certain way of thinking about law and morality that only becomes possible when law has become fully institutionalized. But at such a point the claim that law and morality differ in that one is an institutionalized normative system and the other not claims the truth of a triviality. The fact asserted is a trivial fact, not a deep fact. It can settle debates in legal theory if and only if it is a deep fact.

From the perspective of anti-positivism, we are tempted to think that the scheme embodied in the group's 'sense of justice' is part of the group's 'morality', and therefore that the scheme is supportive of positivism, only because a certain philosophical picture holds us captive. This is the positivist's picture of a 'critical morality' separate from and standing over against *qua* non-institutionalized an institutionalized system of norms identified positivistically by some content-independent test. This picture holds us captive, of course, because, like all such captivating philosophical pictures, it contains a truth. The concept of law is in part the concept of an institutionalized normative system empirically distinguishable from other institutions and other normative systems by the possession of certain empirical properties. Positivism reductionistically identifies the concept of law with being merely the concept of an institution empirically distinguished just by its possession of those properties. None the less, the concept of 'morality' forming a 'circle' 'outside' law has no independent claim on our jurisprudential attention— no claim independent of the context of the particular use made of it by the postulated positivistic account of the foundations of law. Our concept of 'morality', supposedly a theory-neutral concept, is in fact, in so far as it figures in the debate about the nature of law, already a positivistic concept.

Anti-positivism might think that the preceding remarks show positivism guilty of circular reasoning. But, if the remarks are correct, then anti-positivism is in fact in no better a position than positivism. For, if anti-positivism is thought of as the view that there is an essential relationship between law and morality, or the view that law is not law unless it subjects itself to the (prior) dictates of morality, the 'concentric circles' picture still holds sway.[8] The difference is simply that the order of priority between the circles, for purposes of characterizing the nature of law, is reversed. The outer circle of morality now contributes to the determination of the boundary of the inner circle of law, instead of the boundary of that inner circle being internally, or recursively, determined. But we have seen that the concept of 'morality' as deployed in the 'concentric circles' picture is a positivistic concept. It does not cease to be so by being deployed in a 'concentric circles' model with reversed order of priority. An anti-positivism which insists that morality is above the law is employing the positivist's concept of 'morality'. It is unsurprising if legal positivism thinks that anti-positivism requires the positivist con-

---

[8] Cf. Beyleveld and Brownsword, who argue in *Law as a Moral Judgment* that, to be law, a norm must meet the test of consistency with the moral Principle of Generic Consistency. Such a view is also implied by Soper's view in *A Theory of Law*, to the extent that it comprises an anti-positivistic theory.

cept of law even to state its own position. Positivism is not far wrong in so thinking.

What alternative is available? We can grant to anti-positivism that, whatever is the proper name to give to the set of norms acceptance of which is an ingredient in the existence of a prelapsarian social group, it cannot be right to speak of those norms as the group's 'morality'. The myth of the prelapsarian social group shows that the deepest concepts of our present social life are certain notions of social value which precede and inform the whole interaction between morality and law in our society. Therefore, their status is misrepresented if they are thought of as exclusively moral values. Given, however, the interdependence of the concept of law and the concept of morality, the status of those values is equally misrepresented if they are thought of as exclusively legal values. There is as much reason to speak of those norms and values as 'proto-moral', a way of speaking which does not occur to us as natural, as there is to speak of them, as it does seem quite natural to speak of them, as 'proto-legal'. Justice, for example, as a specifically moral value is already an interpretation at a less deep level than that of the fundamental sense of justice to which I have already alluded, as would also be specifically legal justice. The whole conceptual scheme contemplated in that sense of justice is part of the constitutive scaffolding of our form of life: it is part of grammar. We debate within it whether some provision of positive law conforms to some fundamental standard. We cannot get outside that scheme to debate it. It structures both moral and jurisprudential debate. In so far as anti-positivism argues that prelapsarian non-institutionalized justice is legal justice, it is as mistaken as any positivism which insists such justice is moral justice. Each deploys to describe the foundations of social value concepts which are part of the superstructure.

Anti-positivism questions whether positive law is the whole of law. Anti-positivism, however, cannot straightforwardly say that we stand amid the proto-legal/proto-moral values to judge positive law. That those values underlie our social life is a grammatical fact about our social life, and as such can only be shown in that life. The foundational grammar of human social thought has no more substance than the surface of a sphere. We cannot remain human and stand either on that grammar or outside it. Since the holistic scaffolding I have been calling 'the sense of justice' is the very boundary of human social life, it is therefore hard to make sense of the idea of standing at that very point on the boundary in order to judge law. It is hard to make sense of from there judging the justice of one's own legal system, when those values are the values of one's own legality. The distinction between law as an institutionalized normative system and morality as a non-institutionalized normative system emerges exactly within the boundary of the sphere of social thought. It cannot be therefore a simple mistake to say with the positivist, 'There are limits to law'. More than that, that form of words can express a necessary truth. It is not a truth at the foundation of human understanding. It is none the less for that a necessary truth. But then, because of the plausibility of the story of Justice in the Garden of Eden, it cannot either be a simple mistake to say with anti-positivism that there is more to law than positive law, that positive law is essentially rooted in practical reasonableness, natural or divine law, fundamental legality.

We have here a deep conflict between two different pictures of the relation between law, morality, and society. Each deploys at its core spatial metaphors. These metaphors clash irreconcilably. One set of metaphors belongs to positivism and the other to anti-positivism. According to the latter set of metaphors, it is impossible altogether to stand outside law. Law is pervasive; it extends throughout social life; it is an institution of social life, not an institution within social life. The values in which law is rooted are the natural values of legality, not the conventional values of morality. They are the fundamental values of communal social life and of personhood themselves. They are not the values of some point of view within what it is to be a social group and what it is to be a person. Thus, to understand the nature of law is to see the deep connections of positive, institutionalized law with fundamental legality. All this is the way of anti-positivism. According to the former set of metaphors, however, law as a bounded institution is enclosed within social life. The very concept of law itself is the concept of a finite system; to say that background political morality is a part of law is therefore incoherent. We would not have the concept of law at all, it is said, unless there were an area of morality outside it and which contains it. All this is the way of positivism.

The two sets of metaphors are irreconcilable in the following sense. According to anti-positivism, legality and its values are part of the constitutive scaffolding of human social life. One cannot get outside that scheme to pass judgement on all law at once. According to positivism, law is an institution within society. One cannot fail to be able to adopt a point of view outside law in order to judge all law at once. These two claims cannot both be wholly and literally true. But they cannot either one be false, for each of them says what is true. Neither positivism nor anti-positivism therefore can be in any straightforward sense correct as theories of law.

4. LEGAL THEORY AND GENERAL PHILOSOPHY

One further salient fact about fundamental dispute in legal theory is also now coming into view, although there have been already many indications along the way. Legal theory is an idiosyncratic area of philosophy: if it were not so, then a study like the present one, which considers issues strictly within legal theory and the work of persons who are (largely, anyway) strictly legal theorists, would not be possible. But legal theory is not a wholly idiosyncratic area of philosophy. Legal theory is one among many arenas where the grand battles of philosophy itself are fought. Positivism and anti-positivism are in some ways simply the form that some wider theories take when they are applied to the question of the nature of law.

In the first place, positivism, as we saw in Chapters 2.3 and 5 above especially, is a special application of methodological individualism, while anti-positivism in its most plausible forms applies the methods of *verstehen* theory or hermeneutic theory in the domain of the philosophy of social science. For positivism, a legal system is to be understood primarily as an artefact of the decisions of individuals, or of individual groups. That, in fact, explanations in psychology or anthropology or sociology are available which cast doubt on the self-conscious or volitional nature of such 'decisions' (by speaking of law as an instrument of power, for example, or of economic efficiency) does not threaten this artefactuality.[9] The thesis of anti-positivism that law as a social

[9] Thus sociological jurisprudence or Critical Legal Studies can be seen as quite compatible with legal positivism. In such a light they are asking, and answering, quite different questions from positivism.

institution cannot be properly understood from the external point of view is an application of a view that hermeneutic theory will in some form hold about any social institution.

Positivism also has deep connections with empiricism as a theory of knowledge; anti-positivism has affinities with a more holistic and rationalistic approach to human understanding. The emphasis in positivism is on those features of the operation of a legal system which are open to empirical view, even if they are 'institutional', rather than 'brute', facts—the rule-books, the courts, the judges, the legislatures and legislators, as visible entities in the everyday world. In anti-positivism the emphasis is more on such items as natural tendencies, natural function, purposes, goals, values, and so forth, items which are not immediately 'accessible to plain view' by empiricist standards of 'plain view', and whose existence the empiricist is inclined to regard as the product of interpretation or hypothesis or theory, and thus evanescent.

I believe also that positivism has affinities with liberal individualism as a political theory, while anti-positivism has affinities with communitarian political theory as current political theory understands those terms. I say this with some hesitation, and an awareness that I may be starting hares I cannot catch. Raz, after all in *The Morality of Freedom* claims to be a positivist, a liberal, and not an individualist, while Dworkin in many places claims to be a liberal and not a positivist. I have in mind the following. Positivism in the first place sees the task of legal theory as resolutely non-moral and non-political, the task of giving an account from the external point of view of a social institution. The values, goals, purposes, life-plans which may motivate those human choices through which any given municipal legal system takes on the evaluative flavour that it has—all these things lie beyond the limits of law and legal theory. The legal system is 'common' only in the sense that it is the product of aggregated individual choice. Given that law as a social institution is none the less intimately involved with those values, goals, purposes and life-plans, then, if in addition those values and so on are construed non-individualistically as antecedent to individual choice, the isolation of legal theory from those values seems altogether unrealistic. Correspondingly, if law is thought of as in some way an enterprise internally related to certain fundamental values, then, if those values are themselves construed as the product of choices of unencumbered selves, the internal relation becomes pointless through its vulnerability to arbitrary whim and caprice. I am not doubting the importance from the point of view of political theory of attempting to break away from the traditional association of liberalism with individualism and with positivism. My concern here is only with the implications for legal theory, if legal theory is the topic of discussion. In *The Morality of Freedom*, the defence of positivism comes almost three hundred pages before Raz's introduction of a perfectionist and non-individualist liberalism. The compatibility of the two is assumed rather than addressed in the book. In Chapter 4 above questions were raised about the possible anti-positivistic implications of the positivist account of authority in *The Morality of Freedom*. I make no pretence here of definitively answering them; it is sufficient for present purposes that they can be seriously raised. Similarly, in Dworkin's case, he has chosen to keep a distance from positivism in maintaining the centrality to legal theory of the dimension of principle. If the thoughts sketched in this paragraph are correct, it is no coincidence that his most recent writings in political theory have taken on a communitarian mien.[10]

5. SHINER'S THEORY OF LAW

I indicated in the Introduction that I would eventually produce a theory of law. It is time—well past time, even—to keep the promise. The theory has been laid out in the previous pages, although it has not been laid out in the conventional manner of jurisprudential treatises. The theory is, in the first instance, not a theory of law, but a meta-theory about legal theory. I have attempted to present an account of legal theory as condemned eternally to the rivalry between positivist and anti-positivist theories of law. I have tried to show, first, that legal theory must (a conceptual, not a historical, 'must') begin with legal positivism, for positivism is the theory which erects into a philosophical position

[10] I have in mind, for example, 'What is Equality? Part 3: The Place of Liberty', *Iowa Law Review*, 73 (1987); 'What is Equality? Part 4: Political Equality', *University of San Francisco Law Review*, 22 (1987); 'Liberal Community', *California Law Review*, 77 (1989); 'Equality, Democracy and Constitution', *Alberta Law Review*, 28 (1990).

commonplace truisms about the nature of law. I then outlined for purposes of exposition a minimal version of positivism I called 'simple positivism'. In Part II I moved on to a version of positivism I called 'sophisticated positivism', a version designed to mitigate perceived deficiencies in simple positivism. The most substantial part of the book, Part III, argued that the inevitable result of taking seriously the insights of sophisticated positivism was to drive legal theory into an anti-positivist position. But the essay did not end there as a conventional defence of an anti-positivist theory of law. I outlined at the beginning of Part IV a number of considerations which would attract legal theory back again to positivism, thus beginning again the whole movement of thought which Parts I–III of the book constitute, in endless dialectic. I defended further this account of legal theory as condemned to endless dialectic by arguing for the impossibility of compatibilism, attempts to reconcile positivism and anti-positivism, or to have the best of both. I also tried to support the account by representing legal theory as an instantiating philosophical conflict of a deeply fundamental kind.

All this meta-theory gives us a valid constraint on the construction of an adequate legal theory, a constraint no theory examined in this study fulfils. The constraint is that a perspicuous view of mundane law will be obtainable only via the appreciation of why legal theory is condemned eternally to the rivalry between positivist and anti-positivist theories of law. The account presented in this study, however, if correct, does satisfy the constraint. I will show why.

Raz draws a distinction between 'momentary legal systems' and 'continuous legal systems'.[11] These are not two kinds of legal system, as, say, common law systems and civil code systems are two kinds of legal system. Momentary and continuous legal systems are the results of two different ways of viewing any given actual legal system. Viewing a legal system as a momentary legal system, a legal system frozen at a particular point in time, allows one to see clearly structural aspects of a legal system. But, if one

---

[11] *The Authority of Law*, 81. Cf. also Harris, *Law and Legal Science*, 10–14, 41–3, 65–73, 97–102, 111–22. Harris refers to momentary legal systems as 'units of meaning, abstracted from social behaviour-patterns and from psychological events' (ibid. 13), as opposed to a 'historic (non-momentary) collection of written choice-guidance devices, available to officials for settling disputes' (ibid. 65–6).

takes fully on board the notion of law as a social institution, a legal system must be viewed by legal theory as continuous. The social world is situated in history, with a past, a present, and a future inseparably linked, and law as a social institution partakes of this historicity.

The continuous history of law in practice is the history of a dynamic tension between two pairs of poles. The first pair is certainty and flexibility, and the second is procedure or (non-Aristotelian) form and substance.[12] It is no coincidence that the familiar picture of the good judge is as the second platitude of Chapter 11 painted it—the balancing of the claims of settled law and the claims of political morality. In so far as settled law is settled, it represents certainty, and the arguments for the social value of certain law in terms of fairness and the opportunity for personal choice are familiar.[13] Settled law, likewise, though it undoubtedly has a substance and a content, is thought of in inherently procedural terms in that legal validity is thought of as the consequence of a procedure, and as a matter of form. Also familiar are the reasons why the settledness of settled law hampers the pursuit of that end internal to law, the pursuit of justice. Flexibility must be introduced into the operation of law, so that justice may be done when the certainty of form and procedure obstruct justice. The pursuit by law of substantial values, including the values law promotes in its purely co-ordinative and regulatory role, must on occasion require the transcending of the limitations of procedure and form.[14]

The above is a boringly familiar picture of the day-to-day operation of the legal system. The thesis of this study—Shiner's

---

[12] The echo of Duncan Kennedy's well-known paper 'Form and Substance in Private Law Adjudication', *Harvard Law Review*, 89 (1976), is self-conscious. The thesis stated here is different from his, in that its extent goes beyond private law to all law, and it is no part of my view that the implications of the tension at the level of theory are rule-sceptical implications.

[13] This sentence, of course, is shorthand for a very much longer and complex story. It is told at length and with care in Schauer's *Playing By the Rules*, *passim*. He brings out the similarity from the point of view of 'ruledness' between different forms of regime—legislation, common law, etc. In ch. 7 he reviews the main arguments for rules, the arguments from fairness, reliance, efficiency, stability, and from the value of rules as devices for the allocation of decision-making power.

[14] This too is a story which is shorthand for one very much longer. Consider, for example, Finnis's detailed interweaving in *Natural Law and Natural Rights* of the nature of law into standards of practical reasonableness and the basic forms of human good.

theory of law—is the following. Boring the picture may be, platitudinous it may be. None the less, the picture is, as they say, the key to the science of jurisprudence. If the good judge is the one who is able to keep the right balance between the claims of certainty/procedure and the claims of flexibility/substance, then an analogous point may be made about legal theory. Positivism is the prime theory of those aspects of a legal system in virtue of which it is the repository of certainty and procedure. Anti-positivism is the prime theory of those aspects of a legal system in virtue of which it is the repository of flexibility and substance. The good legal theorist, therefore, is the one who is able to keep the right balance between the claims of the theory of certainty and procedure, and the claims of the theory of flexibility and substance. The balance between certainty and procedure at the level of actual legal practice is achievable only in history as a continuous process of adjustment. The legal system in operation moves dialectically between the pole of certainty/procedure and the pole of flexibility/substance. This salient and crucial fact about law can be perspicuously represented only in a theory of law which represents law as thus in dialectical motion. Such a theory, however, will not be a theory of law of the conventional kind. It can only be a meta-theory of legal theories, which shows how legal theory itself is similarly in a constant process of movement and adjustment between theories which glorify certainty/procedure and theories which glorify flexibility/substance.

Just such a meta-theory of legal theories, and therefore just such a theory of law, it has been the goal of the preceding pages to present. The kind of theory this study has aimed to present, if the study is successful, is the only possible legal theory.

SELECTED BIBLIOGRAPHY

ADAMS, JOHN N., and BROWNSWORD, ROGER, 'More in Expectation than in Hope: The Blackpool Airport Case', *Modern Law Review*, 54 (1991), 281–7.

ALEXANDER, LARRY, 'Law and Exclusionary Reasons', *Philosophical Topics*, 18 (1990), 5–22.

ALEXY, ROBERT, *A Theory of Legal Argumentation*, trans. Ruth Adler and Neil MacCormick (Oxford: Clarendon Press, 1989).

ALLEN, C. K., *Law in the Making* (7th edn., Oxford: Clarendon Press, 1964).

ALTMAN, ANDREW, 'Legal Realism, Critical Legal Studies and Dworkin', *Philosophy and Public Affairs*, 15 (1985–6), 205–36.

AQUINAS, ST THOMAS, *On Law, Morality and Politics*, ed. and comp. William P. Baumgarth and Richard J. Regan, S. J. (Indianapolis: Hackett, 1988).

ATIYAH, P. S., *Promises, Morals, and Law* (Oxford: Clarendon Press, 1981).

AUSTIN, J. L., *How To Do Things with Words*, in J. O. Urmson and Marina Sbisà (eds.) (2nd edn., Cambridge, Mass.: Harvard University Press, 1975).

AUSTIN, JOHN, *Lectures on Jurisprudence, Or, The Philosophy of Positive Law*, rev. and ed. Robert Campbell (4th edn., London: J. Murray, 1873).

—— *The Province of Jurisprudence Determined*, with an introduction by H. L. A. Hart (London: Weidenfeld and Nicholson, 1954).

BALKIN, J. M., 'Taking Ideology Seriously: Ronald Dworkin and the CLS Critique', *UMKC Law Review*, 55 (1987), 392–433.

BAMBROUGH, RENFORD, 'Principia Metaphysica', *Philosophy*, 39 (1964), 97–109.

BARNES, ANNETTE, *On Interpretation* (Oxford: Basil Blackwell, 1988).

BAŸEFSKY, ANNE F. (ed.), *Legal Theory Meets Legal Practice* (Edmonton, AB: Academic Printing and Publishing, 1988).

BEEHLER, RODGER, 'The Concept of Law and the Obligation to Obey', *American Journal of Jurisprudence*, 23 (1978), 120–42.

BERLIN, ISAIAH, *Four Essays on Liberty* (London: Oxford University Press, 1969).

BEYLEVELD, DERYCK, and BROWNSWORD, ROGER, *Law As A Moral Judgment* (London: Sweet and Maxwell, 1986).

BLACK, DONALD, *The Behavior of Law* (New York: Academic Press, 1976).

—— 'The Boundaries of Legal Sociology', in id. and Maureen Mileski (eds.), *The Social Organization of Law* (New York: Seminar Press, 1973), 41–56.

BRAMHALL, JOHN, *A Just Vindication of the Church of England from the Unjust Aspersion of Criminal Schism* (Dublin, 1674).

BRINK, DAVID O., 'Legal Theory, Legal Interpretation and Judicial Review', *Philosophy and Public Affairs*, 17 (1988), 105–48.

—— *Moral Realism and the Foundations of Ethics* (Cambridge Cambridge University Press, 1989).

—— 'Semantics and Legal Interpretation (Further Thoughts)', *Canadian Journal of Law and Jurisprudence*, 2 (1989), 181–91.

BURTON, STEVEN J., 'Ronald Dworkin and Legal Positivism', *Iowa Law Review*, 73 (1987), 109–29.

BUTLER, DOUGLAS, 'Character-traits in Explanation', *Philosophy and Phenomenological Research*, 49 (1988), 215–38.

CANE, PETER, 'Economic Loss in Tort: Is the Pendulum Out of Control?', *Modern Law Review*, 52 (1989), 200–14.

CAVELL, STANLEY, *The Claim of Reason: Wittgenstein, Skepticism, Morality, and Tragedy* (Oxford: Clarendon Press, 1979).

COLEMAN, JULES L., 'Negative and Positive Positivism', *Journal of Legal Studies*, 11 (1982), 139–64.

CONKLIN, WILLIAM E., 'Clear Cases', *University of Toronto Law Journal*, 31 (1981), 231–48.

CROSS, RUPERT, *Statutory Interpretation* (London: Butterworths, 1976).

DARE, TIM, 'Raz, Exclusionary Reasons, and Legal Positivism', *Eidos*, 8 (1989), 11–33.

DELANEY, C. F., 'Rawls on Method', In Kai Nielsen and Roger A. Shiner, (eds.) *New Essays on Contract Theory*, Canadian Journal of Philosophy Supplementary Volume No. 3 (Guelph, Ont.: Canadian Association for Publishing in Philosophy, 1977), 153–61.

DEN HARTOGH, GOVERT, 'Rehabilitating Legal Conventionalism', *Law and Philosophy*, 11 (1992) [forthcoming].

DETMOLD, MICHAEL, *The Unity of Law and Morality: A Refutation of Legal Positivism*, (London: Routledge and Kegan Paul, 1984).

DEVLIN, PATRICK, *The Enforcement of Morals* (London: Oxford University Press, 1965).

DUFF, R. A., 'Legal Obligation and the Moral Nature of Law', *Juridical Review* (1980), 61–87.

DWORKIN, RONALD, 'Equality, Democracy and Constitution: We the People in Court', *Alberta Law Review*, 28 (1990), 324–46.

—— *Law's Empire* (Cambridge, Mass.: Harvard University Press, 1986).

—— 'Liberal Community', *California Law Review*, 77 (1989), 479–504.

—— *A Matter of Principle* (Cambridge, Mass.: Harvard University Press, 1985).

—— *Taking Rights Seriously* (2nd edn., Cambridge, Mass.: Harvard University Press, 1978).

—— 'What is Equality? Part 3: The Place of Liberty', *Iowa Law Review*, 73 (1987), 1.

—— 'What is Equality? Part 4: Political Equality', *University of San Francisco Law Review*, 22 (1987), 1.

FELDTHUSEN, BRUCE, *Economic Negligence: The Recovery of Pure Economic Loss* (2nd edn., Toronto: Carswell, 1989).

FINNIS, JOHN, 'The Authority of Law in the Predicament of Contemporary Social Theory', *Notre Dame Journal of Law, Ethics and Public Policy*, 1 (1984), 115–37.

—— *Natural Law and Natural Rights* (Oxford: Clarendon Press, 1980).

—— 'On Reason and Authority in *Law's Empire*', *Law and Philosophy*, 6 (1987), 357–80.

FISH, STANLEY, *Doing What Comes Naturally* (Durham, NC: Duke University Press, 1989).

—— *Is There a Text in This Class? The Authority of Interpretative Communities* (Cambridge, Mass.: Harvard University Press, 1980).

FISS, OWEN, 'Objectivity and Interpretation', *Stanford Law Review*, 34 (1982), 739–63.

FLATHMAN, RICHARD E., *The Practice of Political Authority* (Chicago: University of Chicago Press, 1980).

FULLER, LON L., *The Morality of Law* (2nd edn., New Haven, Conn.: Yale University Press, 1969).

GANS, CHAIM, 'Mandatory Rules and Exclusionary Reasons', *Philosophia*, 15 (1985–6), 373–94.

GAUTHIER, DAVID, *Morals By Agreement* (Oxford: Clarendon Press, 1986).

GEWIRTH, ALAN, *Reason and Morality* (Chicago: University of Chicago Press, 1978).

GIBBS, J. P., 'Definitions of Law and Empirical Questions', *Law and Society Review*, 2 (1968), 429–46.

GOLDSWORTHY, JEFFREY D., 'The Self-destruction of Legal Positivism', *Oxford Journal of Legal Studies*, 10 (1990), 449–86.

GOMBAY, ANDRÉ, 'Commentary', in Anne F. Bayefsky (ed.), *Legal Theory Meets Legal Practice* (Edmonton, AB: Academic Printing and Publishing, 1988), 115–17.

GOODMAN, NELSON, *Fact, Fiction and Forecast* (New York: Bobbs-Merrill, 1965 [1955]).

GOULD, STEPHEN JAY, *The Mismeasure of Man* (New York: W. W. Norton and Co., 1981).

GREEN, LESLIE, *The Authority of the State* (Oxford: Clarendon Press, 1988).

GREEN, LESLIE, 'Law, Co-ordination and the Common Good', *Oxford Journal of Legal Studies*, 3 (1983), 299–324.

HACKER, PETER, 'Hart's Philosophy of Law', in P. M. S. Hacker and J. Raz (eds.), *Law, Morality and Society: Essays in Honour of H. L. A. Hart* (Oxford: Clarendon Press, 1977), 1–25.

HAMPTON, JEAN, 'Should Political Philosophy Be Done Without Metaphysics?', *Ethics*, 99 (1989), 791–814.

HANEN, MARSHA, 'Justification as Coherence', in M. A. Stewart (ed.), *Law, Morality and Rights* (Boston, Mass.: D. Reidel Publishing Co., 1983), 67–92.

HARRÉ, R., and SECORD, P. F., *The Explanation of Social Behaviour* (Oxford: Basil Blackwell, 1972).

HARRIS, J. W., *Law and Legal Science* (Oxford: Clarendon Press, 1977).

—— 'Legal Doctrine and Interests in Land', in John Eekelaar and John Bell (eds.), *Oxford Essays in Jurisprudence*, iii (Oxford: Clarendon Press, 1987), 167–97.

—— 'Unger's Critique of Formalism in Legal Reasoning: Hero, Hercules and Humdrum', *Modern Law Review*, 52 (1989), 42–63.

HART, H. L. A., *The Concept of Law* (Oxford: Clarendon Press, 1961).

—— *Essays in Jurisprudence and Philosophy* (Oxford: Clarendon Press, 1983).

—— *Essays on Bentham: Studies in Jurisprudence and Political Theory* (Oxford: Clarendon Press, 1982).

—— 'Legal and Moral Obligation', in A. I. Melden (ed.), *Essays in Moral Philosophy* (Seattle: University of Washington Press, 1958), 82–107.

HILL, ROSCOE E., 'Legal Validity and Legal Obligation', *Yale Law Journal*, 80 (1970), 47–75.

HODSON, JOHN D., 'Hart on the Internal Aspect of Rules', *Archiv Für Rechts- und Sozialphilosophie*, 62 (1976), 381–99.

HOFFMASTER, BARRY, 'A Holistic Approach to Judicial Justification', *Erkenntnis*, 15 (1980), 158–81.

HOGG, PETER, *Constitutional Law of Canada* (2nd edn., Toronto: Carswell Company, 1985).

HONORÉ, TONY, *Making Law Bind* (Oxford: Clarendon Press, 1987).

HUGHES, GRAHAM, 'The Existence of a Legal System', *New York University Law Review*, 35 (1960), 1001–30.

HULL, C. L., *Principles of Behaviour: An Introduction to Behaviour Theory* (New York: Appleton Century Crofts, 1943).

HUME, DAVID, *Enquiries: Concerning Human Understanding and Concerning the Principles of Morals*, ed. and introd. L. A. Selby-Bigge; rev. and notes by P. H. Nidditch (3rd edn., Oxford: Clarendon Press, 1975 [1777]).

HURLEY, S. L., 'Coherence, Hypothetical Cases and Precedent', *Oxford Journal of Legal Studies*, 10 (1990), 221–51.

HUTCHINSON, ALLAN C., 'Indiana Dworkin and Law's Empire', *Yale Law Journal*, 96 (1987), 637–65.

—— and WAKEFIELD, JOHN N., 'A Hard Look at "Hard Cases"', *Oxford Journal of Legal Studies*, 2 (1982), 86–110.

KELSEN, HANS, *The Pure Theory of Law*, trans. Max Knight (Berkeley and Los Angeles: University of California Press, 1967).

KENNEDY, DUNCAN, 'Form and Substance in Private Law Adjudication', *Harvard Law Review*, 89 (1976), 1685–778.

KOVESI, JULIUS, *Moral Notions* (London: Routledge and Kegan Paul, 1967).

KRYGIER, MARTIN, 'The Concept of Law and Social Theory', *Oxford Journal of Legal Studies*, 2 (1982), 155–80.

LAGERSPITZ, EERIK, *A Conventionalist Theory of Institutions*, Acta Philosophica Fennica, vol. 44 (Helsinki: The Philosophical Society of Finland, 1989).

LEWIS, DAVID, *Convention: A Philosophical Study* (Cambridge, Mass.: Harvard University Press, 1969).

LEWIS, STEPHANIE R., 'Taking Adjudication Seriously', *Australasian Journal of Philosophy*, 58 (1980), 377–87.

LUCE, R. DUNCAN, and RAIFFA, HOWARD, *Games and Decisions* (New York: John Wiley and Sons, 1957).

LYONS, DAVID, 'Comment: The Normativity of Law', in Ruth Gavison (ed.), *Issues in Contemporary Legal Philosophy* (Oxford: Clarendon Press, 1987), 114–26.

—— 'Derivability, Defensibility and the Justification of Judicial Decisions', *Monist*, 68 (1985), 325–46.

—— 'Justification and Judicial Responsibility', *California Law Review*, 72 (1984), 178–99.

—— 'Principles, Positivism and Legal Theory', *Yale Law Journal*, 87 (1977), 415–35.

MACCORMACK, G., 'Anthropology and Legal Theory', *Juridical Review* (1978), 216–32.

MACCORMICK, D. N., 'Coherence in Legal Justification', in Helmut Schelsky, Werner Krawietz, Günther Winkler, and Alfred Schramm (eds.), *Theorie der Normen: Festgabe Für Ota Weinberger Zum 65. Geburtstag* (Berlin: Duncker & Humboldt, 1984), 37–53.

—— 'Comment: The Normativity of Law', in Ruth Gavison (ed.), *Issues in Contemporary Legal Theory* (Oxford: Clarendon Press, 1987), 105–13.

—— *H. L. A. Hart* (Stanford, Calif.: Stanford University Press, 1981).

—— *Legal Reasoning and Legal Theory* (Oxford: Clarendon Press, 1978).

—— and WEINBERGER, OTA, *An Institutional Theory of Law: New Approaches to Legal Positivism* (Boston, Mass.: D. Reidel Publishing Company, 1984).

MACKIE, JOHN L., 'The Third Theory of Law', *Philosophy and Public Affairs*, 7 (1977–8), 3–17.

MACPHERSON, C. B., *The Political Theory of Possessive Individualism: Hobbes to Locke* (London: Oxford University Press, 1962).

MARTIN, MICHAEL, *The Legal Philosophy of H. L. A. Hart* (Philadelphia: Temple University Press, 1987).

MICHELL, JOHN, *Eccentric Lives and Peculiar Notions* (London: Sphere Books, 1989).

MOORE, G. E., *Philosophical Papers* (London: Allen and Unwin, 1959).

MOORE, MICHAEL S., 'Authority, Law, and Razian Reasons', *Southern California Law Review*, 62 (1989), 829–96.

—— 'The Interpretive Turn in Modern Theory: A Turn for the Worse?', *Stanford Law Review*, 41 (1989), 871–957.

—— 'Metaphysics, Epistemology and Legal Theory', *Southern California Law Review*, 60 (1987), 453–506.

—— 'Moral Reality', *Wisconsin Law Review* (1982), 1061.

—— 'A Natural Law Theory of Interpretation', *Southern California Law Review*, 58 (1985), 277–398.

—— 'The Semantics of Judging', *Southern California Law Review*, 54 (1981), 151–294.

MORGAN, DONNA C., 'Controlling Prosecutorial Powers—Judicial Review, Abuse of Process and Section 7 of the Charter', *Criminal Law Quarterly*, 29 (1986–7), 15–65.

PAYNE, MICHAEL A., 'Hart's Concept of a Legal System', *William and Mary Law Review*, 18 (1976), 287–319.

PECZENIK, ALEKSANDR, *On Law and Reason* (Dordrecht: Kluwer Academic Publishers, 1989).

PERRY, STEPHEN R., 'Judicial Obligation, Precedent and the Common Law', *Oxford Journal of Legal Studies*, 7 (1987), 215–57.

—— 'Second-order Reasons, Uncertainty and Legal Theory', *Southern California Law Review*, 62 (1989), 913–94.

POSTEMA, GERALD J., *Bentham and the Common Law Tradition* (Oxford: Clarendon Press, 1986).

—— 'Bentham on the Public Character of Law', *Utilitas*, 1 (1989), 41–61.

—— 'Coordination and Convention at the Foundations of Law', *Journal of Legal Studies*, 11 (1982), 165–203.

—— 'In Defence of "French Nonsense": Fundamental Rights in Constitutional Jurisprudence', in Neil MacCormick and Zenon Bankowski (eds.), *Enlightenment, Rights and Revolution: Essays in Legal and Social Philosophy* (Aberdeen: Aberdeen University Press, 1989), 107–33.

—— 'The Normativity of Law', in Ruth Gavison (ed.), *Issues in Contemporary Legal Philosophy: The Influence of H. L. A. Hart* (Oxford: Clarendon Press, 1987), 81–104.

—— '"Protestant" Interpretation and Social Practices', *Law and Philosophy*, 6 (1987), 283–319.

RAWLS, JOHN, 'The Domain of the Political and Overlapping Consensus', *New York University Law Review*, 64 (1989), 233–55.

—— 'The Idea of an Overlapping Consensus', *Oxford Journal of Legal Studies*, 7 (1987), 1–25.

—— 'The Independence of Moral Theory', *Proceedings and Addresses of the American Philosophical Association*, 47 (1974–5), 5–22.

—— 'Justice as Fairness: Political, Not Metaphysical', *Philosophy and Public Affairs*, 14 (1985), 223–51.

—— 'Kantian Constructivism in Moral Theory: The Dewey Lectures 1980', *Journal of Philosophy*, 77 (1980), 515–72.

—— 'Outline for a Decision Procedure in Ethics', *Philosophical Review*, 60 (1951), 177–97.

—— *A Theory of Justice* (Cambridge, Mass.: Harvard University Press, 1971).

—— 'Two Concepts of Rules', in Philippa Foot (ed.), *Theories of Ethics* (Oxford: Oxford University Press, 1967), 144–70.

RAZ, JOSEPH, 'Authority, Law and Morality', *Monist*, 68 (1985), 295–324.

—— *The Authority of Law* (Oxford: Clarendon Press, 1979).

—— *The Concept of a Legal System: An Introduction to the Theory of Legal System* (2nd edn., Oxford: Clarendon Press, 1980).

—— 'Dworkin: A New Link in the Chain', *California Law Review*, 74 (1986), 1103–19.

—— 'Facing Up: A Reply', *Southern California Law Review*, 62 (1989), 1153–235.

—— 'Legal Principles and the Limits of Law', *Yale Law Journal*, 81 (1972), 823–54.

—— *The Morality of Freedom* (Oxford: Clarendon Press, 1986).

—— *Practical Reasons and Norms* (London: Hutchinson, 1975).

—— 'Promises and Obligations', in P. M. S. Hacker and J. Raz (eds.), Law, Morality, and Society: Essays in Honour of H. L. A. Hart (Oxford: Clarendon Press, 1977), 210–18.

—— 'Reasons for Action, Decisions, and Norms', in id. (ed.), *Practical Reasoning* (Oxford: Oxford University Press, 1978), 128–43.

—— 'Right-based Moralities', in R. G. Frey (ed.), *Utility and Rights* (Minneapolis: University of Minnesota Press, 1984), 42–59.

RÉAUME, DENISE, 'Is Integrity a Virtue? Dworkin's Theory of Legal Obligation', *University of Toronto Law Journal*, 39 (1989), 380–409.

ROSS, W. D., *The Right and the Good* (Oxford: Clarendon Press, 1930).

RYLE, GILBERT, 'On Forgetting the Difference Between Right and Wrong', in A. I. Melden (ed.), *Essays in Moral Philosophy* (Seattle: University of Washington Press, 1958), 147–60.

SARTORIUS, ROLF, 'Hart's Concept of Law', in Robert S. Summers (ed.),

More Essays in Legal Philosophy (Oxford: Basil Blackwell, 1971), 131–61.

—— 'Positivism and the Foundations of Legal Authority', in Ruth Gavison (ed.), *Issues in Contemporary Legal Philosophy: The Influence of H. L. A. Hart* (Oxford: Clarendon Press, 1984), 43–61.

—— 'Social Policy and Judicial Legislation', *American Philosophy Quarterly*, 8 (1971), 151–60.

SCHAUER, FREDERICK, 'Easy Cases', *Southern California Law Review*, 58 (1985), 399–440.

—— 'Exceptions', *University of Chicago Law Review*, 58 (1991), 871–99.

—— 'Formalism', *Yale Law Journal*, 97 (1988), 509–48.

—— 'Is the Common Law Law?', *California Law Review*, 77 (1989), 455–71.

—— 'The Jurisprudence of Reasons', *Michigan Law Review*, 85 (1987), 847–70.

—— *Playing By the Rules: A Philosophical Examination of Rule-Based Decision-Making in Law and in Life* (Oxford: Clarendon Press, 1991).

—— 'Rules and the Rule of Law', *Harvard Journal of Law and Public Policy*, 14 (1991), 645–94.

SCHELLING, THOMAS C., *The Strategy of Conflict* (Oxford: Clarendon Press, 1960).

SHINER, ROGER A., 'Consensus as Foundation', in Carole Stewart (ed.), *Moral Relativism* (Toronto: Agathon Press, 1992) [forthcoming].

—— 'From Epistemology to Romance Via Wisdom', in Ilham Dilman (ed.), *Philosophy and Life: Essays on John Wisdom*, Nijhoff International Philosophy series 17 (Boston, Mass.: Martinus Nijhoff Publishers, 1984), 291–315.

—— 'The Hermeneutics of Adjudication', in Evan Simpson (ed.), *Antifoundationalism and Practical Reasoning: Conversations Between Hermeneutics and Analysis* (Edmonton, AB: Academic Printing and Publishing, 1987), 233–46.

—— 'Justice in the Garden of Eden', *Philosophy*, 63 (1988), 301–16.

—— 'The Metaphysics of Taking Rights Seriously', *Philosophia*, 13 (1982), 223–56.

—— 'Review Essay: Philip Soper, *A Theory of Law*', *Ratio Juris*, 2 (1989), 318–23.

—— 'Review Essay: Stanley Fish, Doing What Comes Naturally', *Journal of Aesthetics and Art Criticism*, 49 (1991), 375–8.

—— 'Wittgenstein and the Foundations of Knowledge', *Proceedings of the Aristotelian Society*, 78 (1977–8), 103–24.

SIMPSON, A. W. B., 'The Common Law and Legal Theory', in id. (ed.), *Oxford Essays in Jurisprudence*, ii (Oxford: Clarendon Press, 1973), 77–99.

SINGER, JOSEPH WILLIAM, 'The Player and the Cards: Nihilism and Legal Theory', *Yale Law Journal*, 94 (1984), 1–70.

SOPER, PHILIP, 'Legal Theory and the Obligation of a Judge: The Hart/ Dworkin Dispute', *Michigan Law Review*, 75 (1977), 473–519.

—— *A Theory of Law* (Cambridge, Mass.: Harvard University Press, 1984).

SPARSHOTT, FRANCIS, *The Theory of the Arts* (Princeton, NJ: Princeton University Press, 1982).

STRAWSON, P. F., *Individuals: An Essay in Descriptive Metaphysics* (Garden City, NY: Doubleday, Anchor, 1963).

SUMNER, L. W., *The Moral Foundation of Rights* (Oxford: Clarendon Press, 1987).

TEN, C. L., 'The Soundest Theory of Law', *Mind*, 88 (1979), 522–37.

ULLMANN-MARGALIT, EDNA, *The Emergence of Norms* (Oxford: Clarendon Press, 1977).

UNGER, ROBERTO M., 'The Critical Legal Studies Movement', *Harvard Law Review*, 96 (1983), 561–675.

VAN ROERMUND, BERT C., 'Narrative Coherence and the Guises of Legalism', in Patrick Nerhot (ed.), *Law, Interpretation and Reality: Essays in Epistemology, Hermeneutics and Jurisprudence*, Law and Philosophy Library, vol. 11 (Norwell, Mass.: Kluwer Academic Publishers, 1990), 310–45.

—— 'On "Narrative Coherence" in Legal Contexts', in Carla Faralli and Enrico Pattaro (eds.), *Reason in Law*, iii (Milan: Dott. A. Giuffrè Editore, 1988), 159–70.

WALUCHOW, WILFRID J., 'Charter Challenges: A Test Case for Theories of Law', *Osgoode Hall Law Journal*, 29 (1991), 183–214.

—— 'Hart, Legal Rules and Palm-tree Justice', *Law and Philosophy*, 4 (1985), 41–70.

—— 'Herculean Positivism', *Oxford Journal of Legal Studies*, 5 (1985), 187–210.

—— 'Strong Discretion', *Philosophical Quarterly*, 33 (1983), 321–39.

—— 'The Weak Social Thesis', *Oxford Journal of Legal Studies*, 9 (1989), 23–55.

WINCH, PETER, 'Eine Einstellung Zur Seele', *Proceedings of the Aristotelian Society*, 81 (1980–1), 1–15.

—— *The Idea of a Social Science and its Relation to Philosophy* (London: Routledge and Kegan Paul, 1958).

WISDOM, JOHN, *Philosophy and Psycho-analysis* (Oxford: Basil Blackwell, 1969).

WITTGENSTEIN, LUDWIG, *On Certainty*, ed. G. E. M. Anscombe and G. H. von Wright, trans. G. E. M. Anscombe and Denis Paul (New York: Harper and Row, Harper Torchbooks, 1972).

—— *Generally Known as the Blue and Brown Books: 'Preliminary Studies for the 'Philosophical Investigations'* (New York: Harper and Row, Harper Torchbooks/Academy Library, 1965).

—— 'Notes for Lectures on "Private Experience" and "Sense-Data"', *Philosophical Review*, 77 (1968), 275–320.

—— *Philosophical Investigations*, trans. G. E. M. Anscombe (Oxford: Basil Blackwell, 1958).

INDEX

This Index does not repeat general information about topics discussed that can be obtained from the Table of Contents